CRAFTING

CIVILIAN CONTROL

OF THE MILITARY

IN VENEZUELA

Crafting Civilian Control of the Military in Venezuela: A Comparative Perspective

Harold A. Trinkunas

CRAFTING CIVILIAN CONTROL OF THE MILITARY IN VENEZUELA

A COMPARATIVE PERSPECTIVE

■

Harold A. Trinkunas

The University of North Carolina Press

Chapel Hill

Manufactured in the United States of America

Designed by Amy Ruth Buchanan

Set in Minion by Tseng Information Systems, Inc.

The paper in this book meets the guidelines for
permanence and durability of the Committee on
Production Guidelines for Book Longevity of
the Council on Library Resources.

Library of Congress Cataloging-in-
Publication Data

Trinkunas, Harold A.

Crafting civilian control of the military in Venezuela :
a comparative perspective / Harold A. Trinkunas.

p. cm.

Includes bibliographical references and index.

ISBN 0-8078-2982-x (cloth : alk. paper) —
ISBN 0-8078-5650-9 (pbk. : alk. paper)

1. Civil-military relations — Venezuela — History —
20th century. 2. Democratization — Venezuela.
3. Venezuela — Politics and government — 20th
century. I. Title.

F2325.T75 2005

322'.5'098709045 — dc22   2005010252

cloth   09 08 07 06 05   5 4 3 2 1
paper   09 08 07 06 05   5 4 3 2 1

TO LUBA AND SOPHIE

CONTENTS

■

Acknowledgments ▪ xi

Abbreviations ▪ xiii

1. Democracy and Civilian Control of the Armed
Forces: *Venezuela in Comparative Perspective* ▪ 1

2. A Lost Opportunity: *The Failure of
Democratization in Venezuela, 1945–1948* ▪ 27

3. The 1958 Transition to Democracy in Venezuela:
Strategizing Civilian Control ▪ 62

4. Statecraft and Military Subordination
in Venezuela, 1959–1973 ▪ 110

5. Civilian Control under Fire: *Resisting Challenges
from the Military in Venezuela, 1992* ▪ 156

6. Revolutionizing Civil-Military Relations?
*Hugo Chávez and the Fifth Republic in Venezuela,
1998–2004* ▪ 206

7. Assessing the Relationship between Civilian
Control of the Military and the Consolidation
of Democracy ▪ 234

Notes ▪ 265

References ▪ 269

Index ▪ 289

FIGURES AND TABLES

■

Figures

1.1 State Jurisdictional Boundaries: Where Is Military Participation Most Threatening to Democracy? 7

1.2 Possible Outcomes in Civil-Military Relations Following a Transition to Democracy 18

1.3 Types of Jurisdictional Boundaries in Emerging Democracies 21

2.1 Civil-Military Jurisdictional Boundaries, ca. 1946: Institutional Reforms Expand Military Autonomy and Jurisdiction 50

2.2 Civil-Military Jurisdictional Boundaries, ca. 1948: The Armed Forces Prepare to Take Power 55

3.1 Civil-Military Jurisdictional Boundaries, ca. June 1958: Prior to Castro León Coup Attempt 95

3.2 Civil-Military Jurisdictional Boundaries, ca. December 1958: Government Strategies Reduce Military Jurisdiction 107

4.1 Civil-Military Jurisdictional Boundaries, ca. 1961: Consolidating Control by Containment of Armed Forces 133

4.2 Civil-Military Jurisdictional Boundaries, ca. 1967: Counterinsurgency Warfare Expands Armed Forces' Jurisdictional Boundaries 146

4.3 Civil-Military Jurisdictional Boundaries, ca. 1970: Civilian Control by Containment Is Consolidated 150

5.1 Civil-Military Jurisdictional Boundaries, ca. 1988: Increased Politicization of Armed Forces Reduces Their Autonomy 169

5.2 Civil-Military Jurisdictional Boundaries, ca. 1991: Armed Forces Drawn into Internal Security 174

5.3 Civil-Military Jurisdictional Boundaries, ca. 1993: Expansive Military Jurisdictions Threaten Civilian Control 197

5.4   Civil-Military Jurisdictional Boundaries, ca. 1997: Civilian Control by Containment Restored 203

6.1   Civil-Military Jurisdictional Boundaries, ca. 2001: Military Jurisdictional Boundaries Expand 217

6.2   Civil-Military Jurisdictional Boundaries, ca. 2003: Institutional Civilian Control Collapses 232

7.1   Outcomes in Civilian Control 237

Tables

5.1   Comparative Government Expenditures per Soldier, 1972–1981 165

5.2   Comparative Government Expenditures per Soldier, 1984–1994 176

ACKNOWLEDGMENTS

■

Writing about Venezuelan civil-military relations has often seemed like an effort to pin down a rapidly moving target, especially when I consider how much Venezuela has changed since the earliest origins of this project in 1991. Although the civil-military system appears to have reached a new equilibrium as of the fall of 2004, there will certainly be new opportunities for instability now that civilian control is no longer institutionalized. Nevertheless, the findings of this book, both for Venezuela and for other emerging democracies, will prove to be enduring since they provide an explanation for how regimes acquire control over their armed forces and a cautionary tale about how democracies can lose that control.

This book would not have been possible without the advice and unstinting support extended to me by my colleagues at the Naval Postgraduate School, particularly Tom Bruneau, Doug Porch, and Jim Wirtz. Their urging me to "get to work!" and "write faster!" helped speed this project to completion. I would also like to thank Terry Karl, Condoleezza Rice, and Philippe Schmitter for encouraging this project from its inception. I am also grateful to Lynn Eden, David Holloway, and Scott Sagan at the Center for International Security and Cooperation and to the staff and scholars of the Center for Latin American Studies at Stanford University for their assistance, financial and other, for this project.

The success of my research in Venezuela was made possible by the cooperation of numerous persons and institutions. I am particularly grateful to all of those who took the time to participate in the interviews on which a large part of this book is based. I would like to thank Jóse Giacopini Zárraga for spending dozens of hours sharing with me his vast knowledge of Venezuelan civilian and military politics in the twentieth century. The scholars at the Fundación Rómulo Betancourt proved instrumental by providing me access to the Betancourt presidential archives. I would also like to recognize the support of the retired and active-duty Venezuelan military officers who took an interest in my work and facilitated my research through their contacts and personal knowledge of this topic.

I would also like to thank all the friends and family who accompanied me during this process for providing an oasis of sanity. I would especially like to express my deep gratitude to my parents, sister, and especially to Luba and Sophie for their unflagging support during the writing of this book. Without their love and encouragement, I would not have been able to complete this project. This book is dedicated to them.

Finally, I would like to thank my editor at the University of North Carolina Press, Elaine Mainer, for all her support and advice. I am also grateful to the outside reviewers for their insightful comments on the original draft of this book.

The views expressed in this book are solely those of the author, and they do not in any way represent the position of the Naval Postgraduate School, the U.S. Department of Defense, or the U.S. government.

ABBREVIATIONS

■

AD	Acción Democrática (Democratic Action Party)
BS.	bolívares (Venezuelan currency)
CEN	Comité Ejecutivo Nacional (AD National Executive Council)
COPEI	Comité de Organización Política Electoral Independiente (Committee of Independent Political Electoral Organizing) (Venezuela Christian Democratic Party)
COPRE	Comisión Presidencial para la Reforma del Estado (Presidential Commission for the Reform of the State)
DIGEPOL	Dirección General de Policia (General Police Directorate)
DISIP	Dirección de Servicios de Inteligencia y Prevención (Intelligence and Prevention Services Directorate)
FALN	Fuerzas Armadas de Liberación Nacional (Armed National Liberation Front)
FARC	Fuerzas Armadas Revolucionarias de Colombia (Revolutionary Armed Forces of Colombia)
FEDECAMARAS	Federación de Cámaras y Asociaciones de Comercio y Producción (Federation of Chambers and Associations of Commerce and Production)
FLN	Frente de Liberación Nacional (National Liberation Front)
GDP	gross domestic product
JRG	Junta Revolucionaria de Gobierno (Revolutionary Governing Council)

MAS	Movimiento al Socialismo (Movement toward Socialism Party)
MBR-200	Movimiento Bolivariano Revolucionario 200 (Bolivarian Revolutionary Movement 200)
MEP	Movimiento Electoral del Pueblo (People's Electoral Movement)
MIR	Movimiento de la Izquierda Revolucionaria (Movement of the Revolutionary Left)
NATO	North Atlantic Treaty Organization
OAS	Organization of American States
PCV	Partido Comunista de Venezuela (Venezuelan Communist Party)
PDVSA	Petroleos de Venezuela, S.A. (Venezuelan Petroleum Corporation)
UPM	Unión Patriótica Militar (Patriotic Military Union)
URD	Unión Republicana Democrática (Democratic Republican Union Party)

CHAPTER 1

■

DEMOCRACY AND CIVILIAN CONTROL

OF THE ARMED FORCES

Venezuela in Comparative Perspective

The failed 1992 coup attempt by Lieutenant Colonel Hugo Chávez Frias came as a surprise to many observers of Venezuela who had long considered it a consolidated democracy. Although the coup attempts were beaten back by forces loyal to the regime, Venezuela's democracy began to unravel. President Carlos Andrés Pérez was impeached in 1993, and presidential elections to select his successor were highly contested. President Rafael Caldera was elected with the support of less than a third of the votes cast; and despite attempts to restabilize the democratic system, he presided over a period characterized by banking crises, economic decay, and political unrest. The persistent crises opened the way for Hugo Chávez to win the 1998 presidential elections on a populist and revolutionary political platform.

Upon coming to power through elections in 1998, Chávez led a sweeping effort to dismantle and replace the democratic institutions that had been established in 1958, often relying on the armed forces to implement and support his agenda for change. Through frequent referenda, President Chávez legitimated the elimination of the Venezuelan Congress and Supreme Court, convened a Constitutional Assembly, and enacted a new constitution that empowered new legislative and judicial actors. Chávez's frequent use of military symbolism to generate support for his regime, along with his reliance on military officers to staff key positions in his administration, has led to great concern among Venezuelan and outside observers over the prospects for democracy in this country. Although President Chávez has argued that he is leading a "peaceful revolution," a failed coup attempt in 2002, mass mobilization by civil society, and violent confrontations among his supporters and detractors indicate that this goal remains wishful thinking.

Thus far, the Venezuelan experience since 1992 does not appear to set it apart from that of any number of unstable democratic regimes; yet Venezuela was once considered a democratic success story, with more than three decades of civilian rule to its credit. Civilian authority over the military was institutionalized, the loyalty of the armed forces to the democratic regime was unquestioned, and officers were focused on their professional missions (Agüero 1990). In fact, while many civilian-led regimes across Latin America were replaced by military authoritarian governments during the 1960s and 1970s, Venezuela's democracy stood apart, apparently immune to the wave of authoritarianism that was sweeping the region. Ironically, it was only during the 1990s, just as Latin America as a region seemed to have achieved stable democratic rule, that Venezuela's democratic regime began to break down.

The contemporary Venezuelan experience addresses two key issues in the debate on democratization: How do democracies achieve control over their armed forces? And how do they lose this control over their armed forces once they have achieved it? Subordinating the military is one of the most difficult tasks faced by democratizers, yet it is also the most critical to the security and stability of the regime. This book draws on the Venezuelan experience to examine the process by which civilians achieve control of the armed forces. It also examines the process by which democratic civilian control can be dismantled. In its conclusion, the book compares the results from the Venezuelan experience against those of better-understood cases of democratization, such as Chile, Argentina, and Spain, each of which provide a perspective on alternative paths to civilian control of the armed forces.

Venezuela's democracy prospered and consolidated during the 1960s and 1970s because its politicians had learned an important lesson: stable democratic rule is impossible without civilian control of the military. Unlike many of their colleagues in other Latin American countries, Venezuelans also learned how to institutionalize civilian control. However, as the last decade of Venezuelan politics has shown, lessons can be forgotten, and institutions unmade. Under the leadership of President Hugo Chávez, Venezuela's democratic institutions have decayed, and most dangerous, its institutions of civilian control of the armed forces have been deliberately dismantled.

Deconsolidating democracy and civilian control was possible because the institutions built in 1958 were flawed by the scarcity of institutional resources and civilian defense expertise available to democratizers. Building on lessons learned from the initial failed democratization attempt in 1945–48, Venezuelan civilian politicians crafted a pattern of civil-military institutions that contained military influence and activities to a narrow range of endeavors closely associated with national defense. This institutional arrangement for civilian control was consolidated during the 1958–73 period. However, civilian control by containment had its limits in Venezuela, namely the inability of elected and appointed civilian officials to truly monitor the activities of the armed forces. As a result, plotting by radical minorities in the military could continue unchecked, erupting into the public eye in the form of the 1992 coup attempts.

The failure of the 1992 coup attempts showed that the institutionalized containment of the armed forces still functioned, but the deterioration of the democratic system that had birthed these institutions eventually led to the election of Lieutenant Colonel Hugo Chávez as president in 1998. President Chávez proceeded to dismantle the institutions of civilian control that had prevented his accession to power by force, but no alternative mechanisms of institutionalized control have replaced them in the new regime. The result has been military discontent and instability, which has already led to one failed coup in 2002 and calls into question the long-term survival of the regime.

What does Venezuela tell us about civilian control in other new democracies? Cases from Latin America and Southern Europe provide a useful check on the conclusions drawn from the Venezuelan experience because they highlight the shortcomings of civilian control by containment of the armed forces. Argentina's efforts to build civilian control by oversight have paid off in times of high political tension and conflict, such as occurred during the 2001–3 economic crisis that led to the resignation of the president and an uncertain succession process. Other Latin American cases suggest that persistent civilian efforts to acquire defense expertise and to build civil-military institutions can eventually overcome unfavorable initial conditions. In Chile civilians have slowly made progress in both institutionalizing their authority over defense issues and limiting the degree of military autonomy. They are thus overcoming the constitutional and political obstacles that empowered the armed forces in the wake of the General Augusto Pinochet dictatorship, which is something that few observers would have predicted from the vantage point of Chile's democratic transition in 1990. Similarly, in Spain the interaction between civilian and military defense professionals who are engaged in institution building has led to a high degree of democratic civilian control over the armed forces and the reorientation of the military toward external defense duties associated with North Atlantic Treaty Organization (NATO) membership, again something few observers would have predicted in the wake of Generalissimo Francisco Franco's dictatorship.

The Puzzle of Civilian Control of the Armed Forces

Why do men with guns obey men without guns? When do soldiers obey politicians, especially in societies that have recently been ruled by the military? How do politicians compel or induce obedience from soldiers? On the face of it, it would seem that emerging democracies would lack the leverage to compel the armed forces to accept civilian control. The military, as a well-armed bureaucracy, is usually well positioned to defend its expanded and autonomous role in security, the economy, and public policy from civilian politicians.

This book argues that transitions away from military dictatorship and toward democracy create an opportunity to craft civilian control, especially when democratizers are backed by high levels of civilian mobilization and their adversaries are weakened by disunity within the incumbent authoritarian regime. Democratizers who act strategically during this moment can maximize their leverage over the armed forces. Their weakest strategy is to appease military commanders, trading off civilian control of the armed forces for short-term regime survival. More robust strategies rely on pitting factions within the armed forces against each other to deter military intervention in politics. The most robust strategy combines high levels of civilian supervision of defense activities with sanctions against military rebellions and dissident officers. The combination of opportunity and successful civilian strategies creates regime leverage over the armed forces, leverage that can be used to eliminate military prerogatives and confine the armed forces to strictly professional tasks.

Civilian control is consolidated when elected officials transform successful strategies into institutions that permanently shift power away from the military and toward elected officials. The regime's capacity to manage defense affairs is what allows democracies to create permanent institutions that sustain their leverage over the military. Regime capacity is the combination of political leadership, institutional resources, and civilian defense expertise required to craft lasting institutions. Democratic leaders who lack the institutional and civilian defense expertise (or choose not to create it) will at best be able to craft institutions of civilian control that dominate the armed forces by restricting their roles and missions. By contrast, emerging democracies that benefit from strong opportunities, successful strategies, and a high degree of regime capacity are likely to achieve a high degree of control of the armed forces, based on the oversight of military activities by elected and appointed civilians.

DEFINING CIVILIAN CONTROL

Today, democratic civilian control of the armed forces is understood to mean military compliance with government authority, rather than the absence of armed rebellion (Pion-Berlin 1992). Civilian control exists when government officials have authority over decisions concerning the missions, organization, and employment of a state's military means. Civilian control also requires that officials have broad decision-making authority over state policy, free from military interference (Agüero 1995b, 19–21).

This definition differs from Samuel Huntington's classic 1957 prescription for civilian control. In Huntington's analysis, civilian control takes subjective and objective forms. Subjective control emerges when political elites protect themselves from military intervention by ensuring that the armed forces share common values and objectives with them — sometimes through a process of politicization of the officer corps. With respect to objective control, which Huntington assesses as most conducive to national security, the military is independent from civilian interference. Instead, it is self-directed through strong norms of professionalism that include subordination toward duly constituted state authority and an apolitical attitude toward civilian government's policies and activities (Huntington 1957).

By contrast, I argue that there are at least two types of institutionalized civilian control. Huntington's objective control of the armed forces tends to produce a division of spheres or labor among civilians and the armed forces. So long as the military's share of the division of labor is narrowly defined and focused on external defense policy, it is possible to conceive of a form of democratic civilian control by containment, where elected officials do not much care about what the military does as long as it does not interfere with civilian prerogatives. I argue, however, that the essential component of contemporary democratic civilian control is institutionalized oversight of military activities by civilian government agencies. In other words, civilian control by oversight exists when politicians and bureaucrats are able to determine defense policies and approve military activities through an institutionalized professional defense bureaucracy. Unlike Huntington's, this understanding of civilian control does not assume that the contents of military professionalization (its ethic of responsibility, from a Weberian perspective) are necessarily compatible with democracy. It requires civilian oversight in a democracy to make them so. Finally, both forms of institutionalized civilian control outlined here differ considerably from the subjective form of civilian control identified by Huntington, which is more likely based on personal relationships and social interactions that create a uniformity of interests and beliefs among civilian and military elites.

Maximizing civilian control in a democracy involves minimizing the areas of state policy in which the armed forces hold exclusive jurisdiction. Broad military prerogatives and high levels of military contestation are incompatible with stable democratic rule (Stepan 1988). The existence of enclaves of military autonomy within the state and institutional vetoes over civilian policymaking threatens regime stability. Armed forces that have exclusive control over state revenues or industries outside the supervision of civilian authorities are more difficult to monitor and control. States in which the armed forces control internal security agencies have found it hard to prevent military intervention in politics (Linz and Stepan 1996, 209–11). Broadly based and autonomous military participation in state activities not only prevents civilian control over the armed forces but also calls into question the very nature of a democratic regime. Furthermore, the military's participation in areas outside its primary mission has historically led to its politicization, friction between politicians and soldiers, and a significant reduction in military effectiveness (Pion-Berlin 1992; Desch 1999).

In sum, I argue that civilian control of the armed forces exists when elected officials or their political appointees have authority to decide the resources, administration, and roles of the armed forces. In emerging democracies, the greater the extent of political authority over military activities and the more focused these activities are on preparing for war, the closer these regimes are to achieving civilian control of the armed forces. In essence, this captures Alfred Stepan's critical insight that maximizing civilian control requires minimizing both the scope of military prerogatives and military contestation of the scope of such prerogatives (Stepan 1988).

Building on Stepan's and David Pion-Berlin's work in this area, this study focuses on three degrees of military autonomy: civilian dominant, shared authority, and military dominant (Stepan 1988; Pion-Berlin 1992, 84–86). By tracing shifts in both military autonomy and participation over time, it is

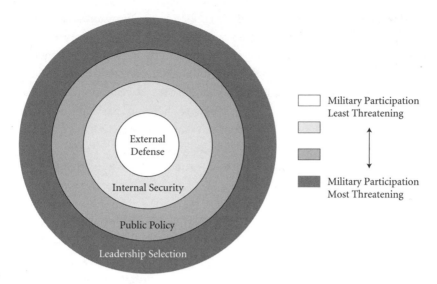

Figure 1.1. State Jurisdictional Boundaries: Where Is Military Participation Most Threatening to Democracy?

possible to track shifts in civil-military jurisdictional boundaries over time. This is the method that will be used to identify movement toward and away from civilian control in Venezuela.

Figure 1.1 illustrates the boundaries between military and civilian jurisdictions by representing four areas of state activity as concentric rings. A civilian government and its military forces can participate in each of these areas, which are arranged by their functional distance from the military's war-fighting mission and by the degree of threat to civilian control posed by military involvement. External defense tasks involve preparing for and conducting war and related military missions, managing the military bureaucracy, training, and strategic planning. Internal security includes the maintenance of public order in emergency situations, preparation for counterinsurgency warfare, the gathering of domestic intelligence, and policing. Public policy covers state budgets, the functioning of government agencies, and the crafting of public policy to achieve social welfare, development, and political objectives. State leadership selection involves decisions concerning the criteria and process by which government officials are recruited, legitimated, and empowered.

Well-established civilian control is principally concerned with excluding autonomous military participation in areas that threaten regime stability and managing the boundaries between civilian and military authority in the state. Yet, civilian control only guarantees that rulers have the ability to make decisions free from the threat or veto of their military institutions (Agüero 1995b). Civilian control, by itself, does not guarantee the rule of law, observance of human rights, regime stability, or the general welfare of the population. All regimes face numerous challenges to their success, legitimacy, and stability as a result of unforeseen crises. Civilian control cannot prevent such regime crises, but it does place decision-making authority concerning these matters in the hands of government leaders and civil society rather than the officer corps.

Crafting Civilian Control

Exogenous shocks have the potential to undermine the basis of support for authoritarian regimes, particularly those of a more personalistic or un-institutionalized nature (Geddes 1999, 138–40; Haggard and Kaufman 1999). Such shocks also create the opportunity to establish (or reestablish) the bases of civilian authority over the armed forces. However, as Philippe Schmitter has argued, simply because a transition to democracy has occurred does not mean that the process of regime consolidation advances in lockstep across all fronts (Schmitter 1995). Even though relations between the state, capital, and labor may be institutionalized relatively rapidly, as in Chile after 1990, civil-military relations may not democratize simultaneously.

In this book, I argue that regime transitions toward democracy provide an extraordinary opportunity for moving in the direction of civilian control, particularly when such transitions occur in combination with other exogenous shocks that undermine the internal cohesion of supporters of the authoritarian ancien régime, such as the military and the intelligence services. The scope of the opportunity structure is determined by the degree of fragmentation and disorder within the armed forces, in comparison to the degree to which civilians have mobilized and established a consensus on democratization.

A broad opportunity structure is characterized by high fragmentation of the armed forces, a high degree of civilian popular mobilization, and an elite consensus on democratization. The nature of the crisis leading up to a transition to democracy determines the breadth of opportunity for democratizers to impose control on the armed forces (O'Donnell and Schmitter 1986; Agüero 2001). Political and economic failures that are attributable to the policies of a dictatorship, particularly if they are compounded by defeat in war, are likely to both hasten the collapse of the regime and increase recrimination and distrust among outgoing ruling elites (Bueno de Mesquita, Siverson, and Woller 1992; Haggard and Kaufman 1999). The fragmentation of the internal cohesion of the coercive apparatus of the state inhibits the ability of the officer corps to resist either democratization or civilian control of the security forces (Agüero 1995b, 101). For example, democratizers in Greece benefited from the internal conflicts that erupted within the officer corps following the defeat of the military dictatorship in war with Turkey over Cyprus in 1974. A high degree of consensus on democratization will reduce the likelihood of significant civilian elites "knocking on the barracks doors" and appealing for renewed military intervention (Stepan 1988, 128). The combination of mass mobilization and elite consensus can provide a powerful counterweight to military threats to the democratic process.

By contrast, narrow opportunity structures are found in transitions that are characterized by a high degree of military unity, a low degree of civilian consensus on democratization, and the absence of a democratic agenda to establish control of the armed forces. The positive performance of an outgoing dictatorship empowers authoritarian elites and the armed forces vis-à-vis democratizers. Furthermore, a legacy of positive government performance under authoritarian rule is likely to deepen divisions among civilians, as occurred in Brazil in the 1980s during its "long" transition, and in Chile following the 1989 elections that resulted in the end of the Pinochet dictatorship. Under these conditions, democratizers face much greater constraints on their power, and they will find greater difficulty in successfully shifting jurisdictional boundaries in the direction of civilian control (Agüero 1995b).

ACTING STRATEGICALLY TO MAXIMIZE REGIME LEVERAGE

Some argue that the nature of the transition, essentially its opportunity structure, overdetermines the outcome in terms of civilian control. Who controls a transition process (the military or the democratizers) essentially determines the limits of civilian authority over the armed forces, as Arceneaux (2001) and even Agüero (1995b) suggest. While conceding the importance of the balance of power between democratizers and authoritarians during the transition, I argue that there is considerable room for agency and strategy during this period. Transitions characterized by broad opportunity structures do not necessarily lead to civilian control. For example, Colombia and Venezuela experienced pacted transitions to democracy almost simultaneously in the late 1950s. The unity among democratizers in each country greatly increased the regime leverage they held vis-à-vis their own militaries. Yet, despite relatively equal leverage, democratizers in Colombia never challenged the prerogatives of their own military, and this armed institution retained a considerably higher degree of autonomy than that of its neighbor until the 1990s. The difference between the Colombian and Venezuelan cases lies not in the configuration of opportunities available to democratizers, but rather in the fact that Venezuelan civilian elites acted strategically to maximize their temporary advantage over the armed forces.

Participation in the armed forces is often associated with a set of cultural norms that values service, self-sacrifice, and honor (Janowitz 1964), yet the military as an institution is fundamentally organized as a rational bureaucracy. Thus, regime leverage exists when democratizers are able to modify the fears, interests, and (eventually) the beliefs of military officers to compel or induce compliance with government orders. Democratizers who benefit from broad opportunity structures, where there is a high degree of civilian unity and mass mobilization in favor of democracy, have a counterweight with which to coerce military leaders, particularly where those leaders are demoralized or divided. However, even civilian leaders who face narrow opportunity structures can benefit from strategic action.

Civilian leaders use strategies of control even in highly consolidated democracies in order to ensure that the actions of the armed forces are in alignment with the preferences of the government (Feaver 2003, 80–86). However, I argue that many of the same strategies can be used to increase the regime's leverage in relation to the armed forces even in the absence of civilian control. The strategies on which civilian leaders have traditionally relied to develop leverage over the military fall conceptually into one of four categories: appeasement, monitoring, divide and conquer, and sanctioning. The object of using these strategies in some mix or phased approach is to co-opt, recruit, or intimidate a sufficiently large number of military officers into supporting the government's agenda so as to prevent the armed forces from acting cohesively to oppose civilian control in a new democracy.

Appeasement strategies rely on governments' adopting policies and budgets that satisfy the institutional and particular interests of the officer corps in the hopes of discouraging military intervention in politics. Used in isolation, these strategies are likely to lead to high levels of military autonomy and little or no reduction in the boundaries of military jurisdiction over the state. Nonetheless, some governments engage in a wide array of patrimonial, remunerative, and clientalistic practices to maintain the loyalty of their armed forces (Decalo 1976, 25–47). These practices include granting officers high salaries and benefits, modern weaponry and equipment, and vetoes over state policymaking. In Ecuador, for example, the armed forces are guaranteed by law a substantial percentage of the profits of the state-owned oil industry (Fitch 1998). In spite of its pernicious effects, appeasement is often the only feasible strategy available to democratic governments with narrow opportunity structures.

A somewhat more robust strategy, monitoring, relies on external and internal agents to maintain surveillance over the armed forces and inform rulers of potential threats. This forewarning may allow civilians to adopt policies and take actions to dissuade military intervention. For example, reliable information on coup plots may allow governments to intervene early, arresting rebellious military officers long before they are prepared to mobilize their units against a democratic regime. Monitoring strategies can be very effective in alerting civilian leaders to problems within the armed forces, but unless they are coupled with more robust strategies, such as divide and conquer or sanctioning, governments may lack sufficient power to head off military threats. In unconsolidated democracies this type of monitoring is essentially concerned with regime security rather than with ensuring that the armed forces are following civilian policy preferences, a characteristic of the institutionalized monitoring that habitually takes place in consolidated regimes.

"Divide and conquer" strategies generate regime leverage by exploiting internal cleavages and encouraging competition within and among state security forces, raising the costs of military intervention. Interservice rivalry is inevitable in military institutions (Feaver 2003, 82), yet civilians can deliberately accentuate such competition by creating new counterbalancing security forces, such as gendarmeries or national police forces, or they can induce existing military units to balance each other, creating deterrence within the armed forces. Faced with the possibility that any coup d'état may lead to open conflict between different security organizations, military leaders are less likely to intervene in politics (Belkin 1998). Furthermore, by introducing competition for power and resources, civilian governments can count on their security forces to monitor each other to prevent any single organization from becoming threatening or dominant. While this may be a difficult strategy to implement, civilians can often rely on the fragmentation of the armed forces in the wake of transitions to democracy, as well as on existing institutional rivalries between armies, navies, and air forces, to practice "divide and conquer" (Farcau 1996).

Sanctioning strategies are designed to use the fear of punishment to induce military cooperation with a democratic regime. Democratizers may be able to use civilian and military courts, loyalists in the military command structure, or internal security forces to suppress military uprisings and punish rebellious officers. In Spain, officers who participated in the only coup attempt (in 1982) against the democratic government were severely sanctioned at the insistence of the civilian leadership (Agüero 1995b). A sanctioning strategy does not require repeated confrontations with the armed forces since, if successful, it has the effect of modifying the interests of the officer corps (Feaver 2003, 87–91). Officers who cooperate with a new democratic regime will tend to have successful careers and rapid advancement. Those who oppose it will find themselves imprisoned or retired if they have taken part in failed rebellions. These new incentives and the fear of punishment lead the armed forces to accept the jurisdictional boundaries set by civilians and cooperate with the government.

Opportunity structures do tend to favor the use of certain strategies. In particular, narrow opportunity structures tempt governments to choose less confrontational strategies, such as appeasement or monitoring. Governments facing relatively fewer possibilities can partially overcome these circumstances by using strategies to maximize regime leverage over the armed forces. In a hypothetical example, civilian leaders could appease the navy in return for its support for a sanctioning strategy against the army. Broad opportunity structures, where there is strong mass and elite civilian support for democratization, allow civilians to use strategies based on forcing the armed forces to achieve rapid changes. It is important to underline that these strategies are not designed to benefit the armed forces but are rather intended to defend a democratic regime from military threats. In transitional democracies where civilian control does not exist, civil-military relations are either characterized by confrontation or by civilian acquiescence to military prerogatives.

The ability of democratizers to act strategically does not preclude the ability of the armed forces to resist since they will correctly perceive these strategies as a means to limit their power and prerogatives. Fortunately for democratizers, the armed forces' use of counterstrategies is often impeded by the dynamics of a transition. This is especially true of broad opportunity structures that fragment the unity of the armed forces. This fragmentation can prevent military commanders from coherently applying counterstrategies to civilian control. Divided armed forces can only effectively defend institutional prerogatives supported by the lowest common denominator of opinion within the officer corps (Agüero 2001, 212–13.) Following the collapse of a military authoritarian regime, many officers disagree over the proper role of the armed forces in society, undermining the ability of their commanders to apply counterstrategies to defend their prerogatives or sustain expanded jurisdictional boundaries.

Overcoming Obstacles to Designing Institutions to Govern Civil-Military Relations

Militaries are Weberian rational bureaucratic organizations par excellence, as Deborah Norden observes (Norden 2001, 111–13). Militaries are rule-bound organizations governed by systems of regulations and standard operating procedures that reward participants for their compliance. This suggests that "rational" military organizations should be particularly amenable to control through regularized incentives and sanctioning mechanisms. Yet, there are numerous political and institutional obstacles to the design of institutions of civilian control, even in cases where democratizers have available the regime leverage necessary to enforce military compliance.

The central role of democratic institutions of civilian control is transmitting information about whether their participants, civilian and military, are abiding by rules, following procedures, and complying with the orders issued by elected officials and their appointees. Yet, all bureaucracies love secrecy because secrets grant them power and protect them from the supervision of their political overseers (Weber 1958, 232–35). The tendency toward secrecy and autonomy that characterizes bureaucracy restricts the information flows that politicians need to control the armed forces. In the absence of accurate information about military activities, elected officials and their appointees are unable to make sure that their orders, rules, and procedures have been followed.

In a more contemporary version of this argument, agency theorists argue that in any principal-agent relationship, the bureaucratic agent tends to shirk the duties imposed by the elected principal and secretly pursue its own interests. Agents also have a strong interest in providing self-serving advice rather than that which best serves the interest of the principal. Thus, elected officials can only check this behavior by either being especially vigilant, becoming highly knowledgeable about the agent's activities, or developing alternative sources of advice and expertise. These alternative mechanisms are time-consuming and defeat the purpose of developing expert bureaucracies in the first place (Feaver 2003, 68–72). Without independent sources of information about how military budgets are being executed, however, civilian defense officials are unable to determine whether the armed forces are "working" (following the defense policies approved by the government) or "shirking" (pursuing their own preferred defense policies) (Feaver 2003, 85).

Compounding the principal-agent problem is a political dilemma for civilian politicians: mastering defense policy is not always electorally rewarding. It is true that in the United States and some other advanced industrialized democracies there are strong electoral incentives to be responsive to defense interests, due to the concentration of defense-related industries and installations in particular electoral districts. These, in turn, generate strong constituent interests and demands on elected representatives (Stockton 1995, 240–44). An electoral incentive for engaging in defense reform is unlikely to exist in countries where external threats are low and where the military-industrial complex is not a source of electoral resources (Hunter 1997, 95–100). From a different perspective, Michael Desch argues that civilian control is only likely to emerge in countries where the external threats to the state create incentives for civilian politicians to take civil-military relations seriously (Desch 1999). Most Latin American countries fall into one or both of these categories since they are not threatened by their neighbors, have negligible defense industries, or ban members of the armed forces from voting. In other words, defense reform is likely to be attractive to politicians only if it is of personal interest (which is possible in any state) (Stockton 1995, 243–44), or if there is a compelling electoral incentive, such as popular demands for reducing military budgets (Hunter 1997) or justice for perpetrators of human rights abuses under previous regimes (Norden 1996a).

Finally, even in emerging democracies where electoral officials are interested in defense oversight and have the regime leverage to enforce institutional change, it is not clear that they would have the resources necessary to populate new systems of civilian control. Huntington's observations regarding the Office of the Secretary of Defense (osd) in the United States are telling. He argues that the main objective of a secretary of defense should be to act as a policy strategist, which requires him or her to have an understanding of defense issues, legal authority to implement policy, and an adequate staff to assist. Yet during the 1950s, when the OSD had nearly two thousand employees, Huntington found that they were mostly of the wrong kind, representing parochial interests of agencies and services rather than providing high-level policy guidance (Huntington 1957, 448–57). Peter Feaver provides further support by contrasting the assistance available to the secretary of defense with that available to the Joint Staff, the armed forces' principal body for high-level policy development (Feaver 2003, 123–26, 159).

Similar issues confront democracies when they attempt to conduct oversight of the armed forces through legislative bodies. Even a legislature as well funded and staffed as the U.S. Congress prefers to conduct oversight via "fire alarms," such as internal whistle-blowers or critical media coverage, rather than "police patrols," such as the Congressional Budget Office or inspectors general. For elected officials and their staff to execute "police patrols," they would need the expertise to evaluate the information they gather about military activities and judge whether it accords with their policy preferences. A "fire alarm" oversight system removes the burden of accumulating expertise from the legislature, yet it still requires a substantial and decentralized array of institutional resources to support the development of civilian defense expertise within the mass media, academia, and civil society (McCubbins and Schwartz 1984; Feaver 2003, 81–84). It is not clear that emerging democracies, particularly following a transition from military rule, would meet these requirements for expertise since most of this kind of knowledge would be possessed by civilian and military supporters of the ancien régime.

Institutionalizing civilian control is thus a costly process, even in advanced industrialized democracies, which requires that democratic regimes possess the capacity to conduct meaningful oversight of military activities. This book defines *regime capacity* as the combination of political leadership, institutional resources, and expert civilian personnel specifically and exclusively committed to matters of civilian control and national defense, in that order of importance. This parallels Huntington's findings about the requirements for civilian authority in the U.S. case (Huntington 1957, 448). Institutional resources and civilian defense expertise may be found within state ministries, legislatures, and courts, as well as in an independent press or nongovernmental organizations focused on military-related issues. Yet, without the commitment of political leadership among democratizers to civilian control, there is little reason for institutional resources to be devoted to this problem, and there will certainly be no institutional home for civilian defense expertise.

The political leadership dimension of regime capacity is difficult to assess from a quantitative perspective, but this study will focus on qualitative measures drawn from interviews and media reports to determine whether civilian control of the armed forces was prominent on the political agenda of the new democracy. The dimension of institutional resources can also be hard to determine since most ministries of defense or legislative committees do not publish detailed breakdowns of civilian versus military personnel and spending. However, the presence or absence of such institutions is usually easy to determine, as is the role that civilians play within them. The third dimension, civilian expertise, can be assessed by focusing on the presence or absence of civilian defense professionals in ministries of defense or congressional defense committee staffs. For example, the members of the congressional defense committees in Venezuela had no permanent or personal staff experts during the period studied here, while Argentina's House and Senate defense committee members quickly acquired personal staff members with defense expertise; yet neither of these arrangements compares in sheer quantity and quality of resources with the dozens of permanent and personal staff experts enjoyed by the members of the U.S. congressional committees that are concerned with the armed forces. The important point is that without these resources, constitutional arrangements for civilian control become paper tigers, unable to contend with the concentrated expertise and interest of the military bureaucracy in defending its prerogatives and interests.

A shortage of regime capacity is a likely characteristic of countries with a low level of external threat and highly autonomous militaries. Both were certainly the case in most of Latin America throughout the twentieth century, and the latter was true in Venezuela prior to 1958. Without an external threat to focus on, civilian politicians in a democracy typically assign defense issues a low priority in favor of economic and political ones that will bring tangible electoral returns. Also, militaries with histories of political autonomy and intervention are reluctant to share defense information with civilian politicians, let alone educate them about these issues, for fear of generating alternative sources of expertise that could threaten their corporate interests. In countries with histories of armed intervention in politics, academic circles tend to be hostile to the study of defense issues, associating them with repression and militarism. Thus, educated civilians who could participate in the supervision of the military are likely to avoid developing the required expertise, for fear of experiencing professional and personal difficulties. Even if they do decide to become involved in studying military issues, they will either have to participate in the sometimes biased training programs run by their own armed forces or seek scarce and expensive overseas training. This suggests that there is a considerable opportunity for advanced industrialized democracies to stabilize emerging democracies by furthering the development of regime capacity, particularly in the area of civilian expertise.

Nevertheless, more recent democratization processes in Argentina, Chile, and Spain suggest that alternative sources of regime capacity can be developed in new democracies where civilian control of the military is high on the political agenda. Groups in civil society that focus on military issues, such as human rights organizations, can provide an external monitoring capacity lacking inside the government. The media can serve a similar purpose, particularly in countries where investigative journalism is relatively well developed. The courts can be used to seek legal redress, generating leverage and capacity in the area of defense. Retired officers who participate in political parties often become additional sources of trained personnel. Even though their training inclines them to favor the armed forces, their pursuit of a career inside political parties after retirement provides incentives for them to shift their loyalties to civilian politicians.

Paths and Outcomes in Civilian Control

The crafting of civilian control is a largely path-dependent process, as Felipe Agüero (2001, 207–9) suggests. As this book will demonstrate, the particular degrees of regime leverage and regime capacity available to an emerging democracy determine the degree to which government control will become institutionalized. Depending on what combination of opportunity, strategy, and institutions is available, an emerging democracy can follow a path toward one of four potential outcomes: a regime at risk, regime persistence, civilian control by containment, or civilian control by oversight. Figure 1.2 includes representative cases for each of the possible outcomes, drawn from Venezuela, which is examined at length in the body of the book, and from comparative studies considered in the concluding chapter. As this figure illustrates, regime capacity and regime leverage vary over time as regimes progress (or fail to progress) toward democratic consolidation.

Regime at Risk: Governments with little leverage over their armed forces

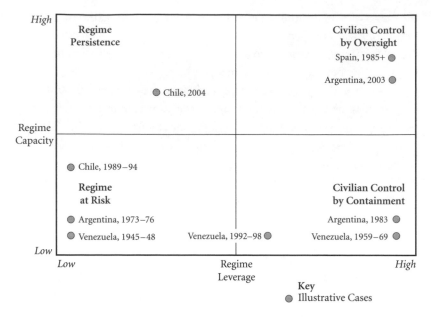

Figure 1.2. Possible Outcomes in Civil-Military Relations Following a Transition to Democracy

and lacking the expertise and resources to manage them are unlikely to *successfully* pursue any strategy other than appeasement. Military autonomy and jurisdictional boundaries will remain high, and democracy will never be fully consolidated. In the face of excessive military demands or a severe crisis in government legitimacy, democracy will be at risk. Venezuela's first attempt at democratization in 1945 and Argentina's turbulent democratic interlude during Juan Perón's second administration (1973–76) represent classic examples of this phenomenon.

Regime Persistence: In this outcome, a government faces constraints on its power and leverage over the armed forces, but its high degree of capacity in defense matters allows it to pursue a combination of monitoring and appeasement strategies. Information derived from monitoring may provide enough forewarning of threats from the armed forces to prevent successful military intervention. A combination of monitoring and appeasement may also allow civilians to negotiate somewhat lower jurisdictional boundaries with the armed forces, but the boundaries between civilian and military authority will be weak. Democracy will not become consolidated, but it is more likely to persist due to growing regime capacity vis-à-vis the armed forces. This outcome should be rare since it is difficult to conceive of cases where elected officials have access to a broad base of civilian expertise in defense affairs yet have not achieved control over the armed forces. However, as this book will show in its conclusion, Chile seems to have followed this path toward democratic consolidation via a slow accumulation of regime capacity that is now creating a new opportunity to move in the direction of institutionalizing civilian control by oversight (Fuentes 2000).

Civilian Control by Containment: Governments with high leverage over the armed forces but low regime capacity will not be able to create sophisticated mechanisms for overseeing military activities but will rather choose to confine these activities to narrow jurisdictional boundaries. Such a "division of spheres" approach comes closest to resembling Huntington's (1957) hypothesized objective control of the armed forces. In practice, there are notable drawbacks since this approach discourages the development of regime capacity. In these cases, civilians will not be able to create the institutional tools necessary to oversee military spending or to define its roles and missions. However, with the threat of military intervention contained, democracy is more likely to become consolidated. As this book will show, Venezuelan democratizers chose to follow this path to civilian control of the armed forces, in part due to an awareness of the shortage of regime capacity.

Civilian Control by Oversight: Democratizers enjoying both high leverage and high regime capacity can pursue any combination of strategies to create civilian control. With appeasement largely unnecessary, governments are likely to institutionalize robust strategies to ensure both the exclusion of the armed forces from political activities and the active civilian supervision of military affairs. Both strong civilian control and democracy are very likely to become consolidated in this outcome. Spain comes closest to following this path to civilian control, aided in part by a cadre of civilian defense experts and political actors interested in defense issues who began to operate even before the conclusion of the Franco dictatorship. Spain's achievements in this area were certainly cemented by its shift to an external defense orientation as it prepared to join NATO (Agüero 1995b).

EXAMINING THE DEPENDENT VARIABLE: CIVILIAN CONTROL

How does a government know when it has achieved civilian control? How can an analyst tell civilian control by oversight apart from its less robust counterpart, control by containment? More important, how does either of them know if a country is moving toward or away from these goals? Although a broad consensus has emerged as to what democratic civilian control is, there have only been a few efforts to measure the degree of civilian control in any given case (Pion-Berlin and Arceneaux 2000). I argue that the presence or absence of civilian control of the armed forces can be measured by the shape of the jurisdictional boundaries separating civilian and military authority within the state.

The concentric circles used in figure 1.1 can be used to derive maps for the jurisdictional boundaries of the four outcomes predicted in figure 1.2: regime collapse, regime persistence, civilian control by containment, and civilian control by oversight. For each map, the presence or absence of military participation and the armed forces' degree of autonomy can be coded by color, ranging from the dark gray of military dominant to the white of civilian dominant. Each map represents the outer limits of the jurisdictional boundaries for a predicted outcome (no map is presented for the first outcome, regime at risk, for the simple reason that the outer limits of jurisdictional boundaries in this case would be represented by military dominance across all areas of state activity). By comparing maps of the jurisdictional boundaries found in particular cases to the ones based on the theoretical outcomes predicted in this chapter, we can determine the presence or absence of civilian control in an emerging democracy.

A comparison of the jurisdictional boundaries in figure 1.3 indicates that achieving civilian control of the armed forces involves both reducing the participation of the armed forces in state activities (shifting jurisdictional boundaries toward the innermost circle, external defense) and reducing the autonomy of the armed forces to such an extent that civilian dominance becomes the norm across most areas of state policymaking. Simply put, so long as we observe that the areas of military jurisdiction in a given case shift toward the center of the concentric circles and become lighter gray (as military autonomy is reduced), civilian control over the armed forces is increasing.

Long-Term Impact of Institutionalized Civilian Control on Democratic Consolidation

The consolidation of civilian control is crucial not only to the survival of emerging democracies but to the quality of their governing institutions. Consolidating democracy requires the institutionalization of partial regimes across a range of areas, from control of the state bureaucracy and the secu-

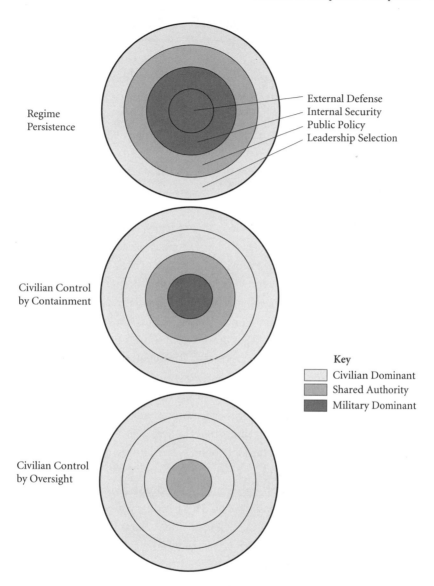

Figure 1.3. Types of Jurisdictional Boundaries in Emerging Democracies

rity forces, to party systems, to economic relations. The failure to craft any one of these institutions, whether it structures civil-military relations or civil society, hinders the full consolidation of democracy (Schmitter 1995). In one sense, civil-military relations are a partial regime much like any other, subject to the same opportunities, processes, and sequences that govern democratization. However, civilian control is also the key tool in the struggle between democratizers and authoritarians over institutional arrangements. If an emerging democracy does not achieve civilian control, supporters of the previous authoritarian regime can continue to credibly threaten the new regime and place limits on its institutional arrangements. Once civilian control is established, authoritarian forces are far less likely to successfully affect the quality of democratic institutions or to place conditions on the consolidation of partial regimes.

Civilian control does not mean that elected officials are free to structure partial regimes as they please, yet it does mean that the limits on this process are imposed within the context of the democratic rules of the game rather than by the use of force. While, theoretically, elected officials should have the authority to make decisions in all areas of state policy, in practice, all democracies face constraints on the power of the authorities. For example, central banks today tend to enjoy a reserved domain over monetary policy, acting relatively free of political constraints in the interests of preserving investor confidence and promoting economic stability and growth. Like independent central banks, militaries hold substantial authority over a critical area of state policy. Even in highly democratic states, the power of civilian politicians constitutionally charged with military oversight is effectively constrained by the greater professional expertise of the officer corps, the military's constituency among the electorate, and the need to preserve a credible defense. However, any limits that the armed forces are able to place on political outcomes occur through lobbies, legislatures, and courts, rather than through the use of force.

Democratic consolidation and democratic regime persistence should also produce changes in the norms associated with military service (especially in the officer corps) and changes in civilian attitudes about the military and its role in democracy. J. Samuel Fitch argues that military norms play a critical role in the consolidation of democratic civil-military relations (Fitch 1998, 2001). Yet most of the existing literature, including Fitch's own work, shows that Latin American military norms on democracy have evolved slowly, if at all. Brian Loveman has argued that the Spanish-American inheritance in Latin American militaries has predisposed them to resist civilian authority, focus on internal security missions, and see themselves as the ultimate guarantors of national sovereignty, standing above the law because they created the state (Loveman 1999). Frederick Nunn's work on the beliefs of Latin

American militaries has shown that the persistence of pre–World War I French and German military traditions in this region has predisposed its militaries to resist civilian authority (Nunn 1983). These beliefs are reproduced through the educational systems of the armed forces and their professional journals, which cultivate hostility toward democracy and civilian authority long after the transition to democracy. This would seem to suggest that any institutional reforms associated with democratic transitions in the struggle for civilian supremacy have to contend with long-ingrained beliefs in Latin American countries.

However, where civilian control is institutionalized, change in military norms and belief systems is the logical consequence. Institutions of civilian control where elected officials are able to define the rules for promotion, reward appropriate beliefs, and punish deviance establish new standards within the officer corps (Feaver 2003, 78–80). Here, Fitch's analysis of military belief systems is especially useful, in that he argues that part of the process of democratic consolidation is an "internal debate" in the officer corps, in which values that favor democracy and civilian policy oversight eventually trump those that favor authoritarianism or a privileged role for the armed forces (Fitch 2001, 101–5). In successful cases of democratic consolidation, officers do not necessarily change their minds, but rather the old generation of officers that is hostile to democracy dies off, is purged, or retires and is replaced by a new cohort of younger officers with views that favor the system.

In parallel to the military internal debate about democracy, this book also suggests that there is an equally important debate among civilians regarding the appropriate form for civil-military relations. During the 1948–58 period of military rule in Venezuela, civilian politicians who opposed the dictatorship engaged in a long-running debate about what to do with the armed forces upon returning to power. More senior and experienced politicians advocated a "divide and conquer" policy toward the armed forces, while more junior activists wanted to politicize the armed forces to ensure a partisan and loyal officer corps. Civilian control by oversight was not one of the options discussed in Venezuela; yet, in the third wave transitions of Chile, Spain, and Argentina, civilian discussion almost completely centered on achieving military subordination through institutions that would allow government oversight of defense policy. Venezuelan politicians could only compare the still evolving post–World War II U.S. system of civilian control with the ideological/party control model used by the Soviet Union. Democratizers in the third wave had more mature examples of civilian control by oversight available in the United States and Europe, and these countries sometimes went to great lengths to export their ideas.

Finally, this book raises questions about the trump value of pro-democracy norms in the military in the absence of institutionalized control. While both the armed forces and democratizers seem to place great weight on the value of education, the 1992 Venezuela case shows that deliberate efforts to alter military norms can misfire. Also, it is quite clear from the experiences of other developing and developed countries that norms of military subordination can break down, as occurred in France at the end of the Algerian war or in Chile during the Salvador Allende administration. The senior military officers and civilian politicians whom I interviewed in Venezuela suggested that democratic norms were not sufficient to prevent armed intervention during severe crises since these norms were vague, subject to misinterpretation and even to deliberate misuse, as occurred during the 1992 and 2002 coup attempts in Venezuela.

A Case of Democratic Civilian Control of the Armed Forces: Venezuela in Perspective

To examine my hypotheses, I structure the book around three cases drawn from the Venezuelan experience with democratic transition: the initial failed democratization attempt in 1945–48, the consolidation of democracy and civilian control during the 1958–73 Punto Fijo period, and the deconsolidation of Punto Fijo democracy and civil-military relations and their replacement by a populist, quasi-democracy with greatly expanded military roles under the presidency of Lieutenant Colonel Hugo Chávez. The selection of three cases from the same historical record has the advantage of minimizing variation caused by difference among states and maximizing my ability to examine the two key variables, regime leverage and regime capacity. I then conclude the volume by examining these conclusions in the light of three better-understood cases of democratic civil-military relations: Chile, Argentina, and Spain.

Venezuela's initial attempt at democratization during the 1945–48 period encapsulates many of the problems faced by democratizers during periods of regime transition. As I will show in chapter 2, Venezuelan civilian politicians made poor strategic and institutional choices regarding civil-military relations from the beginning of this period. As a result, the armed forces remained important political actors in this process, and they were able to intervene against the democratically elected administration of Rómulo Gallegos with ease. The collapse of this initial attempt to democratize initiated a prolonged debate among civilians on the proper role of the armed forces in any future democracy, a theme I pick up in chapter 3.

Chapters 3 and 4 focus on Venezuela's successful democratization experience that began in 1958 with the overthrow of the dictatorship of General Pérez Jiménez. Having learned from the 1948 overthrow of President Gallegos, Venezuelan democratizers made civilian control of the armed forces an early focus of their efforts. Civilian leaders pursued a strategy of "divide and conquer" to weaken military opposition to institutional changes that enhanced government authority over the armed forces. These institutions were designed to contain military influence and activities to a narrow range of endeavors closely focused on national defense. Both the leaders of the transitional government and President Rómulo Betancourt (1959–64) forcefully defended the new institutions of civilian control against military resistance and purged the officer corps of dissidents following a series of revolts in the early 1960s. Even the military effort to combat a leftist insurgency between 1961 and 1969 was framed as a defense of national sovereignty from Cuban infiltration. The overall result was a more professional military, subjected to civilian control by containment.

Chapter 5 explains the surprising eruption of military rebellion in Venezuela in 1992 as a product of the decline of institutionalized civilian control over the armed forces. In this chapter, I argue that civilian control by containment, as practiced by the Venezuelan democratic regime, functioned so long as civilian elites were able to identify and manipulate compliant military elites who would supervise the armed forces as they performed the narrow range of defense-related tasks they were assigned. While civilian and military elites broadly concurred on the wisdom of Venezuela's model of civilian control, its pernicious impact on the junior and mid-ranking officer corps eventually produced cliques of radicalized officers who sought to replace Venezuela's democracy with a more populist alternative. In the absence of civilian control by oversight, military plots against the regime could develop unchecked.

I then examine the militarization of the Venezuelan state during the administration of President Hugo Chávez in chapter 6. After winning the 1998 presidential election, Chávez was able to use his enormous popularity to carry out sweeping reforms of the state, legitimated by referenda. The center-

piece of these reforms was the enactment of a new constitution that, among
other items, considerably weakened the institutional underpinnings of civilian control of the armed forces. At the same time, President Chávez relied on
the armed forces to staff key positions in traditionally civilian government
bureaucracies. The militarization of the state in the absence of civilian control created increased opportunities for corruption and deprofessionalized
the officer corps. Chávez's political program has generated enormous political and economic tension within the society. In this atmosphere, the calls of
pro- and antigovernment civilians on the armed forces have polarized the
officer corps, leading to two military rebellions. In this chapter, I show how
institutionalized civilian control of the armed forces has disappeared.

In the conclusion, I place the findings from the Venezuelan cases in perspective by drawing on findings from other countries that have recently experienced success and failure in establishing civilian control over the armed
forces. Argentina's tumultuous civil-military relations provide a number of
interesting cases that highlight the importance of the choices made by democratizers in the wake of democratic transitions. In particular, the decision by Argentine democratizers after the 1983 transition to seek to develop
civilian control by oversight of the armed forces helps to explain why the
political regime has remained stable in spite of considerable economic and
social turmoil in the late 1980s and early 2000s. Chile after 1990, a case of
regime persistence, shows the importance of developing regime capacity as
a stepping-stone toward civilian control, even though democratizers faced
a narrow and unfavorable opportunity structure in the wake of the Pinochet regime. By contrast, Spain illustrates the importance of both regime
capacity and regime leverage to the development of civilian control by oversight. In this case, Spain was particularly aided by the steps that Franco had
already made in developing civilian authority over the military even prior
to democratization in 1975. Each of these cases helps to validate or place in
context the six main findings I develop based on the Venezuelan experience
of crafting civilian control.

CHAPTER 2

■

A LOST OPPORTUNITY

The Failure of Democratization

in Venezuela, 1945–1948

Following weeks of tension between the armed forces and Venezuela's fledgling democratic government, President Rómulo Gallegos was detained by army officers at his home in Caracas on 24 November 1948. Other officers quickly arrested the leadership of the ruling party, Acción Democrática (AD), along with labor activists, journalists, and prominent civilian supporters of the Gallegos government. Despite having received an impressive mandate in elections nine months earlier, President Gallegos was deposed practically without a struggle. Moreover, the coup was carried out by the minister of defense and chief of the General Staff, the very same officers who had brought Acción Democrática to power in 1945.

On the morning following the coup d'état, Caracas newspapers carried front-page pictures of Jóvito Villalba and Rafael Caldera, leaders of the principal opposition parties, Unión Republicana Democrática (URD) and Comité de Organización Política Electoral Independiente (COPEI), jovially exchanging handshakes with members of the new military junta (Anzola Anzola 1992).[1] The general public responded to the overthrow of the democratic regime with equanimity. The coup against Rómulo Gallegos marked the end of a contentious three-year experiment with democratization in Venezuela. Given the seemingly broad popular support for Gallegos, what then allowed his government to be so easily deposed, with so little resistance? What allowed the armed forces to act against an elected government? Was there anything democratizers could have done to prevent this outcome?

The central mystery surrounding the events of November 1948 is why the officers who had brought Acción Democrática to power in 1945 removed the party from office three years later. There are several different interpretations. Burggraff attributes the collapse to civilian and military unfamiliarity with the institutions of democratic rule, excessive levels of partisanship, and military hostility to civilian attempts to politicize the armed forces (Burggraff 1972, 109–11). Levine blames the collapse of Venezuela's brief democratic experiment on the mutual hostility generated by AD's exclusion of opposition political groups from policymaking and on state-church conflicts over government supervision of education during the 1945–48 period (Levine 1973, 37–41). Avendaño Lugo argues that, while civilian partisanship was an important component of the overthrow of Gallegos, the armed forces acted corporately to overthrow the civilian government, guided by a militarist sense of a "manifest destiny" to rule Venezuela (Avendaño Lugo 1982, 153–60). Others, particularly politicians who participated in the events, have placed greater emphasis on the role of the U.S. embassy and its military attachés, who encouraged and supported a coup against Gallegos in response to U.S. fears of Communist infiltration of the ruling party (Mohr 1976, 213–21, 293–306).

Although these arguments provide partial explanations for the collapse of democratization, they take for granted the power of the armed forces that enabled them to intervene in politics in 1948. Given that these very same armed forces were riven by internal conflicts and factional infighting following their 1945 intervention in politics, it is reasonable to ask why a bloodless coup by a unified military was now possible. In other words, what allowed the institution to regain its internal coherence within three years?

Venezuela (1945–48) is a case of a democracy that failed to establish civilian control over its armed forces, a regime at risk. Even though the failure of Venezuelan democratization in 1948 has been studied before, I argue that by concentrating solely on the civilian politics of this case, analysts have missed the crucial story of how, due to the missteps of democratizers in government, the armed forces were transformed between 1945 and 1948 into an institution prepared to both seize power and govern. This outcome was not foreordained. Although Venezuelan democratizers faced a narrow opportunity structure in 1945, an opportunity for democratization nevertheless existed due to the breakdown of internal cohesion and hierarchy in the armed forces. Facing a more adverse opportunity structure in 1990, Chilean democratizers were able to ensure the persistence of the regime and to craft a slowly broadening scope for their authority over the military. Venezuelan democratizers instead abdicated the pursuit of civilian control and provided an opening for the armed forces by following a perverse civilian strategy of appeasement, which facilitated the overthrow of President Gallegos.

Armed men had often intervened in Venezuelan politics prior to 1945, yet the armed forces as a professional, modern institution were too recent a creation to have had much influence yet over the country's direction. In fact, two military logics coexisted in Venezuela at the time of the October 1945 coup: one based on the armed cronyism of *caudillo* politics and one based on professional bureaucratic norms. Similar to what Fitch (1998) observes in Ecuador and Argentina, this was the beginning of a long-term internal debate in Venezuela, shaped by changes in strategic interaction between military and civilian factions and the institutions they produced.

Democratization began in 1945 when the professional bureaucratic component of the armed forces defeated the remnants of armed cronyism in public administration and the military high command. The resulting disorganization, purges, and internal conflict in the armed forces provided a limited opportunity for Venezuelan democratizers to establish regime leverage over the armed forces. Instead of taking advantage of this upheaval, the leaders of the Acción Democrática party, to whom the military coup plotters handed power in 1945, appeased the officer corps, allowing a faction guided by authoritarian values to seize control of the institution. The transitional government missed this opportunity because civilian control was not on the agenda of the new regime. The combination of a missed opportunity and a perverse strategy led to low levels of regime capacity to counteract military power. In fact, I argue that this approach led to growing military autonomy, increased the hostility of the officer corps to democratization, and provoked the 1948 coup d'état.

The low level of regime leverage over the armed forces during the 1945–48 period was compounded by a total absence of regime capacity, placing the new regime squarely in the "at risk" quadrant of figure 1.2. Political leadership to assert civilian control of the armed forces was absent because the issue was removed from the agenda by the civil-military pact that preceded the 1945 coup. Civilian defense expertise was also almost totally absent; moreover, there was no institutional venue in which it could act by virtue of the military control of the ministry of defense and the low degree of institutionalization of the legislative branch, due to the turmoil of the 1945–47 transition period.

Forging the Modern Venezuelan Armed Forces, 1908–1945

Prior to General Juan Vicente Gómez's seizing power in 1908, Venezuela lacked a professional army, or even one that was truly nationally based. Rather, Venezuela suffered from a network of competing regional warlords, loosely affiliated with the traditional Liberal and Conservative parties, who were able to raise temporary militias by mobilizing and arming the local peasantry. At the turn of the century, this constellation of *caudillos* was swept away by invading forces from the western Andean regions of Venezuela that had been assembled under the leadership of Cipriano Castro. Castro unified the country by seizing Caracas in 1899. He then decisively defeated a revolt by Venezuela's traditional political and military leadership in 1903 at the battle of La Victoria, on the shores of the Orinoco River (Ziems 1979, 65–68; Giacopini Zárraga 1992a). Castro was in turn overthrown in 1908 by his second in command, Juan Vicente Gómez, who set about consolidating Andean hegemony, disarming the regional militias, and developing the institutions of centralized government in Venezuela.

Despite having unified the country, the army that brought Gómez to power was not a professional army, but rather an agglutination of his armed cronies and their followers, recruited through the clientalistic network of political supporters and family members loyal to the dictator. Gómez assigned these loyalists to the management of the public administration and the defense of his government from political challengers. However, rather than rely solely on his armed cronies, Gómez also decreed the creation of a professional bureaucratic army that could provide a counterbalance. This new model army was organized on Weberian principles of rationality, merit, and advancement through professional education, and Colonel Samuel McGill, a Prussian-trained Chilean military officer, was invited to direct the modernization of the Venezuelan armed forces. For the next thirty-five years, these two military logics contended in Venezuela: one based on armed cronyism and one based on professional bureaucratic norms. General Gómez dominated both of them, cowing his opponents to such a degree that he would govern unchecked until his death in 1935.

Venezuela's modern army, based on the Prussian military model, began to function with core institutions designed to educate military officers (the national military academy) and plan the new army (the General Staff). The Academia Militar initially educated officers drawn from all regions of Venezuela, and schools were established to train older officers and sergeants in modern military methods. Officers also began to study abroad in Latin American countries with more advanced military institutions, particularly Chile and Peru. The Ministry of War and the Navy began to function as a center for military administration and reform under the guidance of Colonel McGill. Shortly thereafter, in 1914, Gómez appointed an armed forces inspector general and founded the Venezuelan Armed Forces General Staff to carry out planning and coordination within the new military. A network of barracks was rapidly built to service a growing army, and new military units were organized with weapons purchased abroad from France and Germany (Ziems 1979, 97–135, 175–78). With the institutions of a military academy and the General Staff, the Venezuelan officer corps began to lose its purely clientalistic basis and acquire a modern, meritocratic, and professional overlay.

However, alongside the new professional military, traditional bodies of armed men who were personally loyal to the dictator persisted. Gómez refused to abandon the logic of armed cronyism or subordinate it to the new professional military logic imported from European sources via Chile. Instead of acting as a counterbalance to Gómez's clientalistic network of armed supporters, the professionalized army became one more piece of the feudal apparatus that Gómez controlled. Cadets selected for the Academia Militar were increasingly drawn from Venezuela's Andean states and were principally lower-middle-class youths who belonged to families known to be loyal to the dictator. This selection mechanism gave the officer corps a strongly regional cast and preserved Andean control of the armed forces. Although the Academia Militar continued to operate uninterrupted until 1929, many of the other schools established by Colonel McGill closed. Slowly, despite the efforts of new military missions from France and Peru, the skills acquired by Venezuelan officers in modern areas of military expertise, such as artillery and engineering, degenerated, and the armed forces were increasingly dominated by the infantry (Ziems 1979, 216–17, 232). The professional armed forces were regarded as suspect by Gómez's armed cronies, thus the new military was denied the resources that could have transformed it into a serious threat to the existing system.

By the late 1920s and early 1930s, then, two parallel military forces had developed. The highest ranks of the armed forces were dominated by officers selected on the basis of their personal loyalty to General Gómez; they had trained on the battlefields of Venezuela's civil wars; and they tended to be semiliterate and ignorant of modern military techniques. These officers, termed *"chopo de piedra"* by lower-ranking officers, controlled all key positions in the Venezuelan army.[2] Cronyism, favoritism, and corruption dominated the upper ranks of the army during the 1920s and 1930s. Even though reforms to the laws that governed the armed forces in 1903 and 1923 had established impartial criteria for advancement within the officer corps, Gómez granted promotions on a personalistic basis. Officers who held the same rank were paid differing salaries, depending on the degree of confidence that the government had in their loyalty. Such promotions as were granted were slow in coming, and many of the new professional officers spent more than ten years at the rank of captain. Low salaries and poor living conditions increased officers' discontent. Most galling of all, many officers were assigned to nonmilitary functions, such as serving as agricultural overseers on the dictator's vast farms and ranches and as personal assistants to Gómez's cronies in the highest echelons of government service (Ziems 1979, 184–90, 205–24). The junior officer corps, shaped by the professional bureaucratic standards taught at the Academia Militar, lived in modest conditions, faced poor prospects for promotion, and marked time in provincial garrisons.

Professional officers were institutionally marginalized by the Gómez dictatorship. They also lacked the ability to carry out their missions since they were too ill equipped to provide for the national defense. Conscription was never fully implemented, and army reserves dwindled as the Venezuelan population became increasingly demilitarized. Gómez relied on a civilian secret police known as "La Sagrada," drawn almost entirely from Gómez's home state of Táchira, to track and harass dissidents both among civilians and military officers. Internal and external security duties were almost always carried out by Gómez's armed cronies. Locally recruited paramilitary forces under the control of state governors both repelled "invasions" by Venezuelan exiles and suppressed internal revolts (Giacopini Zárraga 1992a). Under these conditions, it is not surprising that professional officers became alienated from the Gómez regime.

So dominant was the armed clientalistic network that supported the dictator that no rebellion against General Gómez ever succeeded, although several were attempted (Burggraff 1972, 22). The participation of professional officers in one of these rebellions led to the temporary closing of the Academia Militar for several years. It permanently reopened in Maracay in 1931, where the dictator could personally watch over its operations (Capriles Ayala 1985, 157–58). The power of the dictator to shut down the core professional military institution, the Academia Militar, is the strongest indication of the complete absence of autonomy in the new professional armed forces.

The death of Gómez in 1935 began the unraveling of the power of armed cronyism. Unlike Gómez, neither Presidents Eleazar López Contreras nor Isaías Medina Angarita completely dominated the network of families and political clients which sustained the previous regime (Giacopini Zárraga 1992a). They therefore set out to purge many of Gómez's most loyal supporters from public administration, while they simultaneously cultivated the professional elements of the armed forces by improving conditions. Under López Contreras, the influence of old guard military officers, appointed for clientalistic reasons to posts in the civilian government, declined. The number of high-ranking officers in control of state governorships was reduced from nineteen (of twenty-three) in 1937 to only four in 1941.

After 1935, General López improved conditions for the professional officer corps. Wages in the armed forces rose somewhat, the assignment of officers to perform nonmilitary functions in the private sector ended, and corruption in the higher ranks diminished. Promotions and assignments were largely made on the basis of seniority and merit, rather than connections, at least within the lower ranks of the officer corps. The army and navy academies were reorganized, and new military missions from the United States arrived and played an important role in modernizing the armed forces and transmitting democratic ideas, particularly during World War II. While the armed forces retained a constitutionally mandated role in preserving public order and the rule of law, they did not exercise it in practice, except during the brief period of unrest that followed the death of Gómez. Instead, a professional internal security force known as the Guardia Nacional, based on the model of the Spanish Guardia Civil, was created in 1937, and "La Sagrada," Gómez's intelligence service, was dissolved. This allowed the army and navy to concentrate on their external defense mission (Burggraff 1972, 43–45, 50; Giacopini Zárraga 1992a).

In spite of these reforms, the military high command remained a bastion of the pre-professional army, with officers selected for reliability rather than competence, and the junior and mid-ranking officers chafed under them. The statutory age of retirement was often ignored, and lacking a military pension system, colonels and generals preferred to remain in the armed forces well into senescence. Promotions for junior professionalized officers, although fairer, remained glacial. Academy-trained officers found their career paths blocked by time servers in the high command, particularly once they had reached the field grade (middle-level) ranks of major and lieutenant colonel. Officer's salaries rose 12 percent during the Medina administration, yet the consumer price index rose 50 percent during the same period (Baptista 1991, 292), fueling discontent. Many lower-ranking officers felt that large proportions of the military budget vanished due to the corruption of the generals and the Ministry of Defense (Capriles Ayala 1985, 175–78).

Although junior officers faced better prospects under Presidents López and Medina, the pace of change was not fast enough to suit academy-trained officers. As indirect elections for a new president approached in December 1945, groups of junior officers, already associated in secret societies known as *logias militares*, began to conspire in earnest (Burggraff 1972, 43–46; Schaposnik 1985, 29–32).

Generals López Contreras and Medina were engaged in balancing between the demands of an emerging modern Venezuela and the privileges of the Andean network of families and retainers that had brought the regime to power. Lacking Gómez's authority, his successors felt compelled to consult the Andean senior officers in the armed forces and their networks of supporters on key decisions. In fact, López Contreras's choice for a successor, Diogenes Escalante, was blocked by these officers in 1941, who were not prepared to see power transferred to a civilian, even if he was from their region, the Andes (Velásquez 1995). Nevertheless, the shifting balance of power between Venezuela's parallel military forces progressively favored the professional military, depriving the authoritarian elites of the force necessary to defeat new political challenges.

The October 1945 Revolution

The year 1945 provided both a crisis and an opportunity for democratization as President Medina's term drew to an end. The worldwide economic dislocation generated by World War II and internal pressures associated with petroleum-driven modernization led to increasing demands from emerging social and political forces. These forces were able to organize relatively freely as President Medina abandoned the repressive tactics that had characterized the Gómez and López regimes. Unwittingly, Medina faced a classic dilemma: he had begun to modernize and liberalize the political regime in Venezuela, but he was unwilling and unable to cope with the unforeseen consequences of reform, including demands for greater political openness

(Huntington 1968). Medina's concessions to civilian participation in politics were too meager to satisfy democratizers but more than sufficient to drive the remaining members of the governing coalition of Andean cronies into the arms of former president López Contreras.

Adding to challenges by both the left and the right, President Medina's personal choice for his successor generated a full-blown political crisis. Full democratization was not in the cards in the 1945 elections, in which the president was selected indirectly by a Congress packed with pro-Medina supporters. The principal opposition party, Acción Democrática, and a secret society of professional junior officers, the Unión Patriótica Militar (UPM), therefore began to organize a coup d'état. Both factions of the conspiracy had every intention of following through with full democratization, but this narrow window of opportunity was lost due to the divisions among civilians over the rules of the game and their inability to achieve civilian control of the armed forces.

POLITICAL AND ECONOMIC MODERNIZATION
IN VENEZUELA

By the onset of World War II, Venezuela had become a rapidly modernizing society in which the new petroleum industry was transforming the national economy from its traditional rural agricultural basis to one centered on urban commercial interests and state spending derived from oil rents (Baptista 1991, 131, 142). Nearly half of Venezuela's gross domestic product (GDP) stemmed from oil, up from a negligible percentage in 1922. In 1922, shortly after the beginning of commercial oil exploitation, Venezuela's GDP from agriculture was ten times larger than that of oil. By 1945, the GDP derived from oil extraction and refining was nine times that of agriculture, even though the agricultural GDP had nearly doubled in the intervening years.[3] This rapid transformation had led to the rise of new economic and political groups, including a wide array of political parties, professional groups, and foreign and domestic business interest associations (Angulo Rivas 1993, 29–36).

The global restrictions on trade generated by World War II seriously affected the oil-dependent Venezuelan economy, diminishing government rents, generating rising inflation, and leading to shortages in consumer goods. With its large reserves of high-quality oil and close proximity to the United States, Venezuela became the largest foreign supplier of oil to the Allied forces during the war. However, Venezuela had also become heavily dependent on imports as a result of the shift toward an urban commercial economy, importing 50 percent of its food and two-thirds of its manufacturing goods (Valero 1994, 43–54). The semiautarchic conditions induced by the shortage of transportation and the threat of Axis submarines in the Caribbean during the war led to steep rises in the cost of living. While the civilian economy had improved somewhat by 1945, private consumption remained at 60 percent of the levels reached in the boom year of 1940 (Baptista 1991, 135, 292). Poor economic conditions provided ample grounds on which Medina's burgeoning political opposition could criticize the government and recruit new supporters.

This opposition, of which the left-of-center Acción Democrática party was the largest component, was prevented by the existing constitution from effectively participating in the process of selecting the next president. AD's criticism of the government and its influence over many groups in civil society made the party a significant force in Venezuelan politics. In response to this growing political challenge, Medina organized a pro-government party, the Partido Democrático Venezolano, which in a cynical alliance with Venezuelan Communists was able to maintain control of local governments in the municipal elections of 1944. Besides Acción Democrática and a sprinkling of nascent political groups, the only other opposition to the government was found to its political right, headed by the former president General López Contreras, who desired a return to the more conservative policies of his administration (Caballero 1988, 92–94).

Acción Democrática used its substantial lead in political organizing to ensure its dominance over the civilian opposition. It also controlled more than half of the extant labor unions. However, it had only a handful of members in Congress, which left Medina with complete control of both the legislative and executive branches of government (Valero 1994, 63–75). AD's inability to effectively use its political strength to achieve its goals within the existing political system made it a strong candidate for partnering with the restless junior officer corps in a conspiracy to overthrow President Medina.

The succession crisis in 1945 was the catalyst that brought the civilian and military opposition to power together. The powers granted to the president by the 1936 constitution essentially enabled Medina to designate his successor. Initially, Medina came under political pressure from his predecessor, General López Contreras, who wished to return to office for the 1946–51 presidential term. However, the growing popularity of Acción Democrática, Medina's concern for his reputation should he cave to López's demands, and his own liberal instincts led the outgoing president to seek a consensus presidential candidate with the left-center opposition. After some consultations, he selected as his successor the Venezuelan ambassador to the United States, Diogenes Escalante, a person who reportedly favored full democratization of the political system and greater state control over national oil production. Escalante was well received by many civilians in opposition, but his selection alienated a significant sector of conservatives, both in the civil administration and in the armed forces, that had formed the backbone of support for the authoritarian regime (Velásquez 1995).

The prospect of Escalante as president had little appeal for the ambitious conspirators of the professional bureaucratic faction of the armed forces, where the antigovernment secret society, the Unión Patriótica Militar, was gaining adherents. The UPM was founded in 1942 by a group of young officers who had recently returned from the general staff school at Los Chorillos, Peru. It advocated a thorough modernization of the armed forces, the elimination of government corruption, and political liberalization. The UPM also sought redress for the grievances of junior officers, including low salaries, inadequate professionalism in the armed forces, and glacial career advancement. The armed forces had been particularly hard hit by the economic crisis, and the junior officer corps had seen their wages stagnate and living standards decline (Stambouli 1980, 46–47; Giacopini Zárraga 1992a).

The UPM was also strongly influenced by the Allied victory in World War II. Many officers who had trained in the United States during the war returned seeking to improve the professional and technical standards of the Venezuelan armed forces. Their experiences in the United States had also indoctrinated them with a sense of democratic idealism that proved very influential among junior officers (Burggraff 1972, 55–58). Unlike some of their conservative superior officers, who supported former president General López Contreras, officers of the UPM rejected the Escalante candidacy because they foresaw no significant change in the status of the armed forces under what they viewed as a continuation of previous authoritarian regimes. The combination of professional, technocratic, and democratic ideals offered junior military officers a potent alternative vision to the hidebound cronyism and conservatism of the military high command.

Although it was ambitious, the UPM recognized early on that it would have to seek an alliance with civilians to succeed in its aim of overthrowing Medina and reforming Venezuela. It had only recruited 150 officers into the secret society, bringing its membership to approximately 10 percent of the

Venezuelan officer corps (Schaposnik 1985, 32–33). Led by a talented organizer, Major Marcos Pérez Jiménez, the UPM established conspiratorial cells in all major garrisons and developed plans to execute a coup d'état. However, the conspirators were all junior officers, led by six army majors. Major Pérez Jiménez and the other leaders of the UPM knew that they lacked any experience in governing or politics, and they also feared that should they seek to govern alone, they would be perceived at home and abroad as a fascist movement similar to Juan Perón's in Argentina.

This led the UPM to seek an alliance with Acción Democrática, which they saw as the only feasible civilian alternative to the Medina government. They dismissed any possibility of cooperating with the official party, the Partido Democrático Venezolano, who in an ironic twist, was allied during World War II with the Venezuelan Communist Party, one of the few other civilian political parties. General López Contreras was seen by the UPM as a reactionary defender of the logic of armed cronyism who was unlikely to take any steps to modernize the armed forces. Only AD was firmly in the opposition and seemed to have a modernizing, progressive platform consonant with the ideas held by UPM officers. In a meeting arranged by mutual friends, the leaders of the UPM and Acción Democrática began highly secret discussions on the possibility of a joint attempt to overthrow the government.

Initially, Rómulo Betancourt and the other members of the Acción Democrática leadership were highly suspicious of the intentions of the UPM; they did not want to be associated with another iteration of the all too common Venezuelan experience with authoritarian rule. An Escalante presidency offered AD the hope that the authoritarian regime could be reformed from within, ultimately allowing full democratization. Betancourt and his compatriots, however, were also impatient to implement their ideas for modernizing and liberalizing Venezuela's society and economy, and they were eventually persuaded to take a shortcut to power by joining the UPM conspiracy. The rank-and-file members of both the UPM and AD were completely unaware of the growing closeness between their leaders, and they remained mutually hostile and suspicious (Giacopini Zárraga 1992a, 1994c; Anzola Anzola 1992). Only the leaders in AD and the UPM recognized the usefulness of an alliance as a means of gaining power.

The last shreds of reticence toward the conspiracy among AD's leaders dissipated once Diogenes Escalante was incapacitated by a stroke in August 1945 upon his return to Venezuela (Velásquez 1995).[4] Medina, ignoring opposition demands, selected a nondescript lawyer from the Andean re gion, Angel Biaggini, as his successor. Biaggini, then minister of agriculture, was widely seen as a particularly poor choice for the presidency since he had little national political experience. Both the right and the left assumed that Medina had simply selected a pliable individual who would continue to do his bidding once he had retired from office. Withdrawing its support from the government candidate, Acción Democrática decided to commit to the UPM-led coup d'état planned for October or November 1945 rather than endure five more years of semidictatorial rule (Valero 1994, 82–84.)

The arrest of two UPM leaders, Majors Marcos Pérez Jiménez and Julio César Vargas, on 16 October sparked the coup against Medina. Medina had received information from a relative in the officer corps concerning the potential coup d'état and had a list of conspirators in his hands, yet he refused to believe that a large-scale plot existed. Entirely trusting of the junior officer corps, Medina took no special precautions and ordered only a tentative investigation of the actions of UPM leaders Pérez Jiménez and Vargas. The membership of the UPM had previously agreed that the arrest of one of their leaders would be the signal to begin the coup d'état, so on 17 October they contacted their allies in Acción Democrática and set their plans in motion. On 18 October a handful of rebel officers seized one of the principal armories of Caracas, the Cuartel San Carlos, and the presidential palace at Miraflores, almost without firing a shot. Major Carlos Delgado Chalbaud, director of academic studies at the Academia Militar, rallied his cadets to rebel against Medina. Other garrisons in Caracas remained ambivalent, and in the confusion, many seemed to believe that the coup attempt was actually a right-wing effort led by former president López Contreras to remove the more liberal Medina from power (Giacopini Zárraga 1994a; Tarre Murzi 1983, 86–88). The only forces that vigorously supported the government were the Caracas municipal police and the Urdaneta Battalion of the army. Medina, who was completely stunned by the uprising, vacillated in counterattacking. In the face of reports of the addition of airpower to the rebellion, he quickly surrendered.

Medina's indecisiveness in the face of the uprising allowed the outnumbered rebels to succeed. All together, perhaps a few hundred soldiers had participated on the side of the rebels in Caracas, and casualties for all sides, civilian and military, are estimated at approximately 400. By all reports, Medina could have quickly crushed the uprising with only a modicum of decision and common sense, principally by issuing heavier weapons to the loyal Caracas police force and by pressing home the attack against the centers of the rebellion at the Academia Militar and the government palace. Medina could also have made a more deliberate effort to rally his many military supporters to his side. Instead, the military officers of the UPM and the leaders of Acción Democrática almost effortlessly found themselves in control of the Venezuelan government. The authoritarian regime collapsed so quickly that AD had no opportunity to mobilize mass civilian support for the coup, as it had originally planned (Giacopini Zárraga 1992c).

Even though the UPM leadership forthrightly allowed AD take the upper hand in the new government that was formed after the coup, much of the rest of the officer corps was opposed to a civilian-led government, had not participated in the conspiracy, and did not sympathize with its objectives (Giacopini Zárraga 1992a). Even after old-line officers belonging to the "armed cronyism" wing of the military were purged, the professional bureaucratic wing of the officer corps quickly split between those officers who believed in conducting professional modernization within a democratic context and those who advocated a modernizing authoritarian government based on technocratic principles, very similar in spirit to the bureaucratic authoritarianism that Guillermo O'Donnell (1979) identified in the Southern Cone during the 1960s and Brian Loveman and Thomas M. Davies (1989) describe more broadly as characteristic Latin American military "anti-politics."

Internal divisions in the Venezuelan armed forces festered and would shortly fuel a near-constant cycle of conspiracies against the newly formed interim government, the Junta Revolucionaria de Gobierno (JRG). Neither AD nor the UPM had much confidence in the other, leading to tensions within the governing civilian-military coalition. Moreover, AD lacked either the temperament or the experience to successfully exploit the divisions within the armed forces to secure military subordination and institutionalize civilian control of the armed forces. As a result, it followed a perverse strategy of civilian control based on appeasing the armed forces and granting them broad discretion over security affairs, domestic and international. This increased the military's autonomy to such an extent that it endangered democratization.

ACCIÓN DEMOCRÁTICA: EXPLAINING THE ABSENCE
OF AN AGENDA FOR CIVILIAN CONTROL

Although Acción Democrática had developed a broad range of prescriptions for the problems of Venezuelan society, its leaders and intellectual cadres had devoted slight attention to the subject of the armed forces. AD recognized the key role of the armed forces in sustaining past authoritarian regimes in Venezuela, and World War II had heightened its awareness of the importance of modern military forces in the defense of democratic societies. However, neither AD nor other civilian groups addressed military issues other than tangentially since discussions concerning this institution were generally considered taboo in Venezuelan society. Publicly, AD confined itself to a critique of the Andean regionalist bias in the military high command and advocated an apolitical, nondeliberative role for the armed forces, coupled with a thorough modernization of its institutions.[5] Within AD, the armed forces were viewed with suspicion and hostility and were considered creatures of the long Andean hegemony under Presidents Castro, Gómez, López, and Medina. Initially, Betancourt was skeptical of the intentions of the leadership of the UPM since he found it hard to believe that these junior officers, whose families largely originated in the Andean states, could be plotting to overthrow the Andean clique who held power (Anzola Anzola 1992).

Lacking much knowledge of or particular interest in the armed forces, Betancourt and his civilian colleagues reached an agreement with the leaders of the UPM prior to the coup to allow the armed forces autonomy and self-administration. In return, they sought a free hand for Acción Democrática in matters of domestic policy. Once in power, Betancourt and his collaborators relied almost entirely on allies within the armed forces, principally a group of young officers who were sympathetic toward AD, led by Captain Mario Vargas, to prevent the overthrow of the regime (Burggraff 1972, 79–80).

AD limited its efforts to establish formal civilian control of the armed forces to a few clauses of the 1947 constitution. These called on the armed forces to assume an apolitical, nondeliberative role in defense of national sovereignty and withdrew suffrage rights from active-duty armed forces personnel (Burggraff 1972, 92). Although Betancourt and his colleagues favored military modernization, they placed all control over the design and implementation of these reforms in the hands of the minister of defense and the Armed Forces Chief of Staff. Before even entering the government or facing military pressure, Acción Democrática chose, if it engaged in any conscious planning at all, a perverse strategy of appeasement toward the armed forces that would eventually return to haunt it.

OCTOBER 1945: A NARROW OPPORTUNITY STRUCTURE

AD's intellectual disdain toward military affairs and its political inexperience led it to squander the slim opportunity for civilian control created by the transition to democracy. Due to the secrecy of conspiracy to overthrow Medina and its rapid success, there was no significant degree of civilian mobilization nor any elite coalescence around a democratization agenda. This meant that even though the armed forces were divided, so were the civilians. AD made little effort to include nascent civilian political forces in the new regime or to seek a societal consensus in favor of democracy. Instead, its formidable organizational hegemony and its brutal political competitiveness quickly provoked the disloyalty of other political and societal groups. The absence of civilian consensus, mobilization, or an agenda for civilian control provided democratizers with a narrow opportunity structure. Coupled with the absence of civilian strategies, this situation rendered the development of regime leverage over the armed forces impossible. Moreover, AD's inexperience in military affairs fatally undermined regime capacity in this area. The combination of low regime leverage and capacity made the collapse of the democratization process almost inevitable.

Defending Democratization? Military Factionalism, Civilian Partisanship, and a Strategy of Appeasement

AD's abdication of responsibility for civil-military affairs meant that the fate of the new regime would be determined by the internal struggle for supremacy within the armed forces. Once General Medina had been overthrown, two new military logics emerged within the armed forces: democratic professionalism and technocratic authoritarianism. Major Pérez Jiménez, who advocated a technocratic, apolitical, and conservative approach to government, belonged to the latter group and was appointed Chief of the General Staff (Schaposnik 1985, 45–49). Captain Mario Vargas, representative of the junior officers of the UPM and a proponent of democratization and military professionalization, was initially appointed minister of communications. These officers cooperated so long as they faced a substantial threat from disgruntled opponents within the armed forces. After all, Medina's supporters had surrendered without being militarily defeated, and only 10 percent of the officer corps had been sworn to the UPM before the coup. Throughout the two years of the transitional AD-led government, these two military factions defended the regime to prevent their replacement by other factions organized around the formerly dominant logic, armed cronyism. Acción Democrática watched these conspiracies nervously from the sidelines but created no institutions of civilian control that could be used to defend democracy.

THE FACTIONAL STALEMATE INSIDE THE VENEZUELAN ARMED FORCES, 1945–1947

In the weeks following the October 1945 coup, the victorious UPM purged the principal bastion of armed cronyism: the colonels and generals who had risen to power under President-Generals Gómez, López, and Medina. Upon taking power, the JRG decreed the expulsion of all officers of the rank of lieutenant colonel and higher from the armed forces, thus removing over 160 supporters of the ancien régime from the institution. This had the further advantage of creating command billets for most of the officers who had contributed to the October coup d'état (Anzola Anzola 1992). With the most senior remaining officers holding the rank of major, the armed forces were in the hands of young professional officers (both Delgado Chalbaud and Pérez Jiménez were in their early thirties). This led to rapid career advancement as relatively low-ranking officers took over significant positions. The second-, third-, and fourth-year cadets of the Academia Militar were summarily graduated without completing their education and promoted to the rank of sub-lieutenant. Junior officers served on the General Staff, in the Ministry of Defense, as senior garrison commanders, and as heads of the military services (Capriles Ayala 1985, 171–74). For example, Lieutenant Horacio Conde López, still in his early twenties, was appointed to head the Venezuelan state airline, Aeropostal. Military officers were also placed in command of some local police forces, replacing administrators who were loyal to the previous regime. Marquez Añez, only a captain in the army at the time, was appointed the commander of the key Caracas metropolitan police force, with close to two thousand personnel under his supervision. The large majority of junior officers who had not been sworn to the conspiracy gained substantially from the purge of senior officers. This reconciled them to the new armed forces high command; yet, even after the purge the officer corps remained more conservative than the victorious UPM faction, which contained most of the "democratic professional" wing of the officer corps.

Following the purge, the Unión Patriótica Militar agreed to dissolve itself, a move that had serious consequences for the democratic professional faction. The new military leadership argued that abandoning the secret society would erase internal distinctions in the armed forces between those officers who had participated on the victorious side of the coup and those who had opposed it. Former UPM members mostly followed the lead of the popular Captain Mario Vargas, who unconditionally supported democratization. However, without the coordination and prestige provided by the UPM, the democratic professionals in the officer corps found themselves increasingly isolated in a sea of conservative officers. Meanwhile, Major Pérez Jiménez wisely decided to court the far larger number of officers who were never affiliated with the "October revolution" by maintaining his distance from the governing party, Acción Democrática (Giacopini Zárraga 1995b). This accelerated the factionalization of the armed forces between the technocratic authoritarians led by Major Pérez Jiménez and the democratic professionals under Captain Vargas.

In the first months that followed the 18 October 1945 coup, the officers who favored the military logic of democratic professionalism prospered. The victory and technological prowess of the Allies in World War II had raised the prestige of democracy, making democratic professionalism an attractive military ideology (Vargas 1949).[6] Captain Vargas and his supporters differed from many officers in that they were inclined to attribute government missteps during the AD transitional government more to the failings of individual civilians than to the nature of the democratic regime itself. Mario Vargas was eventually promoted and appointed inspector general of the armed forces in 1947. This was the third-highest position in the armed forces, which he revitalized and imbued with great administrative authority, even though he held no direct command over troops. So long as he was inspector general, Vargas was able to maneuver his supporters into key command positions and prevent the military from falling under the control of the technocratic authoritarian faction. Rómulo Betancourt and other leaders of Acción Democrática were well aware of Vargas's pro-democratic attitudes and considered him their principal ally in the armed forces leadership (Burggraff 1972, 92; Giacopini Zárraga 1994b).

However, the longer that AD governed, the more that adherents to the logic of technocratic authoritarianism gained in the officer corps. Many officers were predisposed to oppose civilian rule because they were suspicious of Acción Democrática for its rumored connections to international Communism. Others were simply ambitious, convinced that if the upstarts in the UPM could overthrow a government, they could too (García Villasmil 1995a).

The high levels of partisanship that characterized civilian politics during the transition to democracy made many officers long for a more disciplined and apolitical form of government. These officers either attempted to organize their own conspiracies or gravitated toward the technocratic authoritarian faction. Major Pérez Jiménez, who opposed allowing AD to remain in power, took advantage of this trend and gathered increasing numbers of followers into his fold (Soto Urrútia 1994a). For his followers, the key error of the 1945 coup had been to hand over power to civilians. The military reform process and the increasing strength of his faction gave Pérez Jiménez confidence that the armed forces would be prepared to govern directly under any future authoritarian regime.

Between 1945 and 1947, both the technocratic authoritarian and democratic professional factions of the officer corps shared an interest in suppressing rebellions in the armed forces, although for very different reasons. The latter genuinely desired the preservation of the civilian government and the modernization of the armed forces. The former were principally interested in preventing military rivals from seizing control of government before they were ready to do so themselves (Velásquez 1995). These two factions faced substantial challenges from officers who felt slighted by the outcome of 18 October 1945. Major Julio César Vargas and Lieutenant Colonel Juan Pérez Jiménez, older brothers of the faction leaders, both led failed rebellions against the government in 1946. Lieutenant Colonel Rincón Calcaño led a particularly serious coup attempt on 10 December 1946, in which many of the garrisons of Caracas and Jóvito Villalba, a leader of an opposition political party, were involved. In September 1947 government officials and loyal military officers resorted to impromptu tactics to defeat a coup attempt by Major Eleazar Niño. Former president General López Contreras sponsored two attempts to overthrow the Venezuelan government in 1947. One of his failed plots involved U.S. citizens who purchased and flew war-surplus B-25 bombers from the southeastern United States to Nicaragua, from where they planned to launch an aerial attack on government installations in Caracas in coordination with a local military rebellion (Burggraff 1972, 92–93; Schaposnik 1985, 52–54; Giacopini Zárraga 1994c). At the time, it seemed that hardly a month passed without some sort of internal conspiracy by the remnants of the ancien régime's supporters against the government. These recurring episodes of unrest undermined the stability of the transitional civilian government, so that Betancourt and Acción Democrática stumbled from crisis to crisis, unable to even begin consolidating the new regime.

A PERVERSE STRATEGY: ACCIÓN DEMOCRÁTICA AND
THE APPEASEMENT OF THE ARMED FORCES

AD leaders failed to take advantage of the upheaval in the armed forces
to practice "divide and conquer" strategies, and by adopting a strategy of
appeasement, they relinquished any possibility of establishing regime leverage over the military. AD hoped that the military would resolve its internal
struggles in a manner favorable to the party and democracy, but AD preferred to appease the officer corps rather than intervene in military affairs. In
fact, to label civilian efforts vis-à-vis the armed forces a "strategy" is a considerable overstatement since they were pursued only sporadically and in
the absence of any overall plan for reforming civil-military relations. While
Betancourt was decisive enough in moments of crisis, he was never able to
rid himself of the principal threat to his government: the technocratic authoritarian faction entrenched in the General Staff. In the absence of civilian
checks to military autonomy, Pérez Jiménez and his co-conspirators were
able to consolidate their authority over the armed forces unchallenged.

At first, Acción Democrática sought to buy the loyalty of the officer corps
by remedying the principal sources of military discontent under the Medina
administration. It did so by moving quickly to increase the defense budget and military remuneration. The budget first doubled and then tripled
between 1945 and 1947. Officers' salaries increased by 37 percent and those
of soldiers by 57 percent. Increased allocations for food, lodging, medicine,
and training improved the conditions of service considerably. Both war-
surplus and modern military equipment, including several new destroyers
and squadrons of jet aircraft, were purchased for the army, air force, and
navy. Officers were sent abroad in large numbers to study in the military
establishments of the victorious Allies. Enrollment in the service academies
also doubled and tripled during the 1945–47 period, and the armed forces
expanded rapidly. Even more important, promotions were largely made on
the basis of seniority and merit, ending the clientalist practices that had governed the armed forces during the previous four decades (Burggraff 1972,
81–82, 92; Schaposnik 1985, 52–54). While these measures may have resulted
in some short-term gratitude, Acción Democrática did not achieve any degree of civilian control through them.

Betancourt and AD party activists then attempted to deepen their personal links to progressive military officers, hoping to establish a network of
supporters as their principal defense against military intervention. AD tried
to build ideological commitment in the armed forces by proselytizing the

officer corps and enlisted personnel. The party went so far as to enroll members of its youth wing as cadets in the Academia Militar (Anzola Anzola 1992). However, AD was always constrained by its prearranged division of labor between civilian and military spheres, and it never pressed home any of its efforts to establish civilian authority over the armed forces.

Civilians on the JRG attempted to develop their own intelligence sources and internal security police, but accusations of torture of political prisoners by AD party members led to a backlash by both the military members of the JRG and by the civilian opposition (Fuenmayor 1981, 8:49–56; Giacopini Zárraga 1995b). Furthermore, at the time of the elections for the Constituent Assembly in 1947, the military high command was able to force the resignation of a leading member of AD, Valmore Rodríguez, as minister of interior, alleging that only a nonpartisan independent should hold a position that controlled the national police and internal security forces. Betancourt was also aware of Pérez Jiménez's efforts to promote anti-AD sentiment and recruit followers in the armed forces. He twice maneuvered Pérez Jiménez into taking lengthy trips overseas in an attempt to weaken his hold over the officer corps, but Betancourt did not dare to provoke the principal antigovernment conspirator in the armed forces by taking more decisive action (Giacopini Zárraga 1995b).

Sporadic moves by civilian leaders to ingratiate themselves with the armed forces proved to have a perverse effect, breeding the military's contempt and diminishing regime leverage over the military. A more prepared or experienced civilian administration could have manipulated the military's internal factions to facilitate a strategy of "divide and conquer" and set the 1945–48 democratization effort on the road to civilian control. Instead, the JRG, flawed since its inception by a joint civil-military composition and AD's lack of interest in defense matters, was never able to act strategically to achieve, let alone institutionalize, civilian control.

The government's lack of capacity to manage military affairs allowed the armed forces to act without constraint. By virtue of their control of the most senior positions in the armed forces, the leaders of the technocratic authoritarian faction were able to implement military reform measures that enhanced their institution's autonomy and jurisdictional boundaries. These reforms allowed the technocratic authoritarians in the high command to consolidate their control over the officer corps and position the armed forces to seize power from an essentially defenseless civilian government.

MILITARY REFORM DURING THE JUNTA
REVOLUCIONARIA DE GOBIERNO

Acción Democrática's abdication of responsibility for security affairs allowed the entrepreneurial leaders of the technocratic authoritarian faction of the armed forces to seize control of the defense agenda in the transitional government. While many of the officers who had participated in the coup against Medina were inclined toward a pro-democratic professionalism, the military rebellions that the armed forces leadership fought to suppress during the transitional government period were a constant reminder that conservative officers predominated in the armed forces. Chief of the General Staff, Major Pérez Jiménez, the principal exponent of technocratic rule, used the power of his position to shape the military reform process, weaken the democratic professional faction, and organize conservative officers into a movement he controlled. By acquiescing to these reforms, the civilian government aided and abetted this process.

To secure his faction's dominance of the officer corps, Pérez Jiménez first needed to improve his control over the administration and organization of the armed forces. Together with Lieutenant Colonel Delgado Chalbaud, Pérez Jiménez persuaded the JRG to issue Decrees 348 and 349 on 22 June 1946, which centralized authority over national security in the Armed Forces General Staff. Under previous defense legislation passed in 1939, the armed forces had been defined as the army and the navy, both of which were subordinate to the armed forces inspector general and the General Staff, while the president retained the senior position of commander in chief. Under Decree 349, the Ministry of War and the Navy was renamed the Ministry of National Defense, and the Guardia Nacional and the national police force were both legally incorporated into the overall defense structure as subordinate second-tier (Fuerzas Armadas de Cooperación) and third-tier (Fuerzas Armadas Policiales) components.

This represented a crucial change in the organization of the state security forces since all internal and external security organizations now came under a single command. The rubric of "Fuerzas Armadas" emphasized the military/coercive aspects of the internal security forces as opposed to preventive/policing roles. Decree 349 removed the mission of maintaining public order from among the primary duties of the army and navy and assigned them instead to the police in the first instance and to the Guardia Nacional in emergencies. In practice, the senior military commander of any given district had control of all government forces in emergency situations since the internal security forces were subordinated to the military (Burggraff 1972, 99; Avendaño Lugo 1982, 139–40).

Such centralized military control of state security was particularly dangerous to civilian rulers during this period since the minister of defense and the Chief of the General Staff were the only legal channels by which the president could transmit orders to the armed forces. As established under the 1939 armed forces legislation, active-duty officers assigned to these positions controlled operations, assignments, promotions, and funding allocations, enabling whomever held them to dominate the armed forces (Anzola Anzola 1992). As its chief, Pérez Jiménez revitalized the Armed Forces General Staff and made it the center for planning and administration for all branches of the armed forces, with the chiefs of the navy, air force, and Guardia Nacional having subordinate secretarial roles. The army, to which Pérez Jiménez belonged, achieved supremacy as a result of its greater size and prestige, and the navy, air force, and Guardia Nacional all made do with considerably smaller budgets, manpower, and organizational resources. Furthermore, even though the Venezuelan constitution assigned the role of commander in chief to the president, the minister of defense essentially acted as a vice commander, given his ability to block presidential orders and issue commands directly to the armed forces (Schaposnik 1985, 240–41, 371–78). This placed a civilian president in the position of either having to capitulate or resort to illegal measures in the event of disobedience by his senior military commanders.

The 1945–48 military reform process ensured the victory of the technocratic authoritarian faction in the internal power struggle within the officer corps and placed the democratization process at risk. Pérez Jiménez and his collaborator Delgado Chalbaud were able to use the rationale of modernization to push the acquiescent democratizers in the JRG into issuing decrees that supported the centralization of military authority. The presence of military officers on the JRG and their ability to manipulate civilians into accepting their demands indicate the degree to which these groups shared authority over state leadership during this period, as illustrated in figure 2.1. The purge of senior officers following the October 1945 coup completed the professionalization of the officer corps and undermined a rival source of conservative ideology in the armed forces. Regulations channeled most civilian-military interaction through the minister of defense, effectively preventing any civilian oversight of military activities, just as defense legislation denied democratizers control of external and internal security affairs.

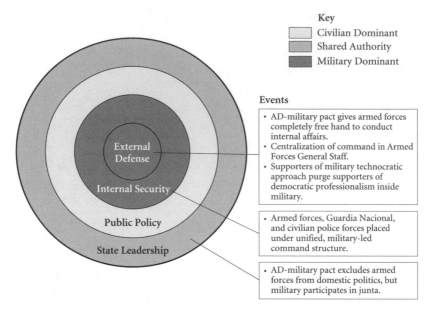

Figure 2.1. Civil-Military Jurisdictional Boundaries, ca. 1946: Institutional Reforms Expand Military Autonomy and Jurisdiction

Given this degree of autonomy, the proponents of technocratic authoritarianism were able to shield themselves from supervision by Acción Democrática. Expanded jurisdictional boundaries were achieved almost effortlessly, since AD had already abdicated responsibility for security affairs through its agreed division of labor with the UPM. Altogether, this represented a substantial expansion of military authority above and beyond the boundaries of the previous authoritarian regimes, effectively insulating the armed forces from regime leverage or supervision and preventing full democratization. Ironically, Venezuela's democracy allowed the military more authority over state affairs than the previous military dictatorships ever had.

The Failure of the Democratic *Trienio*

By failing to create regime leverage during the 1945–48 *Trienio*, as Venezuelans called the three-year experiment with democracy, Acción Democrática contributed to the collapse of the first freely elected government of Venezuela, that of President Rómulo Gallegos. As the new government took office in 1948, the technocratic authoritarian faction of the armed forces was increasingly confident of its ability to impose limits on democratization. Meanwhile, AD's resounding electoral successes in 1946 and 1947 masked the inherent instability of the new regime, encouraging its supporters to take maximalist political positions and engage in vicious partisanship with the civilian opposition. In doing so, AD destroyed whatever support the democratization project had in the larger political and civil society and wrecked the civilian component of regime leverage over the military. With the officer corps increasingly under the sway of the logic of technocratic authoritarianism and the civilian opposition adopting a disloyal stance toward the new regime, President Gallegos had no base of support from which to defend his administration. This state of affairs allowed the newly elected government to be overthrown in a bloodless coup within nine months of its inauguration.

THE DECLINE OF CIVILIAN CONSENSUS
ON DEMOCRATIZATION

The logic of radical partisanship that Acción Democrática practiced during the transition to democracy sowed the seeds of political opposition and disloyalty toward the Gallegos administration in 1948. Rather than wait until an elected government had taken power, AD impatiently set out to modernize Venezuela as rapidly as possible during the 1945–47 transition to democracy and rarely consulted with either the political opposition or the nascent forces in civil society on public policy. The AD-controlled JRG became a "machine for issuing decrees," mandating changes in legislation, state agencies, and public policy that governed all areas of Venezuelan society (Stambouli 1980, 66). The failure to consult other political organizations or conservative sectors of civil society, including the business community, foreign oil companies, and the Catholic Church, created the necessary conditions for the escalation of partisan conflict among civilians.

Acción Democrática came to power too swiftly in 1945, having little experience in cooperation with other political organizations and no particular reason to share power. Civil society and political parties in Venezuela had never mobilized, coordinated, or coalesced around a single democratization project prior to the transition. As a result, they quickly lapsed into partisanship. AD governed as if it were still a part of the squabbling political opposition, rather than in control of the state. Facing the political hegemony of Acción Democrática, other recently formed opposition parties had no incentive to preserve the new democratic system. Furthermore, as a wave of new opportunistic adherents entered the party following 1945, AD became increasingly denatured and undisciplined, which reduced the ability of the party leadership to control its followers (Arreaza 1994). Thus, the democratization process from 1945 to 1948 developed without consensual rules of the political game, without a broad base of civilian support, and amid a climate of political retaliation and mutual recrimination. AD reacted to the perceived disloyalty of its political opposition with the logic of radical partisanship that had preserved the party under authoritarian rule, a logic incompatible with democratic rule.

Important elements of civil society joined the disloyal opposition in reaction to AD's policies, both during the Gallegos administration and during the JRG that preceded it. Foreign and domestic business interests opposed the pro-labor government policies that had led to an explosion in union organizing between 1945 and 1948, and they were unsettled by the increasingly assertive demands of state-protected union leaders and workers. Foreign oil companies were especially concerned by AD policies on petroleum taxation and conservation, which had substantially increased the oil industry's tax burdens and led to restrictions on local exploration and extraction operations (Mohr 1976, 65–69, 298–99). Large landowners were threatened by an AD-imposed agrarian reform that, while moderate in its provisions, was sufficient to turn this small minority within the upper class against the government.

However, by far the most partisan and well-organized attack on AD's control of government came from the Catholic Church, which suspected the organization of being a Communist front. When the AD-controlled JRG acted in 1946 to secularize the Catholic Church–dominated school system, the church hierarchy led a vigorous public protest campaign and attacked AD in extreme terms. AD was labeled a Communistic and atheistic organization bent on extending its totalitarian hegemony over society through its penetration of the private education system. Under pressure from private educators and parents, Acción Democrática eventually recanted, but this political confrontation alienated significant sectors of the middle and upper classes from the democratic system (Levine 1973, 69–88; Stambouli 1980, 69–79.)

Despite intensifying elite political opposition to AD, Rómulo Gallegos was elected to the presidency on 14 December 1947 with the support of over 74 percent of the voters in a very high turnout election. With this victory, Acción Democrática demonstrated its hegemony for the third time in three years, having swept two previous elections for local offices and the Constituent Assembly with over 70 percent of votes cast. Given this immense popular support, AD felt unconstrained by the preferences or opinions of its opposition.

On taking office, Gallegos appointed a cabinet consisting almost exclusively of AD party members, which further reduced whatever stake the opposition might have had in supporting the new regime. The only exception was the minister of national defense, Lieutenant Colonel Delgado Chalbaud. AD's principal opponents, the Christian Democratic party COPEI and the left-center party URD, found themselves completely excluded from government at all levels and constantly harassed by AD's supporters on the streets. They reacted with escalating partisan attacks, accusing AD of corruption, favoritism, gross mismanagement, and Communist sympathies. The COPEI newspaper, *El Gráfico*, was particularly vicious in its attacks on the government, even commenting favorably on the constantly circulating rumors of a coup d'état (Angulo Rivas 1993, 50–53, 55–59; Arreaza 1994).

THE COALESCENCE OF MILITARY OPPOSITION
TO PRESIDENT GALLEGOS

President Gallegos was not well suited to the role of commander in chief of an emerging democracy by reason of his lack of experience and volatile character, a fact that the military high command had long recognized. Gallegos, one of Venezuela's best-known twentieth-century novelists and the nominal leader of AD since the early 1940s, was considered a person of high moral principle and personal probity. Nevertheless, Minister of Defense Delgado Chalbaud warned the actual leader of Acción Democrática, Rómulo Betancourt, that Gallegos was not capable of successfully managing either the presidency or the armed forces (Schaposnik 1985, 98–105; Giacopini Zárraga 1995b).

Gallegos's uncompromising attitude toward the military inflamed many in the officer corps who were already disgusted with Acción Democrática's behavior during the transitional government. Under the influence of the escalating partisanship in civil and political society, officers increasingly felt that the 1945 "revolution" had been betrayed. In particular, charges that AD was a Communist front severely damaged the party's standing within the military, and these beliefs were reinforced by both the efforts of the high command and the U.S. embassy's military attachés (Mohr 1976, 220–22, 293–99).[7]

Appeasement was no longer a tenable strategy with the uncompromising Gallegos as president, and AD's halfhearted proselytization campaign within the armed forces was sufficient to anger the officer corps without gaining any real measure of control. Civilian efforts to displace Lieutenant Colonel Pérez Jiménez and Lieutenant Colonel Delgado Chalbaud from their leadership positions, along with attempts by Gallegos to reassign other officers in the wake of his election, particularly threatened the military. When these resentments were combined with rumors in 1948 of efforts by Acción Democrática to form a party militia of workers and peasants, the armed forces turned almost entirely against Gallegos (Schaposnik 1985, 98–101, 111–13).

Beyond the ideological hostility of military officers toward Acción Democrática, Gallegos's position vis-à-vis the military was further weakened by the collapse of the democratic professional faction of the officer corps. Mario Vargas, by now a lieutenant colonel, remained the leader of the democratic professional wing of the officer corps and defender of the regime as the armed forces inspector general until 1948. He finally succumbed to a persistent pulmonary infection and was forced to leave Venezuela for lengthy medical treatment in the United States in the second half of the year. Lieutenant Colonel Pérez Jiménez, leader of the technocratic authoritarian faction, who had been previously "exiled" by Rómulo Betancourt, was allowed by Gallegos to return from a lengthy military mission to the Southern Cone countries and reassume his duties as Armed Forces Chief of Staff. With Vargas no longer in Venezuela and Pérez Jiménez back in control of the General Staff, the logic of democratic professionalism no longer had high-level protection and encouragement, and the officers who adhered to it were slowly displaced from important positions or recruited to the ranks of technocratic authoritarianism. As Chief of the General Staff, Pérez Jiménez was able to use his administrative powers to grant favors and protect his supporters from punishment, binding anti-AD officers more tightly into his faction. As figure 2.2 illustrates, Pérez Jiménez took advantage of the centralized military institutions he had created to consolidate his control over the officer corps soon after his return from Argentina in early 1948 (Giacopini Zárraga 1995b).

The inauguration of President Gallegos temporarily brought an end to the influential role that the armed forces had held in the outermost circle of civil-military jurisdictional boundaries, state leadership selection. Unlike the JRG, where officers held several ministerial and executive positions, Gallegos appointed no military officers to his cabinet other than to the position of minister of defense. However, the dominance of the military over internal and external security affairs, a direct result of AD's abdication of responsibility over defense-related issues, deprived the civilian government of

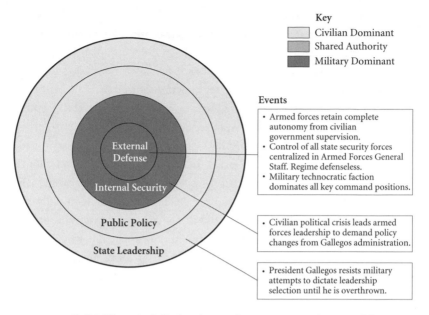

Figure 2.2. Civil-Military Jurisdictional Boundaries, ca. 1948: The Armed Forces Prepare to Take Power

any means by which it could defend itself. In the absence of civilian control, efforts by the armed forces to expand their jurisdictional boundaries were inevitably successful.

ORGANIZING THE COUP AGAINST GALLEGOS

The Gallegos administration survived for nine months before facing a fatal military challenge, despite persistent rumors of conspiracies against the government and the steady drumbeat of political partisanship. By now, the officer corps was sufficiently disaffected to act against the government, yet Delgado Chalbaud and Pérez Jiménez were unsure of how best to proceed. The high command eventually decided to target AD's political hegemony within the regime and the state since it was the most prominent source of civilian and military discontent. They agreed to demand the resignation of Acción Democrática's government ministers and their replacement with a cabinet of political independents. Furthermore, the military leaders also agreed to press for the retirement of the two leading exponents of the logic of democratic professionalism, Lieutenant Colonels Mario Vargas and Gámez Arellano. They also sought the disarming of AD party members, the dissolution of civilian militias, and the expulsion from Venezuela of Rómulo Betancourt, former president of the transitional government (Giacopini Zárraga 1994d). Essentially, the military high command wanted to preserve the presidency of Rómulo Gallegos while stripping it of any substantial power. This would allow the technocratic authoritarian wing of the armed forces to purge the government of any AD influence and control public policy through newly appointed independent government ministers.

Even though the high command had already drawn up plans to confront Gallegos, Pérez Jiménez and Delgado Chalbaud were forced to act sooner than expected by an insurrection led by several junior officers, among them Major Tomás Mendoza, on 16 November 1948. Pérez Jiménez initially believed this uprising to be a radical offshoot of his own conspiracy, but he was quickly disabused of this notion by the insubordinate rebels (Giacopini Zárraga 1994d). On 17 November, in a meeting before assembled officers at the Ambrosio Plaza barracks in Caracas, Gallegos angrily railed against military insubordination and forcefully restated his unconditional rejection of all external pressures on his government. Gallegos's speech so angered the officers that many of those who had attended began pressuring their superiors for immediate action against the government. Facing the possibility of being displaced by more radical junior officers, Pérez Jiménez and Delgado Chalbaud requested a meeting on 19 November with President Gallegos and presented their list of demands. Gallegos flatly refused to accede to this ultimatum, citing his moral and legal obligation to defend the constitution, and thereby set the stage for the collapse of his administration (Capriles Ayala 1985, 234–37; Schaposnik 1985, 88–89, 108).

On 20 November, Gallegos reacted to the military ultimatum by suspending constitutional guarantees of freedom of assembly, speech, and the press, perversely dissuading the mass mobilization that could have saved his government. AD party leaders worked to restrain their activists, hoping to appease the armed forces and to avoid the appearance of a government in crisis. Instead, the leadership of AD brought in two negotiators: the still sickly Mario Vargas, flown in from the United States, and Governor José Giacopini Zárraga from the southern Amazonas territory, a former chief of staff of the JRG and longtime friend of the military high command. Vargas arrived on 20 November, and following negotiations with his fellow officers, he concluded that military sentiment had turned so far against the Gallegos government that resistance was futile. Rather than completely alienate his remaining supporters in the armed forces, a tired Vargas acquiesced to the military efforts to overthrow Gallegos. Vargas decided to preserve the institutional integrity of the armed forces rather than pit the much weakened supporters of democratic professionalism against the dominant technocratic authoritarian wing of the armed forces.

Arriving on 22 November, a more optimistic Giacopini Zárraga pursued a two-track approach to the crisis: organizing a democratic professional counter-coup against the technocratic authoritarians in the General Staff and pursuing negotiations between the technocratic authoritarians and civilian politicians. Initially, Giacopini Zárraga asked the acting inspector general, Lieutenant Colonel Rangél León, to coordinate with Lieutenant Colonel Gámez Arellano, a leader in the democratic professional faction, to defeat the coup attempt. Giacopini Zárraga argued that Rangél León, as the former commander of the armored battalion that protected the presidential palace, could easily take control of this important unit and use it to surround the Ministry of Defense across the street and arrest Pérez Jiménez, Delgado Chalbaud, and the rest of the rebellious military high command. The crucial Maracay garrison was under Gámez Arellano's command, which meant that if Rangel León succeeded, the democratic professional wing of the armed forces would control the two most important garrisons in the country and could prevent any coup. Rangél León agreed with Giacopini Zárraga, but when this plan was presented to Gallegos, the president refused to authorize the operation on two separate occasions, arguing that he could not ask Rangél León to rebel against his legal superiors, Delgado Chalbaud and Pérez Jiménez. As far as Gallegos was concerned, his minister of national defense and Chief of the General Staff should obey him because it was his constitutional due, rather than because they were being coerced. Frustrated, Rangél León and Gámez Arellano refused to act independently, eliminating the possibility of an armed counter-coup against the military high command (Schaposnik 1985, 89–104; Giacopini Zárraga 1994d, 1995a).

Unable to convince Gallegos to take advantage of an armed option to suppress the insurrection, Giacopini Zárraga instead attempted to bypass the president by negotiating a deal directly between the leaderships of the armed forces and of Acción Democrática. Meeting with AD leaders Betancourt, Raul Leoni, and Gonzalo Barrios, Giacopini Zárraga found room for compromise, particularly once Betancourt volunteered to leave the country in hopes of resolving the political crisis. On the evening of 22 November, Giacopini Zárraga met with Delgado Chalbaud and Pérez Jiménez, whom he sensed were nervous and unusually interested in finding a compromise acceptable to both sides. Following two days of negotiations and a face-to-face meeting between Betancourt and Pérez Jiménez, AD and the military high command reached an agreement.[8] Betancourt would leave the country immediately, and AD's government ministers would resign en masse, allowing Gallegos to form a new cabinet with significant representation from political independents. Furthermore, Giacopini Zárraga suggested that existing gun control laws be vigorously applied to all civilians, thereby disarming Acción Democrática without specifically targeting the ruling party as such. Whether or not an AD party militia existed, Giacopini Zárraga argued, disarming all civilians would effectively prevent such a unit from acting effectively and would present a face-saving way out of the crisis for AD.[9] Having reached this deal, the government publicly announced that Gallegos's ministers had resigned on 23 November, hoping to thereby calm the insurgent junior officers (Betancourt 1949a; Giacopini Zárraga 1994d, 1995a).

The logic of authoritarianism had become so dominant in the armed forces, however, that the junior officers continued to agitate single-mindedly for a coup, regardless of whatever agreements their leaders had reached with AD. Gallegos also remained obdurate, refusing to take any actions that could be interpreted as accepting military demands or compromising his powers as president. Lower-ranking AD party members, following their own logic of radical partisanship, increased their pressure on their own superiors for decisive action against the military (Betancourt 1949a; Vargas 1949; Ellner 1989; Angulo Rivas 1993, 65). Despite the imposition of press censorship shortly after the beginning of the civil-military crisis, news and rumors circulated rapidly throughout Caracas concerning the fate of the Gallegos administration. Both civilian leaders and military officers feared that unless the situation were resolved shortly, tensions in Caracas could escalate into a general insurrection, following the example of the bloody "Bogotazo," which had led to severe combat and thousands of casualties in the Colombian capital only months earlier. On the morning of 24 November, in the face of Gallegos's intransigence and fearing the collapse of the negotiated settlement, AD called on its labor unions to mobilize for a nationwide general strike to oppose the threatened military coup. The very same day, at noon, Delgado Chalbaud and Pérez Jiménez gave the orders to arrest Gallegos and overthrow the democratic government.

Once the orders were given, the coup operation proceeded rapidly and bloodlessly, facing almost no civilian resistance. By nightfall, a military triumvirate, composed of Delgado Chalbaud, Pérez Jiménez, and the vice chief of the General Staff, Luis Llovera Páez, held control of the Venezuelan government. Gallegos was overthrown in spite of the best efforts of civilian and military leaders to reach a solution. In the end, their followers had each become so committed to their own military and political logics that the possibility of compromise vanished.

Conclusions

Given the narrow opportunity structure faced by democratizers in 1945 and the absence of regime capacity in defense affairs, Venezuela was a classic case of a "regime at risk." However, the opportunity structure was narrowed further by the actions of democratizers, who undermined civilian consensus and followed a perverse strategy of appeasement toward the military. This strategy had two consequences: it eliminated any possibility of crafting regime leverage over the armed forces, and it allowed the military leadership to reshape its own institution to serve its political objectives. In the face of a disloyal opposition and a growing civilian political crisis, the Gallegos administration found itself defenseless when the armed forces finally intervened to end partisanship and maintain public order.

Despite the narrowness of the opportunity structure during the 1945–48 period, Acción Democrática had an opportunity to consolidate democracy and civilian control of the armed forces. Military factionalism, a precondition for regime leverage over the armed forces, existed as a result of the internal rivalries between factions of officers contending over access to power and alternative visions of the role of the armed forces. The other principal component of regime leverage over the armed forces, broad civilian consensus on democratization, did not exist at the beginning of the transition, but it could have been achieved by a more moderate and inclusive transitional government. By adopting a political style of radical partisanship, AD alienated important sectors of civilian support and antagonized an officer corps unaccustomed to the tumult of democratic politics. Without a civilian consensus on the political rules of the game or persistent military factionalism, AD relinquished all possibility of creating regime leverage over the armed forces and establishing civilian control.

Acción Democrática, by virtue of its political inexperience, lacked the resources to create the regime capacity that would have counseled its leadership to pursue a different strategy vis-à-vis the armed forces. This shortcoming led its leaders to abandon control over the defense policy agenda

to the armed forces in order to avoid antagonizing a largely hostile officer corps. Moreover, there was no room for civilian defense expertise in AD
since its leadership placed its hopes on the success of pro-democratic factions in the armed forces. The lack of government concern with military affairs had the perverse effect of eliminating regime leverage over the armed
forces, while simultaneously preventing the emergence of regime capacity
that might have counseled the regime to act otherwise.

The armed forces' jurisdictional boundaries expanded to such an extent
during the 1945–48 period that the Gallegos administration found itself incapable of resisting new military demands for authority over domestic politics and state leadership selection. The combination of a lack of regime leverage and capacity and a strategy of appeasement in relation to the armed
forces allowed the entrepreneurial leaders of the technocratic authoritarian
faction to establish any jurisdictional boundaries they desired. By consolidating control over all of the coercive power of the state, as figures 2.1 and
2.2 indicate, these military leaders could intervene almost at will in civilian
politics, checked only by their own constituency in the officer corps. When
President Gallegos abandoned his strategy of appeasement and refused to
accede to the military's political demands in November 1948, the armed
forces were able to seize power without any significant opposition.

AD's approach also had a lasting effect on civilian and military beliefs
about the proper role of the military in society. Following a strategy of
appeasement meant that AD had to rely on officers who advocated a pro-
democratic vision of military professionalism. However, appeasement also
meant that AD did not prevent those officers who favored a technocratic
authoritarian vision of the military's role in society from seizing control
of the core military institutions—the Ministry of Defense and the General
Staff. These institutions allowed these officers to refashion the officer corps
to favor a vision of the military that justified its intervention in politics. In
addition, the alliance between the highly partisan AD and the officers in the
armed forces who were sympathetic to democratic rule undermined the appeal of democratic professionalism as a military belief system within the
Venezuelan armed forces.

This failed case of democratization illustrates the perversity of appeasement as a strategy of civilian control of the armed forces and the importance
of narrow jurisdictional boundaries for preserving civilian rule. Rather than
accept civilian appeasement as a quid pro quo for military abstention from
politics, the armed forces leadership took advantage of this strategy to con-

solidate its own power and expand its jurisdiction over state activities. As figures 2.1 and 2.2 suggest, the dominance of the armed forces in both internal and external security affairs is extremely dangerous for any civilian government since it deprives the leaders of a democracy of any coercive means to defend themselves. Moreover, the participation of the armed forces in state leadership selection during the transitional government established a precedent. This precedent encouraged the military high command to place political demands before the Gallegos administration. The rejection of these demands so infuriated the officer corps that a coup d'état overthrew the government in spite of the more moderate preferences of the leaders.

The contrast between two cases that began as "regimes at risk," Venezuela in 1945 and Chile after 1990, is instructive because it demonstrates that alternative paths are possible even in cases where narrow opportunity structures dominate. Chile's transition to democracy in 1990, examined more fully in chapter 7, confronted even worse circumstances than those faced by Venezuela since Chile's democratizers were divided among themselves and faced a successful and unified military. However, by moderating civilian partisanship and placing civilian control of the military on the agenda, Chile's political regime has slowly crafted a considerable degree of regime capacity, placing Chile firmly in the category of "regime persistence" in figure 1.2, rather than "regime at risk." This is the path I argue that Venezuela might have been able to follow in 1945 with a more experienced civilian political leadership, committed to civilian control of the armed forces.

CHAPTER 3

■

THE 1958 TRANSITION

TO DEMOCRACY IN VENEZUELA

Strategizing Civilian Control

In 1958 Venezuela experienced a second opportunity to democratize. Unlike the first attempt in 1945–48, in this case Venezuelan democracy survived and became consolidated, enjoying an unusual degree of political stability by South American standards, at least until 1992. Certainly, the political and economic conditions in Venezuela had not changed sufficiently during the decade of authoritarian rule to lead most observers of the new democracy to expect this radical success. In 1957 Venezuela's population remained nearly 50 percent rural, with a large number of landless, mostly illiterate peasants. Even though the economy had grown during the 1950–57 period at rates that exceeded even those associated with the "German Miracle," per capita income remained low ($660 in 1968 dollars) and poorly distributed (Toro Hardy 1992, 44–50). Politically, the country had endured ten years of military authoritarian rule, and the armed forces had only become larger, better equipped, and more powerful in the years since they took power in 1948. The political opponents of the dictatorial regime were largely in exile or underground, and General Pérez Jiménez seemed firmly entrenched in power as he prepared to extend his rule by referendum in December 1957. Yet within a year, the authoritarian government had collapsed, and a civilian president had been elected. Within a decade, the democratic system showed strong signs of consolidation, as power was transferred peacefully between parties after the 1968 elections.

The 1958 transition to democracy ushered in the first sustained period of civilian rule in Venezuela since the war of independence from Spain.

The four decades that followed the transition have been seen as a successful democratic exception in Latin America, particularly when observers compared the relative political stability of Venezuela with the coups and revolutions that characterized the rest of the continent. What made Venezuela the exception to the rule of political instability in Latin America during the Cold War? And what, then, explains the crisis of the democratic regime in this country during the 1990s, which developed against the backdrop of a continent swiftly moving away from authoritarianism?

Until now, the explanations for the rise and decline of Venezuelan democracy have largely ignored the role of the armed forces and have concentrated on civilian politics. These explanations fall into three groups, which focus on civilian-dominated processes, parties, and institutions.

Those observers closest to Venezuela's transition to democracy in 1958 clearly favored political agency as an explanation for the regime's four decades of success. Alexander (1964) and Martz (1968) argue that the leaders of the principal Venezuelan political parties—AD, COPEI, and URD—were able to sustain the democratization process through their political skills and their control of mass parties with a strong capacity for interest aggregation. Daniel Levine presents a more nuanced version of this argument, suggesting that after decades of ruinous partisanship, by 1958 the Venezuelan political parties had become particularly adept at developing rules and mechanisms for conciliating interests, as well as measures designed to punish political outsiders (Levine 1973, 4–11). In this set of arguments, elite learning and political skill created a system in Venezuela in which political parties dominated society and negotiated among themselves to resolve conflict and maintain stability.

Another version of conventional wisdom about Venezuela, both within the country and abroad, has explained political stability largely as a function of the revenues derived from Venezuela's role as a major international oil producer. In this utilitarian explanation, the Venezuelan government's ability to redistribute state revenues to solve problems and pacify critics has sustained civilian rule. In other words, "petroleum ergo democracy." More sophisticated examinations of Venezuela's political economy argue that the state has been shaped by large inflows of petroleum rents with their consequent distortions. Terry Karl (1986) argues that the elite foundational pacts in Venezuelan democracy were essentially distributive in nature, tasked with assuring that the most important political and social actors received an equitable share of the power and resources that derived from the national oil rents. These pacts froze the political rules of the game into a populist, clientalist, and undemocratic pattern, making the system vulnerable to changes in the international or domestic petroleum economy that could affect the state's ability to continue distributing oil rents (Karl 1986; Romero 1987; Rey 1989; Gil Yepes 1991).

Even accounts that do focus on the armed forces in Venezuela have concentrated on civil-military relations, rather than on civilian control. Burggraff, among the first U.S. scholars of the modern Venezuelan military, suggests that military acquiescence to civilian rule in the 1960s arose out of a growing awareness within the officer corps of broad-based civilian resistance to a return to authoritarian rule and the generally moderate promilitary policies followed by the first Venezuelan presidents after the 1958 transition to democracy (Burggraff 1972). Bigler argues that civilian control of the armed forces was consolidated on the basis of a strong political consensus in favor of democratization and the professionalization of the military (Bigler 1981). Most recently, Felipe Agüero has emphasized even more strongly the role of the civilian democratization consensus in excluding the armed forces from politics, as well as the role of military reforms in creating multiple internal checks to armed attempts to intervene in politics. These checks have carried negative consequences for the effectiveness of the military that have resulted in widespread discontent within the officer corps (Agüero 1995a). This literature has thus identified the basis of civil-military stability in Venezuela during what is known as the Punto Fijo period. It has been less successful in explaining how Venezuelan democratizers developed the institutions that underpinned this stability in 1958 or why these institutions deteriorated during the 1990s.

In 1958 Venezuela started down the path toward civilian control by containment of the armed forces. Much as in Spain after Franco or in Argentina in 1983, democratizers faced a broad opportunity structure, characterized by the fragmentation of military cohesion, high levels of elite consensus in favor of the new regime, and mass mobilization that supported the end of the dictatorship. Democratizers had a well-conceived agenda for removing the armed forces from politics, the product of a lengthy debate carried out among exiled Venezuelan politicians in Cuba, Costa Rica, and Puerto Rico. In particular, the Acción Democrática party made a deliberate effort to take advantage of the opportunity, and it maximized regime leverage over the military through the use of a strategy of "divide and conquer," assisted by the selective appeasement of factions within the armed forces. These strategies later became part of the institutions created by the new democracy to contain the armed forces within narrow and unthreatening jurisdictional boundaries.

Venezuelan democratizers pursued their strategies of civilian control by containment in two stages. The first was carried out by the interim government during the transition to democracy in 1958 and involved the strategy of "divide and conquer." The transitional government faced down military threats and used attempted rebellions to identify and expel officers who opposed democratization. Simultaneously, this government took advantage of the incoherence of the armed forces to decentralize power and authority within the institution, creating multiple safeguards against military intervention. During the second stage, which extended from the inauguration of President Rómulo Betancourt in 1959 to the end of President Rafael Caldera's term in 1970, political leaders added new strategies of civilian control, using appeasement, monitoring, and indoctrination to increase their leverage over the armed forces. The strategies of appeasement and "divide and conquer" required little regime capacity, and they were successfully embedded in new institutions of civilian control, such as the Joint Chiefs of Staff, the military education system, and the generous package of benefits enjoyed by Venezuelan military officers. Unlike the earlier 1945–48 experience, appeasement of the armed forces was relatively selective and designed to disarm opposition to the civilians' overall "divide and conquer" strategy.

However, over time, civilian strategies of indoctrination and monitoring the armed forces were abandoned due to a shortage of regime capacity in military affairs. These strategies required sustained government attention and a high level of civilian expertise, and they faded as the military threat to democracy receded. After the mid-1960s, the officer corps increasingly accepted the constraints imposed by democratization, once it became apparent that rebellion was futile and that the armed forces faced a greater threat in the form of a Cuba-backed insurgency. As a result, by 1973 the Venezuelan democratic regime had consolidated civilian control of the armed forces, but this control lacked institutionalized civilian oversight of military activities.

The crafting of civilian control by containment due to a shortage of regime capacity in Venezuela was not just a matter of circumstances, but also partly a matter of choice. Democratizers in Chile after 1989, Argentina after 1983, and Spain after the death of Franco had relatively low levels of regime capacity at the moment of transition. However, their civilian political leadership was committed to creating such a capacity through the development of institutional resources, including civilian-led ministries of defense, and human resources, in the form of a community of civilian defense professionals. Early investments in these areas provided returns in the form of increased civilian capabilities to oversee military affairs and to ensure civilian control. Venezuela's democratizers did not see such investment as an option available to them in 1958, and instead they chose to pursue a path toward civilian control by containment.

A Return to Armed Cronyism: The Decline of Military Autonomy under Pérez Jiménez

The 1948 coup seemed to confirm the victory of the faction led by Lieutenant Colonel Pérez Jiménez and brought to power officers and civilian collaborators who shared a technocratic authoritarian belief system. However, the 1948 coup did not entirely eliminate contending belief systems within the military. Following the 1948 coup, the officer corps divided into two factions: a majority who agreed with the arguments set forward by Pérez Jiménez about the role of the military, and a minority who was willing to see a return to a restricted form of civilian rule. Although Pérez Jiménez was able to dominate the officer corps until 1957, the possibility of returning to a democratic form of rule remained in the background. As the Pérez Jiménez dictatorship grew increasingly corrupt, the appeal of political alternatives grew as well.

During the interregnum (1948–52) between the overthrow of Gallegos and Pérez Jiménez's assumption of the presidency, Lieutenant Colonel Carlos Delgado Chalbaud competed with Pérez Jiménez for authority and influence within the government, civilian society, and the military (Burggraff 1972, 118). By advocating new elections, the aristocratic Delgado Chalbaud distanced himself from hard-line authoritarians in the military and gained broader support in civil society. By contrast, the technocratic authoritarian credentials of Pérez Jiménez served him well as he consolidated his support in the officer corps by acting as a channel for the concerns of the officer corps vis-à-vis the ruling junta. Once Delgado Chalbaud, the president of the junta, was mysteriously assassinated on 13 November 1950, Pérez Jiménez assumed complete de facto control of the government (Rodríguez Iturbe 1984, 129–36; Soto Tamayo 1986, 116–20).

Having achieved his ambition for de jure presidential power in 1952, Pérez Jiménez moved to reassert government control over the armed forces using a two-level strategy. Publicly, he proclaimed his allegiance to the Nuevo Ideal Nacional (New National Ideal), a regime ideology based on the logic of technocratic authoritarianism. This ideology contained many of the elements that O'Donnell (1979) later used to characterize the military dictatorships of 1960s and 1970s in the Southern Cone region of Latin America: military rule in alliance with civilian technocrats, foreign and domestic, that espoused a "rational efficient" alternative to the messiness of democracy (Müller Rojas 1989). In private, Pérez Jiménez increasingly used the logic of armed cronyism to dominate the armed forces, directing the military through a few favored colleagues, who were kept under the surveillance of his civilian-led secret police, the Seguridad Nacional.

Ironically, Pérez Jiménez was much more successful than his civilian predecessors in minimizing the threat to his government, moving swiftly to restrict the officer corps to narrow military jurisdictional boundaries. During his dictatorship, the officer corps was reacquainted with its professional military tasks. To deepen the military modernization process, Pérez Jiménez established advanced technical training centers, which provided educational opportunities once available only to the few officers who could attend overseas military schools. Pérez Jiménez also improved the capabilities of the Venezuelan army, reorganizing it into modern combat units and adding new equipment. The navy brought modern destroyers into service, and the air force upgraded its squadrons with jet fighters, giving Venezuela the most advanced air arm in Latin America during this period (Celis Noguera 1994). Pérez Jiménez attempted to encourage solidarity among the military forces by also creating the Escuela Básica, which replaced the first two years of military education at the separate army, navy, and air force military academies with one curriculum at a joint institution. All officer cadets, regardless of what service they belonged to, thus shared classes, activities, and living quarters during the first years of their military education. This created a system of lifelong bonds among officers of the same "promoción" or class, across the various branches of service (Giacopini Zárraga 1992d; Néry Arrieta 1992). With this strategy Pérez Jiménez hoped to immunize the armed forces from politics by reprofessionalizing them.

Pérez Jiménez also emphasized the status of the armed forces as a distinctive segment of Venezuelan society, with the intent of isolating the officer corps from larger political and social concerns. At the time, military education in Venezuela focused narrowly on traditional professional issues, with little time in the curriculum devoted to social or political matters. Permission to attend universities, locally or abroad, was tightly restricted for fear of military officers' becoming "polluted" with civilian ideas. The occasional granting of scholarships for such study was used by the Pérez Jiménez regime as a reward for loyalty or to pay off allies within the institution (Schaposnik 1985, 381; Néry Arrieta 1992). This policy contributed to the mutual suspicions and strong divisions that already existed between military and civilian spheres.

Military personnel felt isolated from civilian life for socioeconomic reasons as well. Although they identified with the middle class, their economic condition was precarious due to persistently insufficient salaries and benefits. The bulk of the Venezuelan officer corps was drawn from a rural Andean lower-middle-class background, alienated from the mores and values of the Caracas professional and upper classes. As such, these officers were rejected by the very elements of cosmopolitan Caracas society with whom they most identified. In reaction, military men developed a sense of superiority and disdain toward civilians and their affairs. In fact, in order to compensate for these feelings of inferiority and resentment (and further reinforce military isolation), Pérez Jiménez constructed during his regime what was widely regarded as the most luxurious officers' club (the Círculo Militar) on the continent. The net effect of a narrow military education and exclusion from civilian social circles was the creation of a kind of military caste (Schaposnik 1985, 337–39; Machillanda Pinto 1995).

Individual military officers did maintain some influence over public policy during the 1952–58 Pérez Jiménez administration, particularly as armed forces professionalization programs produced increasing numbers of military engineers and technocrats who could be employed in the management of the wide array of state projects that the dictator pursued during his regime. Pérez Jiménez upgraded the state's planning capacity by creating the Oficina de Proyectos Especiales under a recent graduate from the Argentine war college, Captain Víctor Maldonado Michelena. Other officers were assigned to supervise the most important hydroelectric power and construction projects in the country. Pérez Jiménez's vision for Venezuelan development was shaped by the ideal of a "neutral" technocratic government. Therefore, it seemed only appropriate to use the best-educated military officers in administrative capacities, where their professional training would help insulate them from public and political pressures (Castillo 1994). This limited use of the military also enhanced the veneer of technocratic authoritarianism that publicly justified the dictatorial regime. The small number of officers who were involved in these projects allowed the regime to monitor them for signs of politicization with ease.

Although the Nuevo Ideal Nacional was the official regime ideology, senior government officials, military officers, and their allies in civilian society engaged in crony capitalism, an update of the logic of armed cronyism that had guided the authoritarian regimes of Generals Gómez, López, and Medina. Even though Pérez Jiménez, a military officer, led the government, conservative civilians rapidly gained power over most government policy-making, leaving only the Ministries of Defense and Communication in the hands of Pérez Jiménez loyalists among senior military officers. The alleged corruption of the Pérez Jiménez regime contributed to the disenchantment of the junior officer corps, who perceived hypocrisy in the contrast of the corrupt behavior of the government with the technocratic justifications for the regime.

Fearing threats from both civilian and military opponents, Pérez Jiménez created a new police agency within the Ministry of Interior, the Seguridad Nacional. It was a nonmilitary national force tasked with maintaining internal security, monitoring political activity, and defending the regime from all possible threats, including the armed forces. Although it mostly targeted the civilian political underground resistance, the Seguridad Nacional could arrest and imprison a military officer at any time with the dictator's approval (Müller Rojas 1989, 411–12). The use of torture on both civilian and military prisoners was common. By 1957, military officers who followed the logic of democratic professionalism during the 1945–48 democratization attempt had long since been removed from positions of authority within the armed services, and many had been persecuted as vigorously as Pérez Jiménez's civilian political opponents. Eventually, even officers who subscribed to the regime's technocratic authoritarianism came to see the Seguridad Nacional as a threat to their own careers and the military as an institution. From a bureaucratic standpoint, the different service branches resented the resources lavished on the Seguridad Nacional, which at 5,000 members was almost as large as the army. Rather than using the armed forces as the pillar of his regime's stability, Pérez Jiménez came to rely on the Seguridad Nacional to prevent and eliminate potential threats to his power (Avendaño Lugo 1982, 218–23, 277, 280). As a result, it was increasingly despised by the officer corps.

With the public ideology of the Nuevo Ideal Nacional belied by private corruption, dissent grew within the military, and officers increasingly considered democracy as an alternative to rule by Pérez Jiménez. The dictator also betrayed his promise of military professionalization by interfering in the merit-based promotions process. Officers also felt that the armed forces were being ignored in favor of the regime's civilian spending priorities. While military spending represented 8–9 percent of the national budget during the dictatorship, Pérez Jiménez allocated more than three times as much to the Ministry of Public Works. Meanwhile, younger officers were frustrated by a lack of upward mobility in their careers and social standing and a perceived decline in wages and living conditions. The navy and air force felt overshadowed by the prestige and power of the Venezuelan army. In particular, the leaders of these traditionally junior branches were increasingly at odds with General Rómulo Fernández, Chief of the Armed Forces General Staff (Estado Mayor General de las Fuerzas Armadas). General Fernández, a prominent supporter of Pérez Jiménez in the army, had consistently deflected and denied air force and navy requests for greater autonomy and further professionalization. Given these irritants, it is not surprising that by the end of 1957, a substantial proportion of officers opposed the clique of military officers and upper-class civilians who surrounded Pérez Jiménez and enriched themselves at the state's expense (Stambouli 1980, 133–40). Although cronyism served to cement the loyalty of civilian and military elites to Pérez Jiménez, it had a corrosive effect on the support of the armed forces for the regime they had brought to power in 1948.

As a result of Pérez Jiménez's policies, the majority of military officers had never exercised control over government functions, even though they had participated in bringing the authoritarian regime to power. Pérez Jiménez reserved questions of external security for himself and his supporters in the military, yet in questions of state leadership selection and domestic policy, pro-authoritarian civilians in the government administration clearly dominated through their control of almost all government ministries. The Seguridad Nacional and the Ministry of Interior, both staffed by civilian police agents and functionaries, controlled all matters of internal security, including monitoring the loyalty of the armed forces. Just as Pérez Jiménez attempted to isolate the officer corps from civilian society, he also drastically limited the military's input into government policy. Though Pérez Jiménez was a military officer, his primary concern was for the preservation of his regime rather than the interests of the armed forces.

Growing military dissent made a coup d'état a possibility, yet the isolated position of the armed forces within the regime was such that, when the transition to democracy occurred in 1958, the officer corps was largely unprepared to exert political influence. Rather than defending bloated post-authoritarian jurisdictional boundaries, as many military institutions have been able to do in emerging South American democracies, the armed forces instead found themselves struggling to claim new ones during the transitional process. Unfortunately for the armed forces, and fortunately for Venezuelan democracy, the military high command was in an exceedingly poor position to defend its claims to any given jurisdictional boundaries in 1958, due to the exceedingly rapid collapse of the authoritarian regime and the factionalization of the officer corps that followed.

A New Opportunity to Craft Civilian Control:
The Collapse of the Authoritarian Regime in 1958

Pérez Jiménez, after governing practically unchallenged between 1952 and 1957, saw his regime crumble with almost unprecedented speed. Little more than twenty-three days elapsed between a failed coup attempt on 1 January 1958 and his journey into exile. The suddenness of his regime's collapse seems puzzling in light of his seemingly unassailable position. Pérez Jiménez had governed during a period of unparalleled economic growth in Venezuelan history, had succeeded in eliminating almost all open and underground opposition, and had easily won reelection to the presidency, albeit in a heavily tainted electoral process.

This swift change in fortunes occurred as a result of a sudden shift in the political and economic bases of public support for the regime. The last half of 1957 marked the beginning of an economic recession in Venezuela, brought about by a drop in world petroleum prices. This turn of events shocked and deflated rising popular expectations, particularly among middle- and lower-class Venezuelans. Unfortunately for Pérez Jiménez, this economic shock coincided with the end of his five-year "constitutional" period in office. By mismanaging an attempt to extend his rule, Pérez Jiménez compounded public anger over the deepening economic recession with a crisis over the political legitimacy of his regime. Civil society, which had grown and become more complex during the rapid economic modernization of the previous decade, turned against the dictatorship in the face of these twin crises. Outlawed opposition parties overcame their differences and stepped to the fore of civilian efforts to organize a transition to democracy. Moreover, this time civilian political leaders were clearly aware of the importance of government control of the armed forces and had developed workable strategies to achieve it. Disintegrating military support for Pérez Jiménez and the rapidly developing civilian political consensus provided a broad opportunity to successfully establish democracy and civilian control of the armed forces in 1958.

DEVELOPING AN AGENDA FOR CIVILIAN
CONTROL OF THE ARMED FORCES

Just as there was an internal debate in the Venezuelan armed forces about the military's role in society, civilian politicians in exile or in the resistance movement now engaged in a similar debate among themselves. The question of what to do with the armed forces upon returning to power was among the central issues democratizers faced. The thinking of the leaders of Acción Democrática on the issue of civil-military relations is highly illuminating, not only because of their early failure to consider the armed forces during the 1940s, but also because of AD's future experience in managing the armed forces during the party's two administrations from 1958 to 1968, a crucial period in the eventual consolidation of civilian control.

AD party activists engaged in a great deal of self-criticism in exile, analyzing the political failures that had allowed their government to collapse in 1948. Part of this internal dialogue led to the development of two alternative strategies for dealing with the armed forces. The first, favored by senior AD party leaders, advocated a "divide and conquer" policy toward the armed forces, combined with a policy of moderation and conciliation toward other political parties, with the eventual goal of developing a united civilian front to defend democracy. The second strategy advocated a revolutionary transformation of the armed forces into an AD-dominated organization, supportive of the party's hegemonic role in any future civilian regime. This approach was preferred by the junior ranks of Acción Democrática who bore the brunt of government repression during their participation in armed resistance to the dictatorship (Carnevali 1949).[1] The greater experience and political weight of AD's senior leadership eventually carried the day, and "divide and conquer" became the unofficial strategy of the party toward the armed forces. This conflict between two alternative visions of the role of the military was never truly resolved, however, and drove an important wedge between two generations of Acción Democrática.

The first indication of the emerging moderate "divide and conquer" strategy can be found in a memorandum from party leader Rómulo Betancourt to the Central Executive Committee of AD in exile, dated 1 November 1949.

In it, Betancourt argued that the party should be careful to clearly distinguish between the armed forces as an institution and Pérez Jiménez's clique. Blame for the overthrow of the democratic administration of President Gallegos in 1948 should be laid at the feet of the top leadership rather than the officer corps in general. Otherwise, Betancourt concluded, the party would run the danger of completely alienating the armed forces and seriously diminish the chances that AD might someday return to power (Betancourt 1949b).[2] A separate report from the group of AD exiles based in Mexico (which included former president Gallegos and ex-minister of interior Eligio Anzola Anzola) concluded that the armed forces were fundamentally divided internally, with a significant proportion of the officer corps favoring democratization, a situation that could be used to the eventual advantage of Acción Democrática. In the area of military reform, they specifically argued that in any new government, AD should strengthen the navy and grant it autonomy from the Ministry of Defense (that is, from the army), separate the Guardia Nacional from the army and place it under the control of the Ministry of Interior, and create an independent, well-equipped national police force to allow the army to concentrate on professionalization rather than the maintenance of order (AD exiles 1949). Although these reports contained considerable wishful thinking, it is worth noting that as the first anniversary of the overthrow of the Gallegos administration approached, the party leadership had already decided that establishing control over the armed forces should be a high priority during following a return to democracy.

At more or less the same time, an antimilitary perspective developed among younger members of the party. Domingo Alberto Rangel was the recognized intellectual leader of the younger generation of AD activists and a particularly forceful proponent of the need for a radical transformation of the armed forces. Rangel argued that the original sin of the 1945–48 AD government was to have come to power with the aid of the armed forces. Having failed in this first democratization attempt, he believed that the only remaining path to power was through violence, preferably an insurrection led by workers and students. Further, he advocated the ideological penetration and conversion of the officer corps and the creation of workers' brigades, so as to convert the armed forces into an organization that resembled a party militia rather than a bureaucratized army (Rangel 1949a, 1949b).[3] Unless the allegiance of the officer corps was transferred to the party, any future AD government would be at risk of a coup d'état. Rangel advocated nothing less than the revolutionary transformation of the armed forces into an ideologically committed institution appropriate for defending a future civilian regime dominated by Acción Democrática.

Although these were early statements written within the first year of the coup against President Gallegos, documents from 1957 suggest that positions had not changed in the intervening eight years. Rómulo Betancourt and other political leaders in exile established a conciliatory line toward the armed forces during negotiations in New York. As laid out in a joint memorandum, the exiled politicians acknowledged that the armed forces would remain a basic element of national life and should be a guarantee of order and democratic constitutionality in any new regime (Karl 1986). They therefore called on the armed forces to assume an apolitical character and guaranteed them stability and progress under any future administration. They also called for a general amnesty for political crimes committed during the dictatorship. Most important, the declaration stated that the armed forces should only be at the service of the nation rather than any particular political or military leader. By thus guaranteeing professionalism and an apolitical role, civilian politicians offered the officer corps an attractive alternative military logic to the increasingly intolerable armed cronyism practiced by Pérez Jiménez. By offering amnesty, Betancourt and Jóvito Villalba, the leader of Unión Republicana Democrática, another major party, attempted to assuage military officers who might have otherwise continued to support the dictatorship out of fear of civilian retaliation ("Declaración de los partidos políticos" 1957).[4]

Nevertheless, Rangel and his supporters continued to advocate a strategy of the revolutionary transformation of the armed forces despite the moderate official party line. In a proposal submitted by Rangel to Betancourt and the AD central committee in 1957, Rangel suggested that the party could learn many lessons from the recent Bolivian revolutionary experience. In 1953 the Movimiento Nacional Revolucionario took power in Bolivia and radically politicized the officer corps, shut down the military education system, and, for practical purposes, eliminated the armed forces by creating a party militia (Roquié 1989, 331–32). Only by granting the officer corps political rights and attracting them to Acción Democrática's cause, Rangel argued, would any future regime in Venezuela be secure. He also called for Nuremberg-style trials for military officers and regime collaborators involved in atrocities during the dictatorship and limitations on political freedoms for opponents of any new civilian regime (Rangel 1957a, 1957b). Essentially, Rangel advocated a transition to a civilian single-party authoritarian regime rather than to a democracy.

Rangel's strategy was highly attractive to many of the younger radical party members, particularly those who had participated in the clandestine resistance to the dictatorship between 1948 and 1957. Many of them resented the continuing efforts by the exiles to assert their control over the party from their risk-free position outside Venezuela, as well as the exiles' conservative, conciliatory policies toward the armed forces and their political opponents. The Cuban revolution, which was gaining strength during 1958, was an additional source of radical inspiration for the youth wing of AD. Eventually, Acción Democrática would split over the differences between Betancourt's evolutionary approach to democracy and Rangel's call for revolutionary action.[5] However, in early 1957 AD was still united, and Rómulo Betancourt was still a recognized leader of the party. AD was a party founded on the Leninist principle of democratic centralism, which effectively granted Betancourt the authority to enforce his policy on other party members (Bruni Celli 1992). His divide and conquer approach to the armed forces therefore became the dominant strategy within Acción Democrática.

THE COALESCENCE OF THE CIVILIAN POLITICAL
OPPOSITION TO PÉREZ JIMÉNEZ

Vigorous repression by the authoritarian regime made the years between 1948 and 1957 difficult for the civilian political parties, driving activists into exile or underground. With the overthrow of the Gallegos administration, Acción Democrática's party organization had been severely shaken, and its activists were successfully persecuted by the new regime's secret police, the Seguridad Nacional. Limited attempts at armed resistance in cooperation with the Venezuelan Communist Party (PCV) were quickly defeated. The center-left URD had seen its leadership exiled and its organization dismantled in the wake of its electoral victory (albeit official defeat) in the 1952 elections for a constitutional convention (Rodriguez Iturbe 1984, 129–36; Giacopini Zárraga 1992d). The Christian Democratic party, COPEI, continued to maintain its legal status, but it could only act within severe constraints, under constant surveillance by agents of the Ministry of the Interior. The exiled leaders of AD and URD increasingly lost touch with their party activists in Venezuela and, therefore, their influence over events within their country. Mostly in exile in New York, Havana, and Mexico City, they also maintained a suspicious distance from each other. AD felt betrayed by COPEI and URD in the wake of the 1948 coup against its government, while the other parties felt threatened by the electoral hegemony of AD during the 1945–48 democratic interlude. A history of political antagonism stretching back to the 1930s made it difficult for Venezuela's parties to cooperate.

However, Rómulo Betancourt and Jóvito Villalba, the exiled leaders of AD and URD respectively, began to work together to forge a durable political coalition that would sustain a new democratization process by 1957. Betancourt had reached the conclusion that only a broad front of Venezuela's democratic parties could defend a constitutional regime, and he began work toward developing an understanding with URD and COPEI. The transition to democracy that had begun in Colombia in 1957 was seen as exciting development by the Venezuelan exiles, particularly because of the explicit pledges of mutual support and respect between the Liberal and Conservative parties, which had an enmity dating back to the nineteenth century. Betancourt saw the political pacts that put an end to the long-standing interparty disputes in Colombia as a model for resolving the political conflicts that had aborted the democratic transition begun in 1945 (Betancourt 1957a, 1957c).[6]

In May 1957 Rómulo Betancourt and Jóvito Villalba reached a consensus on a political platform that would eventually become the foundational pact of Venezuelan democracy. The two leaders first explored the possibility of issuing a joint statement of guiding principles for a return to civilian rule in Venezuela. Luis Herrera Campíns, a high-ranking member of COPEI who was then visiting the United States, participated in these discussions. While Herrera Campíns agreed in principle with the contents of the manifesto, he could not commit COPEI to the pact while his party remained the legal opposition to the dictatorship, and certainly not without the approval of other party leaders. This obstacle prevented the early formation of a united opposition front (Betancourt 1957b, 1957c, 1957d). Even so, by June most of the pieces of the pact had been negotiated.

In a final piece of business, the assembled exiles agreed to exclude the PCV, which had acquired a leadership role in the underground resistance to Pérez Jiménez, from any future pacts on democratization or participation in a civilian government. These leaders concluded that Communist influence among younger party activists was dangerous and that their presence in any transitional government would alienate business sectors, the armed forces, the center-right party COPEI, and the U.S. State Department (Karl 1986). Thus, as 1957 drew to a close, all of the major Venezuelan political parties in exile, except the PCV, had effectively entered into a united front.

The dictatorship's announcement of a plebiscitary formula to extend Pérez Jiménez's rule beyond 1958 was the final straw that brought together the political opposition. Even though the constitution enacted by the authoritarian regime had set a five-year limit on presidential terms and prohibited reelection, Pérez Jiménez unwisely believed he could use a rigged referendum as a fig leaf for remaining in power. Rafael Caldera, leader of COPEI, was first jailed and later exiled to the United States for his opposition to the plebiscite, which was to be held on 15 December 1957. Realizing that there was no further advantage to remaining in the legal opposition, Caldera joined the ongoing discussions among the Venezuelan exiles in New York. On 20 January 1958, with news reports from Venezuela raising hopes for an imminent collapse of the dictatorship, Rafael Caldera met with Rómulo Betancourt and Jóvito Villalba and subscribed to a pact to coordinate a transition to democracy. This agreement came to be known as the Pact of New York, and it represented the coalescence of the elite on democratization (Stambouli 1980, 146; Fuenmayor 1981, 10:520–25).

THE JUNTA PATRIÓTICA, THE MOBILIZATION OF CIVIL SOCIETY, AND THE FALL OF PÉREZ JIMÉNEZ

In the years between the collapse of the Gallegos administration and Pérez Jiménez's blundering effort at reelection, the Venezuelan economy and civil society had become much more complex and independent, providing a potential reservoir of opposition to the dictatorship and support for a return to democracy (Toro Hardy 1992, 38–52). Even as the exiled political leadership in New York crafted agreements to support any eventual return to democracy, they remained largely out of touch with the increasingly restless civil society they had left behind. When Pérez Jiménez thoroughly mismanaged government finances in 1957, which prompted a recession and rising unemployment, he alienated the new middle class and worsened relations with important supporters of the regime in the business sector and the Catholic Church. Taking advantage of this unrest, local political activists belonging to the underground parties took the initiative to coordinate opposition to the dictatorship by organized labor, some priests of the Catholic Church, students, middle-class professionals, and businesspeople.

The worsening economic conditions that turned civil society against Pérez Jiménez ironically arose as a result of his regime's own confused attachment to the logics of technocratic authoritarianism and armed cronyism. In accordance with its official technocratic ideology, the dictatorship invested in massive public works projects that were designed to accelerate Venezuela's economic development. However, the logic of armed crony-ism led many of these projects to be built by companies that were owned by prominent civilian supporters of the regime. This infrastructure invest-ment, while popular among important business sectors and the middle class, eventually became an ever-increasing drain on the public treasury. Facing a softening international oil market and reduced government revenues, the regime accumulated ever larger domestic debts, beyond its capacity to easily finance. As public spending slowed and imports became difficult to obtain, private consumption declined and the economy slowed. Unfulfilled govern-ment obligations to local suppliers and contractors spiraled upward, even-tually reaching 4.5 billion bolívares (approximately $1.3 billion at 1958 ex-change rates) (Mayobre 1992, 285–86). Large public projects slowly ground to a halt in late 1957 as many former supporters of Pérez Jiménez refused to extend further credit to his government. These contractors, in turn, laid off thousands of construction workers. The rise in unemployment between 1957 and 1958 (from 7.7 percent to over 10 percent) created a mass of dissatis-fied citizens, particularly in Caracas, who were predisposed to participate in political demonstrations (Toro Hardy 1992, 48–58). Furthermore, local manufacturers and businesspeople, unable to collect on their government debts, began reselling government promissory notes on the secondary finan-cial markets. These financial maneuvers angered Pérez Jiménez, who retali-ated by persecuting important local business leaders, thus pushing many of his most important former supporters into the arms of the burgeoning local opposition (Stambouli 1980, 129–30; Giacopini Zárraga 1992c).

The Pérez Jiménez regime succeeded in alienating almost all sectors of civilian society during the last year of the dictatorship. In particular, the regime lost the support it had initially enjoyed from the Catholic Church, the middle class, and the business community. By 1957, an increasing num-ber of Catholic clergy, influenced by the new doctrines promulgated by Pope Pius XII that promoted social justice and greater equity, had begun to criti-cize the social welfare policies of the Pérez Jiménez regime. The regime, and particularly the minister of interior, Vallenilla Lanz, responded harshly to these criticisms and thereby lost the support of the church hierarchy in Vene-zuela, along with that of many lay Catholics (Stambouli 1980, 105–12). The new middle class, largely made up of urban professionals and small business owners, were hard hit by the economic recession and declining private con-sumption. Labor unions and student groups, traditionally organized by AD or the PCV, had not fared well during the dictatorship. Union organizing had been highly restricted, the national university was closed for several years in the early 1950s to dampen student activism, and leaders of both groups were often harassed by the Seguridad Nacional (Godio 1985, 103–8). Pressure from the regime pushed business, labor, students, the Catholic Church, and professional groups into the opposition.

As Pérez Jiménez antagonized his traditional supporters, local political activists became much more successful at organizing civil resistance. A directorate of members of the major underground political parties, constituted in June 1957 under the name of the Junta Patriótica, controlled organizational activity. The group was originally proposed by Fabricio Ojeda of the URD and Gabriel García Ponte of the PCV, but it eventually included representatives from other parties as well (Fuenmayor 1981, 8:423–28).[7] The Junta Patriótica had strong links to professional associations, student groups, and labor unions, and it was particularly well connected to radio and news journalists (Burggraff 1972, 147–48). Through this growing network of supporters, the Junta Patriótica could carry out successful propaganda efforts, which laid the groundwork for the mobilization of broad segments of civil society.

The Junta Patriótica reached out to the armed forces through its promises of political moderation and amnesty, reflecting the strategies of appeasement and "divide and conquer." In its statements to the public, the Junta Patriótica was always careful to absolve the armed forces as an institution from responsibility for either political repression or support of the dictatorship. Additionally, it reminded members of the military of their own role as victims of political repression by the regime's security police, including torture, imprisonment, and exile.

Once it became clear that Pérez Jiménez would unconstitutionally attempt to extend his term of office, the Junta Patriótica addressed the armed forces directly in a manifesto dated November 1957. In this document, the junta called on the Venezuelan armed forces to defend the constitution and prevent the extension of the Pérez Jiménez dictatorship into the indefinite future. It narrowly concentrated blame for the authoritarian regime on Pérez Jiménez, Vallenilla Lanz, his minister of the interior, and Pedro Estrada, the head of Seguridad Nacional. The Junta Patriótica also reminded military officers of the positive role that other Latin American militaries had played in recent years in restoring or preserving constitutional governments. As several analysts have argued, the Junta Patriótica played a crucial role in the democratization process by signaling to officers in the armed forces that any attempts by the military to oppose the dictatorship would be backed by a politically organized civilian opposition. It also quieted the fear among the officer corps that any future civilian administration would retaliate against them for their participation in the dictatorship (Schaposnik 1985, 173–75). This policy allowed democratizers to drive a wedge between military hard-liners and moderates, preparing the way for a strategy of "divide and con-quer" under a new civilian regime.

By the time that elements of the army and air force acted to overthrow Pérez Jiménez on 1 January 1958, Venezuela's political parties and groups within civil society had already developed the links and mechanisms for coordinated political and economic action in the event of a transition to democracy. Furthermore, both the democratic political parties and civil society had also developed a consensus on the basis of a new political regime and, to a significant degree, on the policies that any future democratic gov-ernment would enact. The collapse of the dictatorship on 23 January 1958 came as a surprise to many Venezuelans, but the foundation and rules for joint action to exclude a future return to dictatorship had already been laid out and were available to the political actors during the transition to democ-racy. This combination of civilian consensus and mobilization capacity pro-vided democratizers with one part of the broad opportunity structure that they would eventually need to carry out their strategies to establish civilian control of the armed forces. The second part of this opportunity structure would emerge from the near-collapse of institutional cohesion in the armed forces during the overthrow of Pérez Jiménez.

OVERTHROWING PÉREZ JIMÉNEZ:
THE COLLAPSE OF INSTITUTIONAL COHESION
IN THE VENEZUELAN ARMED FORCES

The magnitude of the opportunity available to democratizers in 1958 can-not be understood without reference to the self-inflicted wounds that the armed forces absorbed during the final weeks of the dictatorship. By the time that Pérez Jiménez fled to the Dominican Republic on 23 January 1958, his conservative civilian supporters had already been forced into exile by their rivals within the armed forces, and senior military officers had engaged in a vicious internecine struggle which had twice displaced the entire military high command within a three-week period. These events shattered the co-herence of the military and temporarily deprived it of any internal consen-sus on its role, privileges, or interests. The ability of democratizers to both resist threats and establish civilian control of the armed forces was substantially enhanced by the rapid factionalization of the Venezuelan armed forces that ensued in the absence of any coherent authoritarian leadership.

By December 1957, several conspiracies began to coalesce within the armed forces, encouraged by the expansion of popular mobilization and civilian opposition to the regime. The first coup plot to mature developed among mid-ranking air force and army officers. The conspirators, following the announcement of Pérez Jiménez's victory in the national plebiscite on 20 December, agreed to overthrow the government on 6 January 1958, a traditional Venezuelan religious holiday. However, unnerved by the arrest of two fellow officers for treason, air force officers hastily moved up their plans to 1 January. In the early hours of the new year, officers of the Maracay air base, west of the capital, led by Captain Martín Parada, took control of this military installation and arrested Colonel Romero Villate, their commanding officer. In Caracas, Lieutenant Colonel Hugo Trejo, leader of the army component of the conspiracy, successfully took control of the Bermúdez armored battalion and the Ayala artillery group.

Due to resistance by some troops and officers to rebelling, the absence of many of his soldiers on leave for the holidays, and shortages in munitions, however, Trejo was unable to participate effectively in the coup attempt. By the time he was able to deploy his troops, it was already 7 P.M. on 1 January, the presidential palace had been under bombardment by the air force for hours, and Trejo had lost all hope of surprising progovernment forces. Fearing that Pérez Jiménez would be defended by loyalist armored vehicles, Trejo instead decided to retreat toward the nearby city of Los Teques, both to protect Maracay from a Caracas-based counterattack and to establish communications with the air force.

Meanwhile, despite an initial panic over the rebellion, cooler heads among government loyalists prevailed and began organizing the defense of the regime. Pérez Jiménez agreed to order a counterattack against the air force rebels in Maracay and to bring up additional loyal troops to defend the presidential palace, facts he announced by radio to discomfit the rebels. From Maracay, air force planes had been flying bombing missions against Caracas intermittently throughout the day without much evident result. Out of communication with their co-conspirators and aware of an impending attack by ground forces on Maracay, the rebel air force officers decided to flee to Colombia. Shortly thereafter, Trejo surrendered to loyal military forces, ending the rebellion (Molina Vargas 1992). The Seguridad Nacional immediately began investigating suspected civilian and military supporters of the coup attempt (Rodriguez Iturbe 1984, 515–16). Despite the victory of government forces, the coup attempt was a sign that the armed forces, particularly through divisions between junior officers and the high command, were in crisis.

By all accounts, Pérez Jiménez was severely demoralized by the 1 January coup attempt. He felt that he had been betrayed by the armed forces and became uncertain of whom he could trust within his government. People outside the regime saw the coup attempt as a sign of weakness and became increasingly willing to participate in antigovernment activities. The Junta Patriótica, which had generally restricted itself to issuing manifestos prior the January coup attempt, began a campaign of active measures against the dictatorship. Confident of the junta's support among radio and news journalists, it called on them to walk out on strike on 6 January. University professors and intellectuals circulated a manifesto against the government on 7 January. Catholic priests began to speak out as well, and several were arrested during this period by the Seguridad Nacional. Shortly after this, on 9 January, the Junta Patriótica ordered its activists to encourage general civil disobedience and street actions against the security forces. Government security patrols were met by sharpshooters, fire bombs, rocks, bottles, and any other improvised weapons demonstrators could lay their hands on. Violence escalated progressively from this point on (Avendaño Lugo 1982, 280–81).

Within the armed forces, the coup attempt was also seen as a sign of the fragility of the dictatorship, and two different strands of thinking on the future of the government were revealed. Many junior and mid-ranking officers, particularly those in the navy and air force, could conceive of a transition to a civilian or democratic government, albeit one heavily influenced by the armed forces. Others, mostly higher-ranking officers led by General Rómulo Fernández, the Armed Forces Chief of Staff, felt that Pérez Jiménez had betrayed them, was impeding their own ascent to high political offices, and had relied too heavily on a clique of upper-class civilians to rule the country. They wanted to continue full-fledged military rule, with or without Pérez Jiménez. Some have suggested that the idea of Pérez Jiménez and his collaborators maintaining their exclusive access to the government's resources for an additional five years was simply too galling for other generals and admirals, who had waited their turn patiently (Schaposnik 1985, 205–9). Two separate military logics were in conflict in the armed forces as before, with junior, more professional officers once again moving toward professionalism and democratization, while senior officers attempted to maintain authoritarianism and cronyism.

On 8 January, two incidents confirmed the increasing factionalism and unrest in the armed forces and their spread to other military services. Rumors of an imminent coup circulated among navy units based at La Guaira (the port nearest Caracas). To forestall further rebellions, General Llovera Páez ordered several army tanks from the Caracas garrison to La Guaira and forced the navy destroyers docked there to give up their munitions stores at gunpoint. Meanwhile, in Caracas the military high command, led by General Rómulo Fernández, presented an ultimatum to Pérez Jiménez. They demanded a change in the direction of the country through the immediate appointment of an all-military ministerial cabinet. Cowed, Pérez Jiménez acquiesced to their demands, reserving only a few, relatively technical ministries for trusted civilians. Simultaneously, many service chiefs who commanded the armed forces during the January 1958 coup attempt were dismissed for their lack of foresight. General Rómulo Fernández became minister of defense, and Colonel Romero Villate and Colonel Roberto Casanova, who had been instrumental in repressing the 1 January uprising, were named Chief of Staff of the air force and army, respectively (Rodríguez Iturbe 1984, 525–29). These punitive purges against negligent military commanders and the showdown over the composition of the cabinet had the effect of expelling hard-line civilians from the government camp. The open conflict between Pérez Jiménez and the military high command signaled a dangerous new division within the armed forces and the authoritarian elite.

When the cabinet reshuffle was announced to the country, the opposition readily understood the move as a sign of deepening government confusion. As a result, the Junta Patriótica stepped up its plans to destabilize the regime, and student and political activists redoubled their efforts to organize political demonstrations and distribute propaganda. On 13 January, the clandestine executive committee of Acción Democrática joined the Junta Patriótica; all antigovernment parties were now represented in this organization. In the week that followed, associations of business owners, lawyers, engineers, teachers, and students all issued manifestos calling for an end to the dictatorship. With this broad segment of society committed to removing Pérez Jiménez from power, the Junta Patriótica called for a general strike on 21 January (Tarre Murzi 1983, 191–95). As the authoritarian regime and the armed forces progressively fell into chaos, the civilian opposition cohered, creating a power dynamic that would provide democratizers with an unprecedented opportunity to establish civilian rule and control over the military.

Amid the general instability, General Pérez Jiménez contributed to the disintegration of the military hierarchy by striking back at his opponents within the high command. General Rómulo Fernández and the other senior officers who had forced Pérez Jiménez to reshuffle his cabinet on 8 January were arrested and sent into exile on 13 January. Pérez Jiménez again reorganized his cabinet, making himself the minister of defense, hoping in this way to stave off any further military threats to his government (Rodríguez Iturbe 1984, 531). By taking these actions, Pérez Jiménez effectively decimated the hard-line faction within the armed forces, hobbling their opposition to his government and, as a side effect, to any future democratic regime.

Despite General Llovera Páez's action to disarm fleet units based in La Guaira, conspiratorial activity increased among navy officers as pressures from civil society and the growing violence on the streets undermined their willingness to support the dictatorship. The general strike called by the Junta Patriótica for 21 January resulted in the virtual paralysis of economic and social activity in Caracas. Most businesses complied voluntarily, and those that did not were forced to close by political activists and street mobs. Members of the Seguridad Nacional, army units, and the police engaged in running street battles with mobs of demonstrators who had grown progressively bolder during the preceding weeks. Casualties among civilians due to these confrontations with the security forces were estimated at 300 dead and 1,200 wounded over the next three days. On 22 January, navy units based at Puerto Cabello, east of Caracas, rebelled in their entirety. Several destroyers embarked marine infantry units and sailed for La Guaira. By 20 January, some members of the newly appointed military high command had reached the conclusion that Pérez Jiménez should be removed from power (Giacopini Zárraga 1992c). At this point, even hard-liners within the armed forces had abandoned the dictatorial regime and joined the internal struggle for power within the armed forces, fracturing the institutional cohesion of the armed forces beyond immediate repair.

Pérez Jiménez became directly aware of his tenuous position once the armed forces ceased to obey him, and he quickly concluded that his regime would not survive. On being notified of the navy uprising, he ordered elements of the Valencia garrison to move toward La Guaira to repress the insurgent units, but the garrison commander refused to obey orders. Pérez

Jiménez then ordered Major Azuaje, an army officer based in Caracas, to marshal artillery and infantry units to attack La Guaira. Major Azuaje accepted the mission, but instead of attacking La Guaira, he placed his units in the hills between Caracas and the port city to protect the navy. By the afternoon of 22 January, the military academy at Caracas had joined the insurgency. The Bolívar battalion stationed near the academy surrounded the rebellious cadets, but it refused to fire on them. Pérez Jiménez attempted last-ditch negotiations with the army and navy insurgents but found them unwilling to compromise. He also found that his military units were increasingly loath to engage in repressive activities against the civilian population, let alone against other military units. Finally, realizing that he had exhausted his resources, Pérez Jiménez fled into exile on board the presidential plane at 2:30 A.M. on 23 January. He designated no successor to either deal with the continuing civil unrest or create a new government (Stambouli 1980, 159–60; Schaposnik 1985, 214–18).

Statecraft, Strategy, and the Venezuelan Armed Forces during the 1958 Transition

The nature of the collapse of the Pérez Jiménez regime created a broad opportunity structure to craft civilian control of the armed forces by shifting the balance of power away from the military institution and in favor of democratizers. The armed forces occupied a position of weakness during the transition to democracy because the internal factionalization produced by the collapse of the dictatorship prevented any military leader from unifying the institution or using the threat of force to limit the democratization process. The military hierarchy had largely broken down, and junior officers increasingly deliberated before responding to orders from their superiors. Any move by one faction leader to seize power could and would have been opposed by other factions in the military. This allowed the more unified democratizers, backed by a strong political consensus and mass mobilization, to readily use a strategy of "divide and conquer" to create regime leverage and to impose institutional reforms that would eventually lead to civilian control of the armed forces. Because of the mutual suspicions among different factions and historical grievances within the armed forces, democratizers could even recruit large groups within the officer corps to defend democratization and implement military reforms. Nevertheless, hard-liners in the armed forces did attempt to resist this process and initially even claimed expanded jurisdictional boundaries for the military. However, the collapse of military internal consensus on roles and prerogatives prevented the hard-liners from pursuing successful counterstrategies. The outcome of the broad opportunity structure and the ensuing strategic interaction was a high degree of regime leverage over the military.

FORMING THE TRANSITIONAL GOVERNMENT: THE FIRST CHECK TO MILITARY AUTHORITY

The process of establishing the transitional government provided the first evidence of both the newfound power of the civilian democratizers and the degree of incoherence within the armed forces. The struggles of Pérez Jiménez and his opponents in the military high command during the final weeks of his regime purged the armed forces of experienced hard-line leaders who could potentially unify the officer corps and lead resistance to civilian rule. Many Venezuelan military officers were at the very least suspicious of democracy and were often hostile to the idea of unrestrained civilian rule, but they disagreed even more strongly among themselves as to who should lead Venezuela, let alone in what direction. Even though the initial junta that replaced Pérez Jiménez was composed entirely of military officers, civilians in the Junta Patriótica and the opposition political parties moved rapidly to enforce civilian participation in the transition to democracy. These civilian politicians, who readily understood the importance of achieving government authority over the armed forces, acted from the first moments of the interim government to prevent the reestablishment of a military-dominated regime.

No military leader was clearly in charge following the departure of General Pérez Jiménez for Santo Domingo, and as a result, the political situation on the morning of 23 January was exceedingly confused. As local radio stations announced Pérez Jiménez's flight, the populace spilled into the streets to celebrate. Army units and police squads assigned to riot control awaited nervously for decisions by their superior officers. Meanwhile, the highest-ranking members of each of the military services met at the presidential palace, Miraflores, and constituted an all-military provisional government (Junta Militar de Gobierno) to administer the country. Admiral Wolfgang Larrazábal, by virtue of his seniority, was designated president of the junta, and for the first time in Venezuelan history, all military services agreed to exercise power collegially. Colonel Romero Villate and Colonel Roberto Casanova, who had recently rendered sterling service to Pérez Jiménez during the 1 January rebellion, represented the air force and army respectively on the junta. Admiral Carlos Larrazábal, brother to the president of the junta, was appointed commander of the navy. As the military leaders of the old regime sorted out the composition of the new executive authority in the halls of the government palace, members of the economic elite of Caracas lobbied them for positions in prestigious ministries and agencies (Rodríguez Iturbe 1984, 541–42). The decision to form a collegial military government indicated that the junior military services would no longer accept the army's leadership. This boded ill for the future ability of the armed forces to present a united front against the demands of civilian democratizers.

At this point, it was not yet clear what the shape of the new regime would be, let alone whether it would allow a transition to democracy. The military officers who constituted the junta had all gained their high standing for their loyalty to Pérez Jiménez. Casanova and Romero Villate were particularly notable for their support of the dictator during the previous decade. Although most of the senior hard-line military officers had been exiled by Pérez Jiménez himself, a substantial number of his sympathizers remained within the middle and lower ranks of the officer corps; they were suspicious of civilians and firm believers in the idea that democratization would inevitably lead to Communism. On the other hand, political leaders in exile wanted to press for a rapid transition to democracy, with elections in as short a time period as feasible. From New York, Rómulo Betancourt urged the coordinating committee of AD to use all available means to ensure a swift transition (Betancourt 1958). Civilians and insurgent factions within the officer corps moved quickly to prevent the possible formation of another authoritarian regime.

On the morning after the departure of Pérez Jiménez, the president of the Junta Patriótica, addressing the nation by radio, condemned the purely military composition of the new government, demanded the inclusion of civilians in the interim government, and threatened continued mass unrest. Specifically, he targeted Colonels Romero Villate and Casanova for removal due to their well-known participation in repressing the 1 January coup attempt. The Junta Patriótica's vow to continue popular agitation intimidated the all-military junta, who were all too aware of their failure to suppress civil unrest even before Pérez Jiménez had fled the country. Simultaneously, Lieutenant Colonel Hugo Trejo, released from detention on the morning of 23 January following three weeks in military prison, pressured the president of the junta, Admiral Larrazábal, to remove Romero Villate and Casanova from power. It was clearly unacceptable to Trejo and the rebellious junior officers he led that the very colonels who had prevented the 1 January coup attempt from succeeding should now claim to rule as successors to the departed dictator. Facing a twenty-four-hour deadline from Trejo and the indefinite extension of the general strike, Larrazábal acquiesced. The leverage developed by democratizers through mass mobilization, when combined with the fragmentation of the armed forces, thus prevented military commanders from consolidating a new military regime.

The civilians who were nominated to join the new governing executive committee met with the full approval and support of the exiled political leaders in New York. Blas Lamberti, a well-known Caracas engineer, and his employer, wealthy businessman Eugenio Mendoza, became members of the renamed Junta de Gobierno on 24 January. Mendoza had in fact been meeting with opposition leaders during the collapse of the dictatorship and had been present during the final negotiations of the Pact of New York. The two offending colonels were sent into exile, also on 24 January, each with a check for $100,000 to ease their departure.[8] Shortly thereafter, Admiral Larrazábal announced that the goal of the new junta would be to effect a rapid transition to democracy, with presidential elections to be held within the year, thereby marking the capitulation of the armed forces to the civilian democratization project.

FACTIONALISM IN THE VENEZUELAN ARMED FORCES AND THE FAILURE TO DEVELOP COUNTERSTRATEGIES

Factions within the military began to maneuver for advantage and autonomy as soon as the transition to democracy began. Within weeks, the armed forces had split into essentially three competing groups, each with their own agendas concerning political and military power. Efforts by any one faction to affect government policy or restrict the democratization process were met by determined resistance from their opponents within the armed forces. As a result of this competition, the military as a whole was unable to resist government plans to reduce the role and authority of the armed forces within the state.

Wolfgang Larrazábal, as president of the junta and ex-commander of the navy, headed the most coherent and progressive grouping of military forces, the Venezuelan navy. Naval officers shared a commitment to the new Junta de Gobierno due to their loyalty and affection for Larrazábal. Among military officers, the navy had the reputation of being the most constitutionalist and progressive element within the armed forces, perhaps as a result of having fared better under the 1945–48 democratic regime than under Pérez Jiménez (Briceño Linares 1994; García Villasmil 1995c). The navy had participated in only one of the insurrections, the successful one on 22–23 January, and had risen up almost unanimously against the Pérez Jiménez government, which minimized the degree of infighting and mistrust between members of this service. Additionally, Larrazábal could depend on his younger brother, Carlos Larrazábal, commander of the navy, to mobilize forces in his favor in the event of an emergency. While the navy lacked the heavy land-based weaponry of the army and the strategic positions of the army's garrisons in Caracas, it was able to provide a deterrence force through its marine infantry battalions and the guns of its destroyers, based twelve miles away in La Guaira. The very cohesion of the navy, in an otherwise incoherent military, made it more powerful than its capabilities alone would suggest, and its growing commitment to the logic of democratization made it a powerful ally of civilians in the transitional regime. In essence, the navy pursued a counterstrategy against continued army domination of the armed forces, rather than against the new democratic government.

Meanwhile, the officer corps of the army and the Guardia Nacional divided almost immediately after the overthrow of Pérez Jiménez into a progressive populist wing and a technocratic authoritarian wing. Younger progressive officers, particularly those who had participated directly in the January uprisings, tended to look for leadership to Lieutenant Colonel Hugo Trejo (Fuenmayor 1984, 11:208–10). Although he only had an administrative position as vice chief of the General Staff, Trejo provided a moral and political compass for many in the army. Trejo's political views leaned toward themes of national renewal and populist governance, which received widespread civilian attention during his visits to armed forces garrisons in Venezuela's interior. His followers advocated a rather confused populist nationalism, but they remained suspicious of the partisanship of civilian politicians. This confusion over goals and strategies prevented them from developing an effective counterstrategy that would have allowed Trejo to influence the new government and purge his opponents in the armed forces.

Those officers who were still sympathetic to the tenets of the Pérez Jiménez regime sought leadership from the new minister of defense, General Jesús María Castro León. Castro León was never particularly opposed to democratization per se, but rather to the attendant disorders and lack of efficiency involved in the process. His perspective mirrored the mindset of conservative military officers throughout South America, who found in civilian politics a source of national division and corruption. Also, Castro León jealously guarded the presumed prerogatives of the armed forces and resented any attacks on the probity and honor of the military. His early public statements attacked media criticism of the Pérez Jiménez regime and of his institution, and for this reason he was identified as a threat by political leaders. Officers who had supported Pérez Jiménez and desired a return to authoritarian rule thus found Castro León to be an acceptable leader; moreover, he was able to draw on the loyalty of some officers in his own service, the air force (Burggraff 1972, 174–78; Fuenmayor 1984, 11:220). Castro León was largely untainted by the armed cronyism of the dictatorial regime and remained committed to the logic of technocratic authoritarianism that still circulated within the armed forces. Although he wanted to constrain the scope of democratization and preserve the prerogatives of the armed forces, the high degree of military fragmentation was sufficient to prevent him from controlling the number of military units necessary to achieve his goals.

STRATEGIES AND COUNTERSTRATEGIES: THE FAILURE OF MILITARY RESISTANCE TO DEMOCRATIZATION

In spite of this profound factionalization of the armed forces, groups of officers still attempted to mount challenges to the democratization process during 1958 in an attempt to place limits on civilian rule and expand the military's jurisdictional boundaries. In each instance, the Junta de Gobierno was able to use the internal divisions of the military to defeat these threats and turn them to its advantage, identifying and purging pockets of resistance to democratization within the officer corps. Democratizers perceived that the two most significant threats to the junta came from the factions led by Lieutenant Colonel Hugo Trejo, vice chief of the General Staff, and General Castro León, minister of defense. By neutralizing these threats, the Junta de Gobierno removed not only those officers who were most likely to overthrow the government but also those with the leadership skills that could provide a nucleus of resistance to the government's efforts to establish its authority over the armed forces. As a result of these successful government purges, the faction of the officer corps most inclined toward the democratization, led by Larrazábal, gained the upper hand over the conservative and populist wings by the end of the transition process.

With his populist leanings, charismatic speaking style, and strong following among the general public, Trejo was considered a significant problem by civilian politicians within days of the fall of the dictatorship. For many, Trejo was a threat largely because he was critical of the civilian political parties and seemed willing to use his power in the military to shape the democratization process. In particular, though he was always careful to support the junta, he called for a renewal of the political leadership of AD, COPEI, and URD, on par with the purge of the Pérez Jimenista high command that had occurred during the January rebellions. The combination of his popularity in the armed forces and his speeches on domestic issues quickly turned him into a major political phenomenon. Additionally, Trejo reminded many upper-class Venezuelans of Argentina's former dictator, Juan Perón, and even the most conservative were eager to see Trejo undermined (Fuenmayor 1984, 11:211–19; Rangel 1998, 205–18). Venezuela's democratizers also found willing collaborators among Trejo's rivals within the armed forces who wished to rid themselves of him.

Trejo's self-congratulatory claim to the leadership of the officer corps antagonized the military factions who had not participated in the failed 1 January rebellion. Larrazábal resented Trejo's popularity within the armed forces, and he felt that Trejo's early ultimatums to the Junta de Gobierno had been a personal challenge to his authority. Minister of Defense Castro León and his conservative allies saw Trejo's support for democracy as dangerous and divisive, which would undermine their own counterstrategy to place limits on the democratization process. Naively, Trejo never used his apparent power to consolidate his authority over the army, nor does he seem to have made much effort to place his followers in key positions where they could support him. He allowed himself to be appointed vice chief of the General Staff, a subordinate position that removed him from direct command of troops. As a result, Larrazábal was able to force Trejo to accept a gilded exile as ambassador to the friendly government of Costa Rica. Despite wild rumors of armed resistance to this move, Trejo quietly left the country on 29 April 1958 (Burggraff 1972, 176–77; Fuenmayor 1984, 11:219–23; Schaposnik 1985, 249–51;). With his departure, the role played by the populist military faction in politics was eclipsed by the larger contest between the pro-democratization and technocratic authoritarian wings of the armed forces.

Trejo's exile left the field open for the junta's minister of defense, General Castro León, to attempt to direct the transition in a more authoritarian direction. Although he was not initially opposed to democratization as such, Castro León became profoundly opposed to the renewed ascendancy of civilian political parties in Venezuela, particularly the left-of-center

Acción Democrática. He disliked Larrazábal for his presumed presidential ambitions and his closeness to civilians in and out of government. Castro León also resented the pressure from political parties to purge the armed forces of officers who had been affiliated with Pérez Jiménez and, particularly, their demands that officers who had been dismissed for disloyalty during the dictatorship be reinstated in the officer corps with full rank and back pay. Finally, Castro León perceived a leftist conspiracy to undermine the armed forces in the continuous attacks by the media on the officer corps for its participation in the Pérez Jiménez dictatorship and its alleged militarism (Burggraff 1972, 175–78; Rangel 1998, 264–73). For Castro León, democratization posed a threat to public order and the integrity of the armed forces, and this led him to attempt to reassert military guardianship over Venezuela.

Castro León began considering military intervention in earnest in May 1958 as a result of the highly embarrassing mob attack on U.S. vice president Richard Nixon during an official visit to Caracas. In the aftermath of this event, the civilian members of the junta, Eugenio Mendoza and Blas Lamberti, resigned (although they were immediately replaced by two civilians from the ministerial cabinet). As cause for their resignation, they cited their exclusion by military members of the junta from the meetings that determined the Venezuelan government's response to both the popular demonstrations surrounding Nixon's visit and the veiled threat by the United States to intervene with troops to rescue the vice president. Castro León was incensed by Larrazábal's seeming support for the crowds who participated in the mobbing of Nixon's motorcade (Tarre Murzi 1983, 211). Moreover, this event confirmed the minister of defense's perception that democratization was bringing about a collapse in law and order (Fuenmayor 1983, 10:533–34, 544–48). Castro León's fears of a popular uprising were fed by the Servicio de Inteligencia de las Fuerzas Armadas (SIFA), the joint armed forces intelligence service, which warned that Rómulo Betancourt and pro-AD military officers had prepared coup attempts for 1 May and 10 July 1958 (Fuenmayor 1984, 11:289–91; Servicio de Inteligencia de las Fuerzas Armadas 1958).[9] The minister of defense believed that Communist infiltration of the democratization process was increasing, and he considered Acción Democrática its principal conduit.

Fearing an imminent AD-led coup attempt, on 21 July 1958 General Castro León presented an ultimatum to President Larrazábal. Among his demands were (1) reshuffling the ministerial cabinet to eliminate the influence of Acción Democrática in government and create a national unity cabinet; (2)

banning the Venezuelan Communist Party from political life; (3) passing a new press law to restrict media criticism of the armed forces; and (4) authorizing the Ministry of Defense to independently reorganize the armed forces and alter its operating procedures. In effect, Castro León insisted on the exclusion of the most radical political elements from power, including Acción Democrática, and full autonomy for the armed forces from civilian authority. Had his demands been accepted, it would have meant a far-reaching expansion of military jurisdictional boundaries into the areas of public policy and state leadership selection.

Rather than accept these conditions, Larrazábal and his civilian collaborators decided to resist, relying on their allies in the military and their ability to mobilize mass popular support. Larrazábal immediately departed Caracas for a seaside government residence, La Guzmania, conveniently located near the principal installations of the pro-democratic navy. Once he had reached this secure location, he summoned his cabinet and began to organize military resistance to what he saw as a veiled coup attempt. His civilian ministers voted overwhelmingly to reject Castro León's demands, and political activists immediately began organizing mass mobilizations in favor of the transitional government. However, President Larrazábal found that all major military garrisons in Caracas had responded positively to his minister of defense's call to insurrection. With Caracas in rebel hands, the prospect for the survival of the Junta de Gobierno seemed grim.

In Caracas, General Castro León was stunned by the overwhelmingly negative popular reaction to his demands, particularly since he had been assured of widespread civilian support by one of his co-conspirators, Major Juan de Dios Moncada Vidal. Accompanied by 200–300 officers who had gathered in support at the Ministry of Defense, both witnessed crowds of tens of thousands of citizens surging around the building, vociferously supporting the junta and opposing Castro León. Leaders of the major political parties addressed the demonstrators continuously, encouraging popular resistance at all costs. The unions publicly declared a general strike that was widely supported by both workers and businesspeople. Professional groups and, most important, FEDECAMARAS (the Venezuelan chamber of commerce) communicated their opposition to military intervention directly to Castro León and his supporters (Soto Tamayo 1986, 138–43; Briceño Linares 1994). Even though every military garrison in Caracas had joined the coup attempt, Castro León was completely paralyzed and unnerved by the sheer volume of popular opposition (Burggraff 1972, 178–86; Caldera 1992b).

Castro León's confidence eroded as he faced the crowds, waiting for a response from the transitional government. Then, on the evening of 22 July, Castro León was informed that the major military garrisons of Maracay (west of Caracas) had declared for the Junta de Gobierno. Isolated and fearing a civil war, Castro León met with Larrazábal in Caracas and was browbeaten into presenting his resignation as minister of defense in the early hours of 23 July. Castro León ordered the rebellious garrisons to stand down and boarded a plane into exile (Velásquez 1995). In the end, the internal divisions in the armed forces were revealed by the coup attempt, and the sheer size of the civilian mass mobilization signaled to the armed forces that renewed intervention would not be easy.

IMPLICATIONS OF THE DEFEAT OF THE
CASTRO LEÓN REBELLION

The events of 21–23 July 1958 were a high-water mark in the expansion of military jurisdictional boundaries during the transition to democracy. The victory of the Junta de Gobierno marked a definite turning point in the ability of the government to maintain its authority over the armed forces, and military jurisdiction over the state shrank steadily over the next decade. As figure 3.1 illustrates, prior to the Castro León uprising, the armed forces were able to restrict civilian decision making in the interim government at will. Officers in the junta voted or spoke publicly on issues of government domestic policy. The military maintained a dominant role in matters of external security and foreign policy and excluded civilians from critical decisions, such as Venezuela's diplomatic response to U.S. threats of intervention during the attack on Vice President Nixon on his visit to Venezuela in early 1958. Moreover, as minister of defense, Castro León was able to resist important military reform measures, as the next section of this chapter will explore. In matters of internal security, the armed forces predominated as well. Military intelligence gathered information on civilian political activities, and military units participated in policing and riot control. The collapse of civilian security forces after the departure of Pérez Jiménez inevitably pulled the armed forces into an extensive internal security role. Before the events of 21–23 July, military dominance over state activities seemed to be growing rapidly; the armed forces shared authority with civilian politicians only in the areas of domestic policy and state leadership selection.

Following Castro León's exile, no single military leader was able to knit together a sufficient number of military units and officers to credibly

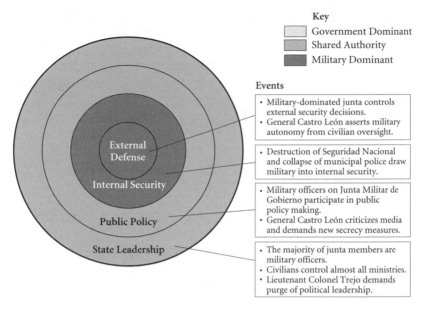

Key
- Government Dominant
- Shared Authority
- Military Dominant

Events

- Military-dominated junta controls external security decisions.
- General Castro León asserts military autonomy from civilian oversight.

- Destruction of Seguridad Nacional and collapse of municipal police draw military into internal security.

- Military officers on Junta Militar de Gobierno participate in public policy making.
- General Castro León criticizes media and demands new secrecy measures.

- The majority of junta members are military officers.
- Civilians control almost all ministries.
- Lieutenant Colonel Trejo demands purge of political leadership.

External Defense

Internal Security

Public Policy

State Leadership

Figure 3.1. Civil-Military Jurisdictional Boundaries, ca. June 1958: Prior to Castro León Coup Attempt

threaten to overthrow the government. The more progressive wing of the officer corps, led by the navy, held the upper hand within the military and readily supported the junta. The Castro León coup attempt also hardened government and civilian attitudes toward military rebellion. Subsequent attempts by military officers to rebel were punished with long prison sentences, rather than exile, as had previously been the norm. These events also led to a reform of the military code of justice, nearly doubling the penalties for rebellion to twenty-five to thirty years of imprisonment (Fuenmayor 1984, 11:420–23).

Most important, the exile of Trejo and the defeat of the Castro León uprising wrote and enforced the new rules defining the military jurisdictional boundaries in Venezuela. Through their actions, democratizers established a narrow range of issues in which military officers could participate. No longer were officers allowed to make political pronouncements, exclude civilians from important decisions in foreign policy or internal security, or resist the transition to democracy. Furthermore, by not accepting Castro León's ultimatum, the Junta de Gobierno effectively ended the possibility that the Venezuelan armed forces would be able either to veto government policy decisions or bar certain groups of civilians from power. Castro León's goal was the expansion of military jurisdiction into the areas of public policy and state leadership selection, which would allow the armed forces to supervise the political process and prevent alleged Communist infiltration. The defeat of these attempts to expand the autonomy and scope of military power, and the punishments inflicted on the officers who participated in them, effectively confronted the officer corps with both the reality of civilian power and the consequences of failure under the new regime. This deterred most from participating in new conspiracies against the interim regime and greatly contributed to the success of the transition to democracy.

CRAFTING INSTITUTIONS OF CIVILIAN CONTROL DURING THE TRANSITION TO DEMOCRACY

During 1958, the Junta de Gobierno found time to practice and begin institutionalizing a strategy of "divide and conquer," even though the interim government was not yet free of the threat of military intervention. It decreed an unusually wide-ranging reform of the administration and command structure of the armed forces, and these decrees, though often shaped by hidden agendas and hurried compromises among civilians and military officers, endured and provided the foundations of civilian authority over the armed forces during the next four decades.

Although neither Acción Democrática nor other civilian political parties were directly represented on the junta, their policy preferences vis-à-vis the armed forces were implemented through the influence of their civilian representatives in the interim government and their allies in the progressive wing of the armed forces. Specifically, the government set out to place a cadre of pro-democratization officers at the helm of the armed forces and to create administrative mechanisms that would weaken the ability of the four armed services branches to cooperate with each other. The junior military services, particularly the air force and navy, endorsed these measures so as to increase their own autonomy from the army and gain access to resources. Democratizers had already demonstrated a high degree of regime leverage by defending the transition from Trejo and Castro León, and they took advantage of this favorable moment to enact permanent institutional barriers to cooperation within the military.

The first part of the strategy involved creating a cadre of loyal military commanders who would be unaffiliated with the traditional power structure of the armed forces and who would provide reliable "insider" information to democratizers. To accomplish this, the junta issued Decree 134 on 7 April 1958, recalling to service scores of military officers who had been exiled, imprisoned, or cashiered during the ten years of dictatorship. Not only were these officers reinstated, but they were also granted seniority and ranks equivalent to what they would have achieved had they been allowed to remain in the armed forces (Tarre Briceño 1994a; Yépez Daza 1995). Many of these officers, termed "*reincorporados*," were known for their democratic tendencies, and some were associated with political parties. The junta also favored these officers in terms of assignments (Müller Rojas 1989, 417). Despite their relatively small numbers, the *reincorporados* caused a great deal of resentment in the Venezuelan officer corps because they tended to receive important command positions and career opportunities. Also, they were viewed as political elements (the equivalent of party commissars) because of their presumed role in monitoring the loyalty of the officer corps (Molina Vargas 1992; Yépez Daza 1995). In practical terms, the hostility between officers who were already in the armed forces and those returning from exile ensured the loyalty of the *reincorporados* to the democratization process and created a new division the government could exploit as it carried out its policy of "divide and conquer." However, the restoration of these officers was also a very risky strategy since it could have caused a backlash within the officer corps.

The most important and far-reaching institutional component of the democratizers' "divide and conquer" strategy was the decentralization of administration and command in the Venezuelan military. On 27 June 1958, the Junta de Gobierno issued Decree 288, which removed administrative authority over the armed forces from the minister of defense and assigned control over operational, financial, and administrative functions to the commanding officers of the army, navy, air force, and Fuerzas Armadas de Cooperación. Military appropriations, once allocated among the services at the discretion of the minister of defense, were thus transformed into separate budgetary line items assigned by Congress to the four military services. The minister of defense no longer had the authority to change allocations among the various branches, nor could he use the threat of reallocation to enforce his will over other service commanders. He was also no longer able to issue orders that directly affected officers or units within a service without transmitting them through its commander (Schaposnik 1985, 238–44). The effect of this decree was to *permanently* fragment the unity of the armed forces. Each service began pursuing its own interests, competing for

resources within the larger political context. The armed forces were transformed from a strong, centralized institution into a diffuse network of feuding military fiefdoms.

From the perspective of achieving civilian control, the policy of weakening the Ministry of Defense only made sense because democratizers had decided to have a military-led Ministry of Defense. Paradoxically, if they had
instead decided to provide for a civilian minister of defense, this individual
would have benefited greatly from the centralization of authority that the
ministry enjoyed prior to Decree 288.

Not only did Decree 288 weaken the power of the Ministry of Defense,
but it completely eliminated the other traditional center of authority in the
Venezuelan military, the Prussian-model General Staff. It was replaced with
a Joint Chiefs of Staff system similar to that of the United States, with an important difference: the new Joint Staff was excluded, for administrative and
operational purposes, from the chain of command. Since no legislation defined the competencies of the new organization (nor would such legislation
exist until 1976), the Venezuelan Joint Staff organized itself on an ad hoc
basis on the pattern of the U.S. Joint Chiefs of Staff, although the Venezuelan
entity had much less authority. Under Decree 288, administrative functions
were assigned to the commanders of each separate military service, while
overall military and strategic planning was given to different officers on the
Joint Staff. Thus, the generals and colonels assigned to the Joint Staff had no
ability to control what type of armed forces Venezuela should have to meet
their plans, how those forces should be based, or what types of operations
they should be trained to accomplish under wartime conditions. As a result
of this split in administrative and strategic responsibility, the commanders
of the military services were free to ignore the requirements of the Joint Staff
and quickly developed their own war plans and drew up their own military
requirements. The new Joint Staff created such a weak central command for
the Venezuelan military that it prevented anyone from using it to gain control of the armed forces, as Pérez Jiménez had done (Yépez Daza 1980, 62–
65; Soto Urrútia 1994a).

The services most supportive of Decree 288 were the navy and the air
force, which had been traditionally relegated to secondary roles by the army-
dominated General Staff and Ministry of Defense. Carlos Larrazábal, commander of the navy, was reportedly the intellectual author of the reform
of the General Staff, while Minister of Defense Castro León, as an air force
officer, had few objections to a decree that could only benefit his service

(Velásquez 1995). Even though these officers' services had received additional equipment and training during the dictatorship, their power, in terms of command positions, and share of the military budget remained small compared to the army. They had been allowed only limited autonomy in their training and educational systems, and the army tended to dominate the higher military educational institutions, such as the Escuela Superior de las Fuerzas Armadas (the General Staff school) (Briceño Linares 1994). By lobbying for the enactment of this decree, the air force and navy sought organizational autonomy, as they viewed the continuing existence of the General Staff as an obstacle to their long-term interests. The army, which had benefited most from the General Staff system, was so disorganized and internally divided by the collapse of the Pérez Jiménez regime that it was unable to resist the transition to the Joint Staff system. As a result of the historical rivalries existing in the armed forces, democratizers were able to deliberately implement legislation that transformed the temporary disunity of the armed forces into permanent barriers to cooperation. After all, Betancourt and other exiled AD politicians had been discussing strategies for dividing the armed forces since 1949, and the Joint Staff system, which they had seen operate in all its competitive glory in the United States during the 1950s, matched their own preferences perfectly (Tarre Briceño 1994b).

As part of institutionalizing its "divide and conquer" strategy, the Junta de Gobierno also closed the Escuela Básica, which provided joint training for cadets from all services, on 22 June 1958. Publicly, the reason given for this action was that the Escuela Básica had become a center for conspiracy against the democratization process. Under the new system, cadets would attend classes and train at separate service academies. The transitional government also took the first steps in the direction of establishing separate advanced training and general staff courses for each of the military services. In the short term, this reform was part of the same drive to grant increased autonomy to the air force and the navy (Giacopini Zárraga 1992c). In the long run, this policy considerably reduced the opportunities for officers to form bonds and develop networks that included colleagues from different service branches. This, in turn, increased the difficulty of coordinating coup attempts. In a coup d'état, rebelling military officers cannot depend on the traditional military hierarchy to ensure the obedience of their co-conspirators and must instead rely on mutual trust and common interests to achieve cooperation. Without the interservice networks of friends and colleagues provided by the Escuela Básica and other training programs, the essential ingredients of trust and mutual interest necessary for an cohesive coup d'état became much more difficult to achieve.

Democratizers retroactively imposed limits on terms of service for military officers to remove the most senior conservative members of the armed forces. This had important unintended consequences that favored civilian "divide and conquer" strategies as well. Admiral Larrazábal and the junta were under great pressure from some politicians, particularly those on the left, to purge conservative and authoritarian officers from the armed forces as soon as possible (Burggraff 1972, 171). While failed coup attempts had identified overtly disloyal officers, civilians had little confidence in the high-ranking commanders of many garrisons, whose attitudes had to be polled prior to the resolution of any major military crisis. Rather than eliminate individual officers, the Junta de Gobierno issued Decree 533 on 17 January 1959, which retroactively set a thirty-year service limit for all military officers, regardless of rank. This enabled the government to remove relatively painlessly key senior officers who had supported Pérez Jiménez, practically all of whom had spent more than thirty years in the armed forces (Schaposnik 1985, 374–75).

Beyond eliminating hard-liners in the short term, Decree 533 further favored civilian control in the long run by decreasing the amount of time an officer served in any one command position. Because of the relatively strict time in grade requirements for each military rank, general rank officers had only a brief opportunity in which to exercise command before retirement, which deprived them of the opportunity to build up a personal following among the officer corps. Furthermore, this shortened length of service meant that rapid rotation of junior and mid-ranking officers through commands was possible and even necessary. While this affected the technical and operational efficiency of the military, it also meant that officers were never allowed to develop an affinity with any particular unit. In fact, this system of rapid rotation and promotion went a long way toward ending the military personalism that had characterized the Venezuelan armed forces until 1958 (Müller Rojas 1989, 416–17). The permanent instability in command positions also hindered the armed forces from achieving the internal coherence that could be used to execute a successful military coup. The support for Decree 533 came mainly from younger mid-ranking officers, who saw this reform as an opportunity to achieve higher rank, prestige, and professional standing more rapidly than had traditionally been possible.

Through its successful statecraft, the Junta de Gobierno was able to embed its strategy of "divide and conquer" into concrete military institutions, namely the reformed Ministry of Defense and Joint Staff, the separate military training centers, and the thirty-year service cap. These reformed institutions were broadly supported by officers in the armed forces, who saw in them new opportunities for service autonomy, accelerated promotions, and professional development. The junta, through the participation of civilians in the enactment and defense of the reform efforts, set precedents for government participation in security issues and for government authority over the shape, mission, and organization of national defense. These precedents reduced military autonomy in the key area of external security. At the same time, the democratizers' strategy of "divide and conquer" made it progressively more difficult for the armed forces to achieve the necessary institutional coherence to expand their jurisdictional boundaries. As military jurisdictional boundaries became narrower and more difficult for the armed forces to change, civilian control of the military became easier for democratizers to achieve.

However, it is important to note that none of the reforms carried out by civilians during this period required a high degree of regime capacity. All of the new institutional arrangements were designed to function without civilian supervision, relying only on the self-interest of military officers to sustain their effectiveness. This would be very important in the future: while civilians were highly focused and motivated to achieve civilian control in 1958, there was little civilian defense expertise available during the transition, nor was there any guarantee that even this amateurish interest could be sustained in the future.

Getting to Democracy: Civil-Military Politics during the 1958 Presidential Elections

Beyond their struggle to preserve the transitional government, civilian politicians faced a key question: would the armed forces accept the victor of the December 1958 presidential elections, no matter how distasteful the results might be to the officer corps? So long as the majority in the Junta de Gobierno was held by senior military commanders, most officers were likely to obey the transitional executive. Once a civilian was elected president, politicians were concerned that the new democracy would be immediately overthrown in a coup d'état. The leading candidates for president were either widely disliked within the armed forces (Rómulo Betancourt) or had been targets of authoritarian repression (Rafael Caldera and Jóvito Villalba), and military officers feared that any of these candidates would be vengeful once he reached office. Achieving the acquiescence of the armed forces to the newly elected president would be the final task of democratizers during the transition from authoritarian rule. Yet, the precedents set by numerous failed military rebellions and repeated shows of strength and unity by democratizers graphically illustrated for the officer corps the degree to which the military had been weakened during the transition. In other words, democratizers had achieved a sufficiently high degree of regime leverage to force the officer corps to accept the distasteful electoral results of December 1958.

In the fall of 1958, as elections approached, the center of political gravity slipped from civil society toward the political parties. The role of the Junta Patriótica, mass mobilizations, and labor strikes in the transition process faded as the traditional civilian parties reasserted their political leadership. Betancourt, Caldera, and Villalba, relying on years of experience in organizing and manipulating party activities, outmaneuvered junior activists and methodically regained control of their political machines. Resisting the temptations of partisanship brought about by the approach of the December elections, the former exiles adhered to the moderate provisions of the Pact of New York. Moreover, they forced their more radical followers to largely adhere to the pact as well. Throughout 1958, despite their differences, senior party members cooperated to prevent the overthrow of the transitional government and preserve their rights to participate in the national elections, scheduled for 7 December 1958 (Caldera 1992b). Civilian unity in defense of democracy remained the key weapon of party leaders against military intervention in the 1958 elections.

Publicly signaling this unity, Betancourt, Caldera, and Villalba met on 31 October 1958 at Caldera's home to affirm the principles of the agreement reached in New York in a new document, termed the Pact of Punto Fijo (Fuenmayor 1983, 10:427–40; Schaposnik 1985, 253–58). A joint political platform, called Programa Mínimo de Gobierno, established a common political and economic program to be carried out by a national unity government, regardless of which of the three political parties won the elections. Among the important points contained in this document was language referring to the Venezuelan armed forces. Echoing the Pact of New York, all parties guaranteed the material and professional improvement of the military in any future democratic administration, but they also agreed to restrict the military's political role to that of defending the constitution and its democratic institutions. The precise language called for the armed forces to be "obedient, apolitical, and nondeliberative" in any future administration (*Constitución de la República de Venezuela* 1994).[10] This foundational pact of Venezuelan democracy contained the key bargain between politicians and the military: narrow jurisdictional boundaries within which the armed forces would have a high degree of autonomy from civilian supervision.

The failure of the Castro León coup attempt in July had demonstrated to the military high command the limits of their power, and as a result, they maintained a low political profile during the fall election campaigns. Publicly, the armed forces supported the transition and the upcoming presidential elections. In private, the commanders of the various services were very concerned over the outcome of the process. The consensus among military officers was that Rómulo Betancourt was a crypto-Communist, whose first task upon winning the presidential elections would be to destroy the armed forces (Soto Tamayo 1986, 149–51). As General Martín García Villasmil recalls, officers in the armed forces at that time believed that many Venezuelan politicians had political "measles" because of their previous association with Communist ideologies in their student days. More important, the high command feared that an AD victory at the polls in December would lead to political reprisals against the armed forces for their role in displacing the Gallegos administration in 1948 (García Villasmil 1995a). No matter how much Betancourt publicly assured the military of his moderation, or privately reiterated the informal amnesty for its participation in the dictatorship, the officer corps were still concerned due to the often brutal past conflict between the political parties and the armed forces.

Many officers believed that politicians would not be able to restrain their more radical party activists or to resist demands for punishment from civil society. However, public demands for justice were never as prominent as they would be in future transitions in other countries, such as Chile, Argentina, and South Africa, due to the nature of the repression under the previous regime and strong penetration of civil society by the political parties. Democratizers were not compelled to publicly defend or abandon their amnesty offer since most civilians did not blame the armed forces for the dictatorship's political repression. Among the citizenry, this repression was largely associated with the former regime's secret police, the Seguridad Nacional, rather than with the armed forces (Pérez 1995). These impressions were reinforced by media accounts that highlighted the degree to which some military officers had suffered at the hands of the secret police. Conveniently, civilian mobs had destroyed the Seguridad Nacional headquarters and carried out extrajudicial killings of its agents and informers during the first days of the transition. The armed forces had despised the Seguridad Nacional, and they stood by while its members were hunted down and eliminated (Fuenmayor 1983, 10:533–34, 544–48). Since the secret police had already been punished, civil society generally did not press for further investigations into the dictatorship's repressive activities, and the new democracy was relieved of the sensitive political task of punishing torturers that has dogged so many other emerging democracies. Nevertheless, this was not yet clear in 1958, so the armed forces still feared that the political parties harbored a secret desire for revenge.

Many military officers were relieved when in the fall of 1958 Wolfgang Larrazábal was offered the center-left URD's nomination as candidate for the presidency. As president of the Junta de Gobierno, Larrazábal had become very popular among average Venezuelans for his folksy charisma, populist political views, and the generous welfare benefits offered under his government. Military officers fully expected that Larrazábal would sweep the elections, breaking the political hegemony of Acción Democrática. Prior to announcing his candidacy, Larrazábal met with the commanders of all the military services to seek their support for his decision to run for office. General Antonio Briceño Linares, then commander of the air force, recalls that at that meeting almost all of the assembled officers voiced their support for his candidacy. Only the Chief of the Joint Staff dissented, arguing that Venezuela would not benefit from another military president (Briceño Linares 1994). Since Larrazábal could be expected to protect the armed forces from gross political interference, the armed forces high command strongly desired his victory in the December 1958 elections. With the support of the navy and other military commanders, Larrazábal stepped down as president of the junta on 15 November and was replaced by Edgar Sanabria, chief of staff of the junta and a professor at the Universidad Central de Venezuela. Larrazábal's entry into the presidential race reduced the amount of concern within the armed forces over the participation of Rómulo Betancourt and AD in the elections.

The December elections were hard fought by all three parties, albeit within the bounds imposed by the Pact of Punto Fijo. URD, with Larrazábal at its head, ran especially strong in the large cities targeted by the transitional government's welfare programs. Yet, in spite of the best efforts of URD and the military high command, Larrazábal was out-organized by the Acción Democrática party machine. On 7 December 1958 Rómulo Betancourt was elected president, with 49 percent of the popular vote (Ewell 1984, 126).

Voting results were strongly skewed regionally, with most of AD's electoral support coming from Venezuela's rural areas where the party controlled most peasant federations. In Caracas, Betancourt carried only 13 percent of the electorate, while Larrazábal won 58 percent. The imbalance between rural and urban election results led to widespread unrest in Caracas. The crowds that had earlier defended the Junta de Gobierno against military threats now called for Larrazábal to replace Betancourt as the elected president. As demonstrations turned violent, military garrisons were awash with rumors of coup plots (Fuenmayor 1983, 10:503–9).

With the elections at risk, the Caracas professional associations, particularly FEDECAMARAS, mobilized in favor of Betancourt, conducting a telephone and media campaign to rally support. They pressured military commanders to endorse the election results and organized a joint television and radio appearance by leading politicians to espouse the democratic process and Betancourt's election. Domingo Alberto Rangel reports that Edgar Sanabria, president of the Junta de Gobierno, called together the commanders of the four military services and ordered them to publicly defend the election results so as to avoid even the appearance that the armed forces would oppose the democratic process (Rangel 1998, 303–8).

In the end, this civilian elite backing was sufficient to convince the armed forces to accept the electoral results. Betancourt's victory in the elections was one of the worst possible election outcomes that could be imagined by the armed forces. Only the victory of the Communists in the December elections would have been worse, but they were not even running their own candidate for president. The civilian elite convinced the military high command that the alternative to Betancourt, annulling the elections, would only have led to a potentially explosive and even revolutionary situation. General Josué López Henrique, minister of defense, and the other service commanders telephoned all major military garrisons to directly order all officers to accept the election results. For example, General García Villasmil, then a colonel serving in the army General Staff, reports that he received a call from the minister of defense, informing him that the military high command had decided to honor Betancourt's election victory (García Villasmil 1995a). Colonel Marco Aurelio Moros, commander of the army, visited the main Caracas garrisons and, in front of the assembled officers, admitted that though Betancourt's election was like a purgative dose of castor oil for the armed forces, they were honor-bound to accept the people's will (Soto Tamayo 1986, 157). Furthermore, the high command told Larrazábal that they would not lead a military intervention to place him in the presidential palace and urged him to be a good sport and accept his defeat in the elections. Larrazábal, whose own initial position on the validity of the election was ambiguous, publicly recognized Betancourt's election victory several days later, which ended the political crisis.[11]

Conclusions

By accepting the election of Rómulo Betancourt, the military high command acknowledged the limits of their power within a democratic society and the high degree of regime leverage that civilians wielded over the military. This regime leverage rested on civilian elite unity, mass mobilization among civil and political society to support democratization, and the successful effort by democratizers to implement strategies that undermined the unity of the armed forces. The deliberate efforts by high-ranking officers to reduce unrest among junior officers and ameliorate the threat of a military coup signaled their acceptance, albeit grudging, that democratic elections were the most legitimate form of selecting a government. Moreover, the coordinated civilian effort to ensure Betancourt's election would stand reminded military officers that the balance of power had shifted toward the democratizers during the transition to democracy. The coup attempt by Minister of Defense Castro León in July 1958 was the last time that a high-ranking officer would attempt to overthrow the government for thirty years. It also marked the high tide of military jurisdictional boundaries in Venezuela. Through the deliberate strategies selected by civilian politicians, the Venezuelan government was able to enhance regime leverage and progressively confine the armed forces to ever narrower jurisdictional boundaries (as shown in figure 3.2), reducing the threat to the new regime. Democratizers also used this leverage to create new institutions of civilian control, thereby making full democratization possible.

The defeat of the various military rebellions against the democratization process was only the first sign that the armed forces would be excluded from jurisdiction in the critical area of state leadership selection. Civilians dominated all government ministries except the Ministry of Defense from the beginning of the transition and, with the appointment of Edgar Sanabria as

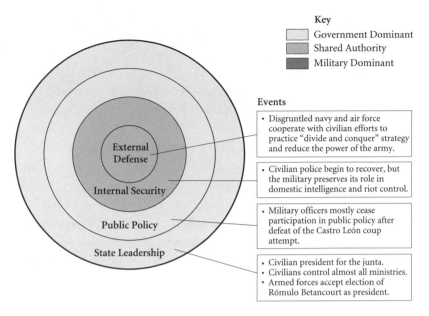

Key
- Government Dominant
- Shared Authority
- Military Dominant

External
Defense

Internal Security

Public Policy

State Leadership

Events

- Disgruntled navy and air force cooperate with civilian efforts to practice "divide and conquer" strategy and reduce the power of the army.

- Civilian police begin to recover, but the military preserves its role in domestic intelligence and riot control.

- Military officers mostly cease participation in public policy after defeat of the Castro León coup attempt.

- Civilian president for the junta.
- Civilians control almost all ministries.
- Armed forces accept election of Rómulo Betancourt as president.

Figure 3.2. Civil-Military Jurisdictional Boundaries, ca. December 1958: Government Strategies Reduce Military Jurisdiction

interim president, demonstrated that the armed forces had abdicated control over this crucial area. By the fall election campaign, military officers who had once intervened significantly in public policy, such as Hugo Trejo and Castro León, had been defeated and exiled. Remaining military officers found the long jail terms received by failed rebels a salutatory lesson in the wisdom of avoiding domestic politics.

At no time during the presidential electoral campaign was the public policy agenda of the political parties either defined by or restricted by the armed forces. Only in internal security and external defense did the armed forces still hold significant power at the conclusion of the transition process. The slow recovery of civilian security forces from their nadir following the collapse of the Pérez Jiménez regime removed some of the burden of daily policing from the armed forces. Furthermore, while military intelligence still gathered information on domestic politics, military commanders refused to act directly on these reports since they were all too aware of the punitive possibilities of the government leverage wielded by democratizers. Within less than a year, civilians had succeeded in ridding themselves of an authoritarian regime, and by aggressively taking advantage of the broad opportunity available, they had prevented the establishment of bloated military jurisdictional boundaries in the emerging democracy.

However, by far the most significant advance in reducing these boundaries was accomplished when civilians participated in the military reform process. These reforms allowed democratizers to penetrate the jurisdictional boundaries of the military's traditional defense role for the first time. The strategy guiding this process was one of "divide and conquer," which encouraged military factions to side with civilians and assist them in crafting the reforms of the governance structure of the armed forces. "Divide and conquer" was a successful strategy largely because it perversely appealed to a wide range of constituencies, both within the officer corps and in civilian political parties. Ranging from junior officers' pursuit of faster advancement to Wolfgang Larrazábal's interest in being elected president to Rómulo Betancourt's desire to avoid future military threats to his own government, the agendas of a preponderant majority of significant actors were satisfied by "divide and conquer." With the defeat of the populist and the technocratic authoritarian military factions, the actors who could and would have opposed the weakening of the army's predominant position were rendered inconsequential. Furthermore, the crafting of these reforms showed the degree to which democratizers could use regime leverage as a fine instrument of statecraft, not just a bludgeon with which to punish the armed forces for transgressing jurisdictional boundaries. These reforms reflected a careful civilian political agenda to shape government control of the armed forces, an agenda that Rómulo Betancourt would skillfully expand on and consolidate during his presidency.

Despite progress in crafting civilian control, it is important to realize that Venezuelan democratizers never intended to achieve much beyond civilian control by containment of the armed forces. Regime capacity at the beginning of the transition was relatively higher than during the 1945 transition by virtue of the political decision to pursue civilian control of the armed forces. However, the lack of civilian defense expertise prior to the transition, the early decision to avoid creating a civilian-led Ministry of Defense, and the inability to foster civilian defense expertise in the legislature meant that regime capacity in Venezuela was stunted from democracy's inception. It is clear that civilian politicians in exile during the 1948–58 period had not conceived of creating institutions for overseeing the activities of the armed forces as a solution to the problem of civilian control.

None of the institutions created by the transitional government required a high degree of regime capacity to sustain, nor would they foster the development of regime capacity in the future. All depended on the self-interest of military officers for their implementation and operation, thus bypassing the shortage of civilian defense expertise in Venezuela. By creating an institutionalized basis for divisions within the armed forces, the transitional government ensured that even if factions within the officer corps desired a larger role or greater autonomy for the armed forces, they would find it difficult to organize resistance to civilian rule. The enduring fractures in the military would make intervening against the new political order both troublesome and risky. However, these institutions did not provide civilians with effective mechanisms to supervise the armed forces in the long run.

By the end of the transition to democracy, civilians had only succeeded in reducing military jurisdiction to boundaries that were marginally compatible with democracy. In addition, it was clear that Rómulo Betancourt, despite his carefully conceived agenda for civilian control, had little desire to muster the regime capacity needed to move beyond these boundaries and achieve civilian control by oversight of the armed forces during his term in office. Regardless of the high degree of regime leverage available in 1958, Venezuela could not achieve civilian control by oversight without sustained government attention, resources, and most important, a pool of trained civilian defense experts, which it lacked. Moreover, unlike the democratizers of Chile, Argentina, and Spain, Venezuelan democratizers never sought to develop regime capacity as a long-range objective.

CHAPTER 4

■

STATECRAFT AND MILITARY

SUBORDINATION IN VENEZUELA,

1959–1973

On 26 December 1958 Rómulo Betancourt addressed a closed-door assembly of 1,200 military officers in Caracas to explain his administration's future policies and to listen to their concerns. It was the high point of his tour as president-elect of the country's major garrisons. As Venezuela's first democratically elected president following the 1958 transition, Betancourt was acutely aware of his need to focus on military policy. He also planned to devote a great deal of his personal time to administering the armed forces and garnering their support, in spite of other urgent demands on his time created by a severe economic recession in the early 1960s and the political and social crises that accompanied democratization.

Betancourt was highly unpopular among military officers at the start of his administration, and he faced a serious threat from right-wing elements in the armed forces and among civilian opponents. During his administration, the threat from left-wing Cuban-backed insurgents grew rapidly, and it became increasingly difficult to sustain the civilian consensus on democratization that had been crafted in 1958. To secure both the survival of his administration and of democracy, Betancourt pursued civilian control of the armed forces using every available strategy at his disposal. He developed a sophisticated personal monitoring network to warn him of potential military threats. He also further institutionalized "divide and conquer" measures, and he worked to deradicalize Venezuelan officers through increased salaries and benefits. He even engaged in long-range efforts to alter the norms of the Venezuelan military, including an intensive program to indoctrinate it with a pro-democratic ideology. However, Betancourt's most impressive political stratagem was to transform a burgeoning Marxist guerrilla threat into an asset, by using it as a new opportunity for regime leverage over the armed forces.

Betancourt laid the cornerstone of civilian control in Venezuela by successfully excluding the armed forces from political life. Although he faced numerous military threats against his government, the armed forces failed to block any significant government policy during his term in office. The repeated failures of military rebellions and Betancourt's tenacity in resisting all threats to his government convinced the officer corps of the futility of resisting civilian rule. Instead, military officers began to take advantage of the professional opportunities and benefits associated with democratization and became increasingly supportive of the new regime. Betancourt also managed to set the foundations for the defeat of Marxist insurgents without diminishing his authority over the armed forces or hindering their prosecution of the counterinsurgency war. His successors, Raul Leoni from AD and Rafael Caldera from COPEI, inherited a military whose officers were largely reconciled to civilian oversight and a democracy in which elected officials faced few constraints on their decision-making authority.

Placing Civilian Control on the Agenda

When he took office in 1959, Rómulo Betancourt was well aware that he had made many errors during his previous experience as a leader of the *Trienio* government between 1945 and 1948, particularly in his dealings with the armed forces. He had entered the *Trienio* with little knowledge of the military and had preferred that commanders manage their own affairs. He had relied on allies in the armed forces to prevent a successful military intervention (Burggraff 1972, 100–111). The collapse of the Gallegos administration in 1948 had shown Betancourt that partisan officers were not a sufficiently dependable guarantee of civilian control. Betancourt began his second administration determined to avoid this mistake (Giacopini Zárraga 1992b).

Betancourt moved away from the transitional government's military policies, characterized by upheaval and radical military reforms, and worked to stabilize the new configuration of civil-military relations in Venezuela. During his exile, Betancourt decided to adopt a moderate, conciliatory policy toward the armed forces. He planned to use increased salaries, benefits, and an emphasis on military modernization to offset opposition to the decentralization and monitoring strategies he also favored. The transitional process had expanded civilian authority over a wide range of state functions and altered the balance of civil-military relations in favor of the executive branch. However, the armed forces that Betancourt inherited were still in a state of ferment. Military officers had spent the years from 1945 to 1958 in nearly constant conspiracy. Simply because a set of "divide and conquer" institutions had been crafted during the transition to democracy, it did not guarantee either the safety of his government or that the armed forces would continue to accept reduced jurisdictional boundaries.

Betancourt adopted a three-part strategy to consolidate the government's authority over the armed forces. He deepened the "divide and conquer" reforms of the transition that had decentralized power within the armed forces, and he established the office of the president as the principal adjudicator among the competing services. To sweeten the bitter pill of civilian control and to reconcile the officer corps to the new democratic system, his administration significantly increased the resources devoted to the material welfare and professional needs of military officers. Unwilling to rely solely on institutional solutions, Betancourt also began an intensive program for transforming the ideology of the armed forces into beliefs more compatible with democratic rule. His goal was to shift the officer corps from a conservative, pro-authoritarian, radicalized force in society to a still conservative but pro-democratic sector that favored civilian governance and the new status quo.

The greatest obstacle to Betancourt's becoming de facto, as well as de jure, commander in chief of the armed forces was his image as a radical, leftist, antimilitary politician. This image dated back to his days as a student activist during the Gómez dictatorship and his membership, while in exile in the early 1930s, in the Costa Rican Communist Party (Sosa A. 1989, 353–57; Briceño Linares 1994; García Villasmil 1995c). The only way to counteract this damning image was for Betancourt to behave in a manner completely contradictory to all expectations of military officers. Betancourt set out to do this by becoming a hard-line anti-Communist president, whose administration provided notable increases in the material well-being of the officer corps, while at the same time severely punishing any and all conspiracies against his government. During his administration, Betancourt faced both reactionary and revolutionary attempts against his government, including a failed assassination and an insurgency. Despite the difficult times that Venezuela experienced in the early 1960s, Betancourt's peculiar skill at neutralizing and co-opting threats against his government contributed immeasurably to the consolidation of democracy.

Shifts in the Opportunity Structure: The Decline of Civilian Consensus and the Rise of Armed Opposition

As one of the key players in writing Venezuela's foundational pacts, Betancourt adhered strictly to these agreements because he saw a national unity government as the principal bulwark against the return of authoritarian rule. Even though Acción Democrática had won by a large majority in the 1958 elections, Betancourt deliberately avoided using this preponderance of political power as a mandate to establish government policy, preferring instead to build consensus among the partners in his national unity administration. His cabinet included representatives of all three major political parties and a number of independents, and he granted his ministers considerable latitude (Karl 1986, 216–18; Arreaza 1994). Despite these efforts, splits soon appeared in Betancourt's political coalition and in his own party, as economic recession and the moderation of the government's domestic and foreign policy distanced the new president from the political left in Venezuela. These divisions were soon so severe that they led to an internal security crisis and the development of a left-wing insurgency. However, rather than allow the breakdown of civilian consensus to diminish his regime leverage over the armed forces, Betancourt used the rise of the Marxist insurgency as a new opportunity to recruit military support for democratic rule and to achieve civilian control of the armed forces.

Betancourt's political moderation was driven as much by fiscal constraints as by his need to manage a fragile coalition government. In all areas of government endeavor, this administration was limited in its first years by a continuing fiscal crisis and economic recession. In 1959 and 1960 the government experienced serious budget deficits, on the order of bs. 850 million (approximately $250 million at the time). Though the economy grew by more than 5 percent in 1959, four years of near stagnation and a decline in real per capita income followed. Unemployment climbed from over 10 percent in 1959 to 14 percent in 1963. Capital flight by both foreign investors and Venezuelans grew dramatically, and Betancourt was forced to order a devaluation of the currency by 30 percent and to implement exchange controls (Toro Hardy 1992, 56–63). Adding to Venezuela's economic problems were a world oil glut and the rapidly evaporating confidence of foreign oil companies in the long-term viability of the country as a fruitful investment opportunity, both of which reduced the government's ability to rely on oil revenues to make up revenue shortfalls (Tugwell 1975, 50–54). The economic recession that Venezuela had experienced during the transition to democracy was transformed into persistent stagnation, with its attendant social unrest.

Fiscal austerity, Betancourt's moderate social policies, and his hard-line anti-Communism drove a wedge between the government and leftist political parties, a division which would have highly significant consequences for internal security and civil-military relations. Even though the PCV had been excluded from the foundational political pacts of 1958, Venezuelan Communists publicly supported the democratization process throughout the first year of the Betancourt administration; however, at the same time they criticized the government for its insufficiently revolutionary political and economic agenda (Tarre Murzi 1983, 158–66, 210–11). The PCV supported mass mobilizations, particularly by university students and the unemployed, against the economic recession and the government's labor, agrarian, and foreign policies. In Betancourt's view, only legally authorized demonstrations by organized sectors of society were legitimate, and any other form of protest was to be met with the full force of the police. Each incident and confrontation allowed Betancourt to escalate his criticism of the left for partisanship and reckless endangerment of the democratization process, as well as send particularly troublesome demonstrators to serve prison sentences building roads in southern Venezuela (Fuenmayor 1985, 12:206).

Betancourt's moderation and internal power struggles within Acción Democrática soon led to a split in the governing party as well. Following an incident in which the senior leadership sanctioned several younger activists for unauthorized public statements, Domingo Alberto Rangel and Simón Sáez Mérida, leaders of AD's youth wing, defected and organized a new political party under the name of the Movimiento de la Izquierda Revolucionaria (MIR), or the Movement of the Revolutionary Left (Rangel 1998, 17–32, 151–66; Stambouli 1980, 147–57).[1] In spite of the party split, AD managed to retain control of most labor federations, peasant organizations, and professional guilds, although it did lose its entire youth movement and several senators and deputies to the new party (Fuenmayor 1985, 12:243–60). The MIR soon joined the PCV in the opposition, both in Congress and in the streets. These two parties would eventually form the core of the Marxist insurgency that Venezuela experienced during the 1960s.

Betancourt's foreign policy added to the friction between his administration and the left, as soon after the split of AD he decided to step up his political opposition to the new revolutionary regime in Cuba. The Cuban revolution and its leader, Fidel Castro, were immensely popular in Venezuela. Occurring only weeks after the 1958 presidential elections in Venezuela, Castro's revolutionary victory over Fulgencio Batista captured the imaginations of many Venezuelans, particularly the young. Castro made a triumphant visit to Caracas on 24 January 1959, addressed the Venezuelan Congress, and was greeted by crowds of tens of thousands wherever he went (Fuenmayor 1985, 12:78–91.). In spite of the Cuban revolution's evident popularity, Betancourt, citing his opposition to authoritarian regimes everywhere in Latin America, severed diplomatic ties with Cuba, as he also would with military dictatorships in the Dominican Republic, Peru, and Argentina.

Though popular with the political right and the armed forces, Betancourt's policy toward revolutionary Cuba cemented the opposition of the left to his administration. Betancourt's policy of equating revolutionary Cuba with military dictatorships elsewhere in the continent incensed the PCV and MIR activists. Furthermore, Betancourt's decision to order his foreign minister, Ignacio Luís Arcaya, to vote in favor of sanctioning Cuba at the VII Inter-American Conference at San José, Costa Rica, on 28 August 1960, led to the withdrawal of URD from the national coalition government. URD, a center-left party, had been an enthusiastic supporter of the Cuban revolution, and its leadership found Betancourt's policy toward Cuba high-handed and provocative. While URD would continue to form part of the loyal opposition and favor democratization, Betancourt could no longer count on political cover from all three major democratic parties, as he had originally intended through the mechanism of the Pact of Punto Fijo.

Betancourt could tolerate dissent against his policies, but he reacted harshly to any perceived threats to the rules of the democratization process. Thus, the PCV and MIR were attacked immediately for disloyalty to the agreed "rules of the game." As Betancourt stated in one of his speeches:

Democracy is a regime which respects public liberties, but does not deal leniently or timidly with those who attack them. Contemporary history is plagued with examples of regimes which, by professing a cowardly and liberaloid conception [of democracy], were annihilated and pulverized by audacious totalitarian minorities. That occurred yesterday with Fascism and is occurring today with Communism. And I feel proud, . . .

that this government has learned the lessons of history and for this reason will not allow itself to be intimidated, corralled, or overthrown by antidemocratic minorities, be they classical Latin American autocrats or those dressed up in the novel raiment of pseudo-revolutionary ideologies, definitely integrated by fifth columnists of the powers which conspire to regiment the world for their own and exclusive benefit with authoritarian structures of government. (Tarre Murzi 1983, 242–43)

In Betancourt's view, being a democrat did not imply weakness in the face of threats, terrorism, or public disorder, which, from his perspective, included many forms of political opposition usually considered legitimate in consolidated democracies. During the first four years of his administration, he ordered the suspension of constitutional guarantees for 761 days (Fuenmayor 1985, 12:403; Soto Tamayo 1986, 234–36). Betancourt saw no contradiction in using undemocratic means to achieve democratic consolidation.

The loss of PCV and MIR support for the democratization process and the new opposition of URD weakened national support for the Betancourt administration and could have potentially undermined regime leverage over the armed forces. Battles between police and demonstrators were weekly events, and terrorist actions by extremists on both the right and left were commonplace throughout the Betancourt administration. The defection of AD's youth wing to the MIR damaged the government's ability to rely on student and lower-class backing and robbed the government of many of its most effective political activists. By 1961, the MIR and the PCV had become semiloyal parties, maintaining their representation in Congress while encouraging the activities of urban and rural guerrillas. Increasingly, Betancourt had to depend on the security forces to sustain the regime against these leftist attacks, even as many in the armed forces remained hostile to the democratization process.

Paradoxically, this division between the administration and the political left, and the ensuing confrontation between state security forces and PCV/MIR insurgency, provided a key opportunity for Betancourt to generate increased leverage over the armed forces. The development of an internal war in Venezuela should have proven extremely dangerous because of the attendant breakdown in civilian consensus on democratization. Several other democracies, such as Juan Perón's second administration in Argentina (1973–75), Uruguay during the 1970s, and Chile under Salvador Allende, have been overthrown in coup d'états that were motivated in part by the growth of domestic insurgencies, often because the government's own security forces have felt constrained by the limits imposed by democracy and the rule of law. Domestic insurgencies often lead to dramatic increases in military autonomy and military jurisdiction over the state, even in cases were civilian rule is not overthrown. In these cases, civilian control of the armed forces becomes uncertain and is often fatally compromised. Betancourt was able to adroitly transform a potentially dangerous shift in the opportunity structure by presenting his own administration as the lesser of two evils. Venezuelan military officers eventually came to believe that the only alternatives they had were to serve and protect a moderate democratic regime or battle without civilian support against a growing Marxist revolutionary movement. Even as civilian consensus on democratization fractured, the military's fear of a Communist takeover strengthened regime leverage over the armed forces. This degree of regime leverage was what allowed Betancourt to sustain a strategy of sanctioning military rebellions even as his administration was under attack for its economic and political policies.

Using a Strategy of Sanctions to Defeat
the Logic of Authoritarianism

Prior to the onset of leftist guerrilla warfare in 1961–62, Betancourt faced significant, albeit disorganized, resistance from substantial minorities in the officer corps. These military revolts, for all their lack of coherence, proved to be quite dangerous to the stability of the Betancourt administration, and they were defeated only through the full support of the military high command for the new regime. In spite of these threats, Betancourt was able to speed the consolidation of civilian control by using these uprisings to identify the most active conspirators within the officer corps and purge them from the ranks. Each new failure further weakened the ability of the armed forces to resist government control, set a precedent for civilian supremacy in Venezuela, and revealed the futility of opposing democratization. Furthermore, as each new revolt uncovered the growing links between Marxist insurgents and the officers involved in conspiring against Betancourt, the conservative majority in the officer corps soon became convinced that supporting the new administration and democratization was the best way to protect the armed forces and Venezuelan society from Communist penetration. Thus, Betancourt was able to sustain a strategy of sanctions, and each successive rebellion strengthened rather than weakened his government.

The success of Betancourt's sanctioning strategy was not foreordained. The consensus among the former politicians and military officers whom I interviewed was that Rómulo Betancourt was an exceedingly difficult president to maintain in power. Ramón J. Velásquez, Betancourt's chief of staff, reports that there were at least eleven civilian and military attempts to remove the president from power during his administration, the great majority of which originated within the Venezuelan armed forces (Velásquez 1995). Both General Antonio Briceño Linares, Betancourt's minister of defense, and General Martín García Villasmil, then chief of the army General Staff, report spending many evenings and weekends on alert in military garrisons, readying themselves to organize counterattacks against imminent coup d'états (Briceño Linares 1994; García Villasmil 1995c). In the face of these threats, Betancourt never publicly wavered from his principal goal — to maintain himself in power long enough to hand over the presidency to his freely elected successor. He faced five full-fledged attacks on his government from military officers before he gained full control over the armed forces.

The first major attempt to overthrow Betancourt occurred on 20 April 1960, when General Castro León, evidently desiring to imitate the actions of General Cipriano Castro and his Andean compatriots in 1899, "invaded" Venezuela through Táchira, a state on the border with Colombia, with a group of retired and exiled army officers. Castro León was granted control of the army garrison of San Cristóbal by local commanders. He then proceeded to declare martial law and broadcast radio appeals for a general uprising by the armed forces. The people of San Cristóbal promptly ignored the martial law decree, and several local political and labor organizations organized demonstrations to protest his actions. Castro León became increasingly nervous at the lack of support from other military garrisons across Venezuela, even though he was under no immediate military threat. Loyalist troops had maintained control of an airport near San Cristóbal, and the government had organized a column of 1,800 troops, moving by road from Caracas toward Táchira. Even so, given the distance between Caracas and San Cristóbal, attacking Castro León, using either option available to the government, would have taken considerable time (Soto Tamayo 1986, 254).

Castro León's erstwhile supporters began to abandon him as the day wore on, as they realized that the hoped-for general uprising would not materialize. The diminished rebel forces were unable to maintain control of San Cristóbal in the face of popular opposition, so Castro León attempted to escape back across the Colombian border. A group of pro-AD peasants captured him, however, and handed him over to civilian authorities. Taking advantage of the uprising, Betancourt jailed twenty military officers for suspected participation in the conspiracy, retired sixteen others, and publicly promised the longest possible prison sentences for the rebels. Within a few years of his arrest, General Castro León died in prison from illness (Fuenmayor 1985, 12:287–303). Betancourt's harsh policy toward the military rebels in this instance set the pattern for his administration. Generally, officers convicted of conspiracy were sentenced to prison terms in excess of twenty years, and none were pardoned until the late 1960s, long after Betancourt's administration had ended. Furthermore, the rapid and well-organized displays of popular support for the new regime and against the reimposition of a dictatorship, previously uncommon in the traditionally conservative state of Táchira, reminded military officers of the widespread civilian consensus favoring democratization.

The most serious right-wing attack on Rómulo Betancourt occurred on 24 June 1960, Venezuela's army day. A group of former military officers and civilians, with the technical assistance of agents of the Dominican dictator, General Rafael Trujillo, attempted to assassinate Betancourt. They detonated a powerful car bomb via remote control as his presidential vehicle made its way down a busy Caracas avenue toward the Academia Militar to join official celebrations. The head of his military household, Colonel Ramón Armas Pérez, was killed instantly. Betancourt's minister of defense, General Josué López Henrique, and the minister's wife were wounded, and Betancourt suffered severe burns to his face and hands. On the following day, covered in bandages, Betancourt addressed Venezuelans by radio and television to reassure them that he was alive and able to exercise power. He publicly singled out General Trujillo, an old friend of Pérez Jiménez, as a co-conspirator in the assassination attempt and vowed to seek sanctions through the Organization of American States (OAS) against the Dominican Republic (Caldera 1992a). In the investigations that followed the assassination attempt, Betancourt retired ten high-ranking officers who were suspected of harboring loyalties for Pérez Jiménez. Other officers under suspicion for sympathizing with the assassination attempt were transferred to less prominent positions within the armed forces or sent overseas as military attachés in Venezuelan embassies (Fuenmayor 1985, 12:451–78).

The failure of these two attempts largely disorganized the most conservative elements of the armed forces. Officers who supported a return of a Pérez Jiménez–style regime were exiled, retired, or shunted into insignificant positions within the military, and the young officers who replaced them did not recall the previous regime fondly. Satisfied with their growing rank and authority, a new cadre of leaders in the armed forces increasingly ignored attempts to organize a return to authoritarian rule.

The third overt attempt by Pérez Jiménez's supporters within the armed forces to seize power occurred on 26 June 1961, when a group of retired officers infiltrated the military garrison of the eastern Venezuelan port of Barcelona, detained progovernment officers, and took control of the marine infantry battalion stationed there. Other officers in the Guardia Nacional and the air force attempted to seize control of installations in La Guaira and at the international airport of Maiquetía, near Caracas. A group of civilians, mostly members of URD, joined in the uprising as well. The government had already been warned of the rebellion by officers who had been contacted to participate in the coup d'état, but Betancourt decided to wait for the uprising to begin so as to arrest the greatest possible number of conspirators. General Briceño Linares, then minister of defense, reports that pamphlets calling for the surrender of the rebels had been printed in advance for air force pilots to drop on insurgent military units (Briceño Linares 1994). Unfortunately for the rebels, other military garrisons rejected the calls for a general uprising, and when the government threatened an air bombardment, the officers in control of Barcelona decided to surrender. As with their predecessors, the officers who participated were sentenced to long jail terms for treason and sedition (Capriles Ayala and del Naranjo 1992, 89–119).

This uprising, popularly known as the "Barcelonazo," marked a turning point in the conspiratorial movements against the new democracy. Prior to the Barcelonazo, military rebellions centered around well-known figures of the previous authoritarian regime, such as General Castro León, Colonel Juan de Dios Moncada Vidal, or Colonel Edito Ramírez. The Barcelonazo was unusual in that both low-level military officers and leftist civilians participated in the uprising with the shared purpose of overthrowing Betancourt. The Barcelonazo also showed that the military was willing to use force in support of the government against rebels in their own ranks.

After the Barcelonazo, the ideological tenor of the armed attacks on the government shifted to the left as the PCV and MIR intensified their armed struggle for power. The decision to do so was made impulsively by the MIR, and somewhat more reluctantly by the PCV. Only a few months earlier, during the week of 10–18 March 1961, the PCV had celebrated its Third Party Congress, in which it decided to undertake a fundamental shift in political strategy. Throughout the transition to democracy and the first years of the Betancourt administration, the PCV and its allies on the left had been supportive of the democratization process but remained very critical of the administration's moderation in social and economic policy and its hard-line position on Cuba. Betancourt had carried out a policy of containing and marginalizing the political left in Venezuela from his first days in office, initiating his rhetorical offensive against the PCV in his inaugural speech. Under constant pressure from the Betancourt administration and threatened with irrelevancy by the revolutionary effervescence of leftist youth organizations (MIR, for example, had attracted significant popular support and competed strongly with the PCV in many student and worker federations), the PCV reluctantly decided to move to an insurrectional strategy to overthrow the new democracy (Blanco Muñoz 1991, 28–31). Essentially, many members of the left deceived themselves into thinking that the objective conditions for a socialist revolution existed in Venezuela, and that in fact the revolution had almost occurred in 1958 but had simply been stolen by Acción Democrática. To maintain its prestige and prevent a drain in members to the newer, more radical parties, the PCV joined the revolutionary bandwagon and founded a military wing (Valsalice 1979, 7–11, 27–31; Blanco Muñoz 1991, 76).

The left's hopes for the participation of at least part of the Venezuelan military in a progressive revolutionary movement were raised by the last two overt military insurrections against the Betancourt administration at Carúpano and Puerto Cabello, both of which featured significant collaboration between military officers and members of the PCV/MIR insurgency (Blanco Muñoz 1991, 74). On 4 May 1962, Captain Jesús Molina Villegas of the navy led an insurrection of the Third Marine Infantry Battalion based at Carúpano, calling for the overthrow of the government and its replacement with a revolutionary alternative. He had been assured of support by fellow officers in La Guaira, and Douglas Bravo of the PCV had convinced him that the people of Caracas would rise up against the government as well. Captain Molina Villegas seized Carúpano without firing a shot, and local students and professors collaborated with the marines to organize a defense of the city. The Betancourt government responded by mobilizing army and navy infantry and artillery troops toward Carúpano and bombarding the rebels with Canberra bombers. After brief fighting, and realizing that other military units had not backed the rebellion, Molina Villegas surrendered his troops. Soon after the Carúpano uprising, the PCV and MIR jointly organized an umbrella organization to combine military and civilian dissidents into a single guerrilla army. Its political wing was known as the Frente de Liberación Nacional (FLN), under Fabricio Ojeda (a former URD member), and the military wing was known as the Fuerzas Armadas de Liberación Nacional (FALN). Captain Molina Villegas later escaped from prison and joined the leftist insurgency, becoming one of the commanders of the FALN.

By far the most worrisome collaboration between the military and the armed left occurred during the insurrection at the Venezuelan navy's principal base at Puerto Cabello on 2 June 1962. Captain Manuel Ponte Rodríguez, at the head of the Second Marine Infantry Battalion, took control of the naval base and the city, freeing and arming sixty Marxist guerrillas imprisoned in the military prison of Castillo Libertador. His appeal to the members of the Second Battalion was explicitly revolutionary, and the marines responded enthusiastically to this message. He expected support from other navy and army units in La Guaira and Caracas, which did not materialize, as well as the support of the PCV, several of whose leaders did in fact participate in the uprising. Political activists took control of the Puerto Cabello radio station and used it to broadcast revolutionary appeals. In spite of these initial successes, other navy and Guardia Nacional units based at Puerto Cabello did not respond to the insurrection, and one of the destroyers, the *Austria*, quickly made its way to sea and, in a cold-blooded display of initiative, began firing its five-inch guns against the rebels in the naval base of Puerto Cabello.

Betancourt had already received some prior notice of a possible coup attempt, and several officers suspected in the conspiracy had been transferred or placed on leave in an attempt to weaken the rebel movement (Fuenmayor 1988, 14:228–44). When Minister of Defense Briceño Linares received the news of the Puerto Cabello insurrection, he quickly mobilized already alerted marine infantry and army tank and artillery units to take back control of city as soon as possible. Due to serious tactical errors by their commanders, loyalist marine and army units suffered severe losses in their first attempt to take back the city and were forced to withdraw until the following morning. As the government brought up more forces, the air force and navy bombarded Puerto Cabello with cannon and rockets. Betancourt ordered the city taken as rapidly as possible, regardless of casualties, because he feared that prolonged resistance would lead to further uprisings and, also, because he wanted to set a harsh example for other conspirators and insurgents. The final casualty list included 300–400 soldiers and civilians, although officially the military dead numbered 72 (Soto Tamayo 1986, 292–310). Approximately 500 soldiers were placed under arrest, and an even larger number of civilians were detained by the DIGEPOL (Dirección General de Policia), the political police. Rebellious officers received sentences ranging from sixteen to thirty years of imprisonment, although several later escaped and joined Marxist insurgents in their rural operating areas (Capriles Ayala and Del Naranjo 1992, 111–14).

The uprising at Puerto Cabello was the last one by military forces against a democratic government for thirty years, and it marked a watershed in the attitudes of the officer corps toward the new regime. The government had responded very severely, and the combat between army and marine units in the city had a cost in casualties that exceeded that of previous insurrections by orders of magnitude. Both Carúpano and Puerto Cabello also signaled a shift in the ideological center of conspiracy within the armed forces, from the army to the more progressive navy, from the right to the left (Capriles Ayala and Del Naranjo 1992, 105–6).

The energy and decision with which government forces attacked the insurgents is a measure of the extent to which Betancourt had been able to extend his control over the Venezuelan armed forces in the years since his election in 1958. The conspiratorial core of the armed forces had largely been expelled or imprisoned by the time of the Puerto Cabello rebellion. The high number of casualties incurred during the suppression of this insurrection set a precedent, making it very clear for any would-be rebel that coup attempts would be dealt with harshly, at great potential risk to life and career. Furthermore, for the high command, the Marxist insurgency and its links to junior officers made the choice very clear: either support Betancourt and defeat the Communists, or allow democracy to fail and possibly face revolutionary firing squads, as had Batista's officers in Cuba in 1959.

Beyond Sanctions: Alternative Strategies and Institutions for Civilian Control

Rómulo Betancourt was keenly aware that he needed to go beyond a pure sanctioning strategy to ensure military loyalty to the new regime. Moreover, he understood that his personal ability to manage military affairs was the key to the success of his administration. Military affairs were the one area of government policymaking where Betancourt reserved all decisions to himself, excluding the participation of his coalition partners, other elements of the executive branch, and the legislative branch. Given the threats to his administration and to the democratization process, Betancourt used any tools

at hand — sanctions, monitoring, "divide and conquer," and appeasement —
to contain the threat of military rebellion and extend civilian control of the
armed forces. He also took the unprecedented step, at least by Venezuelan
standards, of taking a long-term perspective and instituting democratic indoctrination of the officer corps as a way of ending its traditional attachment
to the logic of authoritarianism.

MONITORING THE ARMED FORCES

Betancourt placed a high value on information regarding armed forces
activity. Through Acción Democrática's network of political activists and
supporters, he received information about unusual military movements,
which enabled him to have advance warning of potential trouble (Schaposnik 1985, 378). Furthermore, he reinstated pro-democratic officers who held
key positions in the military command structure and who were able to shed
light on the mood and sentiment of the armed forces (Tarre Briceño 1994b).
Through formal and informal channels, Betancourt was thus able to supervise the activities of the armed forces and avoid potential surprises that
might cost him his administration and the democratic regime.

Betancourt was careful to respect the symbols and ceremonies surrounding the armed forces, but he used these protocols to reinforce his image as
commander in chief and to establish a reputation as a politician who was
concerned with military interests and institutions. He attended graduations
at service academies, participated in ceremonies commemorating important events and battles, and honored holidays dedicated to the armed forces
(Caldera 1992b). Betancourt was well known for his frequent inspections
of military bases, operations, and training installations. He took advantage
of these opportunities to discuss his policies and plans with the officers, as
well as to listen to their needs and complaints (Néry Arrieta 1992). In order
to stress the nonpolitical nature of these visits, Betancourt often undertook
these visits alone, or accompanied only by his military aides, rather than
with other politicians (Schaposnik 1985, 277). Betancourt was also careful
to maintain contact with officers on a more personal level, attending their
weddings and sending condolences for deaths or illnesses in their families
(Machillanda Pinto 1995). Betancourt's presence at these functions allowed
him to gain a personal understanding of the situation in the armed forces,
as well as to communicate directly with lower-ranking officers.

Rómulo Betancourt also initiated the practice, followed by all Venezuelan presidents since, of using his Casa Militar (his military "household," officers selected to act as guards and aides to the president) as a means of communication with the officer corps, bypassing the hierarchical command structure (Soto Tamayo 1986, 349–52). Often, due to the political and personal links that the members of a president's military household established, these officers received increased opportunities for study abroad and command positions, and they generally advanced more rapidly than their peers. Eventually, these officers, with their combination of political and military skills, would reach the highest ranks of the armed forces. Betancourt made himself very accessible to military personnel, and he is reputed to have held weekly office hours for officers of all ranks to discuss personal or institutional problems with him. Whether these problems were financial, personal, or professional, Betancourt often attempted to resolve these matters through the commander of his military household or his chief of staff, Ramón J. Velásquez. Betancourt's concern with the personal needs of officers during these visits became part of the legends surrounding his administration (Bruni Celli 1992; Tarre Briceño 1994b).

Betancourt also improved his standing with the officer corps through his policy of generally overlooking an officer's previous political or repressive activities under the Pérez Jiménez regime. Some officers had participated in the persecution of Acción Democrática during this regime, yet very few attempts were made to punish these individuals for such activities. Prosecution instead focused on Pérez Jiménez and his close associates and was concerned with matters of corruption rather than human rights abuses (Dobrovir 1959). Moreover, the public tended to blame such abuses on the Seguridad Nacional (Soto Tamayo 1986, 231; Bruni Celli 1992). In conjunction with an informal amnesty on these crimes, this policy defused an issue that could potentially have motivated a coup, should justice have been granted to the victims of the Pérez Jiménez regime ("Declaración de los partidos politicos" 1957; Caldera 1992a; Pérez 1995).

"DIVIDE AND CONQUER": MAINTAINING THE DECENTRALIZATION OF THE ARMED FORCES

Unlike many previous presidents, Rómulo Betancourt was careful to take advantage of the formal legal mechanisms of civilian control that were contained in defense legislation and the constitution. The ad hoc military reforms enacted during the 1958 transitional government were of somewhat dubious legality, and they could have fallen by the wayside without Betancourt's intervention to preserve them. The constitutional provisions that granted the president and Congress supervision of military promotions and budget allocations could have easily been undermined if early civilian leaders had preferred to appease the armed forces in these areas rather than enforce the government's legal authority. Betancourt used these provisions to preserve the decentralized nature of command within the armed forces, setting up the president as the last court of appeal in security-related issues.

In particular, Betancourt jealously preserved the legal prerogatives he held as commander in chief and deliberately used his constitutional power to approve promotions to the ranks of colonel and general in order to ensure a reliable military high command (Celis Noguera 1994; García Villasmil 1995c). Ignoring complaints of favoritism and seniority, Betancourt picked two air force generals in succession as his ministers of defense. He also continued the policy of placing officers known to adhere to democratic principles, particularly those who had been reincorporated following the end of the dictatorial regime, in positions of power within the armed forces (Müller Rojas 1989, 417; Tarre Briceño 1994b). With the exception of the *reincorporados*, who were few in number, Betancourt generally had the reputation of allowing lower-level promotions to take place on a purely meritocratic basis, for which he was widely respected within the officer corps (Caldera 1992b; García Villasmil 1995c). Coupled with the rapid promotion and reassignment of officers as required by the thirty-year service limit, this promotion policy meant that most qualified military officers were able to rotate through the postings and assignments necessary to advance their military careers without having to face undue political interference.

Betancourt also took advantage of the autonomy of the various services, which had been engendered by the institutionalization of "divide and conquer" strategies, to shift final decision-making authority in military matters from the Ministry of Defense to the presidency. Betancourt's second minister of defense, General Antonio Briceño Linares, resisted the decentralization of the military high command ordered by Decree 288. He argued that in transferring budgetary, legal, and military authority from his ministry to the services, the decree had stripped him of authority over the armed forces while assigning him the responsibility for their performance. In one incident, General Briceño Linares attempted to issue orders directly to individual naval commanders in La Guaira, relieving certain of their subordinates of their duties and changing their assignments. In another, he also tried to reimpose some Ministry of Defense authority over the budgetary process, changing allocations among the services to the detriment of the navy. The commander of the navy countermanded both orders and threatened to bring charges of misuse of government funds before Congress, arguing that Decree 288 had transferred responsibilities for administering budgets and military assignments to the individual services. Ultimately, President Betancourt had to step in, and he resolved the dispute in favor of the navy in both cases (Schaposnik 1985, 241; Briceño Linares 1994). The impact of this decree was to make the Ministry of Defense, for practical purposes, coequal in authority with the four military services rather than their supervisor. Each service jealously guarded its prerogatives and monitored the behavior of the others, which prevented any one component from gaining too much authority at the expense of the others. Therefore, disagreements among the services could not be easily resolved by built-in institutional mechanisms, such as a General Staff. A "divide and conquer" strategy meant that the only person with the authority to resolve these disputes was the civilian president, and Betancourt carefully availed himself of this fact to enhance his authority.

The final legal component of military reform was codified in the Venezuelan constitution, enacted in 1961, which defined the roles and missions of the armed forces and the president's powers over them. In its preamble, the Venezuelan constitution renounced war, conquest, or economic domination as legitimate instruments of international politics. Although not a "peace" constitution in the same sense as that of the Japanese, the Venezuelan constitution limited the external role of its armed forces to individual or collective defense (Celis Noguera 1994). Specifically, Article 132 of the constitution defined the role of the Venezuelan armed forces as "an apolitical, obedient, and nondeliberative institution, organized by the State to assure the national defense, the stability of its democratic institutions, and respect for the Constitution and its laws, whose enforcement or obedience [acatamiento] shall come before any other obligation." This political definition firmly ensconced the protection of democratic rule as the primary mission of the armed forces (Constitución de la República de Venezuela 1994).

The power of the minister of defense was further weakened under the 1961 constitution, which in Article 190, Section 2, granted the president the right to exercise the role of commander in chief without needing the approval of the Council of Ministers or the approval of the minister of defense. While this may seem normal at face value, such approval (that is, the approval of the Council of Ministers and of the minister whose department was affected) was made necessary for exercising every other power accorded to the president. This seeming legalism allowed the president to issue orders directly to the chiefs of the armed services, as well as to officers within each service, bypassing the military hierarchy as necessary (Caldera 1992b). In the case of a military insurrection, this article also granted legal authority to the president to order officers in the field to defend the government or to suppress rebellions. Officers no longer had to choose between obeying their rebellious superior officers and the president, as had occurred during the 1948 coup against President Gallegos. The president now held, de jure, a trump card that could override the orders of any commanding officer in the armed forces, thereby further emphasizing the decentralized nature of military authority.

Within the new constitutional system the Venezuelan Congress was assigned the functions of approving the yearly list of military promotions to the ranks of colonel and general, once it had been vetted by the president, voting on the armed forces budget, and monitoring the performance of the armed services. In practice, the Congress always voted affirmatively on military promotions, deferring to the president's judgment in this matter. However, over time, the need for officers who expected to be promoted to high ranks to maintain a politically favorable profile tended to increase the informal influence of Congress and the president over the highest ranks. The willingness of colonels, generals, and admirals to cater to the wishes of civilian politicians drew accusations of corruption and undue political interference in the armed forces from junior officers. This, in turn, drove a permanent wedge between the highest- and lowest-ranking officers in the Venezuelan military and created a new barrier to successful military intervention in politics.

Military budgets were initially approved without a great deal of discussion in Congress, again deferring to the plans prepared by each military service within the overall cap set by the treasury and the finance committees of the Senate and Chamber of Deputies. However, the role of civilians in deciding caps on military spending and allocating budgets among the four services was an innovation in Venezuelan civil-military relations. Instead of dealing with a unified military demand for budget allocations, civilian politicians were lobbied by the separate services for increased resources. Once the military counterinsurgency operations began in 1963 and 1964, the Venezuelan Congress approved budgets for these activities as separate line items, again without much debate. However, this did set a precedent for special congressional approval for non-ordinary operating expenses or acquisitions, which created the potential for civilian supervision of military spending plans (Tarre Briceño 1994b).

When added to the decrees issued by the transitional government in 1958, the new constitutional powers radically transformed the pattern of civil-military relations. Instead of dealing one on one with a single, powerful military leader, a civilian president became the arbiter of a complex web of interactions between the commanders of the various security forces. Each of these commanders had relatively equal amounts of power and resources, and they all looked to the president to resolve disputes and provide overall guidance. The minister of defense remained a central figure, who acted as a representative of the armed forces in the civilian government and as an advisor to the president on military affairs. As a high-ranking, active-duty military officer and full participant in the cabinet of ministers, the minister of defense could have input into government decisions on a wide array of political and economic issues (although he mostly abstained) (García Villasmil 1995c). However, the minister of defense no longer had significant legal authority over the military services, nor could he act as the focal point of conspiracies against or pressures on the civilian government.

These military reforms, in their totality, decentralized authority over defense matters across the military, the legislature, and the presidency. In effect, they created multiple independent centers of power within the armed forces and forced the various services to rely on civilian intervention to resolve problems of coordination and distribution of resources. This need to rely on civilians to break logjams and gain access to benefits induced a competitive relationship among and within the various centers of military power. Such competition made it almost impossible for any politically ambitious officer to organize a successful coup without having his plans exposed to civilian politicians by other officers eager to curry favor. Furthermore, the possibility that one or another military faction might gain additional power or resources from a coup d'état led its competitors to discourage any such attempts. Competition increased the uncertainty associated with military intervention in politics, which, in turn, deterred the formation of coup coalitions.

APPEASEMENT AND THE DERADICALIZATION
OF THE OFFICER CORPS

The legal and administrative reforms enacted during the 1958 transition and codified by the 1961 constitution to create civilian authority over the armed forces would not have been enough to preserve democracy without a deliberate effort by Rómulo Betancourt and his successors to integrate the officer corps into the Venezuelan middle class. Betancourt understood that, at its core, the thirty-year period of military unrest, which started with the revolt against Gómez in 1928, had as much to do with the material and professional needs of officers as with the political ideals their leaders espoused. Both in 1945 and in 1958, junior and mid-ranking officers had led coups against senior military officers to demand increases in salaries, benefits, training, and professionalization. Within the constraints of the fiscal austerity imposed by the economic recession, Betancourt set out to satisfy these needs and thereby transform the officer corps from a source of persistent instability into the cornerstone for a democratic status quo.

As a first step, the Betancourt administration increased the funding allocated to officer housing, social security, and related subsidies for food and other necessities. One of the president's principal goals was the expansion of the Instituto de Previsión Social de las Fuerzas Armadas, which provided a wide range of social security benefits to active-duty officers, from low-cost consumer items to reduced interest rate loans and mortgages. To support retired officers, Betancourt also increased the endowment of the OFIDIRE (Office for Detached and Retired Officers) and strengthened the military pension system, which eventually paid retirees nearly 100 percent of their salary upon their withdrawal from the officer corps (Arroyo Talavera 1986, 310–12). With a combination of housing credits and subsidies, the government managed to increase the standard of living of the officer corps to the point where mid- to high-ranking officers could consider themselves members of the upper-middle class. Moreover, the government deliberately opened these housing developments to middle-class civilian families, principally professionals and government employees, in order to integrate military officers into civilian society (Soto Urrútia 1994a). The Betancourt administration also funded the construction of an improved military infrastructure and better conditions for enlisted personnel, including a club for noncommissioned officers (Sub-Oficiales Profesionales de Carrera). Overall military expenditures increased as a percentage of the national budget during the Betancourt administration, even in the context of falling Venezuelan oil income and declining government revenues (Müller Rojas 1989, 419).

Facing an economic recession and committed to a fiscal austerity program, Betancourt was unable to fully implement many of these programs until late in his administration. Military spending on new weapons systems, for example, was severely reduced, and what was allocated served to equip the armed forces for counterinsurgency rather than conventional combat. Much of the money for training and operations was provided by the U.S. mutual assistance program and, again, was targeted at improving the counterinsurgency capabilities of the armed forces. Officers' salaries were cut by 10 percent, paralleling cuts faced by civil servants during the first years of the Betancourt administration (Briceño Linares 1994). However, once the initial period of economic difficulties had been overcome, officers received increasing salaries, benefits, pensions, food allowances, housing subsidies, and generally higher socioeconomic status. In this way, Betancourt and his successors were able to demonstrate to the officer corps the perquisites of living under a democratic system of government and to give them a stake in the new regime (Daniels 1992, 42–47, 52).

Beyond attending to the social and material needs of military officers, the Betancourt administration also improved their professional capabilities. Betancourt approved modernization plans for the army, navy, and air force, including Plan 58-1, which had been developed by the air force during the transition to democracy, and Plan Junín, a long-term restructuring and acquisitions program for the army. The navy renovated its installations in Sucre and Falcón in order to improve its ability to operate in eastern and western Venezuela, away from its main docks near Caracas (Giacopini Zárraga 1992d). These plans addressed long-suppressed desires in the armed forces for modernization, particularly in terms of military infrastructure and the distribution of the armed forces across the national territory (Celis Noguera 1989, 437–38).

As all the military officers whom I interviewed stressed, one of the most important reforms of Betancourt administration was the dramatic expansion of educational opportunities for military officers and its impact on breaking down barriers between military and civilian society. Advanced educational opportunities, particularly in nonmilitary fields, were extremely limited under the Pérez Jiménez regime and were generally restricted to those military officers who were favored by the high command.

Graduates of the Venezuelan military academy were not considered to have university-equivalent degrees, which made it very difficult to pursue post-graduate programs. Under the Betancourt administration, scholarships and opportunities became widely available for officer training in nonmilitary professional fields (Soto Urrútia 1994a). Study in universities at home and abroad became almost de rigueur for ambitious military officers, to the point that today a substantial proportion of generals and colonels have professional training in another field (such as law, medicine, engineering, or business management) when they retire (Müller Rojas 1989, 418). The result of this policy was to "civilianize" the attitudes of members of the armed forces and break down the military caste that had formed in the decades prior to 1958. Furthermore, the opportunity to study abroad was highly appreciated by many young military officers, and it also served as a useful escape valve for the government to informally exile the discontented (Molina Vargas 1992; Néry Arrieta 1992; Montiel 1994).

Rather than increase salaries, benefits, and training under pressure from the armed forces, Betancourt was always careful to categorize these military reforms as appropriate and necessary improvements in the status of the Venezuelan officer corps. Professionalism, a decent standard of living, and improved working conditions were seen as prerequisites of a modern military force by Venezuelan officers. Betancourt presented the reforms of his administration as the natural outgrowth of democratization, contrasting the "modern" military of his administration with the corruption and deceit of the military high command during the Pérez Jiménez government. In all of their public and private appearances before military officers, Betancourt and his successors consistently emphasized the links between military modernization, professionalism, and democratization, hoping to transmit this mental equation to the officer corps.

CONSOLIDATING NEW JURISDICTIONAL BOUNDARIES
DURING THE BETANCOURT ADMINISTRATION

Betancourt's successful defense of his government against military insurrections, combined with his broad array of military reform programs, enforced civilian authority and simultaneously reconciled the armed forces to the new democratic regime. However, the most important effect of Betancourt's strategies was to create a system of cross-cutting cleavages within the officer corps. Enmeshed in this web of conflicting interests and loyalties, dissenting Venezuelan military officers found it impossible to conspire suc-

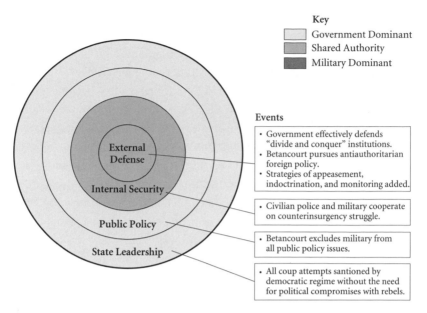

Key
- ☐ Government Dominant
- ▨ Shared Authority
- ■ Military Dominant

External
Defense

Internal Security

Public Policy

State Leadership

Events

- Government effectively defends "divide and conquer" institutions.
- Betancourt pursues antiauthoritarian foreign policy.
- Strategies of appeasement, indoctrination, and monitoring added.

- Civilian police and military cooperate on counterinsurgency struggle.

- Betancourt excludes military from all public policy issues.

- All coup attempts santioned by democratic regime without the need for political compromises with rebels.

Figure 4.1. Civil-Military Jurisdictional Boundaries, ca. 1961: Consolidating Control by Containment of Armed Forces

cessfully, let alone achieve the necessary consensus to carry out a successful coup d'état.

Betancourt also successfully maintained the jurisdictional boundaries he inherited from the transitional government (fig. 4.1). In the public policy arena, Betancourt managed to successfully exclude the armed forces from any significant influence, or even veto power, over his administration's policymaking, confirming civilian dominance. In the area of internal security, Betancourt was forced to rely more heavily on the armed forces than he might have preferred due to the growing threats posed by the PCV/MIR insurgency, as we will see in the next section. Betancourt was successful in restricting military operations to rural areas, where he allowed the military control of specific, limited theaters of operation, while he assigned the task of defeating urban guerrilla bands to civilian police forces, the DIGEPOL, and the Guardia Nacional. Daily policing, as ineffective as it often was following the end of authoritarian rule, was in the hands of civilian police forces, though the Guardia Nacional, a militarized and professional gendarmerie, provided a reserve force in the case of major urban disturbances. The intervention of the armed forces was reserved for emergency situations, as occurred when the army assisted the Guardia Nacional during the general uprising in Caracas in October 1960. As a result, in the area of internal security, civilian authority mostly dominated in the cities, although military influence grew in certain rural areas as guerrilla activity increased.

In the area of external defense policy, Betancourt made substantial progress in interjecting civilian decision-making authority into military affairs, particularly if we consider how small a role politicians had previously played in this area. After 1959, civilian politicians approved overall defense budgets and promotions, and they supervised military education. Betancourt was mainly constrained in his policies by the finite amount of time and resources he could devote to military affairs. Since he could trust no one else with civil-military relations, he centralized security policy decision making in his office. Reflecting the drawbacks of this approach, Betancourt was forced to lean heavily on military-generated plans for the counterinsurgency effort, other defense and security planning, military equipment purchases, and budget allocations. Even under Betancourt, matters that were closely related to professional military tasks were left in the purview of military commanders rather than civilian politicians. This was partly a matter of design, to fulfill the civil-military bargain of professionalization in return for obedience. However, Venezuela's regime capacity was also very low, which prevented civilians from participating intelligently in defense issues in any event.

The success of Betancourt's strategies created a configuration of civil-military jurisdiction over the state that fell within the theoretical boundaries of civilian control defined in chapter 1 (see fig. 1.3). The institutions he created made it difficult for the officer corps to resist the inroads of civilian authority, as Betancourt increasingly divided military officers among themselves: colonels and generals, who needed civilian approval for promotion, versus the junior officers, who did not; the army, navy, and air force against each other in struggles over power and resources; officers who were satisfied with their new material standing versus those who were discontented with the political system; officers who believed in democracy against those who feared civilian rule. In effect, Betancourt achieved multiple and cross-cutting cleavages within the armed forces, which made it nearly impossible for the armed forces to resist his authority in any corporate manner.

Partially by choice, Venezuela never developed a high level of regime capacity to supervise military affairs because democratizers avoided creating a civilian-led ministry of defense or powerful defense committees in Congress.

Instead, civilian authority over the military was concentrated in the office of the president. The system had the virtue of requiring very limited civilian input to maintain control. However, since any civilian president had many demands on his time, the amount of expertise and supervision the government could dedicate to military affairs on a permanent basis was limited. Eventually, this system would restrict the types of institutions of civilian control that the democratic government could consolidate in Venezuela to those based on strategies of "divide and conquer" and appeasement, both of which required little regime capacity to function.

Making Civilian Control Work: Civil-Military Collaboration in the Counterinsurgency War

The final piece of the puzzle of civilian control in Venezuelan was ironically placed by the PCV/MIR insurgency. The Venezuelan armed forces' experience of working under civilian authority and within the scope of the constitution while carrying out military action against what they perceived as a foreign-sponsored insurgency acted powerfully on the officer corps, allowing them to see the new regime as an aid rather than a hindrance to their objectives. Betancourt was able to transform the liability of the left-wing insurgency into an opportunity to increase regime leverage over the armed forces by positioning democracy as a useful alternative to Communism or authoritarianism. However, had the insurgency proven more effective or more dangerous to the armed forces, this opportunity could have quickly become a threat, not only from the dangers of revolution, but also from increased military pressure for unrestricted warfare and increased jurisdictional boundaries.

The PCV/MIR insurgency, with approximately 2,500 combatants, was among the most substantial of the first wave of guerrilla movements that followed the Cuban revolution in Latin America (Wickham-Crowley 1993, 53). Inspired by Castro's example in Cuba, members of the PCV and MIR believed that they could create the revolutionary conditions that would lead to the overthrow of the Betancourt administration. At the very least, they expected that continuous attacks on military and economic targets would provoke a right-wing coup d'état against the democratic government, which would allow them to reenact the experience of clandestine revolutionary activity of 1957–58 that had resulted in the overthrow of Pérez Jiménez. The leadership of these parties believed that in 1958 they had mistakenly allowed oligarchic elements to take control of the democratization process, which defused its revolutionary potential. By provoking a new dictatorship, the left felt it could take the lead in organizing the overthrow of this new authoritarian regime and thereby promote a true revolution. Their guerrilla army was intended both to bring about the overthrow of the Betancourt administration and provide an experienced core of soldiers for a revolutionary army to replace the Venezuelan armed forces (Blanco Muñoz 1991, 89, 103–4, 142–44).

The revolutionary movement first attracted the armed forces' attention during a failed general strike, largely led by university students, that shook Caracas in October 1960. Local police were completely overwhelmed, and army and Guardia Nacional troops were brought into Caracas to restore order. The failure of this uprising, in the minds of several military commanders, forced the insurgents to fall back on urban and rural guerrilla activities (Briceño Linares 1994). Beginning in 1961, urban guerrilla units operating in Caracas started carrying out numerous attacks on police stations, government buildings, and political figures, supplemented by bank robberies. In February 1962 members of these parties had already organized the first guerrilla front in western Venezuela, in Falcón state, called Frente José Leonardo Chirinos. Other fronts soon followed in the states of Lara and Barinas, under the name Frente Simón Bolívar, while smaller units operated in eastern Venezuela in the states of Anzoátegui and Sucre and in Miranda state, within eighty miles of Caracas. The overall direction of these guerrilla units was theoretically in the hands of the FALN, although in practice, an effective centralized command did not exist. The escaped rebel soldiers from the military uprisings of Carúpano and Puerto Cabello added an important leavening of trained combatants to the guerrilla movement. Captain Ponte Rodríguez, the fugitive leader of the Puerto Cabello coup attempt, was named commander in chief of the FALN. After Ponte was recaptured and died in prison, Colonel Juan de Dios Moncada Vidal, an erstwhile supporter of Pérez Jiménez and co-organizer of the July 1958 coup attempt by General Castro León, became the leader of military wing of the insurgency (Valsalice 1979, 145–47).

The initial wave of urban terrorism was aimed at creating a climate of instability and at harassing the government, as well as at providing funding for the movement. Urban guerrillas were so prevalent in the insurgency that this form of combat was considered a specific characteristic of the Venezuelan revolutionary experience, differentiating it from the Cuban or Chinese experiences. In Venezuela, members were mostly university students, leavened with some career criminals who provided useful information on organizing major thefts and evading the police. Besides providing funding, the urban components of the guerrilla movement organized logistics for rural insurgents, many of whom operated in extremely poor areas where supplies were rarely available. The Unidades Tácticas de Combate (UTC), or small terrorist units, also carried out high-profile attacks, including airplane hijackings, piracy (in the case of the Venezuelan transport ship *Anzoátegui*), and attacks on prominent economic and military installations. One of the main targets of the UTC was the local police, 160 of whom were killed between 1961 and 1968. An unintended consequence of this policy was rising popular anger against the guerrillas, mainly due to the humble backgrounds of the murdered police officers, who lived in the poor neighborhoods where the guerrillas had at first found the greatest support. The country was particularly outraged by a guerrilla attack on an excursion train in Los Teques, near Caracas, on 29 September 1963, in which many civilians were wounded and five members of the Guardia Nacional were summarily executed after being captured. President Betancourt ably used this incident to harden public opinion against the PCV/MIR insurgents (Valsalice 1979, 50).

The withdrawal of one of the original coalition partners, URD, from the government, continuous popular unrest in the major cities, and the revolutionary-tinged military uprisings of Carúpano and Puerto Cabello led the activists of the MIR and PCV to believe that the insurgency would be relatively short. They were convinced that the smallest amount of pressure would be enough to topple Rómulo Betancourt. Thus, their rural guerrilla fronts were organized hastily, with insufficient attention given to logistics and sanitation. Small groups, never exceeding 600 combatants in any given front, operated in the rural mountainous regions out of small base camps. Even though these insurgents had received pledges of assistance from Cuba, their material support was intermittent, due in part to the difficulty of landing supplies undetected on the Venezuelan coast. Initially, weapons were limited to those found within the country, stolen during the 1958 uprising against Pérez Jiménez, or manufactured in clandestine facilities. In the years that followed, some war materiel was infiltrated into Venezuela by boat from friendly countries. In addition, Cuba provided training facilities and technical experts for the FALN, including a few regular Cuban army personnel who participated in the guerrilla fronts. Cuba and other socialist countries also provided hard currency to support guerrilla fighters and to pay for more mundane supplies, such as food and medicine. Under the constraint of limited supplies, the guerrillas generally practiced hit-and-run attacks, ambushes, and lightning occupations of isolated villages (Valsalice 1979, 125–43, 152–57; Blanco Muñoz 1991, 80, 151, 157–58).

The Venezuelan armed forces were generally not prepared to fight a counterinsurgency war in 1961. Military training, particularly at the Academia Militar, consisted mainly of preparation for conventional warfare (Machillanda Pinto 1995). From 1961 to 1963, most of the subversive activity seemed to be concentrated in the major cities, and it was generally the responsibility of the police, the DIGEPOL, and the Guardia Nacional to combat it. As the rural insurgency grew, the Venezuelan armed forces during the Betancourt administration adopted a defensive posture and developed their counterinsurgency capabilities. In January 1963 a theater of operations was created in Falcón with the participation of all the military services and the national police forces (Belmonte 1994; Celis Noguera 1994). The Venezuelan army encircled the Falcón guerrilla front (approximately 140 square kilometers) and progressively cut it off from its supply sources. From January through April 1963, the air force bombarded the region, seeking to drive the guerrillas into higher, less hospitable ground. Propaganda leaflets were dropped that offered rewards for information that led to the capture of guerrilla leaders and safe passage for local peasants who desired to leave the area. Army units then instituted a dragnet through the region, which destroyed several base camps but made only limited contact with the highly mobile guerrillas. This operation was nonetheless seen as a success because it prevented the guerrillas from establishing a "liberated" area in Falcón, from which they could have potentially trained and regrouped, secure from army attacks (Valsalice 1979, 100–104).

As the December 1963 presidential elections approached, the attention of the armed forces shifted to the protection of the voting process. On 10 November the FALN called for a national boycott of the elections and declared a general offensive against the government. On 19 November the FALN ordered a general strike in Caracas, and the city was practically paralyzed out of fear of violent demonstrations or guerrilla reprisals. The country also experienced a wave of terrorism and rural guerrilla activity during the month preceding the election, as the FALN attempted to discredit the government and postpone the elections. Regardless, Betancourt was determined that voting would take place on schedule.

In the days leading up to the election, the minister of defense, General Briceño Linares, and the high command publicly announced their support for the electoral process and reminded the public that it would be guarded by the armed forces under the planned Operación República II. This military operation, which has been conducted during every Venezuelan election since 1958, placed soldiers at all the polling stations and provided security during the transportation and counting of ballots (Briceño Linares 1994). All major legal political parties repudiated the violence and campaigned vigorously for elected office. The government's counterinsurgency policy was criticized by all of the opposition parties during the race, particularly by the URD, which advocated a policy of conciliation and pacification. The race was particularly competitive due to divisions in the governing Acción Democrática party, as one of its factions had split off and formed its own political party in 1962 (Tarre Murzi 1983, 248–50).

The elections themselves proceeded without incident on 1 December 1963, and Raul Leoni, the AD presidential candidate, was elected with a bare plurality of 33 percent of the vote, with COPEI coming in second. Electoral turnout exceeded 90 percent, which the government quickly announced as a repudiation of the insurgency's tactics and message. Douglas Bravo, Teodoro Petkoff, and other members of the MIR and PCV later reported they were stunned and demoralized by the level of participation in the elections, which was one of the first signals of how deeply they had misinterpreted popular feelings concerning the democratic process (Tarre 1994b).

CIVILIAN CONTROL ACCOMMODATES MILITARY NECESSITY

Rómulo Betancourt used the threat posed by the PCV/MIR insurgency to cement the loyalty of the Venezuelan armed forces to the democratic system. He was quick to reinforce the contrast between his own administration and that of Fidel Castro, and he would personally use this argument in meetings with military officers as an additional reason for them to support the constitutional government (Betancourt 1960).[2] This argument resonated in the military high command, as they were already concerned by the link between PCV/MIR militants and the rebellious officers who had led the Carúpano and Puerto Cabello uprisings in 1962 (Valsalice 1979, 34–39). For most military commanders, counterinsurgency operations provided a chance to defend Venezuela against a foreign-inspired Communist threat and to exercise their chosen profession. These operations also allowed Betancourt to move beyond defending the redefined jurisdictional boundaries and new institutions of civilian control against challenges from the officer corps to actually making them function in the face of a serious security threat. Even though

Betancourt had to allow some expansion in the jurisdiction of the military during the war, the counterinsurgency effort offered the military a positive role, which balanced the restrictions imposed on them by the democratization process.

Most of the military officers I interviewed for this book participated in the counterinsurgency operations of the 1960s in some capacity, and all agreed that the civilian politicians had been extremely supportive of the armed forces during this effort. As the armed forces reorganized themselves for counterinsurgency operations, Betancourt ensured sufficient funding for new equipment and installations, drawing on both Venezuelan sources and U.S. assistance. The Venezuelan Congress rapidly approved the necessary budgets to cover the increased cost of field operations. By 1963, the military lacked for very little in terms of logistics or training.

In the international arena, the United States broadly supported the counterinsurgency campaign with economic and military assistance, training, and equipment, supporting Venezuelan military operations at a time when the government faced substantial budget deficits. U.S. and French military missions also played an important role in retraining the Venezuelan armed forces (Arroyo Talavera 1986, 312; Molina Vargas 1992). The U.S. military mission placed advisors at almost all levels of the Venezuelan air force and navy, and Venezuelan army field and tactics manuals were direct translations of their U.S. equivalents. A large number of Venezuelan officers, averaging approximately 380 per year between 1959 and 1969, passed through U.S. training schools (Arroyo Talavera 1986, 313). Betancourt developed close ties with the John F. Kennedy administration through the Alliance for Progress, a U.S. economic assistance program, and military assistance programs. The Venezuelan president also used his leverage with the United States and the OAS to push for additional sanctions on Cuba due to its landings of weapons and experts on Venezuelan beaches, and he provided support for anti-Castro Cuban exile organizations.[3] Venezuela's status as a new democracy fighting against a Communist insurgency drew support from a wide range of Western Bloc countries and certainly quieted complaints by U.S. conservatives concerning Betancourt's own Communist-tinged background.

The decentralization of power recently instituted by the strategy of "divide and conquer" was overcome in the field by the creation of local unified military commands (*teatros de operaciones*) that incorporated elements of all four services and the police and operated in geographically restricted areas (Molina Vargas 1992). To coordinate among the different theaters, the armed forces first established the Sistema de Alarmas Electrónica, a central information clearinghouse, on 22 November 1963. A full-fledged central command center, the Centro de Operaciones Conjuntas, was established in February 1965. Despite the increased militarization of the counterinsurgency campaign, Betancourt still maintained his central role as coordinator among the security forces, approving operational plans prepared by the theater commanders and the Joint Staff. He visited military garrisons in the *teatros de operaciones* and listened to the needs of local commanders, thus garnering a personal sense of how the counterinsurgency struggle progressed. These visits also were carefully used by Betancourt to make the argument that the insurgency and its ideology were of foreign derivation, and he accused Castro and the Soviets of supplying and coordinating the guerrillas (Celis Noguera 1994). This argument was not difficult to make once four tons of Cuban-supplied weapons were discovered in a cache on a beach of the Paraguaná peninsula of western Venezuela, a finding that Betancourt announced on 1 December 1963 (Tarre Murzi 1983, 242).

Betancourt also played a role in coordinating cooperation between the military and government leaders in the areas affected by insurgency. The Ministry of the Interior, for example, controlled DIGEPOL and other security forces, particularly in combating urban terrorism. Carlos Andrés Pérez, who would later twice become president, gained a reputation as a ruthless and effective minister of the interior during this time period. On the national political level, Betancourt took the lead in marshaling national sentiment against the guerrillas, by playing up their atrocities and highlighting the role of the armed forces in combating them. When the armed forces presented evidence of participation by PCV and MIR congressmen and senators in the insurgency and requested their arrest, Betancourt responded first by suspending the legal activities of these parties on 10 May 1962, and then, following protests from legal political parties COPEI and URD, by sending a petition for the withdrawal of legal status for the PCV and MIR parties to the Supreme Court in October 1962. In January 1963 PCV/MIR parliamentarians were arrested for participating in subversive activities, although several had been forewarned and escaped. During Betancourt's presidency, measures were also enacted that restricted freedom of the press, assembly, and political activity. For Betancourt, democracy and political rights were a privilege that should only be enjoyed by supporters of the constitutional system. For all others, and especially the PCV/MIR insurgents, Betancourt was willing to take any necessary measures, no matter how undemocratic, to defeat their attempts to overthrow his government (Schaposnik 1985, 310).

In the *teatros de operaciones* military commanders and civilian government officials worked closely together, particularly on civic action projects, infrastructure development, and propaganda activities. Local party organizations provided intelligence and rallied popular sentiment in favor of the government and the armed forces in the areas hit by guerrilla insurgency.[4] Civil-military cooperation at the local level dissolved the traditional military reserve toward the world of civilian politics and created a feeling of mutual regard among officers and government officials. For many officers, civil-military collaboration against the insurgency was a revelation, in that it demonstrated that it was possible for the armed forces to carry out their professional duties and defend the state within a framework of democracy (Celis Noguera 1994).

Additionally, Acción Democrática's political hegemony over the organized peasantry and labor federations assisted the government in defeating the insurgency. Unlike Batista's Cuba, Betancourt's government had a wide base of popular support due to its agrarian reform policies and its consensus-building approach to labor-business disputes. Denied access to these traditional reservoirs of revolutionary support, the guerrilla movement overwhelmingly consisted of students and disaffected military officers. Rather than cooperate with the guerrillas, peasants were more likely to denounce their movements, as occurred in the case of the Paraguaná weapons landing by Cuba (Belmonte 1994; Briceño Linares 1994; Machillanda Pinto 1995).

For Rómulo Betancourt, assigning the armed forces the lead task in fighting the guerrillas was a win-win proposition. In one stroke, Betancourt removed major military units from urban centers in Caracas and Maracay and relocated them to the peripheral areas in the countryside, where they could not be used in attempts to overthrow his administration (Müller Rojas 1989, 420). Combating the Marxist insurgency reoriented the armed forces from political action to military action. More fundamentally, the counterinsurgency experience of the armed forces transformed their organizational mission from one focused largely on domestic politics to one concerned with the defense of the new democratic system against foreign aggression. Finally, it also removed the constant threat of military overthrow of the Betancourt government by establishing in the minds of many military officers, at the very least, that the government was the lesser of two evils.

MANAGING EXPANDED JURISDICTIONAL BOUNDARIES:
PRESIDENT RAUL LEONI AND THE WAR EFFORT

Raul Leoni, one of the founding members of Acción Democrática, won the presidential elections of December 1963, following a hard-fought campaign in which issues of internal security and the fight against the insurgency were very prominent. He took office with a very narrow margin of victory, which seriously limited AD's power in Congress and which forced him to attempt to recreate a national coalition government with URD and other smaller political parties, known as the Gobierno de Ancha Base. COPEI remained in the opposition because its leaders felt that they could not collaborate in a government of which URD formed part. It took nearly eight months of political uncertainty before Leoni could hammer out a deal with URD and a smaller middle-class-oriented party led by a prominent intellectual, Arturo Uslar Pietri (Fuenmayor 1990, 16:47–49, 72–73, 101). Raul Leoni would face considerable difficulty maintaining this political coalition and continuing to prosecute the counterinsurgency campaign, but unlike Betancourt, Leoni never faced a serious military challenge to his rule. Even so, the armed forces expanded their jurisdictional boundaries within the state as they assumed the lead role in combating the PCV/MIR insurgency.

Leoni's government was well received by the armed forces, particularly after that of the controversial figure, Rómulo Betancourt. Unlike Betancourt, Leoni had a reputation as a conciliator and presented a grandfatherly demeanor (Tarre Murzi 1983, 254–55). Leoni's minister of defense, General Florencio Gómez, was generally well liked within the army and made a special point of personally meeting young officers throughout the armed forces in informal breakfasts or lunches, where he exercised his considerable charm to win them over (Machillanda Pinto 1995). Leoni carried on Betancourt's policies of maintaining the government's support for the armed forces, both rhetorically and materially while continuing to enforce the mechanisms and institutions of civilian control, albeit with less overt civil-military friction.

Under Leoni, the armed forces completed their reorganization for counterinsurgency warfare and began offensive actions against the various guerrilla fronts. The Venezuelan army, which had consisted largely of conventional infantry battalions until 1959, was reorganized into thirteen ranger battalions, trained and equipped for mobile warfare. Schools were developed to provide soldiers with jungle warfare and special operations training, which were often taught by U.S. or French instructors (Molina Vargas 1992; García Villasmil 1995c). The Venezuelan army, in cooperation with the other services, began a series of offensives in Lara, Falcón, Miranda, and Anzoátegui to eliminate rural guerrilla fronts. Since the guerrillas lacked either access to secure areas or control over significant territory, the Venezuelan armed forces were able to encircle their opponents by land and sea and confine them to a shrinking perimeter, in which the air force performed reconnaissance missions and bombarded suspected guerrilla camps. Army units then combed through the regions, searching out guerrilla installations and pursuing retreating insurgents (Valsalice 1979, 101–22). As during the Betancourt administration, the armed forces retained a great deal of autonomy in planning and executing missions within the *teatros de operaciones*. However, President Leoni continued to approve the overall counterinsurgency strategy and coordinated political, social, and economic measures to support the military effort (Tarre Murzi 1983, 266–68).

The armed forces also relied on local civilians to provide information on guerrilla movements and bases, which demonstrated the weakness of PCV/MIR support in the countryside. In each *teatro de operaciones*, commanders offered rewards ranging from BS. 15,000 to 30,000 (approximately $3,000 to $8,000) to encourage informers. Military leaders also armed some local militias to defend villages against lightning occupations by guerrilla forces. Military units continued to carry out civic action projects, building schools and dispensaries, organizing agricultural cooperatives, and improving sanitation and water supplies (Soto Tamayo 1986, 327–28). By 1964–65, officers felt that they could rely on rural populations in remote theaters of operation to inform them of guerrilla movements (Machillanda Pinto 1995). Facing such difficult conditions, including sickness, injuries, and the sheer exhaustion of the combatants, the rural guerrilla fronts largely ceased operations by the end of 1965. Constantly harassed and pursued by the armed forces, the PCV/MIR insurgents never had an opportunity to develop roots or support in a significant rural community. As their leaders fell ill or were captured, increasing numbers of rank-and-file guerrillas surrendered.

As a result, the PCV and MIR came under severe internal pressure from dispirited participants in the guerrilla fronts to seek a return to legal political activity and abandon the revolutionary struggle. Leoni was unable to exploit this split due to the deep animosity that had developed between the insurgents and AD. Some combatants, particularly Douglas Bravo, continued to take a hard line and argued for an extended struggle against the government, patterned on the Maoist and Vietnamese revolutionary experiences. The FALN had practically become a separate organization at this time, and it was increasingly unresponsive to political direction by the PCV or the FLN. To resolve the lack of coordination, Fabricio Ojeda, then head of the PCV/MIR umbrella group FLN, attempted to merge his organization with the FALN to create a unified political-military directorate. Seventeen days after issuing this order, Ojeda was captured by the police and imprisoned. Following his capture, the guerrilla organizations slowly disintegrated, and the PCV split into those who were committed to revolutionary warfare and those who sought a return to peaceful political activity. The MIR suffered a similar period of decomposition.

Urban terrorism continued to be a problem in the cities after the collapse of the rural fronts in 1966, but the overall threat from FALN was essentially contained by 1967. Leoni recognized that the military effort had accomplished the goal of removing the insurgency as a threat to democratic stability, and he made an attempt to find a political solution to the revolutionary movement by naming a pacification commission. The military was hostile to the idea of pacification, but more important, AD's role in prosecuting the war made the party an untrustworthy negotiating partner for the guerillas. Thus, this effort never bore fruit, and Leoni's failure to end the war became a major campaign issue during the 1968 elections (Machillanda Pinto 1995).

With the threat of military rebellion against the democratic government abated and the "divide and conquer" strategy well institutionalized, Leoni emphasized strategies of appeasement, indoctrination, and monitoring. To the officer corps he stressed the central role of the armed forces in the defense of democracy and the role of democracy in providing the military with the tools to successfully wage the war against the FALN. Leoni also worked to develop a personal rapport with military officers as a means of monitoring the officer corps. He continued the practice of visiting armed forces garrisons and praised the conduct of military officers in their support of democracy. At graduations at the Academia Militar Leoni handed out copies of the Venezuelan constitution to the cadets and personally congratulated them for their achievements. Through his military household, Leoni continued a policy of informally attending to officers' needs in order to improve his reputation as a concerned commander in chief (Daniels 1992, 18–19, 21).

As economic growth slowly resumed under the Leoni administration, the government was able to increase the budgets assigned to both the *teatros de operaciones* and the overall development of the armed forces. Officers' salaries were on par with those of the U.S. armed forces by 1964, making the

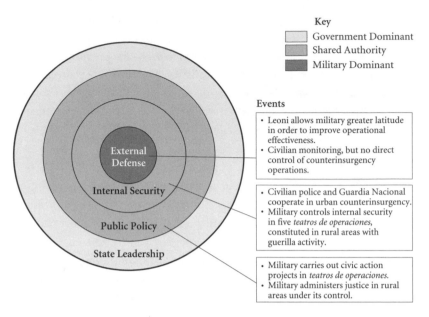

Figure 4.2. Civil-Military Jurisdictional Boundaries, ca. 1967: Counterinsurgency Warfare Expands Armed Forces' Jurisdictional Boundaries

Venezuelan armed forces the best remunerated on the South American continent. Defense allocations remained substantial during the Leoni period, averaging 9 to 10 percent of the total budget. Many officers were able to seek professional training abroad as a step toward advancing their careers. Access to housing and other benefits improved considerably (Arroyo Talavera 1986, 310–13). Leoni inherited a civil-military system in which the mechanisms of government authority had already been successfully crafted, yet by sustaining control even under wartime conditions, he was able to ensure the long-term institutionalization of civilian control of the armed forces.

Given the shortage of regime capacity in his administration, particularly in civilian defense expertise, Leoni was well advised to allow the armed forces wide latitude in pursuing the war in the *teatros de operaciones* (fig. 4.2). These military commanders prepared and carried out military operations, gathered intelligence, and planned infrastructure development and civic action projects. While they held a great deal of independent power within their zones of control, they nevertheless operated under the overall guidance of the president. Some have alleged that human rights abuses were more common during this period, in which several members of left-wing political organizations disappeared (Tarre Murzi 1983, 266–67; Fuenmayor 1990, 16:218–27; Tarre Briceño 1994b).[5] Other than ad hoc investigations of particularly notable events, Congress exerted almost no formal control over the armed forces, and the president's less confrontational attitude toward the military allowed it greater autonomy and jurisdiction over domestic policy.

This expansion of military power could have been problematic if it had become a permanent feature of Venezuelan civil-military relations. However, as David Pion-Berlin and Craig Arceneaux argue, even internal security missions in which the military has some professional latitude are generally not threatening to democratic stability as long as civilians control the overall definition of the mission and control the initiation and termination of the mission (Pion-Berlin and Arceneaux 2000). Leoni governed during the period of fiercest guerrilla activity, particularly in rural areas, and thus, the phase in which the military was most deeply involved. In external defense affairs, civilians encouraged the armed forces to professionalize and manage their own affairs so as to maximize their combat capabilities. This translated into an expansion of military autonomy in this area, although this new power never extended to dominance over foreign policy.

The armed forces also took over some direct government functions in the areas of internal security and domestic politics in its *teatros de operaciones* between 1963 and 1969, although the president still retained overall supervision of military activities. During this period, civilian police forces and the Guardia Nacional had the leading role in combating terrorism in urban areas, which is where Venezuela's population was increasingly concentrated. The combination of military latitude in carrying out operations and civilian overall strategic direction suggests that internal security should be coded as an area of shared authority during the insurgency. The participation of the armed forces in civic action and development projects represented an expansion into the area of public policy, but this was also at the behest of and under the overall strategic direction of civilian authorities. Only state leadership selection remained independent from the participation of the armed forces.

President Leoni had neither the military expertise nor the ability to supervise the widespread activities of the armed forces across five different *teatros de operaciones*. He relied, as had Betancourt before him, on the network of civilian governors and political activists spread out across rural areas to provide him with informal feedback and warnings concerning potential problems. Given the geographic isolation of the insurgency, Leoni was willing to defer to the professional judgment of military commanders to solve what he essentially saw as a military problem, while reserving political dimensions of the counterinsurgency campaign to himself (Machillanda Pinto 1995). In the end, this proved to be a workable solution: once the counterinsurgency campaign ended in 1969, the institutions of civilian control consolidated under President Betancourt provided sufficient regime leverage over the armed forces to enable the civilian president to once again enforce lower military jurisdictional boundaries.

ENDING THE COUNTERINSURGENCY WAR:
RAFAEL CALDERA AND THE CONSOLIDATION
OF CIVILIAN CONTROL OVER THE MILITARY

Rafael Caldera came to power with little experience in the executive branch and a slender margin of victory, yet he was able to end the guerrilla conflict on his terms, against the advice of his military commanders. Caldera won the 1968 presidential election as the candidate for COPEI with 29 percent of the vote; Gonzalo Barrios, AD's candidate, received 27 percent of the vote. Caldera's victory was possible only because of a third split in AD's ranks. Luís Beltrán Prieto Figueroa, who was denied the AD presidential candidacy in 1968 due to internal party maneuvers, announced the formation of a new party, the Movimiento Electoral del Pueblo (MEP), with the support of many AD activists. The MEP attracted 19 percent of the vote and thus denied AD's reelection. Acción Democrática's leaders were stunned by the election results, but they readily conceded victory to COPEI. Caldera's ability to govern Venezuela and, most important, to control the armed forces was a clear indication of how far democratic consolidation and civilian control had advanced since 1958.

Rafael Caldera, a conservative lawyer and former university professor, lacked any experience in military affairs, yet he was respected within the officer corps because of his intellectual gravitas and his reputation for personal probity. His administration was staffed by many COPEI activists who had won admiration for their work in Congress during two AD administrations and their unfaltering support for democracy. However, no one in this party had ever managed civil-military relations or had close ties to the armed forces. COPEI faced military commanders who were accustomed to working with AD politicians and who had established many personal relationships during the previous governments. Furthermore, ten years of rule by Acción Democrática had produced ten "classes" of colonels and generals who had needed civilian (that is, AD) political approval to gain their ranks, and who were therefore likely to be favorably disposed to that political party. As a result, at least initially, Caldera based his military policy on his constitutional authority and institutional channels, rather than on personal relationships (Caldera 1992b; Tarre Briceño 1994b).

During the period between his election and inauguration, Caldera toured the major military garrisons and *teatros de operaciones* to gauge conditions in the field. In each of the theaters, he conducted long discussions with local military commanders on the feasibility of enacting a pacification program to end the guerrilla war. Although they were unhappy about negotiating with their opponents and, in particular, at the possibility of offering amnesty, the group of officers closest to the counterinsurgency war reluctantly agreed that the guerrillas had been militarily defeated and that further offensive actions were not truly necessary to maintain control of the regions in which the FALN guerrillas had operated. This created a space for Caldera to seek a political solution to end the war (Machillanda Pinto 1995). It is important to note that Caldera was careful to consult the military only on the feasibility of ending the counterinsurgency war, not on its desirability.

The new president had campaigned on a policy of reconciliation and was determined to end Venezuela's internal war. In his inaugural address on 11 March 1969, Caldera offered a comprehensive pacification program, which included amnesty for guerrilla combatants, relegalization of the PCV and the MIR, and resettlement overseas for those who wished to leave Venezuela. In return, he required an acceptance of the democratic process as the only legal means of access to political power. Through Cardinal José Quintero Parra of the Catholic Church, the government began negotiations with the guerrilla groups and announced a cease-fire. Soon after, weary guerrillas began coming out of the mountains and hills to accept the government's amnesty program. Some returned to civilian life, some chose resettlement, and others participated in the political system, particularly through the creation of a new political party, Movimiento al Socialismo (MAS). The amnesty program was the last straw for the guerrillas, the vast majority of whom were all too eager to lead normal lives. Only Douglas Bravo, who had always held to the hardest antigovernment line, maintained his guerrilla activities. With the pacification program well under way, the armed forces began winding down their military operations in rural areas and closing the base camps associated with the operational theaters (Herman 1980, 130–33).

Caldera's pacification program closed out the process of consolidation

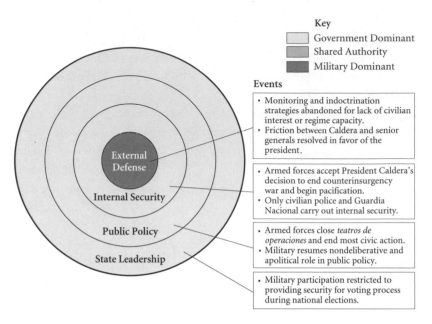

Figure 4.3. Civil-Military Jurisdictional Boundaries, ca. 1970: Civilian Control by Containment Is Consolidated

of civilian control (fig. 4.3). In acquiescing to both Caldera's inauguration and his decision to end the counterinsurgency campaign without demur, the Venezuelan armed forces indicated the extent to which they had accepted an apolitical role within the political system and civilian authority over major security decisions. The counterinsurgency war had brought the armed forces into a wide range of issues concerning economic development, civic action, and internal security. The fact that the armed forces withdrew from a major internal role with little resistance and accepted a more limited role within the Venezuelan political system confirmed the degree to which civilians had been able to set and manage boundaries on military involvement in political and economic affairs. The armed forces had operated against the guerrillas with a great deal of autonomy in their plans and operations, which would seem to indicate expanded military jurisdictional boundaries in both external defense and internal security. However, civilians had the final say in the overall direction of military strategy; they ended the war based on their own political criteria rather than those of the armed forces. High military autonomy in these areas was an effect of Betancourt's, Leoni's, and Caldera's respect for military professionalism, rather than of an inability to maintain control over the armed forces. As the armed forces returned to barracks, they withdrew from the public policy functions they had assumed through civic action and rural development projects and turned over internal security functions to civilian police and the Guardia Nacional. Still, they retained a relatively higher level of autonomy in the external defense area than that to which President Betancourt had originally restricted them. President Caldera's inexperience and lack of interest in substantive military affairs considerably reduced what little regime capacity had been achieved in this area, allowing the armed forces to maintain their expanded boundaries in this one sector. Caldera, like Betancourt, consolidated civilian control of the armed forces by containment.

Conclusions

Although Caldera faced some difficulties in his interactions with the armed forces, the relative ease with which he was able to order the officer corps to accept his pacification policy is an indication of how thoroughly civilian authority over the armed forces had been consolidated by 1969. Only a decade earlier, Rómulo Betancourt had inherited a highly agitated military, torn between supporting the democratic process and attempting an authoritarian counterrevolution and interspersed with a significant number of officers who were interested only in their personal advancement. Civilian control over the Venezuelan armed forces was neither an inevitable nor even a likely outcome of the democratization process. Crafting durable civilian authority required that political leaders have both a broad opportunity structure and a workable agenda, as well as the skill to create appropriate institutions to supervise the military.

The political shock provided by the domestic war against the PCV/MIR insurgency could just as easily have led to increased military autonomy as have provided the additional opportunity for Betancourt and his successors to impose civilian control. As has occurred in many other cases in Latin America, military leaders could have interpreted the growth of the guerrilla movement as an outcome of the disorder and indiscipline of civilian politics and reacted by reimposing authoritarian rule. Betancourt's peculiar genius was to transform the insurgency threat into an additional reason for the armed forces to defend democracy and to accept ever more intrusive measures of civilian authority. The armed forces, already weakened and divided by the dramatic failure of the previous authoritarian regime, faced a more or less consensual democratization process. With no legitimate civilian support for a return to authoritarian rule, and facing their own internal divisions and an incipient leftist revolution, military officers felt they had little choice but to accept democratization and the extension of civilian authority over the armed forces.

However, only by taking advantage of this temporary military weakness could Betancourt have created the means to preserve civilian authority over the military in the long run. Betancourt, due to his experiences in government from 1945 to 1948 and in his decade of exile, readily understood that civilian control was crucial for the survival of Venezuelan democracy and that it had to implemented and defended from the very beginning of his administration. Otherwise, democratizers might miss their brief window of opportunity to establish durable barriers to military intervention. This assessment was particularly perceptive: by the time of the Leoni administration, civilian consensus on democratization had declined, while the armed forces were already beginning to recuperate their original institutional cohesiveness. By acting strategically during his administration, Betancourt created and enforced military obedience to many of the mechanisms for civilian supervision of the armed forces. His harsh, often cold-blooded, sanctioning strategy against any opposition made it clear to any dissident military officer that the only alternatives were to resist and end his career, or to endure and remain a member of the armed forces.

Betancourt and his successors successfully pursued a potentially controversial "divide and conquer" strategy against the armed forces. They went beyond the original cleavages inherited from Pérez Jiménez and created new sources of internal division. In effect, the civilian metastrategy was one of encouraging the growth of multiple cross-cutting schisms in the military. The new institutions divided the services against each other, junior and senior officers among themselves, those who were educated overseas from those who remained behind, those who participated in the counterinsurgency war against officers who remained in Caracas, those who believed in democracy or who affiliated themselves with civilian politicians against those who disdained everything associated with the new regime. These multiple loyalties made it difficult for any political entrepreneur within the armed forces to gather together sufficient forces to carry out a successful coup d'état without meeting opposition from others in the armed forces. Officers who benefited from the new system had too much to risk from the collapse of democracy, and every incentive to ensure that the civilian-led regime survived.

In effect, civilian control over the armed forces endured precisely because, even though the military as an institution lost autonomy and privileges, the officer corps gained immensely in terms of the attractiveness, stability, and professional satisfaction inherent in pursuing their careers. Changes in education and social standing, the improved status of junior services such as the air force, navy, and Guardia Nacional, and the need for senior officers to cater to civilian instructions in order to ensure their uninterrupted ascent through the ranks created an assortment of new interests and career paths in the armed forces. Officers who played by the new rules of the civil-military game enjoyed the support of civilians and rapid progress in their careers, while those who resented civilian control and abhorred party politics found themselves facing a dead end. Furthermore, in comparison with the mixed prospects that military officers had faced under Pérez Jiménez, the benefits and professional opportunities associated with democracy shone even brighter. These advantages, and the new interests they engendered, guaranteed that democratization and civilian control of the armed forces would endure in Venezuela.

The ultimate measure of the consolidation of civilian authority can be found in the degree to which the officer corps accepted the right of a civilian president to set military policy, even against their own wishes, by ending the counterinsurgency war in 1969. Even though COPEI as a party had no experience in administering the armed forces, and President Caldera had no personal ties to the armed forces, he was able to successfully order the implementation of an unpopular policy and force the military to accept amnesty and renewed participation by its former enemies in the political process. In contrast with Betancourt's presidency and its eleven attempts to remove him from office, the relatively timely obedience to Caldera's orders indicates that Venezuelan democracy had consolidated a remarkable degree of civilian authority over its armed forces.

Given the relative power of democratizers over the armed forces in the Venezuelan case, politicians were criticized for relying on excessively personalized methods to monitor and supervise the military, instead of implementing a more objective and professional approach toward civilian control. During the democratic period, officers continued to resent the perceived influence of politics in promotions, the relatively short thirty-year career path, and the decentralized and awkward command structure of the armed forces. Compared to the panoply of mechanisms associated with civilian control by oversight, which relies on civilian defense experts, informed legislative oversight, and broad civilian participation in administering the armed forces, Venezuelan mechanisms of civilian control seem unwieldy and inefficient. Civilian control in Venezuela functioned only because it was centralized in the person of the president, and because it relied on mutual monitoring among the services and cross-cutting cleavages within the officer corps to provide internal counterbalancing and early warnings of potential trouble.

However, as in many emerging democracies today, Venezuelan democratizers lacked the knowledge, resources, and expertise in military affairs required to implement in 1958 the model of civilian control pursued in advanced industrial democracies during the last fifty years. In other words, Venezuela had no regime capacity in 1958, and democratizers inhibited its development by choosing civilian control by containment. Given the absence of regime capacity in defense matters during the period of democratic consolidation in 1958, it is difficult to imagine that Betancourt and his colleagues could have successfully created an effective civilian Ministry of Defense and a competent armed services committee and staff in Congress, let alone depend on external monitors, such as think tanks and newspapers, to provide them with the necessary information to supervise the armed forces. However, evidence from post-Franco Spain and Argentina after 1983 suggests that regime capacity can emerge as an outcome of the transition and consolidation process if the right leadership and institutional resources are made available.

In the early 1960s Venezuelan politicians did not provide the leadership, institutions, or human resources that would have led to a high degree of regime capacity because they had neither the training, nor the interest, nor any electoral incentives to achieve it. Betancourt (and, to a lesser extent, his successors) developed any necessary expertise on military issues personally. They found it much simpler and less risky to centralize civilian control in the presidency, playing the role of prime adjudicator in a decentralized and competitive security establishment. This created a system in which the armed forces enjoyed wide latitude in their professional affairs, yet were strictly circumscribed by presidential oversight as to their political roles and participation in state activities.

This lack of regime capacity meant that democratizers could only institutionalize strategies that required low levels of civilian expertise or attention to function: "divide and conquer" and appeasement. It is important to realize that these strategies only require military capacity (counterbalancing forces) and budgetary resources, both of which were available in Venezuela, but no civilian-led defense institutions or civilian defense professionals. While civilian control by containment placed barriers to the expansion of military jurisdictional boundaries, it did not provide any institutional channels for civilian oversight of the armed forces. As we will see in the next chapter, though Venezuelan civilian control was effective for three decades, it was highly dysfunctional as well. Politicians increasingly relied on illegitimate means to control important internal functions of the armed forces, particularly promotions and assignments. This created perverse new cleavages within the officer corps between politically favored cliques of officers and a resentful majority, which also created the potential for rebellion. As the distributive and consensus-building mechanisms of Venezuelan democracy began to break down in the late 1980s, new opportunities arose for military political entrepreneurs to organize disaffected officers and challenge civilian rule.

CHAPTER 5

■

CIVILIAN CONTROL UNDER FIRE

Resisting Challenges from

the Military in Venezuela, 1992

On the evening of 3 February 1992, army troops led by members of an elite parachute regiment attempted to take control of the government of Venezuela. In Caracas, soldiers under the command of Lieutenant Colonel Hugo Chávez Frias attacked the presidential residence of La Casona, the seat of government at Miraflores palace, the Generalísimo Francisco Miranda air base, and the military headquarters at the Fuerte Tiuna army barracks. Army troops in Venezuela's four other major cities took complete or partial control of vital government and economic installations. Despite achieving most of their operational goals, these rebellious officers failed to overthrow the administration of Carlos Andrés Pérez.

President Pérez, returning from Davos, Switzerland, was met at the airport by his minister of defense, General Fernando Ochoa Antich, and warned of the imminent coup attempt. When paratroopers attacked the presidential residence later in the evening, military officers who were assigned to protect the president successfully held off the rebels, allowing Pérez to escape to a local television station. Initially defended only by the station's security guards and his own civilian escort, Pérez addressed the nation, calling on the rebels to surrender. Paralyzed by indecision and communication failures, the rebellious military officers failed to pursue the president or to terminate his television broadcasts. At President Pérez's direction, General Ochoa Antich then ordered elements of the Third Infantry Brigade, located in Caracas, to attack rebel units at the air base and the presidential palace at Miraflores. Loyal military units accomplished these objectives, and after negotiations, Lieutenant Colonel Chávez Frias agreed to lay down his arms. On the morning of 4 February, upon hearing Chávez's appeal for the end of hostilities, rebels in other cities surrendered as well (Machillanda Pinto 1993, 107–27).

For many who thought of Venezuela as a consolidated democracy, the 1992 coup attempt came as a complete surprise. However, to those who were familiar with the deterioration of its democratic regime, what was more surprising was that the coup did not succeed. Once President Pérez had adopted economic austerity measures in 1989, protests by workers, students, and retirees became a daily occurrence in Venezuela's major cities. During 1991, Venezuela experienced 2,500 labor strikes and demonstrations; 925 large-scale demonstrations, over half of which ended violently, took place between August 1991 and 4 February 1992 (Daniels 1992, 171). While the economy experienced strong growth in 1990 and 1991, it did so amid increasing income inequality and declining real wages (Zambrano Sequín 1995, 100–105). Legislators, including many from the administration's own political party, attacked the neoliberal structural adjustment package. Criticism became particularly severe as thirty-five years of populist and clientalistic government programs were rolled back, directly undermining entrenched party interests (Gil Yepes 1992, 343–60). Within the armed forces, military salaries and benefits declined markedly in real terms. In 1983 a Venezuelan colonel earned the equivalent of a salary of $4,000 per month; in February 1992 he earned barely more than $400 (Tarre Briceño 1994a, 146–54). Even more infuriating to many officers were the rumors and allegations of government corruption and improprieties. Prior to the coup attempt, the approval rating of President Pérez had reached record lows (Romero 1995, 6–11). Under these conditions of extreme political and economic turmoil, a coup d'état should have succeeded.

After February 1992, attempts by military officers to displace civilian rule made no headway despite worsening economic and political conditions. A second, haphazard coup attempt in November 1992 was put down even more rapidly, and at a greater cost in lives, than the one in February. Venezuela experienced no further overt military unrest until April 2002. The return of stability to the military front came in spite of a steady recession, high inflation, a dramatic devaluation of the currency, continuing popular unrest, the deterioration of government services, and the near-collapse of the financial sector (Bottome 1994; Buxton 2003). The problems faced by the armed forces continued, while officers' salaries and benefits struggled to keep pace with inflation. Politically, the country experienced the impeachment of President Pérez, a brief interim administration, and the election of a former president, Rafael Caldera, on the ticket of the new, hastily organized Convergencia party in 1993.

The Puzzles of Venezuelan Democracy

Venezuelan democracy in 1992 presents several puzzles. If Venezuela had been a consolidated democracy before the 1990s, what changes occurred in the regime and its armed forces to create the conditions for a coup attempt? If we instead accept that its democracy had become deconsolidated by 1992, why did the coup attempts fail? Given worsening political, social, and economic conditions since then, why did the military not intervene in politics again during the 1990s?

The 1992 failed coup attempts and the election of the coup leader, Hugo Chávez, in 1998 have forced a wholesale reexamination of Venezuela's democracy, and the emerging consensus regarding the regime is unfavorable. The decreasing governability of Venezuelan society lies at the heart of one group of politics-centered explanations for this crisis. These scholars argue that the instability of the 1990s stemmed from the inability of the traditional party system to effectively integrate alternative organizations that have arisen in both in politics and civil society in response to declining living standards and government services. In a period of increasing scarcity and declining state capacity, traditional political forces were unable to either satisfy or discipline the rising number of independent social and political actors making demands on the system, leading to regime instability (Levine and Crisp 1995). Moreover, the traditional political parties had become informally privatized, ideologically indistinguishable, and deeply corrupt. Thus, they were not able to effectively aggregate interests or manage conflict during this period of economic and political transition (Martz 1995).

Venezuela's political economy also provides an account for the breakdown of democracy, in so far as oil rents have created dysfunctional incentives that have paralyzed the system. From this perspective, the crisis in Venezuela was the inevitable result, first, of an overexpansion of the state during the oil boom of the 1970s, followed by declining oil income. This decline steadily undermined the state's ability to maintain a political model that was dependent on simultaneously satisfying the interests of political parties, labor, capital, civil society, and the armed forces. Efforts to stave off the decline during the 1980s through government controls on the economy further warped incentives and production, which made structural adjustment and economic liberalization programs particularly difficult for the political system to accept during the 1990s and thus paved the way for a populist outsider, Hugo Chávez (Naím and Piñango 1989; Buxton 2003).

Another recent perspective examines the dysfunctional aspects of the political institutions that supported civilian rule in Venezuela prior to 1998, focusing on the role of political parties, social actors, and state institutions in inhibiting economic and political reforms (Coppedge 1994; Crisp 2000). Michael Coppedge argues that Venezuela constituted a "partyarchy," in which the same mechanisms that supported political consensus between the main parties, AD and COPEI, also aided and abetted impunity, corruption, and political paralysis. The Pérez administration's economic program in 1989 challenged the basis of "partyarchy" by aiming to reduce the role of the state in Venezuelan society. In a political system so completely centered and dependent on the state, the result was an inevitable backlash by those sectors most closely tied to the traditional system, including the armed forces (Coppedge 1994). Steve Ellner and Daniel Hellinger have argued that the ability to conduct reforms during the 1990s was a sign of resilience in the system, although it was not sufficient to stave off the deterioration of the party system and growing social polarization (Ellner 2003, 12–23; Hellinger 2003, 35–45). However, given that the economic and civil-military underpinnings of the crisis had been present for years before the 1992 coup attempts, and continue to be present today, this begs the question: why did the military intervene occur when they did, and why did the democratic regime survive?

I argue that the Venezuelan system of civilian control of the armed forces, particularly those institutions based on "divide and conquer" strategies, prevented the collapse of the democratic regime in 1992, but only by a small margin. Explanations based on political economy and political crafting both agree that the crisis led to the breakdown of consensus-driven politics in Venezuela and brought the legitimacy of the democratic regime into question. This crisis created an opening that, in most developing countries, would have drawn the armed forces into politics and led to a coup d'état. I argue that in Venezuela, institutions of civilian control that were developed in the wake of the 1958 transition to democracy created such a large number of cross-cutting cleavages within the armed forces that successful military intervention in politics became nearly impossible. The system worked so well during the 1970s and 1980s that civilians largely abandoned even the minimal supervision they had once exercised over the military. The crisis of Venezuela's development model simultaneously undermined the effectiveness of some of the institutionalized mechanisms for appeasing the armed forces even as civilians increasingly expanded the jurisdictional boundaries of the armed forces into internal security duties. Moreover, institutional developments in the officer corps created a generation of officers with a populist, statist, and nationalist orientation, who were well suited to the political model that sustained democracy for three decades but particularly hostile to the political changes introduced by the Pérez administration. Inattention among senior civilian and military personnel allowed conspiracies to develop unchecked in the junior officer corps, which resulted in the surprise coup attempts of 1992. However, the barriers to intramilitary cooperation created by institutionalized civilian control in Venezuela prevented these military rebellions from succeeding, even in the face of the political weakness of the Pérez administration.

Change and Continuity in Civilian Control
of the Armed Forces, 1973–1989

Venezuela had consolidated control by containment of the armed forces by 1970. The internal divisions and the satisfaction of the officer corps with their professional and personal opportunities inhibited conspiracies and reconciled the armed forces to civilian rule. By institutionalizing strategies of "divide and conquer" and appeasement, civilian rulers felt confident that the threat of military intervention was fully contained, and beginning with the election of Carlos Andrés Pérez in 1974, civilian presidents considerably reduced the amount of attention they dedicated to supervising military affairs. In the absence of any other mechanisms for direct civilian supervision, the armed forces were allowed to freely develop and pursue their own bureaucratic reforms and defense policies. However, several of these policies, adopted for the purpose of enhancing their professional standing and capacity, had unintended consequences that weakened the long-term integrity of the boundaries that separated civilian and military authority.

Under the boundaries that had consolidated by 1973, the armed forces retained a high degree of autonomy within the relatively narrow area of state policy they controlled. In the arena of external defense, the military operated with little civilian oversight, maintaining bureaucratic autonomy and a free hand in the areas of training, organization, and planning. With the end of the counterinsurgency operations against the Cuban-backed PCV/MIR guerrillas in 1973, the armed forces withdrew from direct responsibility over internal security, yet they retained a strong emergency role in responding to civil disturbances and riots. Only the Guardia Nacional continued to participate directly in internal security functions, principally in border control and the protection of state property (Néry Arrieta 1992). Some Guardia Nacional officers were also to command major metropolitan police forces. The armed forces were excluded from any significant role in public policy or leadership selection.

THE UNINTENDED CONSEQUENCES OF THE
MILITARY'S SEARCH FOR A MISSION

After withdrawing from the counterinsurgency mission they had performed during the 1960s, some military officers began to search for a new role for the armed forces in society. Rather than focus on the seemingly theoretical task of external defense, the military sought to become involved in Venezuela's development, drawn by the seemingly limitless possibilities generated by the oil boom of the 1970s. These officers took the initiative and, acting as policy entrepreneurs, carried out significant reforms in the educational system, mission, and governing legislation of the armed forces. While civilian politicians enacted the formal legislation that permitted these reforms, they undermined them in practice, which prevented a substantial de facto expansion in military jurisdiction. Nevertheless, the reforms subtly altered the attitudes of military officers toward democracy, development, and the political system. Many officers overlooked the contradictions between their actual and potential role in society so long as increasing defense budgets made possible larger outlays for salaries, benefits, and military procurement. However, the military reforms of the 1970s had unintended consequences: they created a new generation of Venezuelan officers with a populist, equity-driven, and utilitarian view of democracy and a latent capacity for political activism.

Beginning in the 1970s, the Venezuelan armed forces experienced a generational break within the military hierarchy, as educational reforms in the national military academies produced a new generation of elite, highly trained junior officers with a strong sense of leadership, élan, and nationalism (Tarre Briceño 1994a). Under the army's Andrés Bello plan, Venezuela's Academia Militar was transformed into a university-equivalent institution, graduating its first classes at this level in 1974 (Bigler 1981, 95–97; Müller

Rojas 1995). Implemented under General Jorge Osorio García, who was commandant of the Academia Militar for an unprecedented five-year period, this plan was designed to emphasize leadership training in the new classes of cadets. Not only were the professional aspects of military education reemphasized, but the program aimed to inculcate a mystique of honor, discipline, and self-sacrifice, emphasizing the elite training and role of this new generation of officers. As Gustavo Tarre Briceño argues, this new educational model tended to produce in cadets the mentality of a "soldier-monk" (Tarre Briceño 1994a, 143–46).

The Plan Andrés Bello produced generations of cadets who shared a fervent nationalism, an attachment to the teachings of Venezuelan independence hero Simón Bolívar, and a populist, egalitarian, and ultimately utilitarian perspective toward democracy. Little attention was given to political, economic, or social issues in the new curriculum, and history was taught in a manner that romanticized the wars for independence and the writings of Simón Bolívar. Cadet education continued to emphasize the democratic orientation of the armed forces, but confusion abounded over what democracy was supposed to be and what it was supposed to accomplish, particularly in the areas of equity and development. Out of one hundred classes listed in the 1990 curriculum, there was one class on Venezuelan history, one class on the geography and economy of Venezuela, one class on the political thought of Simón Bolívar, one on philosophy, and one on political doctrines. By contrast, there were three classes on the control of civil disturbances and seven on military law. (Plan Andrés Bello 1990, 12, 43–44). Confronted with the uncertainties and disorder of the Venezuelan political process, which seemed to place party interests ahead of national interests, it is not surprising that most young officers developed a greater attachment to Venezuela's glorious past instead of its inglorious present (Romero 1994; García Villasmil 1995a).

The effect of this curricular reform was to create a new group of young professional officers who saw themselves as morally superior to civilian politicians. They also saw themselves as better soldiers than their own commanders, many of whom had emerged from the Academia Militar with many fewer years of training due to the demands placed on the armed forces during 1960s counterinsurgency conflict. The training and education at the reformed Academia Militar led these young officers to contrast the democratic ideals they had been taught with their perceptions of the dismal democratic practices in Venezuela. Since the democratic regime could not deliver equity, justice, and development as constituted, it became suspect (Tarre Briceño 1994c).

The second educational reform of this period created the Instituto de Altos Estudios de la Defensa Nacional (IAEDN, the Superior Institute for the Study of National Defense), which became the center for the introduction of national security doctrine (NSD) to Venezuela (Manrique 1996, 64–75). The IAEDN, which was patterned on the Inter-American Defense College in Washington, D.C., reinstituted the joint training of military officers and civilians at the highest levels of government and the armed forces. IAEDN doctrine emphasized the links between development and security and the necessity of adapting Venezuela's short-term political goals with its long-term goals of economic development (Celis Noguera 1994). In adapting NSD to a democratic regime, the IAEDN encouraged a populist, equity-oriented vision of development that was well matched to the country's political discourse during the oil boom of the 1970s (Celis Noguera 1994). This focus on development legitimized the armed forces' push for greater participation in infrastructure, state-sponsored industrialization, and colonization of frontier regions. The link between IAEDN and NSD became increasingly important as the armed forces began to lobby in the 1970s for new defense legislation to legitimate their growing participation in economic development projects (Irwin G. 2000, 133–34). These efforts coalesced in the Ley Orgánica de Seguridad y Defensa (LOSD), which passed after much debate by the Venezuelan Congress on 18 August 1976. The LOSD established a formal link between security and development, and it placed frontier regions under the supervision of the Ministry of Defense (Yépez Daza 1980, 116).

Venezuela's new NSD had the potential to dramatically expand the jurisdictional boundaries of the Venezuelan military, but these desires were frustrated by civilian politicians who ensured that all military participation in development planning was confined to ritualistic and formal exercises. "Democratic" NSD became the dominant paradigm in key planning institutions of the armed forces and in the upper echelons of the officer corps, but it never acquired a significant following among civilian government officials (Manrique 1996, 155–58, 178; Müller Rojas 1995). The LOSD fostered among military officers a state-led vision of development, concern for social equity, and a broad definition of security, even as civilian politicians denied the armed forces the institutional channels through which they could carry out their new mission (Machillanda Pinto 1988, 56–57, 175–79).

Frustrated in their efforts to redefine their mission, the Venezuelan officer corps increasingly lost their professional focus and concentrated instead
on the internal power struggles for resources, promotions, and assignments.
By the mid-1970s, the center of gravity in civil-military relations had shifted
to budgetary concerns. The dramatic expansion of government revenues in
the wake of the first and second oil crises had led to the near doubling of
Venezuela's defense budget in the decade between 1967 and 1977.

This augmented allocation was reflected in the salaries and benefits of
military officers and in the equipment procured for the armed forces. Venezuela spent a high proportion of its military budget on salaries and benefits and had the highest per soldier defense expenditure in Latin America
for much of the 1970s. As early as 1963, military salaries had become almost
equivalent to those of their U.S. counterparts at all ranks, and this trend
continued throughout the 1970s, despite rising inflation. The lowest-ranking
officer, a second lieutenant, earned the same salary as a recently graduated engineer from a Venezuelan civilian university. Educational opportunities overseas also expanded rapidly during this same time period, leading
many officers to seek advanced training in the United States and Europe
(Soto Urrútia 1994b; Machillanda Pinto 1997). When health, recreation, and
housing benefits were included, Venezuelan military officers were among the
best compensated in the Western Hemisphere and enjoyed a quality of life
second only to that of U.S. and Canadian officers during this period (Bigler 1981, 102–5, 117–19). The comparative figures presented in table 5.1 illustrate exactly how generous military spending was during this period. Only
Argentina came close to matching Venezuela's military spending, exceeding it only in the late 1970s as Argentina prepared for war against Chile and
Great Britain (U.S. Arms Control and Disarmament Agency 1984).

Not all of this government spending went to salaries and benefits, however, as Venezuela also rearmed during this period, converting the military
from its counterinsurgency orientation to that of external defense. Venezuela's traditional regional rival was Colombia, and illegal immigration,
drug smuggling, and Colombia's left-wing insurgency remained perennial
irritants to the two nations' relationship. Venezuela and Colombia also had
several substantial border disputes, on which most Venezuelan officers took
a hard-line attitude, opposing any concessions. Venezuela also claimed sovereignty over a large portion of the territory of its neighbor Guyana, which
created another potential area for international conflict. Furthermore, as

Table 5.1. Comparative Government Expenditures per Soldier, 1972–1981

	EXPENDITURE PER SOLDIER				
Year	Venezuela	Argentina	Brazil	Colombia	Peru
1972	$31,985	$17,183	$8,270	$9,054	$9,950
1973	29,660	16,742	8,928	9,117	11,885
1974	32,252	20,669	8,419	8,180	10,130
1975	31,874	25,124	7,702	10,178	12,916
1976	30,796	28,835	9,075	6,947	14,347
1977	32,811	31,564	7,812	5,698	16,785
1978	31,520	34,052	7,344	6,218	12,564
1979	25,346	33,085	6,730	8,690	8,017
1980	24,211	30,164	6,813	9,990	11,237
1981	30,050	32,088	6,373	8,790	10,201

Source: U.S. Arms Control and Disarmament Agency 1984.
Note: All figures adjusted to 1994 constant U.S. dollars.

Venezuela experienced an oil boom in the 1970s, the armed forces became increasingly concerned with protecting the shipping routes of Venezuelan oil. These various threats were used to justify major rearmament, and the oil boom provided the revenues with which to carry the program out. The new equipment meshed well with the growing professional sensibilities of many Venezuelan officers and prepared them for their theoretical primary mission of preparing to fight an external war. However, this external defense role was never quite satisfying to some in the officer corps. They viewed international conflict as an unlikely prospect, while they saw internal development as a more immediate and important mission.

An unintended consequence of rearmament, and of the oil boom in general, was the growth in corruption and malfeasance among senior military officers and civilian politicians. In particular, some officers became disgusted by the waste, fraud, and corruption that were associated with government defense contracts. High-level government officials, military procurement officers, and well-placed civilian intermediaries enriched themselves with overpriced defense purchases and suspiciously large commissions (Capriles Méndez 1990; Capriles Ayala 1992). Acquisitions were made with little attention to the compatibility of new military equipment with the existing arsenal or to the suitability of its use in a Venezuelan context (Machillanda Pinto 1995; Müller Rojas 1995).

Venezuela's activist foreign policy during this period, which included financial and military support for Eden Pastora's southern front during the revolution against Nicaraguan dictator Anastasio Somoza in 1979 and for the Christian Democratic government in El Salvador during the early 1980s, provided an additional source of illicit enrichment for civilians and military officers (Belmonte 1994).[1] The anger these practices generated among officers, particularly at the junior level, became an ongoing source of tension within the armed forces and deepened the divisions between the generals and admirals and the new generations of idealistic officers emanating from the national military academies. Moreover, the inability of the government to control corruption began to raise doubts among some officers about the legitimacy of the democratic regime.

Military autonomy, already high due to the absence of civilian interest in security issues, shielded growing corruption from public scrutiny, and it was compounded by legal provisions that protected military budgets and operations from civilian supervision. Congress approved overall defense expenditures by the four services, but it provided no oversight of how the money was spent, and it did not participate in the preparation of detailed military budgets. Even though Congress debated major weapons purchases, such as the 1983 acquisition of U.S.-made F-16 fighter jets, no substantial move was made to modify or block any major decisions in this area. No member of either the Senate or Chamber of Deputies defense committees had (or has) any experience in military affairs (Müller Rojas 1995). Furthermore, rather than falling under the oversight of a civilian inspector general or Congress, the armed forces had their own auditor who reported directly to the president. Sometimes, even the minister of defense did not know how his service chiefs spent their budgets. This allowed military leaders to make decisions, particularly in the area of external defense, with little input from civilian government officials. Secrecy laws prevented the publication of detailed defense expenditures or a thorough discussion of defense policies in the media. As a result, civilian investigation of corruption scandals was discouraged, and the armed forces urged the prosecution of journalists who overstepped these boundaries. Budgetary autonomy and military secrecy laws thus created formidable barriers to civilian participation in defense matters and compounded the ability of the armed forces to act unchecked in the field of external defense (Agüero 1995a, 150–51).

Although military autonomy excluded the participation of civil society in defense matters, politicians soon found ways around this barrier by influencing the promotions process. Particularly at the level of colonel and general, the need for congressional and presidential approval for any promotion created opportunities for political manipulation. While the overall number of promotions affected were small (García Villasmil 1995c), many senior officers felt the need to align themselves informally with one of the two principal parties (AD and COPEI) to protect their careers (Soto Urrútia 1994a). Luis Herrera Campíns, president from 1979 to 1983, confirmed this inclination when he once commented that generals should be appointed on the basis of trust rather than merit (Quiróz Corradi 1992). Moreover, the thirty-year limit on military careers, together with the policy of yearly rotations of officers among different positions and commands, created fierce competition over choice assignments, which well-connected officers could resolve in their favor (Yépez Daza 1995). The requirement for civilian approval of promotions also created a mechanism by which senior military officers practiced self-regulation to avoid offending civilian politicians, which provided the government with a means of controlling the armed forces at very low cost in resources and civilian expertise. Together, civilian oversight of promotions created incentives for ambitious officers and politicians to form insider networks for their mutual advantage, to the detriment of merit and efficiency in the military hierarchy.

The politicization of promotions and assignments was particularly galling to junior officers who were held to strict ethical and professional standards during their careers. Career assignments were made on a competitive basis at lower ranks, based principally on the educational achievements of individual officers (García Villasmil 1995c). Young officers' conduct and their ethical handling of professional and personal duties weighed heavily in the process as well. Upper-level promotion on the basis of political preference instead of merit led young officers, who had recently emerged from the Academia Militar and who were therefore most strongly indoctrinated in professional standards, to lose respect for their military superiors and civilian politicians. Politicization in the military promotion process allowed civilians to overcome institutional autonomy on important issues, but it also increasingly split the civilian and military elite from the junior officer corps (Agüero 1995a, 149).

THE DECONSOLIDATION OF CIVILIAN
CONTROL IN VENEZUELA

By the 1980s, civil-military relations had settled into a stable if somewhat dysfunctional pattern in Venezuela (fig. 5.1). The armed forces' jurisdictional boundaries were restricted to the area of external defense. Even though the armed forces preserved their role in maintaining public order after the conclusion of counterinsurgency warfare in the early 1970s, this role was principally carried out by the Guardia Nacional, a militarized national police, which was viewed with suspicion by other services, particularly the army. Having largely withdrawn from their traditional internal security mission, the armed forces were never really satisfied with their external defense mission. In a country that had not experienced a major war for 150 years, and where political power and energies were focused on economic development, external defense seemed to be a backwater. This mission must have seemed especially stifling to the eager, nationalistic, highly trained officers produced by Venezuelan military academies during this period. When civilians blocked the operationalization of the military's new development mission, the armed forces were left with an unclear and unsatisfying role in society.

So long as institutions based on strategies of appeasement and "divide and conquer" operated, open discontent in the military was avoided, and the armed forces remained confined to their narrow jurisdictional boundaries. Generous benefits, access to higher education, and new weapons systems allowed professionally oriented officers to practice their craft, while the more politicized within the officer corps could happily supplement their income through deals with foreign manufacturers and civilian intermediaries. Institutionalized practices of "divide and conquer" continued to prevent the concentration of authority in the hands of any particular officer throughout the 1970s and 1980s, and they focused military energies on internal armed forces rivalries. The two strategies operated to make it nearly impossible for a critical mass of discontented officers to form or act coherently against the political system. The institutions of civilian control were not particularly efficient, yet they preserved a substantial degree of regime leverage over defense matters, when and if the president chose to exercise it (Soto Urrútia 1994a).

Nevertheless, confusion over the military's mission, civilian inattention to defense issues, growing civilian and military corruption, and the politicization of the armed forces created a latent potential for a break between

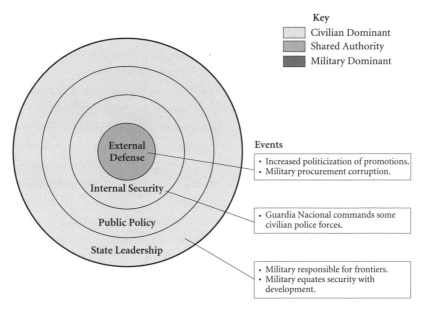

Figure 5.1. Civil-Military Jurisdictional Boundaries, ca. 1988: Increased Politicization of Armed Forces Reduces Their Autonomy

the armed forces and the civilian regime. The Venezuelan armed forces' high degree of autonomy also meant that the growing alienation of many officers went undetected by the civilian government. While Venezuelan institutions of civilian control were useful for restricting the armed forces to narrow jurisdictional boundaries, they provided no institutional channels for monitoring the internal condition of the armed forces. Politicians had become complacent, confident that they could rely on their informal connections with the military high command to maintain supervision over the armed forces. The growing distance between the generals and admirals and their subordinates undermined this means of detecting military unrest. In other words, the "fire alarms" that had traditionally alerted civilians to military unrest following the transition to democracy in 1958 had deteriorated badly during the 1970s and 1980s. As a result, when antigovernment military conspiracies finally began to develop after 1983, the government was caught mostly off guard.

Why Did the 1992 Coups Occur?

The coup attempt of 4 February 1992 caught most people by surprise precisely because the thought of military intervention had become unthinkable after three decades of civilian rule. Despite rising civilian unrest and broad political opposition to the structural adjustment program implemented by President Pérez, no observer seriously considered that the political and economic crisis in Venezuela would be resolved through military means. However, this very crisis of Venezuela's development model had undermined important institutions of civilian control over the armed forces, particularly those concerned with appeasement. The highly autonomous status of the armed forces allowed the development of peculiar factions among junior officers that were vehemently opposed to the Venezuelan political system. Furthermore, the particular policies of the Pérez administration in economic, defense, and foreign policy angered many officers and predisposed them to join these new antigovernment factions within the armed forces. While senior officers continued to firmly support the political regime, they had become so engaged in the internal politics of budgets, promotions, assignments, and corruption that they had lost touch with the rest of the officer corps. In this environment, it was possible for a small group of conspirators to organize a coup d'état relatively unchecked.

SETTING THE STAGE: POLITICAL DECLINE,

ECONOMIC AUSTERITY, AND THE BREAKDOWN

OF CONSENSUAL POLITICS IN VENEZUELA

In the wake of the crisis of the early 1990s, a number of diagnoses for the failures of Venezuela's political system have appeared that share a central theme: political dysfunction. As far back as 1986, Terry Karl argued that the same mechanisms that had allowed democratic consolidation by producing political consensus and reducing conflict during the 1960s had led to a frozen democracy in Venezuela (Karl 1986). Michael Coppedge took these arguments several steps further by documenting the manner in which Venezuela's consensual political system, much admired during the 1960s and 1970s, had become dysfunctional and self-sabotaging. A political duopoly dominated by AD and COPEI shared power and excluded new actors, creating what Coppedge termed a "partyarchy." New generations of political leaders in the principal parties politicized all issues and all actors in civil society, which deprived the political process of flexibility and creativity.

They also demanded strict adherence to party discipline, which stifled all innovation within the two dominant parties. The failures of the political system were linked to Venezuela's economic failures (Coppedge 1994).

When the international price of oil began its steady fall, the Venezuelan political economy, which was based on the maintenance of political stability through state redistribution of oil revenues, was no longer sustainable. During the 1970s, the Venezuelan government had spent unprecedented amounts of money to achieve rapid development, spurred by the exponential expansion of state revenues during the oil booms and reckless foreign borrowing. The government spent without any regard for the limits and bottlenecks imposed by the Venezuela's underdevelopment, and corruption and waste mushroomed.

The sharp drop in international oil prices that began in 1982 deprived the government of the revenues to finance this profligacy, yet Venezuelan elites were unwilling to take the politically painful steps needed to remedy the crisis. Instead, they unsuccessfully attempted to defer reforms in the hopes of experiencing another oil boom. By 1984, capital flight, payments on the foreign debt, and rising imports driven by an artificially strong currency had drained international reserves sufficiently that the Venezuelan government was forced to implement a currency devaluation and a multitiered exchange control system to avoid disaster (Gil Yepes 1992, 338–40). The foreign debt climbed past $33 billion, over 80 percent of which was owed by the state (McCoy and Smith 1995, 124–25). To hold down rising prices, the government reinforced existing price controls, but these failed to dampen inflation and led to shortages in the supplies of many staples. Under the impact of foreign exchange controls, inflation, declining productivity, and negative interest rates, the GDP shrank by 25 percent, and personal incomes were reduced by 15 percent between 1978 and 1985 (Naím 1993, 24–27).

Inequality between rich and poor grew rapidly during this time period, erasing many of the gains made during the 1970s, as the number of people living in critical poverty (defined as those who could afford less than half the basic level of goods and services) expanded from 32.6 percent at the beginning of the 1980s to 53.7 percent in 1989. The crisis was compounded by election-driven spending in 1988, which helped the economy to grow by 5 percent yet was financed by government deficits reaching 9.4 percent of the GDP in 1988 (Naím 1993, 28). Even though Venezuelans by the end of 1988 felt hopeful that the economic crisis had been overcome, the bizarre machinations of their political leaders were no longer economically sustainable. When President Jaime Lusinchi handed over power in 1989 to Carlos Andrés Pérez, he had the highest popularity rating of any outgoing president in Venezuela's democratic history despite his having deepened the economic crisis.

In the face of new indications of the intensifying economic crisis in January 1989, Carlos Andrés Pérez imposed an abrupt and unexpected change in economic policy upon assuming office. He had been elected on a traditional populist platform, promising a return to the "golden" economic conditions of his first presidency (1974–79) that had been generated by the oil boom of the 1970s. Instead, with foreign reserves nearly exhausted, Pérez adopted a radical neoliberal structural adjustment plan, and he staffed his ministerial cabinet with several young technocrats charged with implementing his "Grán Viraje" (the Great Turnabout). This adjustment involved simultaneously eliminating price and currency controls, raising interest rates, reducing tariffs, and beginning a process of privatizing state industries and deregulating the economy. The result was that in 1989 alone, the rate of inflation surged to 80 percent, GDP declined by 10 percent, and personal income dropped 14 percent (Naím 1993, 59–60).

These results of the "Grán Viraje" shocked the population, which had been cushioned by years of populist policies from the harsh economic reality that Venezuela faced. Even though the low point of 1989 was followed by two years of strong economic growth, Pérez's policies led to widespread political discontent, which culminated in almost daily protests against the government. Entrepreneurs, labor unions, government employees, political activists, and the middle and lower classes all found something to dislike about the new economic policies (Rangel 1992; Weyland 2000, 10). Furthermore, the public was infuriated by its perception that government corruption continued unabated while the citizenry suffered the effects of a draconian economic policy. Targeted social benefits failed to reach the poor in a timely fashion, and existing social services collapsed, exacerbating the impact of the adjustment policy on those least able to afford it (Naím 1993, 80–93).

The structural adjustment package also shocked the "partyarchy," which was accustomed to corruption and impunity and which could not believe that the crisis was serious enough to justify abandoning three decades of consensual politics. Many criticized the privatization program as an attack on Venezuelan sovereignty and a recipe for mass unemployment. Privatization and government cutbacks also undercut cozy deals that had existed between the politically well connected and the state, which upset the political relationships that helped the "partyarchy" to maintain control. The rise in opposition both in the legislature and the public at large led to a growing sense of political crisis in the Pérez administration. Even the president's own party, Acción Democrática, turned against him. In national opinion polls taken at the end of 1991, President Pérez and Acción Democrática registered 12.3 percent approval ratings, their lowest ever (Burggraff and Millet 1995, 69). The rising levels of public animosity against the government and its policies undermined the consensual underpinnings of Venezuelan democracy and degraded the legitimacy of the Pérez administration, even as the armed forces were increasingly called on to sustain the regime against popular protests.

UNDERMINING CIVILIAN CONTROL: THE ROLE OF THE
CRISIS IN SHIFTING JURISDICTIONAL BOUNDARIES

The expansion of military jurisdictional boundaries into the arena of internal security occurred nearly simultaneously with the near collapse of the institutions of appeasement on which the civilian government had relied to control the armed forces (fig. 5.2). The increasing use of the armed forces in repressive duties at a time when the Pérez administration's policies and ethics were under attack led some officers to question the legitimacy of the civilian government. Furthermore, the rapid rise in living costs directly affected many junior officers, whose salaries and benefits had completely failed to keep up with inflation due to the budget constraints of the 1980s. Military opposition to the civilian government was aggravated by the perception that Pérez was personally corrupt, excessively concerned with foreign policy, and dovish in his management of relations with Venezuela's traditional rival, Colombia. Junior officers were increasingly hostile to their own military commanders, as new allegations of fraud and abuse in the armed forces high command surfaced. Coup plotters effectively exploited these issues to induce a number of junior officers to support the Movimiento Bolivariano Revolucionario 200 (MBR-200), a secret society within the army that had been quietly plotting for nearly a decade to overthrow Venezuelan democracy. The sense of crisis that followed Pérez's structural adjustment policies created an opportunity for the MBR-200 to take advantage of discontent in the officer corps and attempt a coup d'état.

One of the unintended consequences of President Pérez's economic austerity was to draw the Venezuelan military into internal security functions in the first weeks of his new government (Müller Rojas 1992, 35, 39–39, 48).

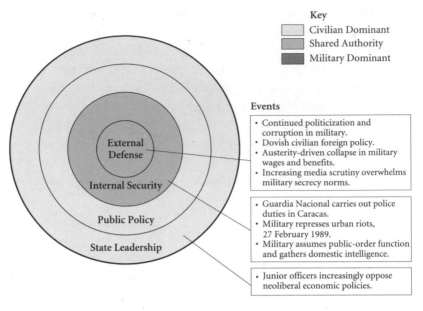

Figure 5.2. Civil-Military Jurisdictional Boundaries, ca. 1991: Armed Forces Drawn into Internal Security

A popular uprising on 27 February 1989 in Caracas shook public confidence in the newly inaugurated administration of Carlos Andrés Pérez. These riots were sparked by austerity measures, mishandled by the new government, that had increased the price of gasoline and transportation. Televised protests by commuters and bus burnings escalated into widespread looting. The police and intelligence services were caught by surprise, and only after a day of unchecked violence were the armed forces ordered to suppress popular unrest. The military reacted rapidly but was ill prepared to deal with large-scale internal security matters. Despite high casualties among civilians, estimated from 300 to 3,000 dead, popular approval for the military's actions was high, particularly within the middle class (Vivas 1994). The ad hoc nature of the army's deployment for riot control, the lack of appropriate equipment, and the ensuing level of civilian casualties were an indication of the extent to which the military had ceased preparing for an internal security role during the 1970s and 1980s.

In the aftermath of the 27 February riots, military commanders, with the support of the civilian government, increased their capacity to deal with public disorder through the purchase of new equipment. They also carried out widely publicized troop exercises that were designed to showcase the military's ability to deal with public disorder. Increasingly, the Guardia Nacional and, on occasion, the army were called on to deploy in force to oppose civil unrest and looting. Six hundred Guardia Nacional soldiers carried out daily police functions in Caracas by 1990, and senior army commanders publicly declared their willingness to suppress riots on short notice to prevent further looting and disorder. Public protests rose rapidly during late 1991 and early 1992, exceeding 900 major events in a seven-month period (Burggraff and Millet 1995, 61). Senior military commanders were principally concerned that the rising tide of lawlessness and public disorder would destabilize the political system and possibly provide an opening for marginalized subversive groups to act.

On the other hand, the employment of the army against the rioters on 27–28 February 1989 disgusted many of the junior officers and soldiers assigned to carry out this duty, leading them to question to value of a democratic system that relied on violence to maintain itself. Even though their branch of service was never as involved as the Guardia Nacional in controlling civil unrest, young army officers privately voiced their opposition to participating in riot suppression in the future (Otaiza 1994). In sum, the military's participation in the 27 February events highlighted the power and efficacy of the armed forces in the public mind, increased the reliance of the civilian government on the military for internal security, and undermined junior officers' confidence in both their superiors and the civilian government.

Structural adjustment measures enacted by Carlos Andrés Pérez exacerbated the steady decline in living standards among many military officers and thereby undermined a fundamental institutionalized strategy of civilian control, that of appeasement. The wages and benefits of military officers, like those of most Venezuelans, completely failed to keep up with the roaring inflation of 1989–90. The armed forces budget had peaked in 1982 at $1.15 billion and had declined steadily during the 1980s, even as the number of soldiers in the Venezuelan armed forces grew from 55,000 to 75,000 over the same period. The large apparent decline in spending seen in table 5.1 and table 5.2 can be explained by the sharp devaluation of the Venezuelan currency, the bolívar, after 1983. Thus, while defense budgets continued to rise in nominal bolívar terms, they declined drastically in real terms.

Government price controls and subsidies to consumers and producers had cushioned the effect of declining military real wages during the 1980s. When the Pérez administration liberated prices and opened the economy in

Table 5.2. Comparative Government Expenditures per Soldier, 1984–1994

	EXPENDITURE PER SOLDIER				
Year	Venezuela	Argentina	Brazil	Colombia	Peru
1984	$16,800	$58,200	$7,900	$8,300	$18,500
1985	13,250	57,200	7,750	9,900	22,100
1986	16,100	79,100	9,100	8,500	25,700
1987	12,300	48,400	10,200	8,200	21,600
1988	14,900	57,800	23,700	11,100	NA
1989	14,100	53,280	26,300	11,000	NA
1990	13,900	44,600	30,800	10,900	6,250
1991	29,000[a]	42,000	24,400	12,600	4,140
1992	20,700	71,800	19,300	9,100	6,650
1993	14,000	66,600	22,300	10,900	6,700
1994	10,000	68,300	32,800	8,200	7,120

Source: U.S. Arms Control and Disarmament Agency 1995.
Note: All figures adjusted to 1994 constant U.S. dollars.
[a] Data inflated by arms acquisitions, not personnel costs.

1989, consumer prices rapidly rose to market levels, and military households experienced a sharp decline in living standards in a very brief period, even though their real wages had been declining for seven years. As government employees, their salaries were even slower to adjust to the new economic realities than those of private sector employees, which caused an extended period of relative economic deprivation.

Suddenly, officers who had once been comfortably upper-middle class found themselves barely able to maintain lower-middle- and working-class living standards. Where even junior officers had once been able to afford housing, new cars, and vacations, their families now had to share apartments in poor neighborhoods under cramped conditions. Salaries that had once approximated those of military officers in advanced industrialized democracies were now insufficient to meet more than basic material needs. A 1991 IAEDN research paper by three senior air force and navy officers found that the salaries and benefits of military officers at all ranks were at least 35 percent below their 1984 incomes in real terms. Military medical and family services had become overburdened and underfunded. Most officers had traditionally sent their children to private schools, but now they could no longer afford to pay for them. In 1991 a lieutenant colonel who purchased the least expensive new sedan could expect to pay 40 percent of his monthly salary in car payments. The maximum subsidized loans available to officers, even the highest ranking, could account for only 10 to 20 percent of the cost of a small apartment in Caracas (Conde Casadiego, Machado Guzmán, and Quintero Torres 1991, 30–40). These disparities affected junior officers the most, and an increasing number abandoned their military careers for employment in the private sector. Furthermore, given that many officers had studied or traveled abroad, they could directly compare their declining socioeconomic status with that of their contemporaries in other countries. As table 5.2 shows, expenditures per soldier rose dramatically in some Latin American countries, particularly Argentina and Brazil, compared to Venezuela (Tarre Briceño 1994a, 149–54). The abrupt decline in living standards in less than a decade sharpened military discontent with democratic rule.

In the context of declining living standards, the growing corruption in military procurement among both civilian politicians and senior military officers simply infuriated many officers. Following a war scare involving Colombia in 1987, the Venezuelan armed forces rapidly increased spending on new weapons systems from 1988 through 1991, which created many new opportunities for official corruption. The Lusinchi and Pérez administrations approved the Plan Global de Adquisiciones (Global Acquisitions Plan), which reportedly included contracts for up to $3 billion, a number of which were suspect due to noncompetitive bidding and allegations of corruption. Some corruption cases were linked back to President Pérez's security chief, Orlando Garcia. Others resulted in arrest warrants being issued against six high-ranking, active-duty and retired admirals and generals in the summer of 1992. Increasingly, allegations of corruption were made by firms that had lost bids to provide services to the armed forces and hoped to use public outrage to force a reexamination of the contract awards process (Tarre Briceño 1994b). Improvements in press freedoms and higher levels of public criticism during the Pérez administration ensured that any corruption allegations received wide coverage, an unusual experience for the armed forces (Rangel 1992). The failure to satisfactorily resolve many of these cases reinforced suspicions among the public and within the officer corps of the incompetence and dishonesty of senior military and political figures. Junior officers, who were expected to exhibit exemplary honesty in their own affairs, were offended by the enrichment of senior military officers and civilian politicians at a time when their own families suffered financial hardship and their troops lacked proper uniforms, food, and lodging (Daniels 1992, 98–103; Naím 1993, 115–19; Tarre Briceño 1994a, 147–54).

President Pérez himself came under severe criticism from some junior officers, not only for the severity of his economic measures and the alleged corruption of his entourage, but also for his handling of external defense issues. His privatization policies, which led to the sale of state industries and the national telecommunications company to foreign investors, were seen as damaging to national sovereignty by many officers who were still influenced by a belief system that equated security with state control of "strategic" industrial sectors. Officers were particularly critical of Venezuela's growing economic integration with Colombia, long seen as the principal foreign threat by the officer corps.

Many within the armed forces also reacted negatively to Pérez's increased reliance on the Venezuelan military to support his foreign policy ventures. A battalion of Venezuelan troops participated in peacekeeping in Nicaragua in 1989–90, and Venezuelan officers served as observers with the United Nations on the Iraq-Kuwait border. Furthermore, following a coup in Haiti in 1991, President Pérez ordered the armed forces to prepare plans for a Venezuelan expeditionary force to join an international military effort then being considered by the United States to restore democracy in that country. Opinion split within the officer corps over Venezuela's participation in United Nations peacekeeping missions: those involved in the Nicaraguan case generally reported positive experiences, while those who remained behind accused the government of using Venezuelan troops as mercenaries. The potential Haiti operation also made some Venezuelan officers uneasy since they regarded this country with special affection for its role in sheltering Simón Bolívar during the wars for independence from Spain (Otaiza 1994; Vivas 1994).

Rounding out this picture of discontent was military outrage over comments by President Pérez that acknowledged that Colombia might have some rights in disputed maritime territory in the Gulf of Venezuela (Tarre Briceño 1994a, 155–57; Soto Urrútia 1994a). Given the military's long-held opposition to any territorial compromises with the neighboring republic, Pérez's comments were particularly damaging to his standing within the officer corps. Since each of these issues involved matters of external defense, an area where Venezuela's presidents had long consulted the military, officers felt justified in criticizing Pérez and disparaging his foreign policy (Machillanda Pinto 1997).

By early 1992, the expansion of military jurisdictional boundaries and the weakening of the institutions of civilian control created both the necessary and sufficient conditions for a coup d'état. Increasing public protest and the broad opposition of all major political parties to President Pérez's economic policies, alleged corruption, and internationalist orientation delegitimized the administration. The growing threat of public disorder had drawn the armed forces into internal security in the role of defending an unpopular regime. In external defense affairs, Pérez's dovish international policies and his failure to consult the armed forces on important questions irritated military officers. This activist foreign policy, civilian political meddling in internal military affairs, and corruption in defense contracts, aggravated by the increasing prominence of these issues in the media, highlighted the military's loss of autonomy. Even as boundaries shifted, one of the principal institutionalized strategies of civilian control in Venezuela, appeasement, collapsed with the decline in officers' salaries and benefits. Under these conditions, the populist, nationalist, and Bolivarian education that many junior army officers had received at the Academia Militar led them to question the legitimacy of the Pérez administration as well as the fitness of their own senior officers to lead them. Their elite orientation also convinced many that they had both the duty and the ability to change the country's political course, a conviction that led some junior officers to organize and prepare for a coup d'état.

THE PERVERSE CONSEQUENCES OF FACTIONALISM
IN THE VENEZUELAN ARMY

Though institutionalized "divide and conquer" policies toward the military shielded the democratic regime, they also had certain perverse consequences, particularly once the divisions between junior and senior officers became extreme. During the 1970s and 1980s, groups of mid-ranking and junior officers had begun to form factions or self-help groups that shared common interests and assisted each other in the competition for assignments and promotions (Müller Rojas 1992, 70–71). One of these groups, the MBR-200, would eventually take advantage of the declining political fortunes of the Pérez administration to lead a coup attempt. The failure of the Venezuelan system of civilian control to institutionalize civilian supervision of military activities, when combined with the divisions between the military high command and their subordinates, allowed this conspiracy to develop practically unhindered.

The MBR-200 was formed in 1983 (on the 200th anniversary of Simón Bolívar's birth) to bring about the transformation of Venezuelan democracy and its armed forces according to Bolivarian ideals (Garrido 2003). These junior army officers, led by then Captain Hugo Chávez Frias, had been among the first graduates of the reformed, university-level Academia Militar in 1974. They had developed a strongly populist, nationalist belief system based on their selective reading of the ideas of Simón Bolívar and other early Venezuelan participants in the wars of independence. Domingo Irwin argues that family ties also brought these junior officers into contact with the followers of the defeated 1960s Marxist insurgency, who were now reintegrated into society after Caldera's pacification, influencing their diagnosis of Venezuela's crisis (Irwin G. 2000, 156–60). Alberto Garrido in particular points to Douglas Bravo, one of the most recalcitrant commanders of the defeated insurgency, as promoting these contacts (Garrido 2003, 28). These contacts ranged from the revolutionary leftist groups Partido Revolucionario Venezolano and Bandera Roja to the more traditional academic left found in Venezuela's universities (López Maya 2003, 74–76). The junior officers of the MBR-200 were particularly opposed to political corruption, neoliberal economic policies, and foreign influences, and they advocated a strong Bolivarian democracy (Tarre Briceño 1994a, 177–83). Members saw themselves as better soldiers than their commanders, contrasting their own university-level professional education with the hasty training their commanders had received during the 1960s. Aníbal Romero characterizes the MBR-200 belief system as nationalist, populist, fundamentalist, and messianic; it invoked the image of Bolívar to justify a radical alteration of the political regime in Venezuela (Romero 1994, 28–34).

Chávez Frias and his co-conspirators began working toward a revolutionary coup to transform Venezuela into a "true democracy" in the early 1980s. Members of the MBR-200 believed that civilian politicians had long ago ceased to act in accordance with the constitution, particularly in their failure to provide justice, equity, and development. For the MBR-200, this justified a coup to "restore" democracy. Several members of the MBR-200 served during the early 1980s as instructors at the Academia Militar, where they were highly popular among cadets. This prestige allowed them to recruit a large number of cadets and junior officers into the MBR-200, and their positions provided considerable cover for their conspiratorial activities. Once their students had graduated and received their first assignments, they extended the reach of the MBR-200 to many major army garrisons. During the years between 1986 and 1992, members of the MBR-200 continued to meet in informal "congresses" to proselytize and solidify the political foundations of their movement (Tarre Briceño 1994b).

The MBR-200 did not go undetected by either senior officers or the Ministry of Defense's Directorate of Military Intelligence (DIM). In 1984 the parents of several cadets at the Academia Militar complained to the academy's director, General Carlos Julio Peñaloza, that several instructors had been advocating a coup d'état. An army investigation uncovered the role of Captain Chávez and others in promoting antiregime ideas and actions at the academy, and these officers were quickly transferred to assignments that removed them from influence over cadets. Even so, they were not dismissed from the armed forces, and they continued to rise through the ranks and to organize their fellow officers.

Senior officers, including Generals Carlos Peñaloza and Pedro Rangel Rojas, commanders of the army in 1989 and 1992, continued to work quietly against the MBR-200 (Romero 1994). General Peñaloza even ordered the interrogation of a large number of suspect mid-ranking officers, including members of the MBR-200, by military intelligence on 3 December 1989, two days prior to local elections. Peñaloza believed that these officers were planning a coup attempt in the event of low voter turnout in these elections, and he recommended to the president the dismissal of these officers from the armed forces. President Pérez did not consider them a serious threat, and so he overruled Peñaloza and instead ordered the MBR-200 officers transferred to new positions (Tarre Briceño 1994a, 174–76; Jiménez Sánchez 1996, 146, 162–64, 204–6). This singular lack of attention to dissent within the officer corps continued throughout the next three years.

Not only were politicians willing to overlook military discontent, but they also deliberately disorganized what institutions existed for monitoring the military, principally the Dirección de Servicios de Inteligencia y Prevención (DISIP) and the DIM. The DISIP, Venezuela's civilian political police, had always played a formal role in monitoring civilian disaffection and an informal role in monitoring military subversion, yet it was rendered ineffective after 1989 by a politically driven reorganization, the same type that occurred whenever a new administration came to power. With the DISIP effectively out of action, senior administration officials lacked timely intelligence on the sentiments and activities of junior and mid-ranking officers. Nearly simultaneously, half of army intelligence and the DIM were reorganized, and their senior commanders were either dismissed or resigned

(Jiménez Sanchez, 163, 168–69). Since the DIM and army intelligence had among their unofficial roles the monitoring of the internal sentiments of the officer corps, Venezuela's high command now had little information on the situation within the officer corps. It is important to note that this monitoring activity by the DIM and the DISIP was not institutionalized through a formal role in the civil-military system, but rather it was one of the many tasks that the intelligence services performed for senior officers and politicians as part of the mutual exchange of "favors." Rather than provide oversight of defense policy, this type of monitoring was intended as a regime protection insurance policy. Nevertheless, this turmoil in the intelligence services provided an opportunity for the MBR-200 to continue to recruit new members unchecked (Molina Vargas 1992; Tarre Briceño 1994b).

Meanwhile, the senior ranks of the army had split over the appointment of General Fernando Ochoa Antich as minister of defense in 1991, distracting senior officers at a critical moment in the MBR-200 conspiracy. Ochoa Antich, who had graduated thirty-ninth in his class at the academy, was part of a faction within the armed forces, known as "Los Notables," that dominated the highest appointments in the army (Jiménez Sánchez 1996, 138–39). His selection over General Carlos Santiago Ramírez, another member of "Los Notables" who had been first in his class, unleashed internal maneuvering among the generals and mutual accusations of corruption, malfeasance, and politicization (Gil Yepes 1994). These accusations received press coverage as generals used friends in the media to publicize their allegations against their opponents. Not only did this damage further the image of senior officers among the rest of the officer corps, but it also meant that the level of attention focused on MBR-200 was considerably reduced.

There is even some circumstantial evidence that senior officers belonging to "Los Notables" may have attempted to manipulate the MBR-200 to serve their own ends in their internal power struggle. General Ochoa Antich intervened to save the career of Lieutenant Colonel Chávez Frias, the MBR-200's leader, by allowing him to retake the army General Staff course's final examination for an unprecedented third time (Jiménez Sánchez 1996, 162–63). When Chávez Frias was assigned to a dead-end position as logistics officer in Cumaná, in eastern Venezuela, Ochoa Antich again intervened and requested that Chávez be given a troop command (Jiménez Sánchez 1996, 162–63; Tarre Briceño 1994b). By February 1992, the leadership of the MBR-200 had been appointed to key troop commands in Venezuela's five major cities, including an elite airborne battalion that Chávez controlled. The membership of the MBR-200 reportedly included 10 percent of all army officers.

The MBR-200 was well positioned to attempt a successful coup d'état in 1992, given the level of public opposition to the government and the ongoing disorganization of civilian and military elites. Chávez and his coconspirators accelerated their planning, initially establishing 1 January 1992 as the start date, later postponing it to mid-February (Otaiza 1994). The conspirators' superior officers were distracted by political infighting, and whatever small measure of the monitoring of the officer corps had once been carried out by senior military and civilian figures had now been rendered ineffective by civilian political meddling in the intelligence services. The MBR-200 expected to receive wide support from junior officers who were alienated from the high command and the Pérez administration. Political opposition to the government and the rising level of street violence also led Lieutenant Colonel Chávez and others to expect that their efforts would receive broad popular support. They also appear to have made contact with some civilian politicians, who informed them that the MBR-200 would find sufficient high-level political support to form a joint civilian-military junta in the wake of a coup. With these advantages, it seemed quite likely that the coup attempt would succeed.

Why Did the 1992 Coup Attempts Fail?

Although bad luck and poor planning played a role, the failure of the two coup attempts of 1992 can largely be attributed to institutionalized crosscutting cleavages in the officer corps, which prevented military rebels from assembling an effective "coup coalition." The very nature of the Venezuelan armed forces made it difficult for any coup to succeed and, even if it had succeeded, to sustain itself for any length of time, as General Müller Rojas suggests (Müller Rojas 1992, 22–23). The failures of these coup attempts can be directly traced to three decades of institutionalized "divide and conquer" policies. Not only did these institutions divide the military services against each other, but they also created firm links between senior military officers and civilian politicians, who actively cooperated on both occasions to suppress rebellions by junior officers. These internal cleavages within the armed forces prevented a cohesive coup against the government and allowed loyal military commanders to find a sufficient number of troops who were willing to mount a counterattack against rebel soldiers. In sum, there were simply too many institutional barriers to cooperation for any subcomponent of the Venezuelan armed forces to successfully organize a coup d'état.

THE IMMEDIATE CAUSES OF THE FAILURE OF
THE 4 FEBRUARY 1992 COUP ATTEMPT

Chance played a significant role in the failure of the 4 February coup attempt (4F). The director of the Academia Militar uncovered the coup plot among his cadets on 3 February and informed the high command, allowing General Ochoa Antich to take preliminary defensive measures. Rebels initially planned to seize the president as he returned to the Generalísimo Francisco Miranda air base in Caracas from Davos, Switzerland. When his plane was delayed in taking off from New York, it was diverted to the civilian international airport to prevent a night landing in Caracas, disrupting the rebels' plans. The MBR-200 instead attempted to seize Pérez upon returning to the presidential residence at La Casona, but a determined defense by the president's military escort prevented rebel paratroopers from seizing him. However, beyond this initial piece of misfortune, the failure of the 4F coup attempt can be traced to poor planning and leadership by rebel army officers in Caracas, the failure to recruit collaborators in other military services, and the loyalty of the military high command to the president.

Planning for the 4F coup appears to have been singularly unimaginative, particularly in the critical city of Caracas. All coups involve a high degree of uncertainty since the participation of any single officer or military unit is only guaranteed by trust among the conspirators rather than an enforceable chain of command. MBR-200 officers were widely considered the best in their class, yet they inexplicably failed to take this uncertainty into account and developed no backup plans in the event of the failure of key units to rebel, technical malfunctions, or unforeseen circumstances. This may have been partly due to the pressure MBR-200 leaders were under from junior officers and noncommissioned officers to act quickly (Otaiza 1994). Many of the units that were originally supposed to join the rebellion failed to do so, and some even fought for the government against the MBR-200 (Jiménez Sánchez 1996, 214–18). Moreover, a videotaped appeal by Chávez was never televised since the officers who took over the station lacked the technical ability to carry out their mission (Tarre Briceño 1994a, 78).

Critically, MBR-200 officers did not attempt to seize control of key communications centers, which allowed the president and a wide range of political leaders to address the nation by television and condemn the coup attempt as it happened. Coup leader Chávez Frias established his headquarters at the Military History Museum in La Planicie, located at some distance from the rebel military operations. When the main Caracas military communications unit failed to join the uprising, the MBR-200 had no alternative plan to maintain contact among rebel units. Chávez therefore remained out of contact with his soldiers throughout the night (Jiménez Sánchez 1996, 206–16). The incompetence and lack of initiative displayed by the elite officers participating in the 4F operations were symptomatic of armed forces that had not engaged in either combat or coup attempts in decades and had therefore never learned the important battlefield skills necessary for coping with uncertainty.

Once the MBR-200 had lost the initiative, President Pérez and the military high command were able to organize a counterattack relatively rapidly, concentrating all their efforts on securing Caracas. Since the MBR-200 had focused its recruiting efforts in the army, General Ochoa Antich was readily able to locate loyal units in the air force, navy, and Guardia Nacional, as well as among the large number of army units in Caracas that had not joined the insurgents. The general then ordered his troops to advance on the Generalísimo Francisco Miranda airbase and the presidential residence, while he simultaneously attempted to negotiate the surrender of Chávez and his fellow rebels. President Pérez placed heavy pressure on his military commanders to order a full-scale assault on rebel units, but his generals were understandably reluctant to increase the casualties among both rebel and loyalist soldiers (Tarre Briceño 1994a). Although heavy combat casualties might have set an example for future military rebels, they might also have induced loyal units to join the rebels or assume neutrality rather than attack fellow Venezuelan soldiers. Under increasing military pressure and lacking air support, Chávez agreed to surrender to loyal military officers on the morning of 4 February, and he broadcast a television appeal to rebel units in other cities to do so as well.

Despite their firmness in dealing with the uprising once it had begun, President Pérez and senior political and military leaders had displayed an almost willful blindness to reports of conspiracies in the armed forces prior to the 4F coup. Senior army commanders had known about plotting by junior officers for years prior to the events in 1992, yet they failed to take serious countermeasures to deter rebellions. Peñaloza had been informed of the forthcoming coup by one of his relatives, a junior officer in the army, on 20 January 1992. Peñaloza transmitted this information to high-ranking members of Acción Democrática, President Pérez's party, but they failed to act on it. Political manipulation of the DIM and DISIP also prevented any meaningful monitoring of the intentions of the MBR-200. Some reports even state that the MBR-200 had recruited an officer in the DIM, who warned that the plot had been uncovered on 3 February. Thirty years of civil-military peace had led all significant civilian and military leaders to conclude that a coup attempt in Venezuela was no longer possible, and they therefore discounted the accumulating evidence to the contrary (Tarre Briceño 1994a, 219–25).

However, by far the most important cause of the failure of the 4F coup attempt was the lack of participation in the rebel movement of any units except those belonging to the army. This seems unusual if we consider that the difficult conditions that sparked the military revolt could be found in every military service. In post-coup interviews and memoirs, MBR-200 members stated that they had sought the cooperation of members from all other military services, but they met with little success. Reportedly, units from the air force were expected to participate, and the armored vehicles belonging to the rebels had been painted with white identifying marks to make it easy to differentiate them from the air during the coup attempt (Jiménez Sánchez 1996, 173–74). However, on 4 February senior air force commanders at the Maracay air base west of Caracas easily suppressed half-hearted attempts by their service members to join the rebellion. Neither navy or Guardia Nacional units appear to have been involved to any significant degree. None of the senior leaders of the MBR-200 belonged to any service other than the army. This made it easy for the president and his military commanders to find loyal troops to attack the positions held by the rebels.

The isolation of the coup plotters from the other services was not necessarily self-imposed but was rather a reflection of the institutionalized policies of "divide and conquer" that had enforced civilian rule for thirty years. The strong bonds of friendship and trust that existed among members of the army, particularly those who attended the Academia Militar at the same time, simply did not exist between officers of different services. Prior to reaching the highest ranks, officers from different services were generally not educated together, and they did not live in concentrated military communities where they could establish firm relationships. Furthermore, since a deliberate effort had been made to integrate military officers into civilian life, army officers were more likely to know engineers, architects, lawyers, and doctors than their counterparts in the navy or air force. The administrative independence of each of the services meant that all training programs and operations were separate from one another, creating both distance and competitiveness for resources. The army in particular saw itself as the senior service, which led its members to minimize the importance of coordinating a coup with the other armed services. Given the importance of secrecy and trust in successfully organizing a coup d'état, members of the MBR-200 found it difficult to overcome institutional barriers to cooperation with members of other services. Acting alone on 4 February, they might have been able to capture President Pérez, but without the support of a broad cross section of the armed forces and the high command, the MBR-200 would have found it impossible to govern.

AFTERMATH OF THE 4F COUP ATTEMPT

Politically, the 4F coup was a disaster for the Pérez administration. Even though senior political figures rapidly rallied to defend the civilian regime, popular opinion seemed fascinated by the actions of the MBR-200. Opinion polls taken in the wake of the uprising seemed to show that while people still favored democracy, they were deeply opposed to the policies of the Pérez administration. For example, in a poll taken among civilians shortly after the 4F coup, 47 percent of respondents stated that they were confident that had the MBR-200 been successful, the military could have reorganized the economy, ended corruption, and called for new elections (Romero 1994, 35). Two events boosted this favorable sentiment toward the 4F rebels. First, in his brief televised speech on the morning of 4 February, Chávez's straightforward demeanor, his unhesitating acceptance of responsibility for the failure of the coup, and his promise of future action against the government electrified many civilians. The contrast with the tired political rhetoric of the civilian leaders who appeared on television defending the democratic regime was notable. Second, in a televised Senate debate over a resolution condemning the 4F coup, former president Rafael Caldera made a speech in which, while he condemned the coup, he appeared to justify the actions of the MBR-200 as an understandable response to the policies of the Pérez administration (Hernández 1995, 70). This speech seemed to echo popular sentiment perfectly and solidified public opinion in favor of the rebels and against the government.

In an attempt to shore up civilian support for his administration and present a unified political front, President Pérez rapidly organized a national unity government within weeks of the 4F coup attempt. Two prominent leaders of the principal opposition party COPEI, Eduardo Fernández and José Ignacio Moreno León, joined Pérez's cabinet, and several of the most visible representatives of the neoliberal economic policies departed. The minister of defense, General Ochoa Antich, had actually demanded that Pérez form a government of national unity, claiming he otherwise could not be responsible for the future actions of the armed forces (Quiróz Corradi 1992). Pérez also called for the formation of a consultative council of leading civilian intellectuals, experts, and politicians to consider political reforms. The civilian political elite belonging to AD and COPEI quickly rallied to the defense of the regime, even if many other organized sectors of society expressed somewhat lukewarm solidarity with the government. Nevertheless, this initial expression of solidarity with the regime prevented public "knocking at the barracks doors" by members of the civilian elite, thereby dampening expectations among conspiring officers that any new coup attempt would meet with broad civilian support.

The international community, led by the United States, responded quickly and effectively to news of the coup attempt. The United States was particularly forceful in communicating to the Venezuelan military that any successful coup would have very serious consequences. Many foreign leaders called with messages of support for President Pérez even as the rebellion was in progress. U.S. ambassador Michael Skol and his superiors in Washington, D.C., publicly announced their support for democracy and threatened drastic sanctions against any military regime that took power in Venezuela. Since the United States was by far the largest consumer of Venezuelan petroleum and since the United States had recently acted forcefully against Iraq in 1990–91, this threat was perceived as credible in some political and military circles. Through private channels, the frequent U.S. civilian and military official visitors repeatedly informed senior military commanders that any coup d'état would be unacceptable, and that such action would have grave consequences for Venezuela's international political and economic standing. The U.S. armed forces immediately increased the flow of training missions to Venezuela, all of which carried the same message to the junior officer corps (Otaiza 1994).

Most Venezuelan generals and admirals did not need much convincing that a coup would be a bad idea since their own personal and professional interests made them among the firmest military supporters of the Pérez administration. However, the firm U.S. position against the coup helped to shore up the coalition between civilian politicians and senior military officers, a critical alliance for the preservation of democracy. On the other hand, U.S. statements against the MBR-200 and the 4F coup attempt did serve to anger some more nationalistic officers and civilians, who saw the statements as evidence of Venezuela's limited sovereignty, U.S. imperialism, and the antinational character of the Pérez administration (Grüber Odremán 1993, 235, 237–38). In the aggregate, U.S. efforts reminded wavering Venezuelan civilians and military officers that their interests lay in supporting the democratic regime.

Nevertheless, Chávez's popularity, rumors of continuing military unrest, and Caldera's speech before the Senate opened the floodgates for civilian criticism of the political system in general and the president in particular. Groups of academics, intellectuals, and elder statesmen were particularly persistent in their calls, widely publicized in the media, for an end to neoliberal reforms, the establishment of a constituent assembly, and new elections. Left-wing opposition parties MAS and La Causa R, a new workers' party, echoed the call for radical political reform by arguing that it was the only means to save democracy. Opinion polls continued to show popular opposition to Pérez's economic policies and increasing support for political reform, which the most vocal civilian opponents used to justify their appeals (Hernández 1995, 77–80). In this atmosphere of political crisis and near hysteria, COPEI withdrew from the national unity administration in the summer of 1992, weakened by months of defending a government with whom they had little influence and significant policy disagreements (Romero 1994). The Pérez administration seemed more isolated than ever, even though COPEI continued to remain in the loyal opposition.

On the military front, Pérez reacted quickly, using the strong links between civilian and military elites to reestablish military order and provide security for his administration. Despite their previous differences, Venezuelan generals and admirals were nearly unanimous in their support for the administration and the regime because they feared public disorder, the disintegration of the military institution into squabbling factions, and the threat posed by rebellious junior officers to the senior command's power and privileges. To maintain the continued support of the minister of defense, General Ochoa Antich, once he retired from service on 5 July 1992, Pérez appointed him minister for foreign relations. Ochoa Antich was replaced as minister of defense by General Iván Jiménez Sánchez of the air force, who was also a firm supporter of the regime.

With the active cooperation of the corps of generals and admirals, President Pérez was able to rely on traditional military institutional mechanisms to attack and remove rebellious officers from the armed forces. Since these efforts were cloaked in appeals to norms, laws, procedures, and respect for hierarchy, many doubtful officers found it easier to obey orders than to vigorously oppose the purge of the MBR-200 from the officer corps. Members of the MBR-200 were rapidly arrested and detained in military prisons, though only 6 percent of the 2,668 service members who participated in the rebellion were indicted in military courts (Daniels 1992, 193–96). Officers belonging to the MBR-200 were tried in military courts, convicted of treason, and sentenced to decades of imprisonment, although these sentences were later overturned on procedural grounds by the civilian Supreme Court.

Pérez also intensified civilian and military monitoring of the officer corps, reviving a strategy that had allowed the first presidents of democratic Venezuela to maintain power during the 1960s. Officers of doubtful loyalty were expelled from the armed forces or sent overseas for lengthy periods of time as students or military attachés. Officers who were permitted to remain in Venezuela were carefully watched and rotated through new commands every three to six months. Junior officers, who were once expected to work long hours and remain on base after their superiors had departed, were sent home promptly at 5 P.M. in order to reduce the potential opportunity for hatching new conspiracies during the unsupervised evening hours. Generals and colonels were assigned to command units once led by lieutenant colonels and majors, and their unit armories were carefully secured and alarmed, preventing any junior officers from having significant access to weapons or, more important, munitions. The DIM swiftly increased its monitoring of subversive activities within the armed forces. Leftist politicians and activists were targeted by the DIM as well; they were outspoken in their support for the MBR-200 and their opposition to the government, and senior military officers believed them to be deeply involved in efforts to organize a new military rebellion. Officer participation in civilian university programs was increasingly discouraged because these universities, particularly the Universidad Central de Venezuela, were seen as centers of left-wing subversion (Müller Rojas 1995).

For President Pérez, senior military commanders, and members of the intelligence community, all of whom had experienced the counterinsurgency war of the 1960s, the MBR-200 and its supporters in the academic and intellectual left were seen as part of a larger left-wing plot against democracy. Although these suspicions may have been unfounded, monitoring and vigilance within the army succeeded in dissuading some officers from conspiratorial activities and aborted several additional plots against President Pérez (Otaiza 1994; Vivas 1994; Jiménez Sánchez 1996, 316–18).

The Pérez administration also reinvigorated the institutions of civilian control that were designed to appease the armed forces, investing a large amount of new resources in the military's social safety net. All officers immediately received 30 percent pay increases, loyal officers were rewarded by having outstanding debts paid off, and housing subsidies and allowances were increased substantially (Rodríguez 1992, 116; Otaiza 1994). As the U.S. Arms Control and Disarmament Agency (1995) reported, Venezuela's military spending was $1.55 billion in 1992, 50 percent higher than average expenditures during the 1988–90 period, even as spending on arms imports declined from an average of $233 million during the same period to $80 million in 1992. This suggests that more of the military budget was apportioned to personnel and operations, rather than new acquisitions, to improve the lot of the officer corps. All the military personnel and civilian experts whom I interviewed noted a sharp rise in spending on the social welfare of the armed forces, which was designed to address one of the principal grievances of the military rebels.

Even with these countermeasures, the possibility of a new coup attempt remained as conspiracies in general, and the MBR-200 in particular, became fashionable in the officer corps. Lieutenant Colonel Chávez and the MBR-200 gained immense prestige among junior officers for their actions during the 4F coup. Internal armed forces polls suggested that up to 90 percent of junior and mid-ranking officers shared the beliefs espoused by the MBR-200 (Tarre Briceño 1994b). Moreover, a significant number of officers who had not participated in the 4F coup attempt were attracted to conspiratorial activities as a result of the example set by rebellious officers. Chávez and his incarcerated co-conspirators maintained contact with their supporters and received numerous civilian and military visitors. Chávez used his new prestige to encourage some conspiracies and veto others, maintaining the leadership role of the MBR-200 within the junior ranks of the officer corps (Otaiza 1994). The Pérez administration attempted to counteract these sentiments by holding pro-democracy conferences for the officers of all the principal military garrisons that featured civilians with prestige within the officer corps defending constitutionalism and democracy (Giacopini Zárraga 1994a). These conferences were often poorly received and met with only

limited success, and they often resulted in little more than the angry public airing of grievances by junior officers against their commanders (Tarre
Briceño 1994a). Essentially, Chávez and the MBR-200 had made antigovernment plotting de rigueur for any self-regarding officer, and many joined the
conspiracy bandwagon.

THE FINAL MILITARY REBELLION? 27 NOVEMBER 1992

The Pérez administration never recovered its political or military footing
after the 4F coup attempt, which created an opening for a new coup attempt.
Mounting civilian criticism of the administration's policies, continuing economic pressure on the middle and lower classes, and the withdrawal of COPEI
from the national unity government isolated Pérez and his team, placing
them on the defensive politically. Civilian opponents publicized allegations
of corruption by Pérez and his entourage, which further decreased the perceived legitimacy of the government. Even though no civilian groups were
openly pushing for military intervention, calls for Pérez's resignation, constitutional reform, and an end to economic austerity measures fashioned an
atmosphere in which the collapse of the government seemed a real possibility. Civilian consensus on the legitimacy of the administration, if not on
the legitimacy of the democracy as a whole, seemed to be crumbling. In the
face of Pérez's unconditional defense of his government and the appropri-
ateness of his policies, some military officers concluded that a coup d'état
was not only viable, but the only way to meet popular demands for an end
to political corruption and a "restored" democracy.

The events of 4 February created the conditions for a more broadly based
coup coalition by once again making military intervention in politics "think-
able" for the many in the officer corps. Military and civilian reaction to the
events of 4F produced an awareness among junior and mid-ranking officers
of just how widespread civilian and military discontent had become and led
some to believe that any new attempt would be met with general approval.
Where disgust with the political system had once been a private matter for
officers, the presence of overt opposition toward the government on military bases reinforced conspiratorial tendencies among the officer corps. The
navy and air force also experienced an upsurge in dissent and plotting among
its junior officers, who eagerly followed the example set by the MBR-200.
In many officers' opinion, the 4F coup had failed because the MBR-200 had
not included a sufficient number of senior officers, approached other military services, or mobilized civilian political support. The spread of dissent

across all branches of the military made it possible for conspirators to identify potential allies in other services.

However, in a military regulated by "divide and conquer" institutions, the spread of military dissent also undermined the possibility of a successful coup by fragmenting opposition to the regime. Even though they achieved great prestige for their leading role in the 4F events, Chávez and the MBR-200 were not able to control the large number of independent conspiracies that developed during the summer and fall of 1992. By virtue of his imprisonment, Chávez no longer had the command of troops, the hierarchical authority, or the freedom of movement to effectively maintain control of the MBR-200 or incorporate new conspirators in its ranks (Jiménez Sánchez 1996, 262–63). Confusion over goals, methods, and ideology among dissident officers contributed to the conspiratorial frenzy of this time period but also hindered the formation of a coherent antigovernment movement. This placed pressure on Chávez to act quickly before his leadership of the radical opposition to the Pérez administration was challenged by an independent military conspiracy to overthrow the government.

Amid this welter of confusion, a new plan to overthrow the government emerged that linked the MBR-200 to two senior officers in the navy and air force. Vice Admiral Hernán Grüber Odremán, a maverick officer who had commanded the navy's small marine infantry group, and Brigadier General Francisco Visconti, who was a key commander at the principal air force base in Maracay, formed a new conspiracy which they called Movimiento Quinto de Julio (the Fifth of July Movement, named after Venezuela's Independence Day) (Tarre Briceño 1994a; Jiménez Sánchez 1996, 248). This group, which included some senior officers, made contact with the MBR-200 and agreed to coordinate a new coup attempt. The MBR-200 saw several advantages in joining Grüber and Visconti: Chávez hoped that their participation in a coup would divide the corps of generals and admirals, split them from the Pérez administration and the civilian elite, and provide protection for the conspiracy at the highest levels of the armed forces (Otaiza 1994).

The difficulty of organizing a coup attempt across the traditional divides between the services was the principal cause for the failure of the 27 November rebellion. Even though members of all four services participated in the planning, it soon became apparent to Visconti and Grüber that the officers representing the army and Guardia Nacional were incapable of delivering on their promises to contribute troops to the rebellion (Grüber Odremán 1993, 100, 113; Otaiza 1994; Jiménez Sánchez 1996, 250). Only the participation of the air force units based in Maracay, west of Caracas, and marine infantry and naval commando units based in Puerto Cabello and Catia, to the east, seemed assured. Without the support of army troops based in Caracas, the conspirators were forced to adopt a complex plan to draw on air force and navy units outside the capital. The MBR-200 would be responsible for taking control of the Caracas television antenna facility, through which most local stations transmitted, and broadcasting a videotaped appeal by Grüber, Visconti, and other senior leaders of the Movimiento Quinto de Julio (Grüber Odremán 1993, 124–26). For the plan to work, Visconti and Grüber would have to coordinate air force, navy, and MBR-200 supporters and hope for an outpouring of popular support. However, the very complexity of the plan and the diverse backgrounds of the conspirators practically guaranteed its failure.

Miscommunication, mistrust, and betrayal characterized the behavior of the participants in the military rebellion of 27 November and brought down the operation before it had even begun. One of the participants in the operation, Captain Luis Manrique Padrón, revealed details of the coup plot to the navy's acting chief of naval operations, Vice Admiral Maucó Quintana, shortly before the coup. Manrique Padrón, a commanding officer in the navy's marine infantry, had played a key role in organizing its participation in the rebellion. His confession allowed Maucó Quintana to order security measures at all marine infantry bases, which deprived Visconti and Grüber of almost all ground troops for the operations in Caracas (Otaiza 1994). As a result of Manrique Padrón's action, the high command was also able to issue a general alert to all military units, which dissuaded ambivalent officers from joining the rebellion and prevented Grüber from receiving promised communications support from the Fuerte Tiuna army barracks in Caracas. Out of touch with General Visconti in Maracay, Grüber had no way of coordinating the rebellion in Caracas.

The MBR-200 successfully seized Caracas television facilities but then proceeded to betray Grüber. Instead of broadcasting the moderate videotaped appeal prepared by leaders of the Fifth of July Movement, the MBR-200 chose to deliver a live harangue by a young army officer, who was bizarrely flanked by two nervous, poorly dressed, civilian guerrillas. Rather than witnessing a traditional military *pronunciamiento* made by Vice Admiral Grüber in the company of senior officers from all four services, the population of Caracas witnessed a poorly prepared revolutionary appeal for a general insurrection. This dampened the sympathy that many civilians, particularly in the middle class, had felt for the military rebels since the earlier 4F coup attempt (Grüber Odremán 1993, 225–30; Jiménez Sánchez 1996, 335–41, 397).

Even in the face of these setbacks, rebellious officers pressed ahead, accomplishing little more than the deaths of 25 soldiers and 308 civilians. Visconti succeeded in seizing control of air force units at the Libertador air base in Maracay and launched a series of air attacks on the presidential palace and key government installations in Caracas. Even so, the presence of two loyal F-16s were sufficient to allow the government to achieve air superiority over Caracas. With loyal army tanks and infantry moving against the Maracay air base, Visconti and his officers boarded an air force transport plane and fled to Peru, while Grüber and his fellow navy officers surrendered to government prosecutors. Both military and civilian rebels were tried and found guilty of treason by courts martial established under Decree 2,669 by President Pérez (Grüber Odremán 1993, 146–51; Jiménez Sánchez 1996, 409–15).

"DIVIDE AND CONQUER" AND THE FAILURE
OF THE 27 NOVEMBER COUP ATTEMPT

The 27 November rebellion failed in spite of the efforts of its military participants to correct the "errors" committed during the 4 February coup attempt. Both civilian commentators and military officers had argued in the wake of the 4F rebellion that the MBR-200 had failed to secure the cooperation of senior officers, other military services, or civilian support, which had allowed the Pérez administration to survive (Tarre Briceño 1994a; Vivas 1994; Soto Urrútia 1995). The leaders of the Fifth of July Movement established contact with civilian politicians and technocrats, other senior officers, the MBR-200 and its civilian allies, and all four military services (Grüber Odremán 1993, 105–8). They even made sure to seize control of the bulk of the television transmitters in Caracas. However, as the process of organizing and executing the coup showed, it was simply too difficult to coordinate among these different groups and sectors. Three decades of "divide and conquer" institutions had deprived the Venezuelan armed forces of the internal cohesion necessary to carry out a coup attempt.

The air force and navy coup leaders found that they could not depend on their co-conspirators in the army to carry out their plans since institutionalized interservice competition and mutual suspicions created incentives for defection. Important commanders of ground units who had originally agreed to participate in the coup abstained from the final operations. According a report prepared by the DIM in February 1993, the army was profoundly divided internally, the navy was alienated from its general command, the air force remained in a state of unrest, and only the Guardia Nacional remained unperturbed by events and loyal to the government (Jiménez Sánchez 1996, 252–53). While these conditions were far from ideal, internal divisions and mistrust in the armed forces also meant that potential conspirators would find it impossible to organize a successful coup.

Only the corps of senior generals and admirals were united since they had too much to lose from opposing the civilian government and everything to gain from suppressing their rebellious subordinates. For junior officers, conspiracy against the government was an attractive proposition in the abstract, yet participating in a coup itself was a risky proposition that could possibly lead to the loss of their careers, or even their lives. A successful coup depended on mutual trust and the coordinated efforts of any number of unrelated military units that had never before acted together. On the other hand, betraying the coup to the military high command and civilian authorities was a sure path to greater rewards. This set of incentives meant that only officers who were particularly ideologically or morally committed to rebelling against the government participated in these operations. Many officers, and certainly almost all senior officers, had simply too much of a stake in the military system and in the continuation of the civilian regime to casually participate in overthrowing the government.

Democracy Survives

Venezuela's democratic regime managed to survive the 1992 coup attempts, even if the Pérez administration did not. President Pérez was removed from office on 21 May 1993, not by a military rebellion, but as a result of an act of impeachment passed by the Venezuelan Senate. Pérez's impeachment occurred immediately following the findings by the Supreme Court that sufficient evidence existed to indict the president on charges of misuse of government funds to provide security services for President Violeta Chamorro of Nicaragua. Pérez was replaced by Ramón J. Velásquez, a noted Venezuelan historian, who served out the remainder of Pérez's term. Velásquez faced a highly uncertain political environment, particularly after he was largely abandoned by his erstwhile electors in the Venezuelan Senate. His outspoken minister of defense, Admiral Radamés Muñoz León, repeatedly sparked coup rumors through his open criticism of leftist political parties, particularly Causa R. Causa R, which hoped to win the forthcoming Decem-

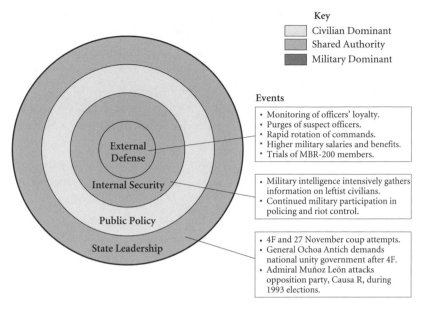

Key
- Civilian Dominant
- Shared Authority
- Military Dominant

External Defense

Internal Security

Public Policy

State Leadership

Events

- Monitoring of officers' loyalty.
- Purges of suspect officers.
- Rapid rotation of commands.
- Higher military salaries and benefits.
- Trials of MBR-200 members.

- Military intelligence intensively gathers information on leftist civilians.
- Continued military participation in policing and riot control.

- 4F and 27 November coup attempts.
- General Ochoa Antich demands national unity government after 4F.
- Admiral Muñoz León attacks opposition party, Causa R, during 1993 elections.

Figure 5.3. Civil-Military Jurisdictional Boundaries, ca. 1993: Expansive Military Jurisdictions Threaten Civilian Control

ber 1993 elections, retaliated against the admiral in the media. Velásquez was also met with a slowing economy, as foreign investors lost confidence and the government's commitment to structural adjustment faltered. Public protests over economic conditions continued, although not quite at the high pace of the Pérez administration. Nevertheless, Velásquez succeeded in delivering power to his elected successor, Rafael Caldera, in March 1994. President Caldera took office with the political project of returning Venezuela to the traditions of "pacted," populist democracy inaugurated in 1958 (Stambouli 1994). Only in the area of civilian control did he succeed in carrying out his agenda.

By the end of 1993, military jurisdictional boundaries had become dangerously bloated, expanding even into the most dangerous sphere of military influence, state leadership selection (fig. 5.3). The two coup attempts of 1992, while unsuccessful in the short term, sufficiently weakened the government of Carlos Andrés Pérez to allow his impeachment in the Senate. General Ochoa Antich and Admiral Muñoz León used their powerful positions as ministers of defense to influence the formation of a national unity government in 1992 and attack one of the principal contenders in the 1993 elections, Causa R.

Events palpably demonstrated the degree to which the armed forces had come to penetrate state leadership selection. Civilian politicians were too disorganized and delegitimized to easily counteract these expanded boundaries. The suspicions by senior military officers of connections between traditional leftists politicians and activists and the MBR-200 fueled a network of domestic espionage, which reportedly enabled General Muñoz León to compile evidence on two hundred Venezuelans associated with the political left. Continuing public unrest during these administrations led the armed forces to emphasize their internal security mission, much to the distaste of some of the officers. On the other hand, determined efforts by the civilian administrations of Pérez and Velásquez to contain military rebellion, which included extensive manipulation of promotions, assignments, and overseas duties for military officers, allowed civilian input into the military's core area of competence, external security. The corps of generals and admirals collaborated with this intrusion into their traditional jurisdiction to prevent a military rebellion by junior officers that could displace those on top.

Given this picture of rapidly shifting and expanding jurisdictional boundaries, why were there no further military threats to democracy during the 1990s? Certainly, President Caldera's economic and social policies cannot explain why the military threat receded. These policies proved to have a greater negative impact on Venezuelans, particularly poorer Venezuelans, than the neoliberal policies of the Pérez administration.

Rafael Caldera, who had already served as president from 1969 to 1974, was elected in 1993 on a populist political platform that promised a renewed commitment to social equity and justice and an end to corruption and neoliberal economic reforms. Among his first executive decrees was a suspension of the constitutional guarantees of the citizenry, stating this was a necessary measure to effectively prosecute the corrupt politicians and businesspeople responsible for the crisis. In an attempt to halt soaring inflation, a deepening recession, and capital flight, the government imposed new exchange and price controls. The Ley de Emergencia Financiera (Law on the Financial Emergency), which followed shortly, established severe criminal penalties for evading these banking and exchange controls. Soon after, the government halted privatization and abandoned the neoliberal aspects of President Pérez's economic policies. Foreign investment dropped off, the stock market declined sharply, and the shaky banking system nearly collapsed. Caldera responded with billions of dollars in bailout funds, which led to soaring inflation due to excess liquidity in the money supply (Buxton 2003, 120–22). Inflation rose from the low twenties under Carlos Andrés Pérez to 73 percent in 1994, reaching over 100 percent in 1995. The economy, after stagnating in 1993, entered a steep recession in 1994 with a reduction of 3.3 percent in GDP (Hernández 1995, 109–12). In 1995, 41 percent of Venezuelans lived in critical poverty, while another 39 percent lived below the poverty line. These economic conditions cannot explain why the armed forces once again returned to the barracks in Venezuela.

The military threat to Venezuela's civilian government receded for three principal reasons: the reinforcement of traditional mechanisms of civilian control, the enactment of public policies compatible with the desires of most Venezuelans, and the growing realization among military officers that they were incapable of supplying an effective alternative to the policies of the civilian government. Caldera instituted a return to a traditional model of civilian control based on institutions of appeasement and "divide and conquer," as part of his overall return to the model of "pacted" democracy. He believed that the democratic institutions he had helped craft in 1958 would save Venezuelan democracy in the 1990s.

Immediately upon taking office, Caldera reestablished himself as the commander in chief of the armed forces by summarily dismissing Admiral Muñoz León as minister of defense several months prior to his official retirement date. The president also selected a relatively junior army general as his new minister of defense, a move that forced nearly a dozen more senior generals to resign (Villegas Poljak 1996).[2] In one stroke, Caldera reasserted civilian authority over the military high command, purged it of AD-leaning officers, and eased some of the resentments of junior officers toward their commanders. Caldera also eliminated a source of discontent among junior officers by issuing presidential pardons for all soldiers who were convicted of participating in the 1992 coups on the condition that these officers retire immediately from the armed forces. This move was criticized by some for sending a terrible signal to future conspirators, but it did remove the issue of the imprisonment from the public debate, depriving MBR-200 supporters on the left of opportunities to attack the government. Moreover, as civilians, Chávez and other former rebels had many fewer opportunities to influence the junior officer corps, and their forced retirement signaled to active-duty military officers that participation in conspiracies would carry consequences. By expelling both the military high command and the MBR-200, Caldera purged the officer corps of its two most politicized extremes and allowed the rest to return to their professional duties.

Caldera reemphasized these duties by focusing the military on controlling the Colombian border and acting as an emergency reserve force to meet public crises. Increasing activities by Fuerzas Armadas Revolucionarias de Colombia (FARC) guerrillas in Venezuela's frontier regions resulted in numerous attacks on military outposts and significant casualties between 1994 and 1998. Caldera responded by creating two military theaters of operation to actively combat guerrillas along the Colombian frontier, redeploying Venezuelan soldiers from all services to the region for external and internal security duties. This hard-line stance toward Colombia was well received by the armed forces, and it established a contrast between Caldera and his dovish predecessor Pérez. In a more potentially politicizing step, Caldera began to use the military to resolve public policy crises by deploying soldiers to maintain emergency services in the face of strikes by public sector employees. Air traffic controllers at major airports were replaced by their air force counterparts in one instance, while a doctors' strike was met by the militarization of government hospitals and their temporary staffing with physicians from the armed forces. Rather than allow Caracas public transportation to be shut down during a strike by subway employees, Caldera ordered the army to keep the trains running. Paradoxically, rather than increasing overt military hostility toward the government, this participation in public service at Caldera's behest appears to have been well received both by the public and within the armed forces. Additionally, military participation in external defense and public policy arenas provided sufficient meaningful employment for the armed forces to overcome the existential crisis generated by their diffuse mission during the 1970s and 1980s.

Meanwhile, Caldera once again subjected the officer corps to the twin strategies of civilian control: appeasement and "divide and conquer." Military officers received pay raises that at least matched inflation in 1994, and even exceeded inflation in 1995, leading the minister of defense to declare that the officer corps was receiving the best salaries in history (Montiel 1994). While the defense budget dropped, most spending was targeted at the military's social needs (Alliegro 1994). Caldera also maintained the policy of rotating officers frequently through different commands and appointed a new minister of defense on schedule every year, which hindered effective plotting by potential rebels. Outgoing ministers of defense were appointed to senior civilian positions in the government, including several ministries and ambassadorships, thereby retaining their loyalty. Collectively, these reinvigorated measures of appeasement pacified the officer corps by restoring to them a measure of economic security and reinforcing the president's image as a concerned commander in chief.

Military opposition to the government also dropped off because the policies of the Caldera administration were more congenial to the armed forces' traditional statist and developmentalist mentality. Caldera had a reputation for personal integrity, and his policies were antiprivatization and antimarket. His efforts to direct the economy through subsidies and through price and exchange controls matched the expectations of most Venezuelans, including the military, as polling data from the period suggests. Even his decision to suspend constitutional guarantees for more than a year in the (ineffective) pursuit of corruption met with the approval of 62 percent of Venezuelans. The effective end of privatization efforts and the nationalization of collapsing banks increased the state's role in the economy. Caldera's economic policies and anticorruption rhetoric also met with approval from the officer corps, steeped as they were in the idea that state-led development brought national security. Moreover, the long public opinion honeymoon of the Caldera administration, indicated by the fact that its approval ratings increased 30 percent in the eight months following the inauguration, temporarily reduced public protest and sustained the legitimacy of the regime (Romero 1995, 15, 25). This led potential conspirators in the armed forces to refrain from new plots, both out of respect for Caldera and approval for his policies. In other words, the military in 1994 also believed in Caldera's attempt to return to a traditional Venezuelan model of consensual politics and state-led development.

When Caldera's efforts to reintroduce the post-1958 model failed, the government's position vis-à-vis the armed forces paradoxically became more, rather than less, secure. The return to a state-centered economy worsened the material conditions of most Venezuelans after 1995, and public approval ratings for President Caldera decreased rapidly. Antigovernment protests and strikes once again became the norm. However, no new signs of military discontent appeared, as they once had under Carlos Andrés Pérez. In part, renewed government commitment to military social welfare dampened the impact of the worsening economy on military personnel. On the other hand, many in the armed forces, particularly in the high command, saw no policy alternatives to those presented by the government. In part, civilian and military opposition to Pérez's neoliberal economic policies was driven by the comparison between the hardships experienced during 1989–90 and the rising living standards of the 1970s and 1980s, when state-centered development policies were the norm. As it became obvious that the attempt to "return to the past" by the Caldera administration had failed, no one in the military could offer policy alternatives, and no one in the high command wanted to try to pick up the pieces.

REASSERTING CIVILIAN CONTROL DURING
THE CALDERA ADMINISTRATION?

Despite the grudging implementation of market-centered economic policies by the Caldera administration, in some ways similar to the ones that had precipitated a crisis during the Pérez administration, the armed forces remained tranquil between 1994 and 1999. Even the increasing opening of the state-owned oil sector, once a sacred cow for all Venezuelan nationalists, to foreign investment failed to stir much public protest. The jurisdictional boundaries of the armed forces retreated under the Caldera administration, and the armed forces no longer played a role in state leadership selection, as was indicated by their bland acceptance of former Venezuelan guerrilla leaders (now members of the socialist MAS party) as government ministers (fig. 5.4).

Although the armed forces increasingly were called upon to maintain public services under emergency conditions, this did not lead to any significant military influence over public policy. The armed forces maintained their increased role in internal security, although its locus had been transferred to dealing with the cross-border insurgency led by Colombian FARC rebels rather than the maintenance of public order. The armed forces even accepted some reduction in their level of autonomy in external security issues and their internal functions. Civilian alertness to signs of military rebellion continued, and economic austerity forced the congressional armed services and finance committees to work much more closely with the military high command to resolve budgetary issues, particularly when it came to finding appropriations for major maintenance and munitions purchases (Alliegro 1994; Tarre Briceño 1994b).

It was a positive sign that Caldera was able to shift civil-military boundaries toward civilian control with relative ease at the beginning of his term. This indicated that the armed forces were not interested, as an institution, in achieving expanded control over public policy. Furthermore, the mission of controlling guerrilla attacks along the river and land borders with Colombia provided a useful external defense mission in which all of the military services could participate. However, as events during the Chávez adminis-

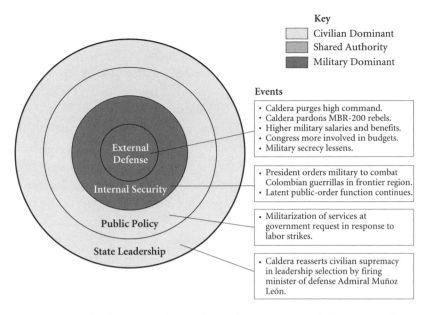

Key
Civilian Dominant
Shared Authority
Military Dominant

Events

- Caldera purges high command.
- Caldera pardons MBR-200 rebels.
- Higher military salaries and benefits.
- Congress more involved in budgets.
- Military secrecy lessens.

- President orders military to combat Colombian guerrillas in frontier region.
- Latent public-order function continues.

- Militarization of services at government request in response to labor strikes.

- Caldera reasserts civilian supremacy in leadership selection by firing minister of defense Admiral Muñoz León.

External Defense

Internal Security

Public Policy

State Leadership

Figure 5.4. Civil-Military Jurisdictional Boundaries, ca. 1997: Civilian Control by Containment Restored

tration would show, military jurisdictional boundaries were as institutionalized as they had been after the consolidation of democracy in Venezuela during the 1960s. The increasing use of the armed forces to deal with public policy crises, particularly to replace strikers, was problematic because it drew the military into the center of Venezuela's social and economic problems. Given the trained personnel available to the military, it would be almost impossible for the Caldera administration to avoid drawing on this institution to resolve breakdowns in public services. Caldera's appointment of retired generals to manage particularly troublesome civilian agencies, such as the Ministry of Transport and Communications, raised concerns that the armed forces would become repoliticized, which could lead to full-fledged military interventions.

1992: A MISSED OPPORTUNITY FOR CIVILIAN CONTROL BY OVERSIGHT?

Although 1992 could be seen as a new opportunity to restructure civil-military relations, Venezuela did not move to civilian control by oversight because it still lacked, as in 1958, any significant regime capacity to manage defense issues. Establishing institutions of monitoring and indoctrination compatible with Venezuelan democracy would have required major reforms in the manner in which civilians managed military affairs. In particular, Venezuela would have needed a significant pool of civilian defense experts to staff the new congressional and executive branch agencies needed to successfully monitor military activities. Civilian control by oversight would have also required civilian penetration of key military institutions, particularly the Ministry of Defense. Major educational institutions within the armed forces, such as the military academies, would have had to emphasize democratic constitutionalism in their curriculum and abandon their attachment to particular national security development models that predisposed officers to favor statist economic and social policies. The establishment of civilian control by oversight would also have necessitated a commitment to monitoring by civil society and the media and to increasing the transparency of security issues in Venezuela. The armed forces would have had to give up some of the protections provided by military secrecy laws to achieve this transparency. Ultimately, achieving a western model of civilian control of the armed forces would require a major transformation in the way in which the Venezuelan armed forces interacted with the state and a major commitment of government resources to participating in security issues on a permanent basis.

Civilian control by oversight was not achieved in Venezuela after 1992 because too many vested political and military interests depended on the maintenance of the traditional form of control by containment. In the wake of the 1992 coup attempts, politicians avoided testing new mechanisms of control for fear of being unable to defend themselves against future rebellions. The increased transparency and efficiency of a version of civilian control by oversight would have required politicians to give up certain institutions, including the thirty-year limit on military service and rapid rotation of officers through multiple postings, on which they had come to rely. Transparency would also have prevented politicians from manipulating the internal promotions system for their personal benefit and that of favored officers. Officers who depended on achieving their posts through connections rather than merit would have also opposed these reforms. While many in the officer corps would have supported a transparent and professional military bureaucracy, it is unclear whether they would have welcomed the increasing intrusion of civilian experts into defense affairs that this would require.

Just as in 1945 and 1958, Venezuela lacked the necessary civilian expertise and institutional resources to seriously reform the defense sector, and it chose to avoid creating them in a moment of crisis. Even when the regime was under threat, there were few incentives for the government, political parties, and civilian society to acquire such expertise. Improving civilian control was not on the agenda, particularly during the deepening social and economic crisis of the 1990s, and it did not generate the political-military coalition or attract the necessary resources to create strong institutional government authority over the armed forces.

The greatest threat to the continued stability of Venezuelan democracy was that civilians chose to return to institutionalized civilian control by containment. By restoring institutions of "divide and conquer" and appeasement, the Caldera government managed to stave off further military intervention. The temporary increase in civilian vigilance that took place after the 1992 coup attempts was not institutionalized, and it dissipated as the threat of military intervention receded. The underlying grievances of the officer corps generated by the politicization of the military bureaucracy were not addressed, providing future military conspirators with a ready-made issue with which to justify their rebellion and recruit new supporters. Venezuela's continuing political and economic problems in the late 1990s provided many of the necessary conditions for a new bout of military intervention, particularly as they became aggravated during the future administration of President Hugo Chávez.

CHAPTER 6

■

REVOLUTIONIZING

CIVIL-MILITARY RELATIONS?

Hugo Chávez and the Fifth Republic

in Venezuela, 1998–2004

On the evening of 11 April 2002, the third day of a general strike, elements of the Venezuelan armed forces rebelled against their commander in chief, President Hugo Chávez Frias. Reacting to the bloody outcome of clashes between pro- and antigovernment demonstrators near the presidential palace, the commander of the army, General Efraín Vásquez Velasco, announced in a nationally televised address that he would no longer obey presidential orders. General Vásquez accused Hugo Chávez of preparing widespread repression of antigovernment strikers and demonstrators, and he ordered military units under his command to disregard further government orders and remain confined to base. High-ranking generals and admirals soon followed Vásquez to the airwaves, expressing their solidarity with his position and their refusal to support President Chávez. In the early hours of 12 April 2002, the senior military officer in the Venezuelan armed forces, General Lucas Rincón Romero, announced the resignation of President Chávez and the formation of a transitional government under the leadership of Pedro Carmona Estanga, president of FEDECAMARAS, the national federation of chambers of commerce (Hernandez 2002).

Less than twenty-four hours after becoming the head of a transitional government, Pedro Carmona was forced to flee the presidential palace to make way for pro-Chávez civilian and military forces. These swiftly engineered Chávez's return to power, and the generals and admirals who had so recently refused to support his government reversed their positions, many scrambling to provide explanations for their behavior during the rebellion. Amid the celebrations of his supporters, Chávez advocated a new policy of national reconciliation, but he also ordered the detention of high-profile military officers associated with the events of 11 April 2002 (Olivares 2002b).

The military rebellion against the democratically elected government, the first since 1992 and only the third since 1963, is of great significance since it confirms that the armed forces have reemerged as a political actor. Despite President Caldera's best efforts to restore civilian control by containment, the system failed to prevent military politicization. This chapter explores the linkages between the growing role of the military in Venezuelan politics, the deinstitutionalization of civilian control of the armed forces, and political destabilization in Venezuela. It argues that the deliberate expansion of military jurisdictional boundaries by President Chávez has been accompanied by a breakdown in the institutions designed to control and oversee military activities. Moreover, disputes over the control of civilian security forces and the emergence of armed civilian political groups have eroded the state's monopoly on organized violence. These events have taken place in a regime that increasingly lacks institutionalized mechanisms for political dispute resolution among pro- and anti-Chávez forces. In combination, these factors suggest that a politicized military and political violence will become an increasingly prominent feature of Venezuelan politics, and they call into question whether democracy as such will persist.

Venezuela's political crisis during the Chávez administration, the use of the armed forces in domestic operations, the deterioration of civil-military relations, and the growth in civilian political violence are not directly linked in a causal fashion but are rather all the product of the transformational political project of President Hugo Chávez. The expanded jurisdiction of the armed forces is only a reflection of the elected leadership's efforts to secure military support for its political agenda, rather than the result of an internal desire for role expansion by the officer corps. The reaction that the government's use of the military in domestic operations has provoked, both within the military and in civil society, indicates that the armed forces are not a reliable ally of either the Chávez administration or its political opposition. This suggests that the violence that accompanies this political confrontation is increasingly likely to be organized by civilians, which further erodes the state's monopoly of the use of force in society.

The Election of Hugo Chávez and the Transformation
of the Venezuelan Political System

Former coup leader Lieutenant Colonel Hugo Chávez was elected president of Venezuela on 6 December 1998 by 56 percent of voters. This victory marked a year of unprecedented changes in the Venezuelan political environment. Chávez's electoral fortunes had risen from his near-invisibility in the polls in December 1997 to his maintaining a consistent lead by September 1998. The traditionally dominant parties, COPEI and AD, polled single digits in this presidential election, where they had once captured over 90 percent of voters only a decade before. Similarly, whereas 45 percent of the electorate identified themselves with one of the two major parties in 1973, less than 14 percent did so in 1998. This shift in voter preferences and party loyalty is highly unusual, and it is a sign of the depth of crisis experienced by Venezuelans during the 1990s (Molina Vega 2000, 7; Canache 2002, 146–51).

A number of attempts at reform of the democratic system were initiated, beginning in the 1980s, but their failure increasingly disillusioned voters and drove them to seek radical electoral alternatives. Beginning with the Comisión Presidencial para la Reforma del Estado (COPRE) appointed by President Jaime Lusinchi in 1984, Venezuelan academics and activists generated a number of proposals to address the malaise of the system. The diagnosis was that the state was too centralized and unaccountable, which encouraged impunity and corruption. Decentralization was the solution that gained the widest degree of support among political and academic elites during the 1980s. In practical terms, the initial mechanism for achieving decentralization was the revitalization of federalism, enacted in 1988 (Penfold Becerra 2000, 14–19). As part of a strategy of devolving power to the states, many more elected executive and legislative positions were created at the state and municipal levels. Furthermore, to improve the accountability of state officials, the electoral system moved away from closed-list proportional representation toward a mixed system that allowed citizens to vote for many of their elected officials by name, rather than as part of a party (Canache and Kulisheck 1998, 44–47). Although these two efforts corrected some of the vices of the democratic system, they had the unintended consequence of greatly increasing the levels of political contestation associated with elections and politics. This political contestation in turn contributed to undermining the already fragile legitimacy of the Punto Fijo system.

Electoral scandals associated with the 1993 election, the failure of the Caldera administration to address the core issues of poverty and a lack of economic growth, and the decline of the two-party system all set the stage for the implosion of the democratic system. Voter impatience with the traditional system grew rapidly, as is evidenced by the rise in abstention from single digits in the 1970s to close to 40 percent in 1993. Voters increasingly chose nontraditional parties to represent them, as the surprising strength of the leftist Causa R party in the 1993 elections suggested (Hellinger 2003, 35–37). It is also telling that the three candidates with the most significant showing in polls during the 1998 election year (Irene Saenz, Hugo Chávez, and Salas Romer) were all political outsiders with few connections to traditional elites. There was also considerable volatility in voters' preferences for presidential candidates. The mayor of Chacao municipality, Irene Saenz, led the polls with 40 percent of voters in December 1997, but by August 1998 her support had descended into single digits. Similarly, both of the eventual principal presidential candidates in the December 1998 elections, Hugo Chávez and Salas Romer, had registered in the single digits in voter preference polls taken a year earlier. (McCoy and Trinkunas 1999, 122–23).

Chávez's political campaign resonated with voters because of its call for a radical change. His main campaign themes were a condemnation of the existing democracy and a promise to conduct major changes to reduce poverty and create a new participative and Bolivarian democracy. The highly popular centerpiece of his agenda was the convening of a constituent assembly to rewrite the 1961 constitution (McCoy and Trinkunas 1999; Molina Vega 2000, 13.) Coppedge was correct when he described Chávez's 1998 victory as a filling of a political vacuum. Venezuelan voters had been looking for alternatives to the two traditional parties for nearly a decade. Their choices shifted to the political left, and they eventually selected the candidate who offered a populist alternative (Coppedge 2003).

The voters' choice of a populist alternative was a reflection of the increasing social polarization of Venezuelan society, and Chávez's populist discourse appealed to the subaltern classes and members of the middle class who felt excluded by the preceding partyarchy. Chávez most closely fit the mold of a traditional populist politician, and he rejected the fusion of neopopulism and neoliberalism that Roberts and Weyland found in the Argentine and Peruvian cases (Roberts 1996, 2003; Weyland 2000). In his political discourse, Chávez downgraded the importance of intermediary institutions and instead advocated a direct relationship between the people (or the *soberano* [sovereign], a term he prefers) and himself as leader. He called for a participative democracy, and the 1999 constitution reflected many of these changes. His populism extended to the military sphere, particularly through the use of the armed forces in civic action programs and the use of the state to ameliorate poverty. However, in political practice Venezuela under Chávez has become an extreme version of a delegative democracy, one increasingly sustained only with the support of the armed forces (Coppedge 2002). Under these conditions of low horizontal accountability, Chávez's approach to the use of the key source of state coercion, the armed forces, is critically important for understanding the likelihood that some form of democracy in Venezuela will persist.

The Impact of the Election of President Hugo Chávez on the Venezuelan Armed Forces

Chávez's electoral victory and his political agenda brought about major transformations in civil-military relations in Venezuela, expanding military jurisdiction to an unprecedented extent for a democracy. First, Chávez repeatedly justified the 1992 coup attempt as legal, he relied on active and retired military officers to perform civilian political and administrative functions, and he intervened directly in officer promotions and assignments, all of which significantly increased the level of politicization in the armed forces and created a popular expectation for direct military participation in politics. Second, at his direction, military roles and missions were substantially reoriented from national defense to internal security and development, which again contributed to the politicization of the armed forces. Third, the 1999 constitution, written at his behest, created a legal basis for the military's expanded role in state affairs while simultaneously dismantling the admittedly problematic institutional mechanisms of civilian control developed during the Punto Fijo period. This combination would prove explosive for Venezuelan democracy.

IMPACT OF THE 1999 CONSTITUTION ON THE VENEZUELAN ARMED FORCES

The 1999 constitution, whose design was guided by President Chávez, provided the legal underpinnings for a sweeping expansion of military jurisdictional boundaries. In some respects, such as providing officers with the right to vote, the new constitution represented a significant step forward in democratizing Venezuelan politics. However, it also institutionalized civil-military conflict by failing to replace the dysfunctional institutions of the 1961 constitution with new avenues for elected officials to oversee and command the armed forces.

In 1999 the Asamblea Nacional Constituyente (National Constituent Assembly) introduced four principal changes in the constitutional standing of the armed forces. Under the new constitution, active-duty soldiers and officers gained the right to vote, a right they had been denied in the 1961 constitution. At least theoretically, this reform had the merit of encouraging military personnel to participate individually in politics rather than corporately as part of an armed institution. However, Norden points out that the vagueness of the phrasing of this new right in the 1999 constitution (which only bans political militancy, connoting official card-carrying party membership in the Venezuelan context) actually provides for a lot of latitude for military officers to carry out partisan activities (Norden 2003, 99–100).

Of greater importance was Article 328, which redefined the mission of the armed forces to include cooperation in the maintenance of internal order and active participation in national development. Moreover, in Article 330, the constitution specifically provided the armed forces with the right to perform administrative police and investigative activities. While the Venezuelan armed forces had legally acquired a development role as a result of the Ley Orgánica de Seguridad y Defensa in 1976, the 1999 constitution gave this mission constitutional ranking. This made altering or restricting these missions by future governments much more difficult than in the past. Article 331 contained a third critical change since it eliminated the right of the legislature to approve military promotions, leaving this task entirely to the armed forces and the president. The final important change enacted by the new constitution was the unification of the armed forces into a single command structure.

President Chávez also became the ultimate arbiter of military promotions by virtue of Article 236 of the new constitution, which gave him the right to approve promotions of officers at the ranks of colonel and general (or their naval equivalents). The proposed new organic law governing the armed forces extended this power by requiring the president's signature for the promotion of all officers at all ranks (Ley Orgánica de la Fuerza Armada 2002). This has removed a check on the power of the presidency and has made military officers much more likely to align themselves with the preferences of the political party that holds the presidency than was likely during the Punto Fijo system, where there were at least two choices (Angel E. Alvarez 2003).

Taken together, these reforms eliminated two of the underpinnings for civilian control inherited from Punto Fijo democracy. The first of these was the constitutional requirement for legislative approval of military promotions for the ranks of colonel and general. Legislative approval of military promotions overtly affected less than 5 percent of officers in any given year, according to former minister of defense Martín García Villasmil (1995c). However, it had the important effect of self-censoring ambitious military officers into compliance with the policies of elected officials. The elimination of this requirement meant that the only elected official with any constitutional relationship to the armed forces was the president. The second underpinning for civilian control of the armed forces was the decentralization of command authority within the armed forces, originally brought about by Decree 288 of the 1958 transitional government. This had deterred military intervention by increasing the risk that a coup d'état would fail due to lack of coordination, and it had encouraged each service to compete with the others for resources and attention from elected officials. In the absence of these two mechanisms or any alternatives that could facilitate civilian control, the Venezuelan armed forces became substantially more autonomous from political oversight.

POLITICIZATION OF THE ARMED FORCES

President Chávez made his experiences as a military officer and a coup leader integral to his image as a politician, but his ennobling of these "virtues" generated considerable discontent within the armed forces over his blurring of the boundaries between civilian and military roles. During the first years of his administration, Chávez's frequent use of military uniforms in public ceremonies drew widespread civilian and military criticism since it was unprecedented (and possibly illegal) in Venezuela for a civilian elected leader to wear a military uniform (Betancourt 2000). Moreover, by vindicating the failed 1992 coup attempts, Chávez created an opening for military deliberation on the legitimacy of civilian regimes and future rebellions against constituted authority, a position he would later have cause to regret (Villegas Poljak 1999).

Public discussion of the role of the armed forces in politics, unusual prior to the Chávez administration, was sharpened by the events of the 2000 presidential election campaign, in which Chávez sought reelection for a lengthened six-year term under the new 1999 constitution. His opponent, Francisco Arias Cardenas, was a former co-conspirator in the February 1992 coup attempt who later participated in democratic politics, winning election as governor of Zulia state. Arias's decision to run for president was motivated by personal disagreements with Chávez over the direction of the "Bolivarian revolution," and his defection from the government's camp surprisingly had the support of the other three "*comandantes*" (lieutenant colonels) who had conspired with Chávez and Arias to carry out the February 1992 coup. Furthermore, the split between Chávez and the other leaders of the 1992 coups raised the possibility of an internal division within the military. The surprise emergence of Arias as the main opposition presidential candidate led to a bitter political debate in which Arias and Chávez accused each other of treason and incompetence in their professional military careers. The 2000 presidential elections were also the first in which armed forces personnel had the right to vote and, therefore, had to decide between two candidates who were both former military officers and aggressively sought the military vote. This led to reports of the factionalization of the armed forces between "aristas" and "chavistas," which repeatedly surfaced in the press during the campaign (Sanoja Hernández 2000; Norden 2003, 101–3.)

Chávez's administration was noted for its reliance on active-duty and retired military officers to staff political and bureaucratic positions. During the first year of the Chávez administration, retired and active-duty military officers held up to one-third of the portfolios in the presidential cabinet, including the Ministry of Interior, Ministry of Infrastructure, and the governorship of the federal district. As of October 2000, over twenty-nine active-duty military officers held senior ministerial or administrative positions within the government. Military officers were appointed as president and vice president of PDVSA (Petroleos de Venezuela, S.A.), the state oil company, as well as chief executive officer of its U.S. subsidiary, CITGO (Wilson 2000). Active-duty military officers held positions as the president's chief of staff and personal secretary. An active-duty general headed the state agency that was charged with building public housing, including new homes for victims of the 1999 disastrous mudslides and floods in the state of Vargas, as well as the Office of the Budget. Chávez was also careful to appoint officers who supported him in the 1992 coups to head the political and judicial police forces. A number of mid-ranking officers were also transferred to administrative functions in traditionally civilian bureaucracies, particularly in tax collection and customs posts. More controversially, the president encouraged several active-duty military officers to run for office in the 2000 elections on his party's ticket ("Los militares que son" 1999; Colomine 2000). This phenomenon reemerged as the 2004 recall referendum, with President

Chávez calling on voters to recall opposition politicians and nominate military officers in their place.

Chávez retained control over the armed forces by exercising his presidential prerogative to promote officers who were sympathetic to his cause and expel those who were suspected of opposing him. Officers who had reached prominent positions under the previous administration were retired once Chávez assumed the presidency. Following the enactment of the 1999 constitution, Chávez took full control of military promotions, alleging that the legislature's role in this process during the previous four decades had politicized it. Instead, all military promotions were to be approved directly by the president and his minister of defense (Trinkunas 2002b, 65–72; Angel E. Alvarez 2003).

During the first three years of the Chávez presidency, the politicization of the armed forces (both for and against the new regime) became increasingly visible. Senior military officers began using traditional military functions and celebrations to make public statements of support for the "Bolivarian revolution." Junior officers began to conspire in small groups and to distribute samizdat-style anti-Chávez literature and videotapes. Others retired from the armed forces in protest of political manipulation of the officer promotions process (Mayorca 2000). Similarly, a group of retired senior military officers, known as the Frente Institucional Militar (Institutional Military Front), organized themselves for the purpose of opposing the government's use of the armed forces in political and social programs ("Frente Institucional Militar" 2000). Rumors of military conspiracies repeatedly surfaced in the press during this period, which forced the government to deny any dissent within the armed forces (Leal 2000). This level of activity by military officers for and against the new government was unprecedented by the standards of the Punto Fijo period, and it revealed the increasing stress that had been generated within the officer corps by President Chávez's reforms.

EXPANDING MILITARY ROLES AND MISSIONS

In the Fifth Republic, as President Hugo Chávez called his new regime, the armed forces became one of the principal executors of government social and political policy. From the beginning of his term, President Chávez argued that the only way to address the national crisis was to take advantage of the human and technical resources provided by the armed forces. Furthermore, Chávez explicitly called on the armed forces to join and support his revolutionary project (Trinkunas 2002a). The reform of the organic law of the armed forces, prepared by the Ministry of Defense, identified eighteen functions for the armed forces, as compared to the six identified in legislation prior to the election of President Chávez (Ley Orgánica de la Fuerza Armada 2002). The military played its most prominent role in public policy through the Plan Bolívar 2000 social program (Norden 2003, 100–105).

The Plan Bolívar 2000, among the first programs announced by President Chávez, aimed at the broad incorporation of the armed forces into domestic political and economic affairs. Plan Bolívar 2000 included infrastructure refurbishment and construction, health care for the poor, combating illiteracy and unemployment, and food distribution. Initially established as a six-month emergency program that hired unemployed civilians and placed them under the direction of military officers, it became a permanent part of the Chávez administration's policies (Comando General del Ejercito 2000). Under the Plan Bolívar 2000, the armed forces went so far as to use soldiers to sell basic goods at below-market prices to hold down costs in lower- and working-class marketplaces (Norden 2003). The air force provided low cost rural air transport through its Rutas Sociales, and the navy became involved in aiding the fishing industry through the program Pescar 2000. Approximately 29,000 soldiers (out of a total force of 85,000) participated in Plan Bolívar 2000 in its first year (Cardona Marrero 2001a).

While these military-led efforts at poverty alleviation and economic development provided significant public benefits, they came at the expense of expanded military jurisdictional boundaries and a reduction in the civilian capacity to develop and implement public policy. As a case in point, the Chávez administration starved opposition governors and mayors of resources with which to address these problems, preferring to fund military-led social programs that were controlled by local garrison commanders (Maracara 1999). This occurred even as Venezuela was benefiting from a sharp rise in world oil prices after 1999, to over $44 per barrel in 2004, and generated a large sum of windfall revenues with which the central government could fund discretionary spending. Even though the government was legally required to channel a substantial amount of this funding to the state and local governments, it failed to do so (Monaldi Marturet 2005). Specifically, President Chávez avoided disbursing windfall profits from the sale of oil set aside in a macroeconomic stabilization fund, part of which was originally destined for the use of regional governments. Military garrisons, as principal executors of the Plan Bolívar 2000 in each state, instead benefited from these revenues and were able to replace the state and municipal governments as the principal agents for regional development and poverty alleviation (Bottome 1999).

The initial expansion of military roles and missions between 1999 and 2001 generated considerable debate within Venezuela. Retired military officers critiqued the expansion of the military's role as a threat to the professionalism of the institution (Norden 2003, 106–7). Former prosecutor general Eduardo Roche Lander reported several cases of corruption in relation to irregularities in the administration of Plan Bolívar monies (Yánez Mondragón 2004). Former presidential candidate Francisco Arias Cardenas accused the government of decreasing military readiness due to its excessive emphasis on the Plan Bolívar 2000. Other critics questioned the diversion of government resources into funding a civic action plan under the auspices of the military, which used secrecy regulations to shield its activities under the plan from scrutiny ("El gobierno debe" 2000). Although all of these critics had valid grounds for their specific concerns, the danger lay not only in the expansion of the military's role, but in that such expansion occurred at the same time as institutional mechanisms of civilian control were being dismantled.

IMPACT OF EXPANDING JURISDICTIONAL BOUNDARIES

The growth in the military's domestic role under the first two years of the Chávez administration had a mixed impact on the armed forces. The greatest negative impact came in the area of readiness, with persistent reports of the inoperability of military equipment due to the stagnation of the portions of the defense budget apportioned to operations and acquisitions. In the army, it was reported, 25 to 30 percent of armored assets were not operable. The air force and the navy were reportedly worse off in terms of readiness (Romero and Romero 2002a, 2002b, 2002c). Also, some retired officers alleged that military preparedness was affected by the diversion of personnel to support the activities of the Plan Bolívar 2000.[1] The Ministry of Defense spent more on salaries for personnel and made large budgets available to garrison commanders to execute activities related to the Plan Bolívar 2000 (approximately BS. 200 billion in 1999–2002), but the overall budget declined in 2001 and 2002, which meant that operational and acquisition budgets were squeezed (Cardona Marrero 2001a; Armas 2003).

Until 2002, the role of the armed forces in domestic "internal security" missions was relatively restricted, although there were allegations by local human rights organizations that the military used excessive force during its

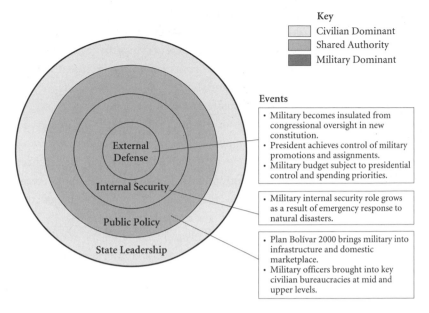

Key
Civilian Dominant
Shared Authority
Military Dominant

Events

External Defense

Internal Security

Public Policy

State Leadership

- Military becomes insulated from congressional oversight in new constitution.
- President achieves control of military promotions and assignments.
- Military budget subject to presidential control and spending priorities.

- Military internal security role grows as a result of emergency response to natural disasters.

- Plan Bolívar 2000 brings military into infrastructure and domestic marketplace.
- Military officers brought into key civilian bureaucracies at mid and upper levels.

Figure 6.1. Civil-Military Jurisdictional Boundaries, ca. 2001: Military Jurisdictional Boundaries Expand

operations to support civilian authorities following the massive landslides that occurred on Venezuela's littoral in 1999. However, the main use of the military prior to 2002 was to perform domestic humanitarian operations in support of President Chávez's policies (Norden 2003, 104–6).

In aggregate, the result was a substantial revision of Venezuelan military jurisdictional boundaries. As figure 6.1 shows, Venezuelan civil-military relations showed a clear trend away from civilian control, presaging the conflicts that would erupt in 2002.

The 11 April 2002 Coup Attempt

Although President Chávez's popularity had been declining throughout 2001, the successful general strike held on 10 December of that year demonstrated that the opposition, led by an unusual coalition of major business and labor federations, was finally coherent enough to raise a successful challenge to the government. The opposition's criticism of the Chávez administration centered on the government's policies toward land use, education, organized labor, and the economy. The opposition also attacked the administration's foreign policy, which included closer links with countries such as Cuba, Libya, and Saddam Hussein's Iraq, criticism of U.S. foreign policy after 11 September 2001, and expressions of sympathy for the Colombian FARC guerrillas ("Gobierno evalua denuncias" 2002). President Chávez responded to his critics with characteristically tempestuous and aggressive language, which heightened the tension between pro- and antigovernment forces. The opposition's criticisms of the president found sympathizers in the armed forces, and a small number of senior military officers from all services began publicly to denounce Chávez in a series of press conferences (Alvarez 2002c). Although these individual actions were not a serious threat to the administration's grip on power, they did undermine the president's claim of unconditional support from the armed forces.

Opposition to Chávez became especially trenchant after the administration began to make changes in the senior leadership of the state-owned oil industry. Although this had always been a prerogative of past governments, senior positions in PDVSA had traditionally been reserved for technocrats promoted from within and a leavening of outsiders with business experience (Mommer 2003). The appointment of Gastón Parra, an academic who was highly critical of PDVSA, to its presidency detonated a rebellion by the middle management that found support in civil society at large. A cycle of civilian protests against the government began as a means to pressure Chávez into reversing this decision. President Chávez went as far as to summarily dismiss many senior technocrats, announcing the decision on his weekly radio show, "Aló Presidente," which many took as an effort to heap insult on injury (Leal and Garbarini 2002).

After it became clear that President Chávez would continue his efforts to seize political control of the oil industry, the civilian leaders of the opposition called for a new general strike for 9 April 2002. Highly successful, the strike was extended indefinitely by the leader of the national labor confederation, Carlos Ortega, on 10 April. Progressively larger antigovernment demonstrations were held on successive days in Caracas, which led to a conflict between the private sector media and the Chávez administration over news coverage of the strike. Tragically, the massive antigovernment march of nearly 500,000 people on 11 April ended in violence when protesters converged on the presidential palace. Here, they clashed with members of the Círculos Bolivarianos, a popular movement of supporters of President Chávez, and were fired on by unidentified snipers. An estimated twelve persons died and over a hundred were injured. Live coverage of the bloody events, shown in a split-screen format simultaneously with President Chávez's televised address to the nation, prompted the administration to close down private television transmissions. At this time Chávez also ordered the armed forces to take military control of the capital, an order that rebel officers claim led them to begin the coup (Olivares 2002b).

In the face of a worsening crisis, the military acted, although their intervention at first resembled a sit-down strike rather than a coup. There were initial reports on the evening of 11 April that a number of senior officers had attempted to broadcast a message against the government. Censorship of television and radio broadcasts began to break down as the coup gathered momentum. The turning point of the rebellion occurred when General Efraín Vásquez Velasco, surrounded by his officers, stated in a televised address that he would not obey presidential directives to suppress antigovernment demonstrations and ordered all of his troops to remain confined to base. In his speech he characterized President Chávez's directives as illegal, and in short order, senior generals in the Guardia Nacional and admirals in the navy echoed Vásquez Velasco's sentiments in radio and television broadcasts (Alvarez 2002a). Active-duty officers who served in the government, such as the minister of finance and the vice minister of citizen security, resigned their positions. Although President Chávez claimed in his national address of 11 April that he would hold out in the presidential palace with his honor guard and supporters to the bitter end, General Lucas Rincón Romero, inspector general of the armed forces, announced Chávez's resignation in the early hours of 12 April (Weffer Cifuentes 2002). A transitional government soon formed under Pedro Carmona, leader of the national business federation FEDECAMARAS.

General Vásquez Velasco's refusal to obey the president made it appear that the armed forces had turned decisively against the Chávez administration, yet the military rebellion never extended very far beyond the upper ranks of the officer corps. Venezuelan investigative reporter Patricia Poleo, in her published account of how the coup was hijacked by conservative elements of the civilian opposition, reveals that the rebellious elements of the armed forces controlled almost no combat troops (Poleo 2002). Although some senior officers admitted after the rebellion that they had been conspiring since the summer of 2001, they did not secure support from officers outside Caracas. The strategic military installations in the city of Maracay, where Venezuela's armored, airborne, and air forces were concentrated, never accepted the new government, and rebel military control in Caracas was spotty at best (Mayorca 2002). The military consensus in favor of deposing President Chávez rested on the shared conviction among officers that they should not be involved in repressing civilian antigovernment demonstrators. Once the unconstitutional nature of the transitional government became clear, this consensus fell apart.

Pedro Carmona's interim government committed a number of key political errors during its brief existence. First, it was drawn from a narrow right-wing slice of the political spectrum that excluded key elements of the opposition to Hugo Chávez, most notably organized labor. Images of the well-heeled participants in the televised self-proclamation of Pedro Carmona as president quickly confirmed the sectarian upper-class nature of the new government, particularly to poor and working-class Venezuelans where pro-Chávez sentiments were concentrated. Second, Carmona's decree to dissolve the National Assembly and the Supreme Court made it clear to many military officers that the new government was completely unconstitutional and not prepared to meet even minimum democratic criteria. Third, Carmona erred in the military arena, appointing as minister of defense an admiral who had very little authority within the officer corps rather than a senior army general. Carmona also selected a recently cashiered officer, Admiral Carlos Molina Tamayo, as head of presidential security. These appointments, which also contravened military views on seniority and merit, angered a number of senior officers who had initially supported the Carmona government (Zapata 2002a).

In another critical miscalculation, nobody in the Carmona administration thought of replacing the troops in charge of security at Miraflores, the presidential palace. Once pro-Chavez demonstrations and riots began on 13 April 2002, loyal presidential security troops ejected the Carmona administration from Miraflores and allowed President Chávez's ministers to enter, reconvene the National Assembly, and temporarily swear in the vice president, Diosdado Cabello, as interim president. As Pedro Carmona took shelter at a nearby military base, the junior and mid-ranking officers who actually commanded the combat units of the armed forces made it clear to their superiors that they would only support efforts to restore constitutional rule. This paved the way for a swift return of Hugo Chávez Frias to power on 14 April 2002 (Poleo 2002; Romero 2002a).

CONSEQUENCES OF THE 11 APRIL COUP FOR
VENEZUELAN CIVIL-MILITARY RELATIONS

Even though military participation in the domestic arena was the leading cause of the 11 April coup attempt, it was President Chávez's orders to the military to employ violence against civilian demonstrators that precipitated the rebellion. On the face of it, the rebel military officers argued that they were disobeying illegal and unconstitutional orders from the president to repress demonstrators. Even if the motives of some of these officers were suspect, they took advantage of the crisis created within the armed forces by these orders to pursue their agenda of removing Chávez from power. Either way, domestic roles for the military led to substantial negative consequences for the armed forces, loyal and disloyal alike. In the long run, military unrest also meant that the Chávez administration could not fully rely on the armed forces to defend the regime, opening the way for greater civilian participation in the use of force for political purposes.

The anti-Chávez faction, which was concentrated among senior officers, was hard hit by their defeat during the rebellion. Their association with the Carmona government discredited them among their subordinates, and the Chávez administration pursued a policy of legal action against these officers. Initially, military prosecutors detained fifty-eight officers, twenty-four of whom were generals or admirals. In the army, these detentions were largely concentrated in the logistics and aviation branches, an indication of the president's success in shuffling his opponents in the military into positions where they did not command significant numbers of troops (Trinkunas 2002b, 165–72; Olivares 2004). As the generals who participated in or sympathized with the 11 April coup attempt were cashiered, a substantial number joined the civilian opposition or formed their own political interest groups (Hernández 2003). The government also cracked down on any public dissent from administration policy, including jailing some senior officers (Olivares 2004).

The government had some success in pursuing administrative channels to punish or sideline rebellious officers. Many of the officers who participated actively in the 11 April coup attempts were involuntarily retired by the Ministry of Defense. Together with a policy of rapid rotation and the promotion of politically reliable junior officers to senior positions, the Chávez administration secured renewed control over the armed forces. This control was strengthened by the presence of several of Chávez's military academy classmates in command of the army ("Chávez ordenó" 2002). At least some observers in Venezuela report that as many as 980 officers have been removed from the armed forces since 2001 (Olivares 2003). The accelerated promotion of officers based on political loyalty rather than professionalism increased dissatisfaction with the government among the institutionalist wing of the military.

The success of Chávez's punitive tactics in the wake of 11 April eventually produced a reaction within the armed forces. A substantial number of officers who had been affected by the administrative and judicial maneuvers began an open-air vigil at a plaza in the Altamira neighborhood of Caracas in October 2002. They criticized the government both for its left-wing policies and for its politicization of the armed forces. Other officers and enlisted personnel joined them, and their numbers eventually exceeded one hundred. Their peaceful "sit-down strike" also attracted large numbers of civilian supporters who joined them in Plaza Altamira, provided food and shelter, and helped to stand watch against the government efforts at dislodgement that President Chávez publicly threatened to order more than once (La Rotta Moran 2002; Pérez Rodríguez 2002). This movement continued unabated until the conclusion of the larger general strike in February 2003.

From the perspective of civil-military relations in Venezuela, the most troubling aspect of these developments was the accretion of a popular civilian movement around the rebellious officers and the increasingly political nature of the their pronouncements. Not only did they call repeatedly on President Chávez to resign, but they also began to take a leadership role in the political opposition to the administration, going as far as holding joint events with the Coordinadora Democrática, a civilian opposition umbrella organization. As the "peaceful" military rebellion extended for months, the accusations against the government became more pointed, including attempts to link Chávez to support for Al Qaeda terrorism, a clear attempt to influence U.S. government opinion on developments in Venezuela.[2]

Pro-Chávez forces emerged from the rebellion with a mixed record. Senior officers who were closely identified with the president's program, such as General Manuel Rosendo, the commander of the armed forces unified command (CUFAN), sided with the rebels on 11 April (Zapata 2002b). As a result, almost the entire military high command was replaced in the days following President Chávez's return to power, and there was a further shakeup of the armed forces leadership in the summer of 2002. The coup attempt did allow the government to place officers that it considered most loyal, such as General Jorge Garcia Carneiro, into the key control positions in the armed forces. These officers have done a great deal to ensure the quiescence of most military officers in political matters. However, their high visibility has made them the target of virulent protests by civilian opponents of the government, including "*cacerolazos*" (banging on pots, tables, glasses) whenever these officials appear in public places such as restaurants and civilian airplanes. Civilian distaste for these particular military officers has the potential to turn into a broader civilian disdain of the armed forces, once the most prestigious public institution in Venezuela (Pew Center Global Attitudes Project 2002).

The institutionalist majority in the Venezuelan armed forces emerged as a key actor, one that remains a threat to the Chávez administration in the long run. By standing by during the overthrow of the president in the first place, it showed that it was willing to place limits on the actions of the president and prevent him from using force to achieve his political objectives. However, the support for democratic principles and the constitution also show that the Venezuelan armed forces were not willing to support an outright dictatorship (Olivares 2002a). The Chávez administration's need for military support in order to remain in power has meant that it has intensified its vigilance over the armed forces, ironically using many of the same tactics that were used against the pro-Chávez military in the wake of the 1992 coup attempts.

The credibility of the civilian opposition to President Chávez was undermined by its antidemocratic actions during the 11–14 April period, and this will have a negative impact on its future relations with the military. The hijacking of the transitional government by the most conservative elements in Venezuelan civil society, its mistakes in handling civil-military relations, and the subsequent failure of the coup can only create doubts within the officer corps about the wisdom of working with the opposition. More important, the unconstitutional decrees of the Carmona government confirmed for many officers the truth of President Chávez's claims about the opposition, namely, that it is led by a right-wing conspiracy between a corrupt oligarchy and the owners of the media. The coup also confirmed that an important element of the civilian opposition does not view the Chávez administration as legitimate and is more than willing to subvert the state's control over the armed forces to overthrow the government.[3]

The Chávez administration was initially weakened by the military rebellion because it revealed the seams in the alliance between the revolution and the armed forces. During the first two years of his administration, President Chávez repeatedly asserted the solidarity of the armed forces with his revolutionary project as one of the strengths of his regime: the guns of the military, he stated, were on the side of the people (and by extension his programs). This claim of a seamless connection between military support and government authority was no longer credible after 11 April. Moreover, as critics of his military policy predicted, Chávez's efforts to manipulate the officer promotion process to favor his revolutionary project accentuated the splits in the armed forces. Although he did have sufficient supporters in key positions as a result of this policy, his personal control of the armed forces was not enough to prevent a nearly successful military rebellion.

THE DECEMBER 2002 GENERAL STRIKE

Government restraint on the use of the armed forces in internal security roles broke down during the sixty-three days of the general strike that began on 2 December 2002. Organized by the Coordinadora Democrática (the umbrella civilian opposition organization), the Confederación General de Trabajadores (the national labor union federation), and FEDECAMARAS, the general strike was intended to force President Chávez from power, either by his resignation or his acquiescence to a recall referendum ("Oposición convocó" 2002). President Chávez's popularity among the general public plummeted, with his approval ratings dropping to 29 percent (Giusti 2002). To survive the general strike, Chávez turned to the armed forces to provide internal security, distribute goods and services, and assist in the restoration of oil production. Military officers, many of whom perceived the interruption of oil production as a direct threat to national security, proved willing to support the government in this confrontation. For those who were not as enthusiastic, the purge of the officer corps following the 11 April 2002 coup proved a salutatory reminder.

Political tension between the government and the opposition had reached a peak in the fall of 2002 when President Chávez ordered the armed forces to take over the Caracas metropolitan police force, which was under the control of the opposition mayor, Alfredo Peña. The government accused the police force of being partial to the opposition because it protected their demonstrations from clashes with pro-Chávez activists, such as the Círculos Bolivarianos. The government went so far as to accuse the metropolitan police of deliberately targeting its supporters. The armed forces prevented the police from operating and put troops on the streets of Caracas to ensure their control of the city. This striking use by the government of the armed forces to intervene in domestic politics formed the backdrop to the decision to call a general strike (Ruiz Pantin 2002).

The December 2002 general strike received broad backing from civil society, and economic activity was nearly paralyzed in certain sectors. The strike gained real momentum when the management and workers of the state-owned oil company, PDVSA, joined the strike, which critically undermined Venezuela's ability to export oil (Castro and Ventura Nicolas 2002). Estimates of the impact on the Venezuelan economy varied wildly, ranging from an 80 percent stoppage rate reported by the opposition to a 20 percent rate reported by the government (Salieron 2002). During the height of the general strike, Venezuela was even forced to import gasoline from Brazil, an operation for which its port facilities had never been designed since Venezuela was a long-established leading oil producer.

Initially, the Coordinadora Democrática hoped to force Chávez to resign, but the group eventually settled on a strategy of calling for a referendum on his presidency. Venezuela witnessed the longest period of social mobilization since its transition to democracy in 1958, as literally millions turned out in antigovernment demonstrations. The government turned out its own supporters in counterdemonstrations, and social and political tension rose to such an extent that OAS secretary general Cesar Gaviria committed his personal prestige and authority to a prolonged negotiation process between the government and its opponents ("Gaviria instó" 2002). Most of the opposition placed its hope in a proposed referendum on President Chávez scheduled for 2 February 2003. Over 1.5 million signatures were gathered and delivered to the Consejo Nacional Electoral (CNE), as required by law, and the CNE began the process of organizing a nationwide referendum (Martinez 2002). This process continued even in the face of the obstacles placed by President Chávez, such as the denial of additional funding for electoral organization and the refusal to provide military support and security to the electoral process (as had occurred in every election since 1958). Only the decision of the Tribunal Supremo de Justicia (Supreme Court) declaring the 2 February referendum nonbinding and the board of the national electoral council invalid brought the process to a halt (Irma Alvarez 2003). Discouraged, the civilian opposition called off the general strike on 3 February 2003.

THE ARMED FORCES IN THE WAKE
OF THE GENERAL STRIKE

The armed forces enabled President Chávez to remain in power during the general strike. The armed forces, particularly the Guardia Nacional and the army military police, acted to quell civilian opposition demonstrations on a number of occasions (Gonzalez 2003), and the military was used to intimidate civilian food producers who were participating in the general strike (Camel Anderson 2003c). The armed forces occupied the police stations of the Caracas metropolitan police force to prevent the civilian police from operating. The military occupied oil facilities and assisted in breaking the production strike by PDVSA workers. When the oil tankers of the Venezuelan merchant marine refused to load oil or operate, they were boarded by naval commandos, and their crews were reportedly intimidated ("Armada toma control" 2002). After President Chávez took the step of breaking up the existing organization of PDVSA and firing almost half of its employees, military officers were brought in to support the progovernment minority of oil workers and managers who returned to work (Camel Anderson 2003a, 2003b). Finally, as supplies and services ran short in most metropolitan areas of Venezuela, the navy was used to ship supplies from neighboring countries, and the army was used to organize street fairs in which citizens could buy basic necessities and access health and government services ("Buque cargado de alimentos" 2003).

With the rest of the state largely inoperative, wavering (the Supreme Court), or actively opposing the Chávez administration (CNE), only the armed forces allowed the government to continue operating with some measure of physical security, access to resources, and the threat of violence to compel its adversaries to end the general strike. However, it is very significant that the use of the armed forces in internal security missions was limited to specialized units, such as the Guardia Nacional, military police, and the naval commandos, rather than to units of the regular military as a whole.

In the short term, the armed forces did not benefit much as a result of their core role in supporting the government during the general strike, at least in terms of autonomy and resources. The size of the armed forces did not increase. In 2004 discussion began on finding alternative sources for re-equipping the armed forces, such as Russian and Chinese armaments. President Chávez announced acquisition programs in late 2004 to introduce Russian-produced military helicopters and a large number of small arms into Venezuela's military inventory, with a potential follow-up acquisition of antitank and antiaircraft systems ("Venezuela planea comprar" 2004). Similar plans were announced in 2005 to acquire Brazilian and Spanish air and maritime defense equipment ("Rodríguez Araque: Venezuela no tiene" 2005).

The general trend in the employment of the armed forces, however, has been in internal affairs at the service of the Chávez administration's political agenda. The consolidation of the internal role of the armed forces was apparent in the speech by the commander of the army, General Raúl Baduel, on the occasion of Army Day 2003, which provided some confirmation of the shift in the thinking of the military high command. In this speech, on the most important public appearance of the army chief in any given year, Baduel called on the armed forces to assume greater readiness to defend Venezuela. Enumerating the threats to the state that he saw, Baduel listed subversion by internal groups or external powers, separatist movements, coups d'état, or invasion by the United States under a United Nations or OAS mandate. With the exception of this last item, nothing in this discourse distinguishes it from the declarations of other military governors in the Southern Cone during the 1970s. Interestingly, General Baduel's prescription was an integrated national defense in which all elements of the society (economic, cultural, social, political, environmental, geographic, and military) would contribute, again reminiscent of the internally focused national security doctrines of Argentina, Chile, and Brazil during the 1960s and 1970s (Rojas 2004).

THE 2004 PRESIDENTIAL RECALL REFERENDUM: MILITARY SUBORDINATION TO THE "PEACEFUL REVOLUTION"

The continuing importance of the armed forces' internal role, even its political role, was confirmed during 2004, when the opposition to President Chávez attempted to remove him from office by means of a recall referendum. One of the innovations of the 1999 Venezuelan constitution was the ability for citizens to recall the president at any point after the first half of his term had been completed. One of the prerequisites was that 20 percent of registered voters had to petition the CNE for this referendum to be conducted. Beginning in November 2003, opposition groups claimed to have collected sufficient signatures. The leadership of the CNE, often accused of being biased in favor of the Chávez administration, required the opposition to overcome substantial procedural hurdles, including a process by which citizens had to reconfirm their signatures on recall petitions (the so-called Reafirmazo). The opposition cleared this last set of obstacles, finally forcing the CNE to announce that a recall referendum would be held on 15 August 2004.

President Chávez defeated the opposition in August 2004 referendum by a margin of almost 20 percent (59 to 41), despite polling data that had shown his government's popularity among voters waning in the first quarter of the year. International election observers from the OAS and the Carter Center announced that they had found the polling to be free and fair, but the opposition, still led by the Coordinadora Democrática, quickly cried foul. The opposition alleged massive fraud at the polls, where electronic voting machines were used, and in the postelection audit conducted by international observers. However, the international community quickly accepted the legitimacy of the voting outcome, confirming Chávez's increasingly firm hold on power.

Regardless of the allegations of fraud, two other factors undermined the opposition's campaign to remove President Chávez. The first was the economic turnaround driven by high oil prices, which surged for the first time past $50 per barrel. The Chávez administration was able to directly access these revenues due to its iron grip on the post–general strike PDVSA. The government in turn invested these revenues in programs (known as *misiones*) designed to improve literacy and to provide access to health care, basic food, housing, and even university education. Although disorganized, these programs were highly visible and popular among the poorer sectors of the electorate, who were Chávez's core supporters. The second factor was the disorganization of the opposition. Despite the existence of the Coordinadora Democrática, the opposition's referendum strategy was often murky and directionless. The opposition was particularly hurt by its inability to present potential alternatives to Chávez. With no single figure around whom disaffected voters could coalesce, the opposition faced an uphill battle to oust the president (McCoy 2004).

The armed forces played a low-key role during the 2004 recall referendum. The important senior commands were all in the hands of Chávez loyalists, and significantly, two of the officers who had restored the president to power in April 2002, General Garcia Carneiro and General Baduel, now headed the Ministry of Defense and the army, respectively. The military reprised its traditional role of executing the Plán República to provide logistics and security support to the CNE as it conducted the election. No instances of military unrest, common in 2001 and 2002, were reported in the lead-up to the referendum process, although the ongoing prosecution of participants in the 2002 coup attempts must have served as a deterrent. Moreover, with the official results of the referendum apparently granting the president a landslide victory, military subordination to the Chávez administration was never seriously tested.

Conclusions

The remilitarization of politics and the rise in organized violence are a consequence of the growing gap between the Chávez administration and the opposition, neither of which see the other as legitimate. In the absence of legitimacy, both the government and the opposition have tried to lay claim to the most powerful organization in society, the armed forces. So far, neither side has entirely won this tug-of-war, yet the struggle has clearly had a deleterious effect on Venezuelan democracy. The armed forces have not been a reliable source of compulsion and force for either the government or the opposition, and the result has been increasing civilian-on-civilian violence, with the expected negative impact on democracy.

The heated and often apocalyptic rhetoric that the government and the opposition use to refer to each other is more than a political tactic; it is a reflection of the growing fear with which political actors in Venezuela regard one another, as both PROVEA and COFAVIC, both local human rights organizations, have noted. The most recent example of the impact of this phenomenon can be found in the prolonged negotiations that followed the conclusion of the 2002–3 general strike. These discussions, which focused on restoring political peace in Venezuela and addressed the terms under which the government would hold a referendum on President Chávez's term of office, revealed two sides with almost no common ground politically. The participation in these negotiations of the secretary general of the OAS, Cesar Gaviria, on a daily basis over a period of months was unprecedented in the history of that organization. Gaviria's statements during this process confirm the depths of mistrust among participants. At their conclusion, the negotiations produced an agreement with little substance, and it was almost immediately disavowed by important political actors from both the pro- and anti-Chávez movement (BBCMundo.com 2003).

Civilians' growing use of violence to achieve political ends, often legitimized or excused by political leaders in their daily discourse, confirms the breakdown on the state's monopoly on the use of force. The psychological sense of insecurity experienced by many Venezuelan citizens and the growth in organized and armed groups are reflections of this phenomenon. The re-emergence of urban guerrilla organizations is especially troubling since it may lead to a spiral of organization and violence as political actors engage in an arms race to protect themselves and deter their opponents. The armed forces have attempted to remain at the margin of the growing violence in Venezuelan society, and even the 11 April 2002 coup attempt was notable for the fact that almost all of the violent acts that occurred during this period involved civilian rather than military use of force. However, if violence continues to escalate, the armed forces may be compelled into another untenable scenario in which they have to choose between supporting elected authorities and using force against their fellow citizens.

The greatest effect of current political and criminal violence is on the legitimacy of the government. Pro- and anti-Chávez factions in Venezuela see in each other an existential threat. The government points to the 11 April coup attempt and the general strikes that have been convened against the administration as evidence of the opposition's goal of overthrowing the regime. In light of this, the government discredits every proposal made by the opposition and rejects all efforts to reach political consensus. The president's references to the opposition as a "squalid oligarchy" and "destabilizers" summarize effectively the government's view of the opposition. The opposition points to the repeated violations of the Venezuelan constitution by the government, ongoing violations of legislative procedures to favor government legal proposals, widespread corruption and impunity, and government repression of political demonstrations as evidence that the country is no longer democratic. From the opposition's perspective, since President Chávez's political agenda leads to dictatorship, the regime is not legitimate and must be removed, legally or otherwise. The mutual withdrawal of legitimacy by each side is of particular concern since the government has few policy successes to point to that could reconcile the opposition to the new regime. The limited economic growth achieved in 2000 and 2001 was erased by an 8.9 percent decline in GDP in 2002 and a 17 percent decline in 2003. Venezuela's strong recovery in 2004, with 17 percent GDP growth, may set the stage for a modus vivendi between the government and business sectors, which have so far supported the opposition (Sarmiento 2003; Markey 2005).

Since the 2002–3 general strike, the government and the opposition have confined their conflict to the institutional boundaries set forth in the 1999 constitution by focusing once again on the possibility of a recall referendum against President Chávez. Tensions in the run-up to the 2004 recall referendum confirmed that civilian political tensions continued to run high, with mutual accusations of electoral fraud and political chicanery common in Venezuelan political discourse. Efforts by the opposition Coordinadora Democrática finally bore fruit after a second round of recall petitions were completed in May 2004, despite the best efforts of the government to delay the process (Carter Center 2004). The government countered by circulating recall petitions for opposition governors and legislators. At the same time, the Chávez administration pushed through an expansion of the Supreme Court in what many perceived as an effort at packing the court prior to the recall referendum in August 2004.[4]

In this highly politically charged atmosphere, the Venezuelan armed forces have not actively sought an expanded role in domestic affairs. Rather, they initially responded to the president's request to support the government's programs and, later, became the centerpiece of a political tug-of-war between the government and the opposition. Although there has always been a development role enshrined in the armed forces' organic laws and in the 1999 constitution, the preferences of the military have usually run in other directions, as revealed by their desire for sophisticated defense materiel appropriate to an external defense role. It was not until newly inaugurated president Chávez ordered the development of Plan Bolívar 2000 that the armed forces expanded their efforts into domestic affairs. Chávez ordered each of the expansions in the armed forces' domestic role that followed, particularly during the general strike. Moreover, the ability of elected officials to manipulate the military promotion system on the basis of personal loyalties and politics, even after the 11 April coup, and their ability to prosecute officers and punish them administratively indicate that likelihood of the overt military resistance in Venezuela is low.

The failure of the 11 April coup indicated that, even though there was discontent in the officer corps, the sentiment in favor of military intervention in politics was limited to a small number of senior officers, now expelled from the institution. Furthermore, the fact that the armed forces did not intervene against the president during the 2002–3 general strike, a period of intense social conflict when the president was most vulnerable, also suggested that the officer corps would prefer to avoid politics (although it may also indicate that Chávez's manipulation of promotions and assignments is especially effective). In any event, pro-Chávez military officers still base their support for the president on the constitution. What is most disturbing and remains a great threat to Venezuelan democracy is the persistent appeal by civilians

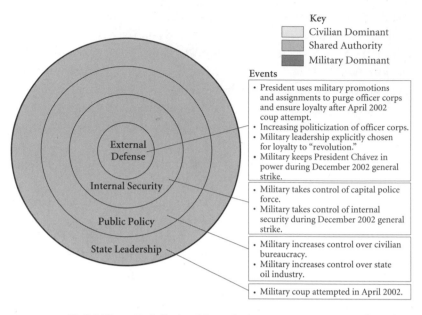

Key
☐ Civilian Dominant
▨ Shared Authority
■ Military Dominant

Events

External
Defense
- President uses military promotions and assignments to purge officer corps and ensure loyalty after April 2002 coup attempt.
- Increasing politicization of officer corps.
- Military leadership explicitly chosen for loyalty to "revolution."
- Military keeps President Chávez in power during December 2002 general strike.

Internal Security
- Military takes control of capital police force.
- Military takes control of internal security during December 2002 general strike.

Public Policy

State Leadership
- Military increases control over civilian bureaucracy.
- Military increases control over state oil industry.

- Military coup attempted in April 2002.

Figure 6.2. Civil-Military Jurisdictional Boundaries, ca. 2003: Institutional Civilian Control Collapses

on both sides for support from the armed forces, which recalls the "knocking on the barracks door" phenomenon that Alfred Stepan (1974) described in the Brazilian case during the 1960s.

Figure 6.2 illustrates the extent to which institutionalized civilian control has collapsed in Venezuela. There are few jurisdictional boundaries between civilian and military roles in the Venezuelan state. The civilian government's thorough manipulation of military promotions and assignments to reward "revolutionary" virtue suggests that the Venezuelan armed forces lack institutional autonomy in their core functions. Military participation in internal security and public policy is well documented, and even though jurisdictional boundaries were expanded at the behest of civilians, these new missions are open-ended and bereft of civilian oversight, neither of which is conducive to democratic stability (Pion-Berlin and Arceneaux 2000). The role the armed forces played in sustaining, displacing, and reinstating Chávez during the April 2002 coup confirmed the new political role of the armed forces, even though they were largely subservient during the subsequent two years. This pattern of intermingled civilian and military responsibilities is noninstitutionalized and does not resemble either civilian control by oversight or civilian control by containment but rather a particularly extreme version of the form of subjective control of the armed forces documented by Huntington (1957).

The bottom line is that the remilitarization of Venezuelan politics has had a negative impact on the Venezuelan armed forces and on Venezuelan society. Expanded domestic roles for the armed forces during the Chávez administration has led to internal division, politicization, attempted coups, and declining operational readiness in the military. However, the expansion of the military's domestic social and political roles had its source in the guidance provided to the armed forces by its democratically elected leadership. Moreover, the results of the manner in which President Chávez managed the armed forces were entirely predictable because they were mostly more extreme versions of the strategies his predecessors used vis-à-vis the armed forces as a means of keeping them in check. Ironically, one of the goals of Chávez's 1992 coup attempt was to put an end to the harmful (yet much milder) civil-military practices that democratic governments had pursued during the Punto Fijo period.

In many ways, President Chávez's transformational political project has been both the source of the military's participation in domestic roles and a catalyst for the burgeoning civilian opposition. The result has been escalating violence and conflict in both civil society and the armed forces. However, the government is in a quandary. The events of 11 April 2002 show that the armed forces are not necessarily a reliable ally, particularly when it comes to deploying force against the civilian opposition. Maintaining control of the military in the wake of the coup required increased politicization of the officer corps and personal control of promotions and assignments by the president. On the other hand, the role of the military during the 2002–3 general strike also shows that it would be difficult for the Chávez administration to survive the efforts of the opposition to remove it from power without support from the military. Rather than putting further strain on civil-military relations, the logical response by the government has been to avoid using the armed forces in any large-scale repressive activities that might once again provoke the officer corps to reexamine their loyalties.

CHAPTER 7

■

ASSESSING THE RELATIONSHIP

BETWEEN CIVILIAN CONTROL OF THE

MILITARY AND THE CONSOLIDATION

OF DEMOCRACY

The key to establishing civilian control is the use by democratizers of regime leverage to define narrow boundaries for military authority and to institutionalize supervision of the armed forces. After all, regime leverage over the military is what allows civilians to resist conditions placed by outgoing authoritarian elites on the institutions of a new democracy, and it is what allows governments to compel the armed forces to accept institutions of civilian control. These institutions, when put into place at a time in which the domestic "balance of power" favors democratizers, perpetuate civilian authority over the military long after a regime transition by altering the armed forces' incentives and, eventually, their belief system.

An important constraint on the ability of civilians to institutionalize control over the armed forces is the shortage of regime capacity in defense affairs that is often found in emerging democracies. This shortage is true not only of Venezuela, but as the cases presented in this chapter confirm, it also appears to be a common feature of new democracies. A shortage of regime capacity prevented the deepening of the institutions of civilian control in Venezuela's case; however, as the cases of Argentina, Chile, and Spain suggest, this is an obstacle that can be overcome to achieve civilian control by oversight. These comparative cases illustrate the process by which political leadership can provide the institutional resources that produce and sustain the civilian defense expertise that is at the core of regime capacity.

Civilian control is a key barrier to the collapse of democracy, as the Venezuelan experience in 1992 suggests, yet the presence of consolidated control is not, by itself, sufficient to ensure the stability of the regime. Narrow military jurisdictional boundaries can also become deinstitutionalized under the pressure of changes in the domestic and international context or by the deliberate efforts of individuals, as occurred in Venezuela during the 1980s and 1990s. Moreover, the breakdown of civilian control over the armed forces is likely to form part of a larger deinstitutionalization of all of the partial regimes of a democracy. In Chile under President Salvador Allende (1970–73), civilian control of the armed forces became deinstitutionalized as the partial regimes that governed the party system, interest representation, and economic relations unraveled. Domestic political forces and international pressures expanded the jurisdictional boundaries of military authority in response to a crisis of legitimacy, internal security, and the economy (Valenzuela 1978). The Venezuelan experience between 1992 and 2004 suggests that institutionalized civilian control may be enough to prevent the overthrow of democracy but not sufficient to preserve the regime against changes brought about civilians themselves. These examples serve to remind us that civilians play a considerable role in decisions about whether to bring the armed forces back into politics after they have been successfully excluded.

In this chapter I validate the findings on the development of civilian control in new democracies by examining the Venezuelan cases in a comparative context that includes the cases of Chile (1989 and after), Argentina (1983 and after) and Spain (1975 and after). In each of these cases, I compare the impact of regime leverage by assessing opportunity structures and strategic interaction between civilians and the armed forces. I then compare the degree of regime capacity developed by examining the degree to which civilian control of the military was featured on the political agenda of democratizers and by analyzing the availability of institutional resources and civilian sources of defense expertise. Placing the Venezuelan cases in a wider context is particularly illuminating because it illustrates vividly the role that regime capacity plays in developing civilian control by oversight.

Reassessing the Venezuelan Experience
in Comparative Perspective

In contrast to the Argentine, Spanish, and Chilean cases, Venezuelan democratizers never sought as a goal to develop civilian control by oversight. This
dissimilarity cannot be traced solely to differences in opportunity structure
or strategies (that is, regime leverage), although both vary widely among the
cases. There were also major differences in regime capacity, particularly in
how political leaders approached the development of such a capacity. Democratizers in Chile, Spain, and Argentina all sought as their ultimate goal
civilian control by oversight, even in the absence of extensive civilian expertise and institutional resources at the moment of regime transition. In 1958,
as I have argued, Venezuelan democratizers had the regime leverage necessary to implement civilian control by oversight, but they never developed
the regime capacity to do so. In fact, they conceptualized civilian control in
a very different fashion from democratizers in the third wave, as the Chilean,
Argentine, and Spanish cases illustrate. In Venezuela, the result was civilian
control by containment, a largely self-regulating civil-military system based
on the principle of divide and conquer that successfully excluded the military from politics but did not provide civilians with the tools to meaning-
fully control defense policy.

The experiences of Spain and Argentina are useful checks on the conclusions drawn from the 1958 Venezuelan case because they demonstrate
what can be accomplished by democratizers who benefit from higher degrees of regime capacity. In both cases, the decision to pursue the full panoply of mechanisms of civilian control that are found in advanced industrialized democracies, including a civilian-led ministry of defense and legislative
oversight of military activities, produced enduring democratic civil-military
institutions that benefited both countries in moments of crisis. Chile also
serves as a useful contrast to the failed 1945–48 Venezuelan attempt to democratize because it demonstrates that an alternative path to democratic
consolidation is possible even in cases where democratizers face a narrow
opportunity structure and entrenched authoritarian elements. Figure 7.1
serves to summarize in very schematic fashion the causal pathway that each
of the cases presented here took toward the eventual configuration of institutionalized civilian control or its absence.

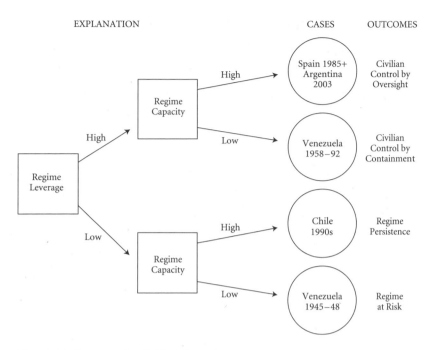

EXPLANATION

CASES   OUTCOMES

Figure 7.1. Outcomes in Civilian Control

VENEZUELAN CIVIL-MILITARY RELATIONS
IN COMPARISON: APPEASEMENT (1948) VERSUS
CIVILIAN CONTROL BY CONTAINMENT (1958)

Venezuela's first attempt to democratize in the twentieth century (1945–48) failed due to a fundamental imbalance in the power of civilian and military forces within the government. In that government, conceived from its inception as a civil-military partnership, the civilian leadership abdicated its authority over the armed forces, and the result was an absence of regime leverage and an inability to defend the new democratic regime. The surprise regime transition that resulted from the October 1945 military coup created a situation in which both civilian political forces and the armed forces themselves were internally divided and at odds. The fracture between authoritarian and democratic elements in Venezuelan civil-military relations was never healed, in part because authoritarian forces that supported of the pre-1945 regime never accepted their defeat. This subjected the democratic regime to constant subversive attacks from the political right. Civilian political parties of the center and left, such as URD and COPEI, never coalesced in support of the democratic rules of the game that had been crafted by the preponderant party, Acción Democrática.

The narrow opportunity structure created by the 1945 transition slowly closed in the ensuing three years as the armed forces recovered their internal coherence and unity of action, in contrast to the civilian political parties, which succumbed to extreme partisanship. Regime leverage was further undermined by the perverse strategies pursued by civilian democratizers that appeased the armed forces rather than establish control. Appeasement was an essentially defensive strategy, designed to ensure regime survival rather than democratic consolidation. Once the presidency changed hands from AD's politically adroit Rómulo Betancourt to the party's less flexible elder statesman, Rómulo Gallegos, the weakness of ad hoc strategic appeasement of the military was revealed.

A total absence of regime capacity compounded democratizers' regime leverage during the 1945–48 period, something that might have allowed democratizers to choose a more effective power-maximizing strategy vis-à-vis the armed forces than appeasement. Venezuela had almost no civilian defense expertise available at that time, nor was there any prospect of quickly developing such a capacity given the absence of available educational programs or career paths for such personnel. Institutionally, the decision to maintain a military-dominated ministry of defense ensured that no such civilian defense expertise would even have an institutional "home" within the government. Similarly, the constitutional convention of 1947 and the first elected legislature in 1948 had no civilian politicians or staff with defense expertise. The civil-military pact between AD and the UPM in 1945 ensured the continuity of this situation by depositing responsibility for all defense matters in the hands of the officer corps. Venezuela's new democracy was thus shorn of all potential instruments for civilian control of the armed forces.

By contrast, democratizers in 1958 benefited greatly from a broad opportunity structure, one that in combination with effective power-maximizing strategies, resulted in a high degree of regime leverage over the armed forces. Democratizers in 1958 faced a considerably broader opportunity structure that included a coherent civilian coalition of democratizers, reinforced through political pacting, mass popular mobilization in favor of the new regime, and disorganization and fragmentation among authoritarian elements in Venezuelan society. The death throes of the Pérez Jiménez regime — the perceived economic difficulties of the ancien régime and its repression of popular forces — contributed to the accretion of support around the democratization project. Before he fled, the outgoing dictator also contributed to the dissolution of the ties that bound together the civilian and military elements of his authoritarian coalition. Factionalized, opponents of democratization in the armed forces were thus picked off one by one as they rebelled during the transitional period, and every coup attempt was met by a unified elite front of civilian democratizers, buoyed up by mass popular mobilization.

Democratizers in Venezuela, particularly the AD party leader Rómulo Betancourt, transformed the temporary advantage they held over the armed forces through the use of a blend of power-maximizing strategies that had as its cornerstone a "divide and conquer" approach. Playing on the internal divisions of the armed forces, Betancourt was able to play the army, air, and naval services against each other, as well as exploit divisions between more professional junior officers and senior officers who were tainted by their association with the corruption of the former dictatorship. Each coup attempt provided a new opportunity for civilian democratizers to purge the armed forces of sympathizers of both the ancien régime and the emerging left-wing threat to the new democracy, a Cuban-backed Marxist insurgency. Adeptly using appeasement and monitoring strategies to complement a "divide and conquer" approach, the democratic government was able to reshape the officer corps to provide power and authority to those who most closely adhered to the principles of the new regime.

Even though Venezuela's democratizers were much more skillful at deploying regime leverage in 1958, they still lacked the regime capacity to institutionalize civilian control by oversight. Well aware of the shortcomings in civilian defense expertise, Venezuelan democratizers never sought to develop institutionalized mechanisms for overseeing the activities of the armed forces or even for controlling military spending except at the most aggregate levels. The Ministry of Defense continued to be headed by military officers, and the Congress lacked the requisite expert staff to advise the members of the legislative defense committee, nominally charged with reviewing military activities and approving officer promotions. The result was a system that discouraged the accumulation of civilian defense expertise or persistent attention to military matters, thus permanently inhibiting the development of regime capacity.

Democratizers instead institutionalized mechanisms of civilian control that contained the sphere of military action within the state to levels that were perceived as nonthreatening to consolidated democratic institutions.

These mechanisms perpetuated the transition-engendered fragmentation of the armed forces and set the services against one another. The Ministry of Defense was essentially stripped of its coordinating functions and was made to compete with the services themselves for missions and resources. The air force and navy were aggrandized at the expense of the traditionally preponderant army. Institutions that had been designed to conduct intelligence against foreign powers were instead encouraged to monitor the armed forces for loyalty to the democratic system. Military hostility to these measures was assuaged by the generous provision of professional development opportunities for officers and increased budgets for the services. By the mid- to late 1960s, loyalty to the regime was cemented by the provision of a new role, the defense of democracy against a Cuban-backed leftist insurgency.

After 1972, democratic consolidation was thus accompanied by the development of a new civil-military relationship that contained the armed forces to activities related to national defense and a limited array of internal security duties but that provided considerable autonomy for the armed forces. Government leaders essentially relied on "fire alarms," activated by the various services themselves, to alert them to any problems in the civil-military relationship. The resulting system provided Venezuela with democratic stability and an adequate degree of civilian control, at the expense of any future development of civilian regime capacity that might one day engender civilian control by oversight. Civil-military institutional arrangements discouraged further civilian attention to defense issues and created opportunities for military factions in the armed forces to collude among themselves to achieve private and public ends. When Venezuela entered a new political crisis at the end of the 1980s, these institutions would prove deficient in extremis.

CASE OF CIVILIAN CONTROL BY OVERSIGHT?
ARGENTINA, 1983–1991

Democratizers in Argentina in 1983 and Venezuela in 1958 both achieved a high degree of regime leverage. Paradoxically, Argentina suffered more civil-military turmoil than Venezuela during the transition and consolidation of democracy. As this next section suggests, Argentina's democratization is a cautionary tale, both about the way poor civilian choices about strategy can sabotage regime leverage and about the importance of developing regime capacity to institutionalize civilian control by oversight.

Argentine democratizers benefited from the near-collapse of the armed forces' cohesion in the wake of the military, economic, and political failures associated with El Proceso (1976–83), the country's longest and harshest military-led dictatorship. Although Argentina's opportunity structure provided even more possibilities for initiating civilian control, Argentine democratizers pursued substantially different strategies than those in Venezuela. In Argentina President Raúl Alfonsín had made a policy of sanctions against the armed forces, including a judicial review of the crimes committed by the armed forces during El Proceso, a centerpiece of his successful 1983 election campaign. Yet, he attempted to reconcile the armed forces to his sanctions strategy through selective appeasement. This approach satisfied neither the officer corps nor the human rights community, both of whom worked to undermine Alfonsín's strategies.

A second difference between Argentina and Venezuela was that both faced an initial deficiency of regime capacity, yet Argentina's democratizers sought to remedy this lack while Venezuelan democratizers abdicated responsibility. In Argentina civilians sought control of the military by oversight, and they deliberately set out to craft defense institutions that were similar to those found in advanced industrialized democracies. This approach meant that Argentina's leaders were initially successful at shrinking military jurisdictional boundaries in 1984, yet the new democracy lacked the regime capacity to operationalize civilian oversight. Without institutionalized civilian control, the Alfonsín administration could not effectively prevent rebellions, let alone address the military unrest caused by reduced budgets and low morale. Only under the Carlos Ménem administration was civilian control institutionalized, but through peculiar channels that tended to undermine the role of the Ministry of Defense.

Squandering Regime Leverage in Argentina, 1983–1989 • One of the main lessons of the Argentine transition is that the nature of the opportunity structure produced by a particular mode of transition is not enough to ensure civilian authority over the armed forces. After taking office, President Alfonsín was in a quandary: he had unexpectedly won the election, in large part by campaigning on a platform of punishment for human rights abuses, yet the achievement of his stated objectives would likely lead to a violent military reaction. Furthermore, the president and his advisors knew they faced an unprecedented opportunity to establish civilian control due to the manner in which the military-in-government had been defeated abroad, in the 1982 Malvinas conflict with the United Kingdom, and at home, where its policies had engendered massive human rights abuses and had triggered an economic crisis. Yet, the new president believed that prosecuting large numbers of military officers would undermine the reforms his administration planned to implement.

To sustain regime leverage, the Alfonsín administration planned to selectively combine strategies of sanctioning and appeasement. The sanctioning strategy would take advantage of the relative weakness of the military following the transition to empower the civilian Ministry of Defense and drastically reduce the defense budget. The appeasement strategy was designed to prevent a military rebellion by prosecuting only those officers who had given orders to commit human rights abuses and those who had exceeded their authority in carrying out orders (Pion-Berlin 1997, 80–81). Unaware of the sheer scope of the number of officers who had participated and the crimes committed during the "Dirty War," the Alfonsín administration failed to understand that it would be impossible to limit the number of military trials through administrative measures (Verbitsky 1987, 43–47, 51–55).

The government's strategies, sanctioning and appeasement, worked at cross-purposes. The officer corps interpreted the sanctioning strategy as revenge and the government's appeasement strategy as weakness. Appeasement also allowed urgently needed military reforms to become blocked by interservice rivalries and bureaucratic inertia. Most critically, though, the president directed the armed forces' judicial system to conduct the initial trials of officers who were accused of torture and disappearances. This allowed the military to obstruct justice long enough for parts of the officer corps to reacquire sufficient cohesion to rebel.

Civilian and Military Counterstrategies in Argentina ▪ The only objective on which the Argentine officer corps wholeheartedly agreed was to prevent a judicial revision of the repression the military had conducted during the "Dirty War." Other priorities, such as using the lessons of the Malvinas war to reorganize the armed forces, were rapidly abandoned due to the inability to reach a consensus on military reform (Acuña and Smúlovitz 1995, 162). Although not all officers had participated in the "Dirty War," a large enough percentage had been involved that many felt that either they or colleagues were at risk of standing trial. According to Deborah Norden, between 900 and 1,300 officers directly participated in the repression, although the figure may have been much higher (Norden 1996a, 58–60). In the army the officer corps was split generationally. Junior officers advocated a proactive defense of the institution and vindicated their role in the "Dirty War," while the military high command favored a defensive "judicial battle" that would minimize convictions. Despite this divergence in specific preferences, both junior and senior officers initially supported a counterstrategy of delay in the face of civilian pressure to prosecute human rights abuses (Verbitsky 1995; Norden 1996a, 107–19, 127–30).

Human rights organizations also rejected President Alfonsín's strategy toward the armed forces, and they used the courts to pursue their own strategy of "unlimited" sanctions. Given the openness of Argentina's judicial system to citizen-initiated prosecutions, these groups were highly successful in expanding the scope of judicial review. The moral authority and popularity of the human rights organizations made them an effective pressure group, which was able to strongly influence public opinion against the Alfonsín administration. Also, by assembling evidence and providing legal expertise in support of the prosecutions of military officers, human rights organizations could force the pace of the government's policies toward the military. Indictments of officers rapidly reached more than 400 by 1987 (Pion-Berlin 1997, 97–98).

Outflanked politically by human rights organizations and the progressive wing of the Peronist party, Alfonsín postponed making decisions on military issues that he knew would be unpopular. Though a successful electoral strategy, Alfonsín's approach had the effect of delaying a resolution of the human rights trials until a time when the government no longer had a strong hand against the military. In addition, it alienated the army's junior officers, setting up the conditions for the Holy Week rebellion of 1987 (López 1994, 108–10). The regime's massive leverage over the armed forces at the beginning of the transition had thus been undermined through a set of strategies that had provoked divisions among civilians on military policy and forced the feuding factions of the armed forces to band together in self-defense.

The Collapse of Regime Leverage under Alfonsín and Its Reconstruction under Ménem • Regime leverage could only remain high so long as the majority of the officer corps felt it was useless to resist government authority. Between 1984 and 1987, senior officers saw no point in open rebellion as a means to resist civilian efforts to sanction the armed forces (Alonso 1995). However, by 1986 growing overt and covert resistance by junior and midranking officers led Alfonsín to place greater emphasis on appeasing the officer corps through legal measures such as the Full Stop Law, which halted judicial proceedings against the armed forces (Pion-Berlin 1997, 97–99). Unappeased, military resistance culminated in the 1987 Holy Week rebellion by a small group of military officers (Norden 1996a, 128–30; McSherry 1997, 213–16).

The extent of the failure of Alfonsín's strategy was exposed by the inability of the government to secure any military support to repress the small numbers of officers who actively participated in the Holy Week rebellion in 1987. Confronting a hostile and newly confident military, the president was forced to negotiate a humiliating end to the uprising by eventually asking the legislature to pass the unpopular Law of Due Obedience, which established strict limits on who could be prosecuted for the human rights abuses of the dictatorship (Jaunarena 1995).

The rebellion of 1987, and the two that followed in 1988 and 1989, also provided the armed forces with enough leverage to expand their jurisdictional boundaries into internal security and halt the process of the institutionalization of civilian control. As the Argentine economy began to collapse and social unrest grew after 1987, civilian politicians became increasingly unwilling to defend narrow jurisdictional boundaries for fear that the military would be needed to contain public disorders. In the face of his declining ability to govern effectively, Alfonsín decided to step down six months early and transfer power to the newly elected Peronist president, Carlos Ménem, in 1989 (McSherry 1997, 194–97, 214–17).

President Ménem was able to resurrect regime leverage over the armed forces by repackaging the civilian strategies of sanctions and appeasement into a quid pro quo: blanket pardons for convicted officers in return for military obedience. Almost immediately after taking office, Ménem issued two amnesties that covered all officers who were threatened with prosecutions for their actions during the "Dirty War." By accepting the political cost of this action, President Ménem gained the confidence of many military officers. Amnesty also removed the only common ground that had provided some degree of military cohesion against civilian strategies of control. When junior officers and sergeants under Colonel Mohamed Seineldín rebelled in December 1990, President Ménem had little trouble securing the support of the military high command for the use of force to repress them (Ferreira Pinho 1995). With renewed support from senior military officers, Ménem was able to reshape the military from an expensive source of instability into a cheaper instrument compatible with his neoliberal economic policies and useful in his realignment of Argentine foreign policy toward cooperation with the United States (Trinkunas 1999a, 250–55).

The Peculiar Institutionalization of Civilian Control in Argentina • Even though its strategies failed, the Alfonsín administration came to office with a mandate to achieve authority over the armed forces, and early on it created the institutional conditions for the growth of regime capacity. It reinvigorated the Ministry of Defense by placing it in the chain of command and granting the civilian minister the power to supervise joint military activities and discipline higher-ranking officers. New civilian secretariats were created to oversee military spending, planning, and operations. Military influence over public policy, exercised through officers who had been appointed to head defense industries and state enterprises, was reduced by transferring control of these endeavors from the armed services to the civilian-led ministry. Internal security forces that were previously controlled by the army and navy were also placed under civilian supervision. Military budgets, which had peaked during the dictatorship at 5.1 percent of GDP, were slashed within two years to their historic level of approximately 2.3 percent of GDP. The army was hit hardest since its budget sank from 1.8 percent of GDP in 1983 to 0.6 percent in 1989, all within the context of a contracting economy (López 1994, 123).

However, Argentine democratizers initially lacked the defense expertise and resources to effectively staff these new institutions of control. This shortage of regime capacity operated against civilian authority in several instances: in the inability of Defense Ministry officials to reform the military force structure in light of budget cuts, the failure to pass new defense legislation until 1988, and the government's mistakes in managing the prosecutions of officers for human rights abuses. For example, defense reform measures were never enacted not only because civilians lacked the capacity to generate their own plan for downsizing the armed forces but also because they could not judge which military proposal would promote greater defense efficiency without hindering government control (Pion-Berlin 1997, 164–66). Meanwhile, defense legislation to restrict the armed forces to external defense duties was not passed for four years due to partisan bickering among legislators and a shortage of expertise among congressional staffers. In fact, congressional productivity in defense legislation was notably low until after the 1987 Holy Week rebellion (Druetta 1990, 232–43). Throughout this period, the staff of institutions for controlling the security forces, the military, and the intelligence agencies continued to be recruited largely from active-duty or retired members of the same agencies or institutions, which rendered their advice suspect to elected officials.

As a result, civilian oversight of the armed forces by the Ministry of Defense never became fully operational in Argentina during the Alfonsín administration. This prevented the government from monitoring military activities for signs of rebellion or addressing the roots of military discontent through effective reform measures. After the Holy Week uprising in 1987, the institutions of civilian control largely ceased to function, and the civilian minister of defense was reduced to role of a mediator between the newly confident military high command and a demoralized President Alfonsín (Jaunarena 1995; Pion-Berlin 1997, 158–59).

President Ménem, moreover, contributed to the undermining of regime capacity through his penchant for favoring personalistic or noninstitutional channels to administer the armed forces. Ménem bypassed the authority of the minister of defense by establishing personal relationships with the commanders of the armed forces as a means of resolving civil-military questions. The Ministry of Defense, theoretically the leading institution of civilian control, was further weakened by the rapid succession of ministers, six of whom were appointed between 1989 and 1995. Amid this turmoil in the leadership of the ministry, it was difficult to develop a stable cadre of experienced civilian defense experts. The authority of these ministers was called into question since some were accused of sympathizing with the "*carapintada*" rebels (until the final uprising in 1990), while another was convicted of corruption (Trinkunas 1999a, 264–71). Taking advantage of the presidentialist nature of Argentine democracy, Ménem often bypassed the congressional committees that were tasked with supervising the armed forces, even though these committees were increasingly acquiring the expertise necessary to pass effective defense legislation (Behrongaray 1995; Vaca 1995).

Thus, the two principal channels associated with supervision of the armed forces in states with strong civilian control (the Ministry of Defense and the legislature) were shunted aside during the Ménem administration. Instead, the Ministry of the Economy and the Ministry of Foreign Affairs became key players in conducting oversight of the armed forces and the repositories of some degree of regime capacity (Pion-Berlin 1997, 122–36). Indirectly, the Ministry of the Economy set the limits for the overall size and structure of the military. Similarly, the Ministry of Foreign Affairs now played an unprecedented role in determining the deployment of Argentine military forces through its focus on peacekeeping operations and regional collective security (Pion-Berlin 1997).

The Ménem legacy for civil-military relations endured, for good or bad, well after the reforms were consolidated during the 1990s. The fact that Argentina's democracy survived its 2001–2 economic and political crises without a murmur of military unrest and that President Nestor Kirchner was able to cashier the military high command with no opposition on his taking office in 2003 are both signs of the consolidation, peculiar or not, of civilian control. Regime capacity, whether found in the much abused Ministry of Defense or the more prestigious Ministries of the Economy and Foreign Affairs, has an institutional setting that sustains and reproduces it. The continuity in civil-military relations and the absence of expansion in military jurisdiction during a period of rapid turnover in political leaders are suggestive of the institutionally bound nature of this relationship. Unlike Ménem, Presidents Fernando De la Rua and Nestor Kirchner and the five interim presidents who held office between 2001 and 2003 never had the means or the opportunity to establish personalistic relationships and were forced to rely (successfully) on the peculiar institutions of civilian control that they had inherited.

THE IMPORTANCE OF REGIME CAPACITY: CHILE, 1990–2005

On the face of it, Chile seems to have faced the worst prospects of establishing civilian control of the military of any of the third wave democracies in Latin America. The authoritarian regime led by General Augusto Pinochet handed power to civilians in an orderly fashion in 1990 after losing a national referendum, avoiding the collapse that many other Latin American dictatorships had suffered. The Pinochet regime was perceived as having succeeded politically and economically, and it retained strong backing from a significant minority of the general population. General Pinochet had succeeded in embedding authoritarian features in Chile's constitution that were designed to preserve the institutional autonomy of the armed forces and shield them from civilian control. For example, the armed forces were constitutionally guaranteed a fixed percentage of state revenues from the sale of one of Chile's major exports, copper, and an inflation-adjusted defense budget to insulate them from civilian oversight. They were also provided with representation in the legislature through a fixed quota of Senate seats. They were also protected from civilian control through their participation on the National Security Council, where the armed forces controlled half the seats (Fuentes 1999, 15–17).

Observers predicted that these arrangements would permanently give the armed forces the upper hand over the civilian government and prevent the consolidation of democracy. Yet fifteen years later, civilian authority has slowly extended itself to such an extent that the prerogatives and autonomy of the armed forces have seriously eroded (Fuentes 1999, 14; Hunter 1996). A good deal of this change can be attributed to the systematic development of regime capacity during the 1990s, which was institutionalized in the civilian-led Ministry of Defense and paralleled by the emergence of a community of civilian defense intellectuals in Chile's universities and think tanks.

Perhaps the most difficult challenge that Chile's democratizers faced as they confronted the prospect of establishing civilian control of the military was the narrowness of the opportunity structure. In contrast to Venezuela's transition in 1958, the Chilean military was united behind a single figure who was perceived by some significant conservative sectors of the general population as having led a successful regime (Huneeus 1997, 91–93). Civilians were divided between a left-center political coalition, the Concertación, which was committed to full democratization, and conservative parties that preferred to preserve the achievements of the dictatorship. These conservative parties also had an interest in preserving the institutional autonomy of the armed forces as a counterweight to the political dominance of the Concertación political coalition that had won the first three presidential contests of Chile's contemporary democratic period (Hunter 1997, 457). Elite cleavages placed the armed forces in a favorable position to resist civilian efforts to establish control (Fuentes 1999, 12–14). In many ways, the opportunity structure was even less favorable than the situation facing Acción Democrática in Venezuela in 1945, where democratizers could at least benefit from the lack of cohesion in the military.

Chile's democratic leaders acted strategically to minimize the power imbalance vis-à-vis the armed forces far beyond what the opportunity structure might appear to allow, as Fuentes (1999) argues. Rather than pursue a pure appeasement strategy, as did democratizers in Venezuela, Chile's presidents sometimes chose more confrontational strategies, ranging from the monitoring of military activities to the use of their limited constitutional sanctioning power. For example, President Patricio Aylwin (1990–95) was particularly effective in using his control over the more discretionary elements of the military budget, and the armed forces found that their constitutionally guaranteed budget floor would become a ceiling if they refused to cooperate with the civilian government. Civilians also held power over officer promotions and weapons acquisitions, which provided counterleverage to military pressures on the civilian government (Hunter 1997, 157–58). On the other hand, President Eduardo Frei (1995–2000) pursued a strategy of engagement that enabled civilians in the Defense Ministry and the legislature to slowly gain the trust of their counterparts in the armed forces. In particular, civilians sought to develop collaboratively with the military an explicit national defense policy, to be published as a government "white book." The objective of this strategy was to seek out areas of common agreement between civilians in government and the armed forces rather than to focus on areas of tension, such as those surrounding prosecution for past human rights abuses by the Pinochet regime or cases of corruption (Fuentes 1999, 18–34). Civilian leverage over the armed forces remained relatively low and rested largely on formal legal grounds, but the strategies pursued by the Aylwin and Frei administrations allowed incremental progress toward democratic civilian control of the armed forces.

Chile's democratizers nevertheless faced considerable resistance from the armed forces, including some rather overt military mobilizations during the Aylwin administration that were designed to remind the civilian leadership that the armed forces still had the power to make or break the government. The inability of civilian governments to retaliate against these military threats emphasized the precariousness of Chile's democratization in the carly 1990s (Agüero 1998, 392).

However, part of what gave Chile's civilian leaders a chance to pursue strategies other than appeasement were a supportive international environment and a military adversary that quickly discovered that it, too, had developed a stake in the success of Chile's new democracy. Chile's democracy benefited from an explicit focus on supporting democracy that came to the forefront of U.S. policy toward Latin America during the George Bush (1988–92) and Bill Clinton (1992–2000) administrations. Support for democracy came to be understood by U.S. administrations during this period as support for civilian control of the armed forces, a position the United States reinforced during a series of hemispheric defense ministerials during the 1990s. The Organization of American States and the European Union also joined in with their support for democratization in Latin America (Millett 1994). Chile's armed forces also came to understand that their efforts to defend the economic and political "achievements" of the Pinochet regime also meant that they could not overthrow the democratic system that had followed. The military rights, privileges, and autonomy that the Pinochet period had produced were in a sense legitimized by the democratic regime that followed, and overthrowing the regime at a time when democratization was sweeping the world would have made the armed forces the target of international hostility and discrimination.

One of the long-term advantages that Chilean democratizers possessed compared to their Venezuelan counterparts in 1945 and 1958 was an elected government committed to building regime capacity in defense issues. This is not to say that Chile's democracy began with high levels of regime capacity, but in two of three categories (placement of civil-military issues on the political agenda and institutional resources), there was a foundation for growth. Civilian defense expertise developed more slowly during the following decade.

Civil-military issues remained prominent on Chile's political agenda during the 1990s because of the interest of civilians in government in asserting control over the military institution and because of the interest of elements of civil society in prosecuting human rights abuses committed during the Pinochet period. President Aylwin signaled the importance he attributed to military policy by appointing one of his longtime collaborators in the Christian Democratic party, Patricio Rojas, as minister of defense. The president also made an effort to introduce legislation to minimize the autonomy of the armed forces, but he faced obstacles from conservative civilian opponents in the legislature (Hunter 1997, 156). He was more successful in using the existing powers of the president to contain military spending and divert the state's growing budget toward social and developmental agendas. He was also able to assert his authority to veto military promotions, even if he could not control officer selection processes. Similarly, President Frei kept civilian control of the armed forces on the agenda, although he attempted to achieve progress through a more cooperative approach that was designed to transform the tensions of civil-military relations into a more routinized and collaborative approach to defense issues.

The civilian administrations of Aylwin and Frei managed the process by which the issues raised by the past human rights abuses of the dictatorship were addressed to produce justice "within the limits of the possible." Aylwin's most prominent action in this area was the convening of a government-sponsored truth commission to examine the record of the Pinochet administration in the area of human rights, which again raised the profile of civil-military issues. Although the truth commission was unable to prosecute wrongs perpetrated during the dictatorship, it provided documentation of the abuses committed under General Pinochet's watch and helped to raise civilian awareness of the continuing high levels of military autonomy.

Ongoing attempts by human rights groups to prosecute members of the dictatorship eventually proved successful in the case of former intelligence chief General Manuel Contreras, who was sentenced in 1995, but these prosecutions led to renewed tension between the government and the armed forces (Hunter 1997, 160–62). The arrest of Pinochet in London in 1998 on an international arrest warrant issued in Spain by Judge Baltazar Garzón for responsibility for human rights violations also kept the issue of civil-military relations prominent on the Chilean government's agenda. This particular event caused great consternation in the armed forces, which could do little about the arrest because it had happened outside of Chile. Nevertheless, it forced both sides of the civil-military divide to reexamine their relationship and work cooperatively to resolve the crisis, particularly since the foreign policy dimension of the crisis brought civilian diplomatic expertise to the fore (Fuentes 1999, 35). The ongoing issues raised by the pursuit of justice for past victims of the military also sustained civilian interest in civil-military issues, something that quickly declined in other cases, including Venezuela during the 1960s and Argentina during the 1990s.

The creation of institutional settings in which civilian defense expertise could accumulate contributed to bolstering regime capacity in Chile. One key element that Chile shared with Spain and Argentina, although not with Venezuela, was the development of a civilian leadership cadre for the Ministry of Defense. The ministry had been composed almost entirely of military personnel during the Pinochet period, but the new minister, Patricio Rojas, created room for civilian leadership in the ministry through the appointment of civilian vice-ministers and the creation of a policy advisory council (the Consejo de Asesores). The ministry had few positions for civilians, either as political appointees to leadership positions or as career civil service staff, so the council was central to providing an arena in which civilian defense experts could find long-term employment and engage in their vocation. The council eventually led to a trust-based working relationship between civilian and military experts at the policy level (Robledo 2004).

The second key institutional setting that fostered regime capacity was the defense "white book" development process. Begun under the Frei administration, the production of a defense white book was one of the centerpieces of the government's cooperative approach to civil-military relations. A defense white book elaborates on the basic principles of national defense and the rationales for a country's forces, force structures, acquisitions, and other defense policies. In Chile this process was conducted jointly by the minister of defense, the Consejo de Asesores, and the General Staff of the armed forces. The first white book was published in 1997, the culmination of a multiyear process, and its table of contributors reveals the broad scope of participation in this first attempt at joint civil-military defense policymaking. Since the table of contributors lists active and retired military officers by their ranks, it is easy to distinguish the relative composition of the participants. In the 1997 edition, the executive secretariat of the white book project was evenly balanced between civilian (2) and military (2) participants, and not surprisingly, the list of regular participants was also balanced, including 19 civilians, 21 active-duty or retired military officers, 10 legislators from the Chamber of Deputies, and 9 representatives from academic institutions or think tanks. Representatives from 4 civilian bodies, in addition to the Ministry of Defense — the Ministries of the Economy, Foreign Affairs, and National Planning, and the presidency — were also contributors (Libro Blanco 1997).

In the 2002 edition, a much wider array of participants was included. The executive secretariat was still perfectly balanced (7 civilian to 7 military members). Government participants were 49 civilians from 10 civilian ministries (including defense) and 55 active-duty or retired military and police officers, although it is interesting to note that the divisions between civilians and military elements were less neatly drawn than in the 1997 edition. The nongovernmental civilian participants included for the first time 9 representatives from political parties. Sixteen academic institutions contributed 21 participants (compared to 9 in 1997). The 2002 white book also lists the participation of 4 environmental nongovernmental organizations and 6 defense industry representatives (Libro Blanco 2002). Although these numbers provide only a sketchy insight into the evolution of civilian participation in the defense policymaking process, what is clear is the civilian defense experts and civilian institutions that participated in this process were much greater in number and broader in scope after only a five-year period. The 2002 white book also shows a higher level of detail and addresses a wider range of defense policy issues, rather than focusing on descriptions of the functions of the various military services.

The growth of regime capacity in Chile, particularly in the form of civilian defense expertise in government, academia, and the private sector, is part of the key to understanding the progress that Chile has been able to make toward civilian control. It is instructive that the inauguration of President Ricardo Lagos in 2000, Chile's first socialist executive since Allende in 1973, produced no overt military discontent. The armed forces have proved to be more amenable to providing information on past human rights abuses; and even issues that once provoked military threats to civilian rule, such as the possibility of prosecuting military officers, are received with relative equanimity. Chile's civilian government does not yet have control over its armed forces to the degree that would be considered desirable in well-established Western democracies. One important task that has yet to be accomplished is the restructuring of the ministry itself to institutionally codify the role of the Consejo de Asesores in the policy development structure (Robledo 2004). Chile's civilian government also has yet to achieve authority over other significant elements of defense policy, including military doctrine and education. Yet, to date, it has achieved a great deal more than all observers who witnessed the 1990 military-dominated regime transition would have expected.

CRAFTING CIVILIAN CONTROL BY OVERSIGHT: THE CASE OF SPAIN

Of all the cases considered here, Spain comes closest to representing the ideal type of civilian control by oversight, yet its transition to democracy differs in important ways from those of Venezuela, Argentina, and Chile. The key difference is that Spain's transition toward democracy took place from a civilian-led authoritarian government, rather than in the wake of a military dictatorship. In a certain sense, civilians had already established substantial authority over the armed forces within the context of the Francisco Franco dictatorship, and this authority provided the foundation of the leverage they developed over the armed forces. Whether pro- or anti-Franco, civilian political elites in control of the Spanish transition understood that the armed forces should remain subordinate to their authority.

In the civil-military arena, the problem that Spain's democratizers faced was how to sustain civilian authority over the military and popular support for democracy long enough to replace the relatively weak institutions of civilian control inherited from the Franco period with ones appropriate to a democracy. In terms of regime capacity, Spain's democratic regime focused important political and institutional resources on developing mechanisms to control the military, principally through the creation of a Ministry of Defense, but this was a process that did not truly achieve fruition until after the assumption of power by the Socialist party in 1984. In other words, Spain's democracy took over ten years to develop the level of regime capacity appropriate to civilian control by oversight.

Regime leverage in Spain rested less on strategic interactions among civilians and the armed forces than on the nature of the opportunity structure created by the death of Generalissimo Franco in 1974. Having led an institutionalized authoritarian regime for almost four decades, Franco had already created an institutional place for the armed forces that subordinated them to civilian leadership and reinstituted the monarchy under King Juan Carlos II as the focus of their institutional loyalty (Rodríguez 1989, 37–39, 84–89). This did not mean that the Spanish military lacked substantial autonomy in the area of external defense and internal security. It did mean that when the civilians leading the post-Franco government decided to negotiate a pacted transition to democracy, there were almost no institutional avenues through which the armed forces could influence the process (Agüero 1995b, 45–54). The armed forces had numerous members scattered throughout the administration of the Spanish state, but there were no institutional or ideological methods to bring cohesion to their efforts (Rodríguez 1989, 52). The options facing the military were either to operate within the legal framework inherited from Franco, which they had spent four decades defending, or overthrow the whole system to stop the democratization of Spain (Agüero 1995b, 104–8). The inevitable result was deep divisions between conservatives who opposed democratization but preferred to operate within the law and a minority who favored violent resistance. Adding to these divisions within the armed forces, there was also an important segment of the officer corps who favored defense reforms.

The main strategic choice faced by civilians, both democratizers and authoritaritarians, was how far and fast could they push the democratization process before they provoked violent military resistance. The armed forces were essentially put on the defensive throughout the transition process, caught off guard by measures that legalized trade unions and civilian opposition parties, including their nemesis, the Communist Party. Spain's new constitution also caught the armed forces off guard because it empowered regions and ethnic minorities, a taboo during the Franco period, and diminished the role of the armed forces in internal security (Rodríguez 1989, 184–95). To the extent that civilians did act strategically during the democratization process, it was to reinforce the internal divisions that existed in the military by working with reformers who sought to modernize the armed forces by focusing their mission on external defense rather than internal security (Rodríguez 1989, 202–4). At various points during the transition and early consolidation process, there were overt displays of military indiscipline among senior officers who were unhappy over the direction that Spain was taking toward democracy. However, civilians remained highly unified, and their efforts culminated in the constitution-writing process that successfully produced a rupture between the Francoist past and the democratic future.

The coalescence of civilians around the democratization process at both the mass and elite levels of society provided little opportunity for the armed forces to intervene except by resorting to extralegal violence. The only overt act of violence against the new government, the 1981 seizure of the parliament (Cortes) by Colonel Antonio Tejero Molina and a unit of Guardia Civil gendarmes, initially gained some support from hard-liners in the armed forces, but it fell apart in the face of opposition from Spain's monarch and the vast majority of civil and political society (Agüero 1995, 156–74). Democratizers did act strategically in the wake of this coup attempt by seeking hasher sanctions for those who had participated in the revolts, even appealing to civilian courts when military courts returned verdicts that they considered too lenient (Zaverucha 1993, 295).

After forty years of dictatorship, it would be unreasonable to expect that Spain would possess much in the way of civilian expertise, but it did possess a political leadership that understood the importance of achieving civilian control over the armed forces. During its transition and consolidation process, Spain went through two distinct phases in the development of regime capacity. The first took place during the conservative governments of presidents (prime ministers) Adolfo Suarez and Leopoldo Calvo Sotelo (1976–83), which mostly focused on the reforms necessary to democratize Spain's political process. However, during this first phase, a civilian-led Ministry of Defense was created, the armed forces' role in internal security was downgraded, and the police were moved from military to civilian jurisdiction (Rodríguez 1989, 251–60; Zaverucha 1993, 292–94). The new Ministry of Defense remained relatively weak because most of the critical staff functions associated with personnel, budgets, and acquisitions were still controlled by each armed service (Agüero 1995b, 147–50).

The second phase in the development of regime capacity occurred during the presidency of the Socialist party leader Felipe González. His government passed new organic laws that delineated the command authority of the president and his minister of defense, reformed the armed forces' command structure, and reapportioned powers between the Ministry of Defense and the military (Agüero 1995b, 188–90). Minister of Defense Narciso Serra progressively enforced his authority over military strategy, plans, acquisitions, and personnel. One of the main axes of effort during Serra's tenure was to empower the civilian leadership in the ministry in relation to their counterparts in the military staffs, which was eventually codified in law. However, legislative participation in defense issues remained mainly confined to the approval of laws proposed by the government rather than any form of intrusive oversight (Marquina 1991; Esparza Valiente 1993).

Minister of Defense Serra worked progressively with military reformers to modernize the armed forces and prepared them for Spain's accession to NATO. The move to join NATO was controversial among the general public and within the armed forces, but it was the cornerstone for the continued growth of regime capacity and cemented civilian control of the armed forces. Civilians and military defense professionals were now forced to interact with and catch up to the defense establishments of NATO countries, which had enjoyed democratic civil-military relations for decades. In the wake of a successful referendum on joining NATO, Spanish civil-military relations increasingly became focused on defense policy rather than contestation over authority (Marquina 1991; Agüero 1995b, 203–15).

Paradoxically, Spain's democratization benefited from the commitment of its military to the institutionality created by the Franco regime and by the commitment of Franco's heirs to the liberalization of Spanish politics. The armed forces could not halt the process toward liberalization without casting aside the institutions that Franco had bid them defend in the name of the new monarch. The dynamics of the transition tended to drive civilian elites together as they engaged in political pacts that guaranteed their mutual interests. At the same time, the armed forces were driven apart by disagreements over the nature of the new Spanish state and military reform as well as fears over the cultural transformations produced by democratization. This put regime leverage squarely in the hands of the new democratic government, yet that government still faced significant shortcomings in the area of regime capacity. Political will to reform civil-military relations was strong during the conservative governments of Suarez and Calvo Sotelo, but the drive to build institutions and develop civilian defense expertise truly came to fruition during the Socialist administration of Felipe González. Spain's accession to the NATO alliance cemented both the external defense orientation of the armed forces and civilian supremacy over the military.

Conclusion: Comparing Cases of Civilian Control

If we contrast the Venezuelan cases of democratic transition in 1945 and 1958 with the Argentine, Chilean, and Spanish cases, we can draw conclusions on six major issues in civil-military relations: the impact of the opportunity structures created by democratic transitions, the importance of strategy selection in crafting civilian control, the sources of regime capacity, the role of ideas in crafting civilian control, the role of civil-military jurisdictional boundaries, and the weakness of civilian control by containment.

THE NATURE OF THE OPPORTUNITY STRUCTURE
DOES NOT OVERDETERMINE THE OUTCOME

If we were to examine the opportunity structures in the two Venezuelan cases of transition and even in the Spanish case, it might be easy to conclude that the dominant variable in explaining the crafting of civilian control was the nature of the opportunity structure. In 1945–48 Venezuela, civilian disunity and fragmentation prevented the consolidation of democracy and eventually created the conditions for a reunified and newly confident military to take power and lead the country back into a decade-long military dictatorship. The pacted nature of the Spanish and Venezuelan transitions created broad opportunity structures in which civilians held the upper hand over the armed forces when decisions about the role of the military in the new democracy were made.

Yet, Venezuela in 1958 and Spain after 1975 produced very different forms of civilian control, despite some substantial similarities in opportunity structures. Venezuelan democratizers chose to craft a system of civilian control that contained military activities within a narrow range of permissible behavior, while the Spanish regime chose to institutionalize government oversight through a civilian-led Ministry of Defense. Turning to the Argentine and Chilean cases, it becomes even clearer that opportunity structures are only one part of any explanation for variation in outcomes in civil-military relations. Argentina had the broadest opportunity structure of all the cases considered here, yet it experienced a very high degree of civil-military turmoil during its consolidation period, and even today, the peculiar configuration of its institutions of civilian control do not provide the same degree of oversight as is found in Spain. Focusing solely on Chile's narrow opportunity structure would not explain the relative success that democratizers were able to achieve in institutionalizing some elements of oversight over military activities, nor would it explain the growth in regime capacity that the country has experienced since 1989. These comparative cases suggest that the mode of transition or opportunity structure does not overdetermine the outcome of civil-military relations in new democracies. Rather, they are only a departure point on the path toward civilian control.

CIVILIAN STRATEGIC CHOICES AFFECT THE SUCCESS OF EFFORTS TO CRAFT CIVILIAN CONTROL

The choices that democratizers make regarding strategies is important not only because those decisions affect the distribution of power between the civilian and military sides of the equation, but also because they affect long-term choices regarding institutional design. Moreover, it is quite clear that democratizers can choose strategies that diminish their leverage over the armed forces, either because they choose suboptimal strategies based on an incomplete or erroneous understanding of the situation they confront, or because the strategic choices slip out of the hands of civilian politicians and are driven instead by the actions of civil society.

The civil-military outcomes in Venezuela (1958) and Argentina (1983) provide a useful illustration of the importance of strategy selection. By blending a dominant strategy of "divide and conquer" with elements of sanctioning and appeasement, Venezuelan democratizers were able to maximize their leverage over the armed forces during the transition and consolidation phase of democratization. However, the success of their strategies was not sufficient to lead to the implementation of civilian control by oversight. Instead, the strategy of "divide and conquer" itself was embedded in civil-military institutions. Argentine democratizers, despite benefiting from the broadest opportunity structure of any of the cases examined in this chapter, chose poorly by following a strategy in which sanctioning predominated with only a leavening of appeasement; they misread the condition of civil-military relations. The Alfonsín administration also subordinated strategy selection to its larger political strategy for maintaining electoral power vis-à-vis other political parties. The Alfonsín administration thus missed the implications of the growing power of civil society, particularly in the form of human rights organizations, and it lost control over the timing and pace of its military policy. This led to the debacle of three coup attempts in three years by armed forces that had been thoroughly defeated politically, economically, and militarily only four years earlier.

The contrast between the failure of Venezuelan democratizers in 1945–48 and the relative success of Chile after 1990 is also instructive in that it shows the extent to which appropriate strategy selection can overcome even weak opportunity structures. On coming to power in October 1945, Venezuela's Acción Democrática party abdicated its responsibility for civilian control of the armed forces and relied instead on allies within the military establishment for regime preservation. As long as the military remained divided, AD's allies in the officer corps had a chance of defending the new democracy on an ad hoc, noninstitutionalized basis. Once the officer corps reunited behind the authoritarian program advocated by Colonel Marcos Pérez Jiménez, the new democracy was defenseless and collapsed without resistance. Chilean democratizers were in an even more difficult position in 1990 than AD in 1945 because of the General Pinochet's success in consolidating his control over the officer corps. Nevertheless, the Aylwin and Frei administrations were able to move progressively toward civilian authority by judiciously blending the necessary elements of appeasement, which were the inevitable products of a narrow opportunity structure, with the sanctioning powers that the Pinochet-devised 1980 constitution provided.

THE SOURCES OF REGIME CAPACITY

The absence of resources, civilian expertise, and government attention to defense issues prevented the development of effective oversight agencies for defense affairs in both Venezuelan cases. In 1958 Venezuela's Betancourt ruled out a substantive civilian supervision of the military from the beginning. Instead, he chose to transfer the burden of surveillance to the armed forces themselves by institutionalizing the dynamics of "divide and conquer" among the different services. He also kept civilian control of the military largely off the public agenda and preserved control over defense policy in the hands of the presidency. The Venezuelan experience stands in contrast to the Chilean, Spanish, and Argentinean cases where, even though civilian defense expertise was modest at best at the beginning of democratization, governments did feature the goal of civilian authority over the armed forces prominently on the national political agenda and provided the institutional resources to promote regime capacity, principally through the creation or imposition of a civilian-led Ministry of Defense.

Without civilian institutions inside or outside of government concerned with defense policy, regime capacity never had a chance to flower in Venezuela. What is more important is that this absence was the result of civilian policy decisions made by Venezuelan democratizers in 1958 and 1959. The conceptualization of regime capacity as something that is subject to political agency rather than something that should only be treated as a structural feature of a new democracy is important. The Spanish, Argentine, and Chilean cases suggest that regime capacity can develop from initially low levels through a combination of political leadership, a prominent place on the national political agenda (particularly over the issue of human rights in Argentina and Chile), and the creation of institutional settings where civilian defense expertise can mature (such as the defense white book project in Chile or the Ministry of Defense in Spain).

It is interesting to note that Chile, Spain, and Argentina began with high levels of political commitment but low levels of civilian defense expertise. As I pointed out in the introduction, a shortage of civilian interest or expertise in defense issues is characteristic of countries with a low level of external threat and highly autonomous militaries, found in all of the cases analyzed in this chapter. In the Chilean and Argentinean cases, government attention to civil-military issues was a matter of political necessity, given the influential role of the human rights community in shaping political debate and electoral results. Spain's accession to NATO is instructive since in this case democratizers deliberately sought out a formal external alliance system that conveniently provided them with an adversary. By contrast, the issue of civil-military relations dropped off the political map relatively quickly in Venezuela since there was neither an external threat nor an internal political debate over human rights to force civilians' attention to defense issues.

THE ROLE OF IDEAS IN CRAFTING CIVILIAN CONTROL

One of the characteristics revealed by the analysis of the Venezuelan cases is the evolution of both a military debate on democracy and civilian debate on the military. J. Samuel Fitch (1998) has argued that the resolution of the internal military debate in favor of democracy is important for democratic consolidation, yet the cases examined in this book suggest that there is an equally important civilian debate about military policy that influences the nature of civil-military relations. Prior to the 1945 coup in Venezuela, both civilian and military debates about democracy and the role of the armed forces were relatively sparse, surfacing only during the 1940s as Venezuelan politicians began a general debate about democracy in the context of the post–World War II era and the Allied victory over fascism. Once a new generation of civilian and military leaders took power in 1945, the debate within the military quickly focused on the arguments put forth by pro-democracy

officers, perceived as partisans of AD, and by the supporters of a technocratic vision of military rule. The victory of the military technocrats in 1948
ushered in a decade of debate not within the military but among civilian
politicians driven underground or into exile. This debate took place between
civilian politicians in exile, such as Betancourt, who advocated rendering
the military politically neutral through institutional means, and younger
activists in Venezuela, such as Domingo Alberto Rangel, who advocated a
politically partisan and loyal military. The advocates of a partisan military
were sidelined politically during the 1958 transition and eventually became
the leaders of the Marxist insurgency that fought the armed forces during
the 1960s. Paradoxically, their ideas survived their bearers' defeat in the insurgency to influence a generation of junior officers, most notably the future
president Hugo Chávez.

One of the interesting findings from the Venezuelan case is the role of
institutions in shaping the civilian debate over time. Among civilian politicians of the post-Betancourt generation, debate about defense and military policy almost ceased. The institutional containment of the armed forces
lulled these politicians into the false security that a military threat to the
regime could never reemerge. Within the military the combination of "divide and conquer," appeasement, and sanctions strategies drove out those
officers who adhered to beliefs that were political or antidemocratic.

However, beginning with the generation of officers who are the contemporaries of President Hugo Chávez, it became increasingly difficult to find
institutional obstacles to the emergence and spread of radical military ideas
about repoliticizing the officer corps. With civilian monitoring essentially
absent, it was up to the armed forces to monitor the ideological content
of their own officer corps and sanction their homegrown radicals, something that the senior military leadership in the 1980s failed to do. Now, the
Chávez administration is repoliticizing the officer corps, beginning with the
education of cadets in the military academy, and rewarding "revolutionary"
officers with promotions and assignments beyond their professional merits.
Once again, we can see the means by which institutions serve as vehicles to
propagate military beliefs.

THE IMPORTANCE OF JURISDICTIONAL BOUNDARIES

The maps of jurisdictional boundaries used throughout the book illustrate the shifts in civil-military relations that take place during democratic
rule. In emerging democracies, the figures show the shifts toward civilian

control and, in the absence of such shifts, predict which democratization processes are unlikely to succeed. As each Venezuela case shows, comparing the final configuration of the limits of military and civilian authority over the state with the ideal-type boundaries proposed in figure 1.3 helps to identify whether civilian control has been achieved. Moreover, by systematically tracing the areas of conflict and agreement over jurisdiction between democratizers and the military, we can determine which issues have been settled and institutionalized and which remain latent threats to the democratization process.

In the case of the first Venezuelan case (1945–48), democratizers never attempted to shift these boundaries, making the outcome of regime collapse inevitable. Military boundaries acquired a perverse configuration that secured military control over all instruments of coercion and deprived the emerging democracy of any defense against armed intervention. The map of the jurisdictional boundaries in this case settled relatively quickly into a pattern of military dominance over internal security and external defense (see figure 2.2). This pattern of civil-military relations is likely to be common across a wide range of transitions in which democratizers lack the opportunity and the leverage to establish control over the military. It is also particularly dangerous to the persistence of a civilian regime. Jurisdictional boundary maps also show the difference between the civilian control by containment of the 1958 Venezuelan case from the absence of civilian control in the 1948 case. In addition, the maps show the residual internal security role of the armed forces and the absence of institutionalized civilian supervision in external defense matters, which created a latent opportunity for renewed civil-military conflict in 1992.

Just as the jurisdictional shifts mapped in the figures illustrate moves toward civilian control, they can show moves away from it. As the armed forces are drawn into missions and roles outside their primary focus on external defense, they are increasingly exposed to the political dynamics of a democracy. In moments of severe crisis, this exposure makes it more likely for the armed forces to become politicized, possibly prompting military intervention. The events leading up to the 1992 coup attempts in Venezuela illustrate this phenomenon. The economic and political crisis associated with the breakdown of the foundations of pacted democracy led politicians to assign the armed forces to internal security duties. Tracking changes in military jurisdictional boundaries during the 1980s helps to explain the sudden reemergence of military interventionism in a democracy that had been thought to be consolidated until 1992. Expanded jurisdictional boundaries during the Chávez administration in 2001 preceded the burst of military dissent and insurrection that the regime experienced in 2002. Similar studies of other democratic regimes during periods of crisis may provide insights into whether civilian control is becoming deinstitutionalized and a military coup more likely.

THE FLAWS OF CIVILIAN CONTROL BY CONTAINMENT

The Venezuelan experience in the wake of the 1992 coups runs counter to the general regional trend toward democratization and a diminished role of the armed forces in national politics. Its experience with crafting civilian control of the armed forces also runs counter to the trend toward civilian control by oversight present in Spain, Argentina, and even Chile. Democracy in Venezuela survived for forty years after the 1958 transition to democracy, and this country's experience reminds us that the institutional arrangements developed during the transitional period are enduring and may carry the seeds of the regime's eventual destruction. In particular, the institutional arrangement of civilian control, designed to contain the military rather than oversee its activities, created some unfortunate incentives that allowed renewed militarism to germinate within the armed forces. However, civilian leadership also played a crucial role in breaking down civilian control during the 1990s. The institutional arrangements that allowed democracy to survive in 1992 had to be deliberately dismantled during the Chávez administration in order to allow the president to achieve direct and personal control of the armed forces.

Venezuelan civil-military arrangements after 1958 succeeded admirably in removing the armed forces from the political equation. For a period of two decades, they also allowed for the professionalization of the armed forces. However, they created a barrier between civilians and the armed forces that prevented politicians and members of civil society from acquiring knowledge pertinent to defense issues. Regime capacity would have enabled civil-military institutional reform during the 1980s and 1990s that could have removed the incentives for factionalism and conspiracy within the armed forces while simultaneously constructing civilian control by oversight. Instead, the withdrawal of attention by senior political figures from defense issues was eventually followed by the withdrawal of senior military leaders from the governance of the armed forces, allowing the MBR-200 conspiracy to develop unchecked. The results were the 1992 coup attempts that revealed the depth of discontent with the present institutional arrangements and set off the downward slide toward the deconsolidation of democracy.

The evolution of civil-military relations following the election of President Chávez in 1998 also suggests the important role that leaders play in sustaining democratic consolidation. President Chávez deliberately dismantled institutions of civilian control and fostered a set of institutional arrangements, embedded in the 1999 constitution, that provided for direct and personal presidential power over the armed forces. It is a testament to the success of efforts by previous presidents to consolidate civilian control that the Venezuelan armed forces initially did not resist, bureaucratically or politically, the president's efforts to politicize the officer corps. In fact, many military leaders were eager to cooperate in reforming the armed forces, although not always in the manner preferred by President Chávez. It was not until 2002 that senior military leaders turned against the president, and only in small numbers, as the coup attempt of April demonstrated. As a result of the purge of the officer corps in the wake of the April 2002 coup, the officer corps was fragmented between the politicized and revolutionary faction in the ascendancy and officers who still cling to an apolitical vision of a professional military. The fragmentation of the officer corps, previously experienced during the 1945–48 period and the 1958–63 period, promised further episodes of military rebellion and resistance to civilian authority.

The Venezuelan experience after 1998 reminds us that the dangers to consolidated democracies in the region do not necessarily come from their own armed forces, as was once the case during the 1960s and 1970s. Instead, the Venezuelan experience may be a forerunner of the repoliticization of military forces by populist or neopopulist leaders, much as occurred during the Alberto Fujimori regime in Peru between 1992 and 2000. However, it may hopefully also serve as a warning to other civilian leaders as they consider using the armed forces for their own political benefit.

NOTES

■

Chapter Two

1 *El Nacional*, 25 November 1948, 1. I would like to thank Eligio Anzola Anzola for bringing this photograph to my attention.

2 The literal translation of "*chopo de piedra*" is "stone ax," but when the term was used by junior professional officers in reference to the senior officers of the Gómez regime, it implied that these were Neanderthals or cave men.

3 Venezuela's agricultural GDP in 1922 was Bs. 2.6 billion, while the combined oil-derived GDP was Bs. 243 million. In 1945 agricultural GDP had risen to Bs. 3.9 billion, while combined oil GDP had risen to Bs. 3.7868 billion. In 1945 Venezuela's GDP index (100.0 = 1920) had risen to 1,053, of which 556.1 was derived from non-petroleum-related economic activity. (All figures given in inflation-adjusted 1984 bolívares or otherwise indexed to 1984.)

4 Ramón J. Velásquez served as Escalante's private secretary shortly before his stroke.

5 An internal memorandum from the Comité Ejecutivo Nacional of Acción Democrática (CEN Memorandum) dating from the early 1940s indicates that AD's position toward the armed forces ranged from outright suspicion and antimilitarism to a desire for the improvement of the technical capacity of the armed forces so that Venezuela would be able to maintain an armed, pro–Allied Forces neutrality.

6 Vargas and other officers who adhered to a democratic professional perspective have since been accused of being partisan to Acción Democrática, although many of them appear to have been sincere in their commitment to democratization and modernization.

7 Sources, including U.S. State Department memoranda from this time period, report a split within the U.S. embassy in Venezuela between pro-AD civilian staffers and the military attachés, who were firmly convinced that AD was a Communist front. Given their direct links to the Venezuelan military through assistance and training programs, it seems likely that the views held by the U.S. military attachés circulated widely within the officer corps (Mohr 1976).

8 The meeting between Pérez Jiménez and Rómulo Betancourt, which successfully negotiated a compromise, was confirmed by Giacopini Zárraga (who was present), and in a letter from Betancourt to a Venezuelan army officer, Captain Tomás Pérez Tenreiro, dated 20 April 1949.

9 Ellner (1989) suggests that part of the reason that rumors concerning the existence of an AD party militia may have arisen was a result of actions by members of AD's youth wing, led by Domingo Alberto Rangel, to use weapons seized during the 1945 coup attempt to organize armed student and labor groups to defend the Gallegos administration. In letters written to Venezuelan army Captain Tomás Pérez Tenreiro shortly after the November 1948 coup, both Rómulo Betancourt and Mario Vargas denied that AD ever formed a party militia (Betancourt 1949a; Vargas 1949).

Chapter Three

1 In this letter to Rómulo Betancourt, dated 24 July 1949, Alberto Carnevali discussed the widespread feeling among party members, both those in prison (from which he had recently been released) and independents and activists in exile, that violence was the only means that AD could rely on to return to power. He suggested strengthening the party organizations among the labor unions, possibly arming them, and using them to seize power. Carnevali also suggested playing on the divisions in the armed forces to neutralize their power during any overthrow of the military dictatorship.

2 In this letter Betancourt argues, "[we] should not blame the national armed forces as an institution, but concretely the three and their clique [a reference to the junta], because to fall into extreme civilianism and an antiseptic allergy to the 'caps' [soldiers] would reveal us to be ingenues deserving of remaining in limbo." Unless otherwise indicated, all translations are the work of the author.

3 Rangel expressed these ideas in a series of letters, dated June and August 1949, to another member of AD in exile in the United States, Rubén Castellanos. For example, in a letter dated 27 June 1949, Rangel stated, "taking up the rifle until we bloody the country is the rough but indispensable solution to the Venezuelan drama that will come about once the party [AD] is tempered and improves its belligerence." Later, Rangel argued, "The day that we have in our illegal organization—as affiliates or adherents—substantial military commanders, and that the lower ranks of the officer corps either become militants or are propagandized periodically, the revolution will face no problems once it is in power. If we add to this the presence of thousands of militia members, who would not put down their arms but would instead would become regular units in the army with their own politicized officer corps, we would have a Virgilian scenario for permanent peace and prosperity."

4 This declaration was prepared in June 1957, but it was never released due to the failure to reach complete agreement with COPEI.

5 Domingo Alberto Rangel and the bulk of the party's youth wing separated from Acción Democrática, formed a new party, the Movimiento de la Izquierda Revolucionaria (MIR), and commenced guerrilla operations against the Betancourt government in 1960.

6 In letters to Alvarez (13 May 1957) and to Roberto García (2 June 1957), Rómulo

Betancourt mentioned that he thought the fall of General Rojas Pinilla in Colombia damaged the government of Pérez Jiménez, and he cited the political arrangements in Colombia as an inspiration for his own effort to reach a joint declaration or pact with URD's Jóvito Villalba and COPEI's Luis Herrera Campíns in New York later in June.

7 Fuenmayor reports that the idea of organizing the Junta Patriótica came from Jóvito Villalba, the leader of URD in exile, as a means to deemphasize the public image of Acción Democrática as the main resistance to the dictatorship. By organizing an all-party coordinating committee, Villalba hoped to weaken the hegemony of AD in any future democratic regime.

8 These checks were issued by the newly appointed minister of finance, Arturo Sosa, at the request of Edgar Sanabria, chief of staff of the Junta de Gobierno (interview by the author with a source whose name has been withheld, 1992, Caracas, Venezuela).

9 In the Betancourt presidential archives there is a collection of intelligence reports to military high command from the summer of 1958. These reports describe plans by Rómulo Betancourt to dismember the armed forces, instigate a revolution, and even to destroy the oil fields. They also link him with international Communism.

10 This is similar to the language in the "Declaración de los partidos políticos al pueblo Venezolano" (1957). This language also reflects the political approach to the armed forces advocated by Betancourt, as opposed to that urged by Domingo A. Rangel and the radical members of AD.

11 Interview by the author of a retired Venezuelan flag officer, 1995, Caracas, Venezuela.

Chapter Four

1 During the dictatorship, AD's clandestine resistance movement had been uncovered and decapitated so frequently that Simón Sáez Mérida, the leader of the party cadres in Venezuela, had never even met Rómulo Betancourt, the founder and president of AD, prior to his return in 1958.

2 Betancourt referred to this link between the domestic insurgency and international Communism on multiple occasions in speeches to groups of military officers and in missives to his cabinet. For example, in a letter to his minister of defense, General Antonio Briceño Linares, on 19 November 1960, Betancourt congratulated Briceño Linares on the success of the military's efforts to control rioting in Caracas, which had "prevented the creation of a New Cuba" in Venezuela.

3 See the intelligence report concerning status of Cuban exile groups prepared for Rómulo Betancourt, Doc. 92, Vol. 39, Fundación Rómulo Betancourt, Caracas, Venezuela.

4 One military officer I interviewed stated that most of the "arm twisting" involved in intelligence work (interrogations, torture, and other human rights abuses) was

carried out by civilians, particularly in the DIGEPOL. Another officer mentioned that political abuses and corruption led to the police's complete exclusion from the second *teatro de operaciones*, established at El Tocuyo in the Lara/Barinas/Trujillo guerilla front. However, this move also led to predominantly military interrogations of guerrilla prisoners, with their attendant abuses. Physical duress and psychological pressures were often used, along with incentives for informers and double agents such as cash rewards and relocation to friendly foreign countries, particularly Chile and Uruguay (interviews by the author with sources whose names have been withheld, 1994 and 1995, Caracas, Venezuela).

5 A subcommittee of the lower house of the Venezuelan Congress issued a report on 10 November 1964 that denounced the use of torture and extreme duress to extract information from prisoners by the police and, specifically, by the DIGEPOL.

Chapter Five

1 Also on this point, interview by the author with a U.S. Army Foreign Area Officer whose name has been withheld, 1995.

2 It is customary in Venezuela for more senior generals to resign rather than serve under a more junior officer appointed to the top position of minister of defense.

Chapter Six

1 Retired officers belonging to the Frente Institucional Militar have consistently argued that military preparedness has been negatively affected by President Chávez's policies. However, General Garcia Ordoñez, then a senior army general and commander of the armed forces unified command (CUFAN), stated in May 2000 that participation in the Plan Bolívar 2000 involved less then a third of his force's duty time and thus had little impact on readiness. Officers in the U.S. Military Assistance Group in Venezuela told me in June 2001 that the truth lay closer to the arguments of the Frente Institucional Militar.

2 For examples of these accusations, see the website of the dissident military officers, <http://www.militaresdemocraticos.com> (accessed February 2005).

3 For an example of the government perspective on the 11 April coup, see the National Assembly's report, "Informe de la Comisión Parlamentaria Especial para investigar los sucesos de abril de 2002" (Asamblea Nacional 2002).

4 See the government-opposition negotiated agreement, "Acuerdo entre la representación del gobierno de la República Bolivariana de Venezuela y los factores políticos y sociales que lo apoyan y la Coordinadora Democrática y las organizaciones políticas y de la sociedad civil que la conforman," signed 23 May 2003 in Caracas, Venezuela, <http://www.analitica.com/bitblioteca/varios/acuerdo_gobierto-oposicion.asp> (accessed February 2005).

REFERENCES

■

Acuña, Carlos, and Catalina Smúlovitz. 1995. "Militares en la transición Argentina: Del gobierno a la subordinación constitucional." In *La nueva matriz política Argentina*, edited by Carlos Acuña, 153–202. Buenos Aires: Ediciones Nueva Visión.

AD exiles in Mexico. 1949. "Memorándum confidencial, situación en Venezuela." Memorandum to Rómulo Betancourt, 30 November. Doc. 90, Vol. 9, Fundación Rómulo Betancourt, Caracas, Venezuela.

Agüero, Felipe. 1990. "The Military and Democracy in Venezuela." In *The Military and Democracy*, edited by Louis Goodman, Johanna Mendelson, and Juan Rial, 257–75. Lexington, Mass.: Lexington Books.

———. 1993. "Las fuerzas armadas y el debilitamiento de la democracia en Venezuela." In *Venezuela: La democracia bajo presión*, edited by Andrés Serbín, Andrés Stambouli, Jennifer McCoy, and William Smith, 187–203. Caracas: INVESP/Nueva Sociedad.

———. 1995a. "Debilitating Democracy: Political Elites and Military Rebels." In *Lessons from the Venezuelan Experience*, edited by Louis Goodman, Johanna Mendelson Forman, Moisés Naím, Joseph S. Tulchin, and Gary Bland, 136–63. Baltimore: Johns Hopkins University Press.

———. 1995b. *Soldiers, Civilians, and Democracy*. Baltimore: Johns Hopkins University Press.

———. 1998. "Legacies of Transition: Institutionalization, the Military, and Democracy in South America." *Mershon International Studies Review* 42 (November): 383–404.

———. 2001. "Institutions, Transitions, and Bargaining: Civilians and the Military in Shaping Post-Authoritarian Regimes." In *Civil-Military Relations in Latin America: New Analytical Perspectives*, edited by David Pion-Berlin, 194–222. Chapel Hill: University of North Carolina Press.

Alexander, Robert J. 1964. *Venezuela's Democratic Revolution*. New Brunswick, N.J.: Rutgers University Press.

Alfonso Ravard, General Rafael. 1995. Former president, Petroleos de Venezuela. Interview by the author, 20 February, Caracas, Venezuela.

Alliegro, General Italo del Valle. 1994. Speech, TECNOFAN '94 conference, November, Caracas, Venezuela.

Allison, Graham. 1971. *The Essence of Decision*. Boston: Little, Brown and Company.

Alonso, Lieutenant Colonel Santiago. 1995. Former *carapintada* military rebel. Interview by the author, 12 July, Buenos Aires, Argentina.

Alvarez, Angel E. 2003. "State Reform Before and After Chávez's Election." In *Venezuelan Politics in the Chávez Era*, edited by Steve Ellner and Daniel Hellinger, 147–60. Boulder, Colo.: Lynne Rienner.

Alvarez, Irma. 2002a. "La constitución guió a Efraín Vásquez Velasco." *El Universal*, 14 August.

———. 2002b. "Cuatro equipos para 20 magistrados." *El Universal*, 14 August.

———. 2002c. "Deliberancia de la FAN pone en riesgo seguridad de la nación." *El Universal*, 25 February.

———. 2003. "Cero comicios hasta designación del CNE." *El Universal*, 23 January.

"Amnistia Internacional: La violencia y polarización política aumentaron la inestabilidad." 2003. *El Universal*, 28 May.

Angulo Rivas, Alfredo. 1993. *Adiós a la utopía*. Caracas: Alfadíl Ediciones.

Anzola Anzola, Eligio. 1992. Minister of interior under President Rómulo Gallegos. Interview by the author, 5 August, Caracas, Venezuela.

Arceneaux, Craig. 2001. *Bounded Missions: Military Regimes and Democratization in the Southern Cone and Brazil*. University Park: Pennsylvania State University Press.

"Armada toma control del Pilín Leon." 2002. *El Universal*, 8 December.

Armas, Mayela. 2003. "Recortan asignación para las regiones." *El Universal*, 15 February.

Arreaza, Julio César. 1994. Ministry of Hydrocarbons and Mines official and Acción Democrática activist since 1940s. Interview by the author, 8 September, Caracas, Venezuela.

Arroyo Talavera, Eduardo. 1986. *Elecciones y negociaciones: Los limites de la democracia en Venezuela*. Caracas: Fondo Editorial Conicit/Pomaire.

Asamblea Nacional. 2002. "Informe de la Comisión Parlamentaria Especial para investigar los sucesos de abril de 2002." <http://abrilonce.tripod.com/texto111.html> Accessed March 2005.

Avendaño Lugo, José Ramón. 1982. *El militarismo en Venezuela: La dictadura de Pérez Jiménez*. Caracas: Ediciones Centauro.

Baptista, Asdrúbal. 1991. *Bases cuantitativas de la economía Venezolana: 1830–1989*. Caracas: Ediciones Comunicaciones Corporativas D.

Baumann, Frank. 1960. Confidential memorandum to Harold Wright, 1 September. Doc. 194, Vol. 35, Fundación Rómulo Betancourt, Caracas, Venezuela.

BBCMundo.com. 2003. "Venezuela: Gaviria no quiere polémica." 1 March. <http://news.bbc.co.uk/hi/spanish/latin_america/newsid_2810000/2810219.stm>. Accessed February 2005.

Behrongaray, Deputy Antonio. 1995. Unión Causa Radical (UCR) member of the national defense committee of Chamber of Deputies and former chair of Senate National Defense committee during the Alfonsín administration. Interview by the author, 20 June, Buenos Aires, Argentina.

Belkin, Aaron. 1998. "Domestic Survival and International Conflict: The Relationship between Coup d'Etat and War." Ph.D. diss., University of California at Berkeley.

Belmonte, Amalio. 1994. Chair, Department of Sociology, Universidad Central de Venezuela. Interview by the author, 6 October, Caracas, Venezuela.

Betancourt, Johanne. 2000. "Comandante en jefe y teniente coronel, o viceversa." *Tal Cual Digital*, 19 September.

Betancourt, Rómulo. Ca. 1949. Letter to Comando del Exterior. Doc. 251, Vol. 8, Fundación Rómulo Betancourt, Caracas, Venezuela.

———. 1949a. Letter to Captain Tomás Pérez Tenreiro, 20 April. Doc. 154, Vol. 7, Annex A, Fundación Rómulo Betancourt, Caracas, Venezuela.

———. 1949b. "Memorándum para el Centro (AD)," 1 November. Doc. 6, Vol. 9, Fundación Rómulo Betancourt, Caracas, Venezuela.

———. 1957a. Letter to "Alvarez," 13 May. Doc. 14, Vol. 33, Fundación Rómulo Betancourt, Caracas, Venezuela.

———. 1957b. Letter from Mata to "Alvarez," 15 May. Doc. 17, Vol. 33, Fundación Rómulo Betancourt, Caracas, Venezuela.

———. 1957c. Letter to Roberto García, 2 June. Doc. 40, Vol. 33, Fundación Rómulo Betancourt, Caracas, Venezuela.

———. 1957d. Memorandum to Central Committee of Acción Democrática, 20 June. Doc. 60, Vol. 33, Fundación Rómulo Betancourt, Caracas, Venezuela.

———. 1958. Memorandum to AD Coordinating Committee, 27 January. Doc. 133, Vol. 35, Fundación Rómulo Betancourt, Caracas, Venezuela.

———. 1960. Letter to General Antonio Briceño Linares, minister of defense, 19 November. Doc. 77, Vol. 40, Fundación Rómulo Betancourt, Caracas, Venezuela.

———. 1963. Letter to General Antonio Briceño Linares, minister of defense, December. Doc. 146, Vol. 40, Fundación Rómulo Betancourt, Caracas, Venezuela.

Biddle, Stephen, and Robert Zirkle. 1993. "Technology, Civil-Military Relations, and Warfare in the Developing World." Paper presented at the annual meeting of the American Political Science Association, Washington, D.C.

Bigler, Gene. 1981. "La restricción política y la profesionalización militar en Venezuela," trans. Colonel Carlos A. Pérez Garcia. *Politeia* 10: 85–142.

Blanco Muñoz, Agustin. 1991. *La lucha armada: La izquierda revolucionaria insurge.* Caracas: Ediciones FACES/UCV.

Blank, David E. 1984. *Venezuela: Politics in a Petroleum Republic.* New York: Praeger.

Bottome, Roberto. 1994. Director, Veneconomía. Interview by the author, September, Caracas, Venezuela.

———. 1999. Interview by the author, 28 July, Caracas, Venezuela.

Briceño Linares, General Antonio. 1994. Minister of defense under President Rómulo Betancourt. Interview by the author, 26 October, Caracas, Venezuela.

Bruni Celli, Marco Tulio. 1980. *Los primeros programas políticos*. Caracas: Acción Democrática, Departamento de Estudios, Doctrina y Capacitación.

———. 1992. Interview by the author, 13 July, Caracas, Venezuela.

Bueno de Mesquita, Bruce, Randolph M. Siverson, and Gary Woller. 1992. "War and the Fate of Regimes: A Comparative Analysis." *American Political Science Review* 86 (September): 638–46.

"Buque cargado de alimentos llega el viernes a la Guaira desde Colombia." 2003. *El Universal*, 13 January.

Burggraff, Winfield. 1972. *The Venezuelan Armed Forces in Politics, 1935–1959*. Columbia: University of Missouri Press.

Burggraff, Winfield, and Richard L. Millet. 1995. "More Than Failed Coups: The Crisis in Venezuelan Civil-Military Relations." In *Lessons from the Venezuelan Experience*, edited by Louis Goodman, Johanna Mendelson Forman, Moisés Naím, Joseph S. Tulchin, and Gary Bland, 54–77. Baltimore: Johns Hopkins University Press.

Buxton, Julia. 2003. "Economic Policy and the Rise of Hugo Chávez." In *Venezuelan Politics in the Chávez Era*, edited by Steve Ellner and Daniel Hellinger, 113–30. Boulder, Colo.: Lynne Rienner.

Caballero, Manuel. 1988. *Las Venezuelas del siglo XX*. Caracas: Editorial Grijalbo.

Caldera, Rafael. 1992a. President of Venezuela, 1969–74 and 1994–99. Interview by the author, 4 August, Caracas, Venezuela.

———. 1992b. Interview by the author, 18 August, Caracas, Venezuela.

Camel Anderson, Eduardo. 2003a. "Bloquean a empleados de PDVSA." *El Universal*, 7 January.

———. 2003b. "Deficit de ONG contra la probreza." *El Universal*, 15 June.

———. 2003c. "Venamcham denuncia terrorismo de estado contra el empresariado." *El Universal*, 23 January.

Canache, Damarys. 2002. *Venezuela: Public Opinion and Protest in a Fragile Democracy*. Miami, Fla.: North-South Center Press.

Canache, Damarys, and Michael R. Kulisheck. 1998. *Reinventing Legitimacy: Democracy and Political Change in Venezuela*. Westport, Conn.: Greenwood Press.

Capriles Ayala, Carlos. 1985. *Los años treinta y cuarenta*. Caracas: Editorial Capriles.

———, ed. 1992. *Diccionario de la corrupción en Venezuela*, vol. 3. Caracas: Consorcio de Ediciones Capriles.

Capriles Ayala, Carlos, and Rafael Del Naranjo. 1992. *Todos los golpes a las democracia Venezolana*. Caracas: Consorcio de Ediciones Capriles.

Capriles Méndez, Ruth, ed. 1990. *Diccionario de la corrupción en Venezuela*, vol. 2. Caracas: Consorcio de Ediciones Capriles.

Cardona Marrero, Rodolfo. 2001a. "Plan Bolívar manejó 200 millardos." *El Universal*, 18 August.

———. 2001b. "Recorte de presupuesto afecta aviación militar." *El Universal*, 31 October.

———. 2002. "Toma de la PM 'fue impecable.'" *El Universal*, 18 November.

Carnevali, Alberto. 1949. Letter to Rómulo Betancourt, 24 July. Doc. 315, Vol. 7, Annex A, Fundación Rómulo Betancourt, Caracas, Venezuela.

Cartay Ramírez, Gehard. 1983. *Política y partidos modernos en Venezuela*. Caracas: Ediciones Centauro.

Carter Center. 2004. "Informe del viaje del presidente Carter a Venezuela, del 29 de mayo al 1 de junio, 2004." Caracas, Venezuela.<http://www.el-nacional.com/ref erencia/documentos/pdf/carter.pdf>. Accessed March 2005.

Castillo, Ocarina. 1994. Professor, Department of Sociology, Universidad Central de Venezuela. Interview by the author, 4 October, Caracas, Venezuela.

Castro, Monica, and Patricia Ventura Nicolas. 2002. "Petroleros responden otra vez." *El Universal*, 3 December.

Celis Noguera, General Carlos. 1989. "Comentario." In *Rómulo Betancourt: Historia y contemporaneidad*, 435–40. Caracas: Editorial Fundación Rómulo Betancourt.

———. 1991. "El IAEDN." Speech given at a seminar conducted by the secretariat of the National Security and Defense Council for the Acarigua Chamber of Commerce, 5 October.

———. 1994. Director emeritus of Instituto de Altos Estudios de la Defensa Nacional. Interview by the author, 10 October, Caracas, Venezuela.

CEN Memorandum, Acción Democrática. ca. early 1940s. Doc. 172, Vol. 4, Fundación Rómulo Betancourt, Caracas, Venezuela.

"Chávez ordenó retiro a 300 oficiales de la FAN." 2002. *Tal Cual*, 3 September.

Chief of the first section of the Air Force General Staff. Not dated. Memorandum to President Rómulo Betancourt. Vol. 37, Annex C, Fundación Rómulo Betancourt, Caracas, Venezuela.

Chilcote, Ronald H. 1981. *Theories of Comparative Politics: The Search for a Paradigm Reconsidered*. Boulder, Colo.: Westview Press.

COFAVIC. 2002. "Venezuela: Democracia y derechos humanos. Informe semestral enero–agosto 2002." <http://www.cofavic.org.ve/InformeENE-AGO2002.pdf>. Accessed March 2005.

———. 2003. "La democracia en Venezuela está seriamente amenazada (periodo septiembre 2002 a febrero 2003)." <http://www.cofavic.org.ve/informe2.doc>. Accessed March 2005.

Colomine, Luisana. 2000. "Militares activos no deben optar a elección popular." *El Universal*, 1 March.

Colton, Timothy J. 1979. *Commissars, Commanders, and Civilian Authority: The Structure of Soviet Military Politics*. Cambridge, Mass.: Harvard University Press.

Comando General del Ejército. 2000. *Plan Bolívar 2000*. No. 2. Caracas: Impresas Mundo Gráfico.

Conde Casadiego, Colonel Antonio M., Colonel Jose G. Machado Guzmán, and Capitán de Navio Omar Quintero Torres. 1991. "Situacion socio-económica del personal de oficiales y sub-oficiales de las Fuerzas Armadas y su incidencia sobre la Defensa Nacional." IAEDN Thesis, XX National Defense Superior Course.

Constitución de la República de Venezuela. 1994. Caracas: Distribuidora Escolar.

Coppedge, Michael. 1994. *Strong Parties and Lame Ducks: Presidential Partyarchy and Factionalism in Venezuela.* Stanford, Calif.: Stanford University Press.

————. 2003. "Venezuela: Popular Sovereignty versus Liberal Democracy." In *Constructing Democratic Governance*, edited by Jorge I. Dominguez and Michael Shifter, 165–92. 2d ed. Baltimore: Johns Hopkins University Press.

Crisp, Brian. 2000. *Democratic Institutional Design: The Powers and Incentives of Venezuelan Politicians and Interest Groups.* Stanford, Calif.: Stanford University Press.

Dahl, Robert. 1971. *Polyarchy.* New Haven, Conn.: Yale University Press.

Daniels, Elias R. 1992. *Militares y democracia.* Caracas: Ediciones Centauro.

Danopoulos, Constantine. 1988. "Beating a Hasty Retreat: The Greek Military Withdraws from Power." In *The Decline of Military Regimes*, edited by Constantine Danopoulos, 225–58. Boulder, Colo.: Westview Press.

Decalo, Samuel. 1976. *Coups and Army Rule in Africa: Studies in Military Style.* New Haven, Conn.: Yale University Press.

"Declaración de los partidos políticos al pueblo Venezolano." 1957. Draft document jointly subscribed by Rómulo Betancourt (AD) and Jóvito Villalba (URD). Doc. 84, Vol. 33, Fundación Rómulo Betancourt, Caracas, Venezuela.

Desch, Michael. 1999. *Civilian Control of the Military: The Changing Security Environment.* Baltimore: Johns Hopkins University Press.

Diamond, Larry, and Marc Plattner. 1993. "Introduction." In *The Global Resurgence of Democracy*, edited by Larry Diamond and Marc Plattner, ix–xxvi. Baltimore: Johns Hopkins University Press.

Dix, Robert H. 1994. "Military Coups and Military Rule in Latin America." *Armed Forces and Society* 20 (Spring): 439–56.

Dobrovir, William A. 1959. Letter and memorandum to Rómulo Betancourt, 11 December. Vol. 37, Fundación Rómulo Betancourt, Caracas, Venezuela.

Druetta, Gustavo. 1990. "Diputados y defensa: Radiografia de un poder tenue." In *Defensa y democracia*, edited by Gustavo Druetta, Eduardo Estévez, Ernesto López, and José Enrique Miguens, 196–243. Buenos Aires: Punto Sur.

"El gobierno debe." 2000. *El Nacional*, 12 September.

Ellner, Steve. 1989. *De la derrota guerillera a la política inovadora.* Caracas: Monte Avila Editores.

————. 2003. "Introduction: The Search for Explanations." In *Venezuelan Politics in the Chávez Era*, edited by Steve Ellner and Daniel Hellinger, 7–26. Boulder, Colo.: Lynne Rienner.

Esparza Valiente, Colonel Juan Martinez. 1993. Deputy director general for defense policy—international affairs, Ministry of Defense. Interview by Thomas Bruneau, 17 February, Madrid, Spain.

Ewell, Judith. 1984. *Venezuela: A Century of Change*. Stanford, Calif.: Stanford University Press.

Farcau, Bruce. 1996. *The Transition to Democracy in Latin America*. Westport, Conn.: Praeger.

Feaver, Peter D. 1996. "Delegation, Monitoring, and Civilian Control of the Military: Agency Theory and American Civil-Military Relations." Project on U.S. Post–Cold War Civil-Military Relations, John M. Olin Institute Working Paper No. 4.

———. 2003. *Armed Servants: Agency, Oversight, and Civil-Military Relations*. Cambridge, Mass.: Harvard University Press.

Feng, Yi. 1995. "Regime, Polity, and Economic Growth: The Latin American Experience." *Growth and Change* 26 (Winter): 77–104.

Ferreira Pinho, Juan A. 1995. Secretary of defense under Minister Ermán González and President Carlos Ménem. Interview by the author, 17 May, Buenos Aires, Argentina.

Finer, S. E. (1962) 1988. *The Man on Horseback: The Role of the Military in Politics*. Boulder, Colo.: Westview Press.

Fitch, J. Samuel. 1986. "Armies and Politics in Latin America: 1975–1985." In *Armies and Politics in Latin America*, edited by Abraham Lowenthal and J. Samuel Fitch, 26–55. New York: Holmes and Meier.

———. 1998. *The Armed Forces and Democracy in Latin America*. Baltimore: Johns Hopkins University Press.

———. 2001. "Military Attitudes toward Democracy in Latin America: How Do We Know If Anything Has Changed?" In *Civil-Military Relations in Latin America: New Analytical Perspectives*, edited by David Pion-Berlin, 59–87. Chapel Hill: University of North Carolina Press.

Fitch, J. Samuel, and Andrés Fontana. 1991. "Military Policy and Democratic Consolidation." Paper presented to the Sixteenth International Congress of the Latin American Studies Association, Washington, D.C.

"Frente Institucional Militar niega vinculación con capitán García." 2000. *El Nacional*, 30 June.

Fuenmayor, Juan Bautista. 1981–93. *Historia de la Venezuela Política Contemporanea*. 20 vols. Caracas: Talleres Miguel Angel García e Hijo.

Fuentes, Claudio. 1999. "After Pinochet: Civilian Unity, Political Institutions, and the Military in Chile (1990–1998)". Durham, N.C.: Duke–University of North Carolina Program in Latin American Studies Working Paper No. 28.

———. 2000. "After Pinochet: Civilian Policies toward the Military in 1990s Chilean Democracy." *Journal of Interamerican Studies and World Affairs* 42 (Fall): 111–42.

García Villasmil, General Martín. 1961. "Adoctrinamiento institucional: Aspectos de la educación cívica que interesan a las Fuerzas Armadas en la actualidad." 3 July, Caracas, Venezuela. In author's possession.

———. 1995a. Minister of defense under President Rafael Caldera, 1969–72. Interview by the author, 16 February, Caracas, Venezuela.

————. 1995b. Interview by the author, 5 April, Caracas, Venezuela.

————. 1995c. Interview by the author, 19 April, Caracas, Venezuela.

Garrido, Alberto. 2003. *Notas sobre la revolución Bolivariana*. Merida, Venezuela: Ediciones del Autor (self-published).

"Gaviria instó a las partes a poner mas voluntad política." 2002. *El Universal*, 28 December.

Geddes, Barbara. 1999. "What Do We Know about Democratization after Twenty Years?" *Annual Review of Political Science* 2 (June): 115–44.

Giacopini Zárraga, José. 1992a. Chief of staff of the Junta Revolucionaria de Gobierno, 1947, and minister of finance for Pérez Jiménez regime. Interview by the author, 29 July, Caracas, Venezuela.

————. 1992b. Interview by the author, 20 August, Caracas, Venezuela.

————. 1992c. Interview by the author, 23 August, Caracas, Venezuela.

————. 1992d. Interview by the author, 25 August, Caracas, Venezuela.

————. 1994a. Interview by the author, 2 September, Caracas, Venezuela.

————. 1994b. Interview by the author, 29 September, Caracas, Venezuela.

————. 1994c. Interview by the author, 16 October, Caracas, Venezuela.

————. 1994d. Interview by the author, 1 November, Caracas, Venezuela.

————. 1995a. Interview by the author, 24 January, Caracas, Venezuela.

————. 1995b. Interview by the author, 2 February, Caracas, Venezuela.

Gil Yepes, José Antonio. 1978. *El reto de las élites*. Madrid: Editorial Tecnos.

————. 1991. "El encaje político en el sector militar." *Nueva Sociedad* 81.

————. 1992. "De 1976 a nuestros dias." In *Política y economía en Venezuela: 1810–1991*, edited by Alfredo Boulton, 293–379. 2d ed. Caracas: Fundación John Boulton.

————. 1994. Pollster and political analyst. Interview by the author, 14 October, Caracas, Venezuela.

Giusti, Roberto. 2002. "El 71% del pais rechaza a Chávez." *El Universal*, 3 November.

"Gobierno evalua denuncias sobre presencia de la FARC en Venezuela." 2002. *El Universal*, 25 March.

"Gobierno y PM exigen a fiscalia investigar violencia en el Petarazo." 2003. *El Nacional*, 16 June.

Godio, Julio. 1985. *El movimiento obrero Venezolano, 1945–1964*. Caracas: ILDIS.

González, David. 2003. "Dispersaron con bombas lacrimógenas nueva marcha opositora en Los Próceres." *El Nacional*, 13 January.

Grüber Odremán, Hernán. 1993. *Insurreción militar del 27-N-1992*. Caracas: Editorial Centauro.

Haggard, Stephan, and Robert R. Kaufman. 1992a. "Economic Adjustment and the Prospects for Democracy." In *Politics of Economic Adjustment*, edited by Stephan Haggard and Robert R. Kaufman, 319–50. Princeton, N.J.: Princeton University Press.

————. 1992b. "The Political Economy of Inflation and Stabilization in Middle Income Countries." In *Politics of Economic Adjustment*, edited by Stephan Haggard and Robert R. Kaufman, 270–318. Princeton, N.J.: Princeton University Press.

———. 1999. "The Political Economy of Democratic Transitions." In *Transitions to Democracy*, edited by Lisa Anderson, 72–96. New York: Columbia University Press.

Hartlyn, Jonathan. 1984. "Military Governments and the Transition to Civilian Rule: The Colombian Experience, 1957–1958." *Journal of Interamerican Studies and World Affairs* 26 (May): 29–60.

Hellinger, Daniel. 2003. "Political Overview: The Breakdown of *Puntofijismo* and the Rise of *Chavismo.*" In *Venezuelan Politics in the Chávez Era*, edited by Steve Ellner and Daniel Hellinger, 27–53. Boulder, Colo.: Lynne Rienner.

Heper, Martin, and Aylin Guney. 1996. "The Military and Democracy in the Third Turkish Republic." *Armed Forces and Society* 22 (Summer): 619–42.

Herman, Donald L. 1980. *Christian Democracy in Venezuela*. Chapel Hill: University of North Carolina Press.

———, ed. 1988. *Democracy in Latin America*. New York: Praeger.

Hernández, Alejandra M. 2003. "Disidentes exhortan a la FAN desconocer autoridad de Chávez." *El Universal*, 13 June.

Hernández, Carlos Raúl. 1995. *El motín de los dinosaurios*. Caracas: Editorial Panapo.

Hernández, Clodovaldo. 2002. "Tarde de sangre, noche de golpe." *El Universal*, 20 April.

Horowitz, Donald L. 1980. *Coup Theories and Officer Motives. Sri Lanka in Comparative Perspective*. Princeton, N.J.: Princeton University Press.

Human Rights Watch. 2003. "Informe Annual 2003: Venezuela." <http://www.hrw.org /spanish/inf_anual/2003/venezuala.html#venezuela>. Accessed June 2004.

Huneeus, Carlos. 1997. "The Pinochet Regime: A Comparative Analysis with the Franco Regime." In *Politics, Society, and Democracy: Latin America*, edited by Scott Mainwaring and Arturo Valenzuela, 71–99. Boulder, Colo.: Westview Press.

Hunter, Wendy. 1996. *State and Soldier in Latin America: Redefining the Military's Role in Argentina, Brazil, and Chile*. Washington D.C.: United States Institute for Peace, Peaceworks No. 10.

———. 1997. *Eroding Military Influence in Brazil: Politicians against Soldiers*. Chapel Hill: University of North Carolina Press.

Huntington, Samuel P. 1957. *The Soldier and the State*. Cambridge, Mass.: Harvard University Press.

———. 1968. *Political Order in Changing Societies*. New Haven, Conn.: Yale University Press.

———. 1991. *The Third Wave*. Norman: University of Oklahoma Press.

Intelligence report concerning status of Cuban exile groups prepared for Rómulo Betancourt, ca. 1963–64. Doc. 92, Vol. 39, Fundación Rómulo Betancourt, Caracas, Venezuela.

Irwin G., Domingo. 2000. *Relaciones civiles-militares en el siglo XX*. Caracas: Ediciones El Centauro.

Janowitz, Morris. 1964. *The Military in the Political Development of New Nations*. Chicago: University of Chicago Press.

Jaunarena, Deputy Horacio. 1995. Minister of defense, Alfonsín administration. Interview by the author, 6 May, Buenos Aires, Argentina.

Jiménez Sánchez, General Iván. 1996. *Los golpes de estado de Castro hasta Caldera*. Caracas: Centralca.

Joseph, Richard. 1993. "Africa: The Rebirth of Political Freedom." In *The Global Resurgence of Democracy*, edited by Larry Diamond and Marc Plattner, 307–20. Baltimore: Johns Hopkins University Press.

Karl, Terry L. 1986. "Petroleum and Political Pacts: The Transition to Democracy in Venezuela." In *Transitions from Authoritarian Rule: Latin America*, edited by Guillermo O'Donnell, Philippe Schmitter, and Lawrence Whitehead, 196–219. Baltimore: Johns Hopkins University Press.

———. 1990. "Dilemmas of Democratization in Latin America." *Comparative Politics* 23 (October): 1–21.

———. 1995. "The Hybrid Regimes of Central America." *Journal of Democracy* 6 (July): 72–96.

———. 1997. *The Paradox of Plenty*. Berkeley: University of California Press.

Karl, Terry L., and Philippe Schmitter. 1993. "What Democracy Is . . . and Is Not." In *The Global Resurgence of Democracy*, edited by Larry Diamond and Marc Plattner, 39–52. Baltimore: Johns Hopkins University Press.

Kebschull, Harvey G. 1994. "Operation 'Just Missed': Lessons from Failed Coup Attempts." *Armed Forces and Society* 20 (Summer): 565–79.

Kier, Elizabeth, and Jonathan Mercer. 1996. "Setting Precedents in Anarchy: Military Interventions and Weapons of Mass Destruction." *International Security* 20 (Spring): 77–106.

Krispin, Karl. 1994. *Golpe de estado Venezuela, 1945–1948*, Caracas: Editorial Panapo.

La Rotta Moran, Alicia. 2002. "Desconocen gobierno de Chávez." *El Universal*, 23 October.

Lagos, Marta. 2003. "A Road with No Return?" *Journal of Democracy* 14 (no. 2): 163–73.

Leal, Adela. 2000. "No hay ni la más remota posibilidad de fraccionamiento en la Fuerza Armada." *El Nacional*, 3 March.

Leal, Adela, and Pablo Aiquel Garbarini. 2002. "Chávez admite errors y pide perdón a los gerentes removidos de PDVSA." *El Nacional*, 16 April.

Levine, Daniel. 1973. *Conflict and Political Change in Venezuela*. Princeton, N.J.: Princeton University Press.

Levine, Daniel, and Brian F. Crisp. 1995. "Legitimacy, Governability, and Reform in Venezuela." In *Lessons from the Venezuelan Experience*, edited by Louis Goodman, Johanna Mendelson Forman, Moisés Naím, Joseph S. Tulchin, and Gary Bland, 223–51. Baltimore: Johns Hopkins University Press.

Ley Orgánica de la Fuerza Armada Nacional. 2002. Asamblea Nacional, Segundo Ordinario, 9 September. Expediente 234. <http://www.asambleanacional.gov.ve/ns2/leyes.asp>. Accessed 12 January 2004.

Libro Blanco de la Defensa Nacional. 1997. Ministerio de la Defensa Nacional. Chile.

Libro Blanco de la Defensa Nacional. 2002. Ministerio de la Defensa Nacional. Chile.

Linz, Juan. 1978. *Crisis, Breakdown, and Reequilibration*. Baltimore: Johns Hopkins University Press.

Linz, Juan, and Alfred Stepan. 1996. *Problems of Democratic Transition and Consolidation*. Baltimore: Johns Hopkins University Press.

Looney, Robert E. 1990. "Militarization, Military Regimes, and the General Quality of Life in the Third World." *Armed Forces and Society* 17 (Fall): 127–39.

López, Ernesto. 1994. *Ni la ceniza, ni la gloria*. Buenos Aires: Editorial Universidad Nacional de Quilmes.

López, Natálio. 1992. Acción Democrática activist. Interview by the author, 12 July, Caracas, Venezuela.

López Henrique, General Josué. 1960. Ministry of Defense radiogram to all military garrisons (draft), September. Doc. 197, Vol. 35, Fundación Rómulo Betancourt, Caracas, Venezuela.

———. 1961. Letter to Colonel Pablo A. Flores, June. Doc. 79, Vol. 39, Fundación Rómulo Betancourt, Caracas, Venezuela.

López Maya, Margarita. 2003. "Hugo Chávez Frias: His Movement and His Presidency." In *Venezuelan Politics in the Chávez Era*, edited by Steve Ellner and Daniel Hellinger, 73–92. Boulder, Colo.: Lynne Rienner.

López Maya, Margarita, Luis Gómez Calcaño, and Thaís Maingón. 1989. *De punto fijo al pacto social*. Caracas: Fondo Editorial Acta Científica Venezolana.

"Los militares que son y donde están." 1999. *El Universal*, 28 February.

Loveman, Brian. 1999. *For la Patria*. Wilmington, Del.: Scholarly Resources Books.

———. 2001. "Historical Foundations of Civil-Military Relations in Spanish America." In *Civil-Military Relations in Latin America: New Analytical Perspectives*, edited by David Pion-Berlin, 246–74. Chapel Hill: University of North Carolina Press.

Loveman, Brian, and Thomas M. Davies Jr. 1989. *The Politics of Anti-Politics*. Lincoln: University of Nebraska Press.

Machillanda Pinto, José. 1988. *Poder político y poder militar*. Caracas: Ediciones Centauro.

———. 1993. *Cinísmo político y golpe de estado*. Caracas: Italgráfica.

———. 1995. Retired army lieutenant colonel and political scientist. Interview by the author, 3 March, Caracas, Venezuela.

———. 1997. Interview by the author, 10 March, Caracas, Venezuela.

Maldonado Michelena, General Victor. 1992. Member of the secretariat of the Venezuelan National Security Council. Interview by the author, 28 July, Caracas, Venezuela.

Manrique, Miguel. 1996. *La seguridad en las Fuerzas Armadas Venezolanas*. Caracas: Fondo Editorial Tropykos.

Maracara, Luisa Amelia. 1999. "Gobernadores pedirán a Chávez reforma del FEM." *El Universal*, 30 June.

Markey, Patrick. 2005. "Oil-Rich Venezuela's Economy Grew 17.3 Pct. in 2004." *Reuters*, 16 February. <http://www.reuters.com>. Accessed 2 March 2005.

Marquina, Antonio. 1991. "Spanish Defense and Foreign Policy since Democratization." In *Spanish Foreign and Defense Policy*, edited by Kenneth Maxwell, 19–62. Boulder, Colo.: Westview Press.

Martinez, Eugenio. 2002. "Referendo se realizará el 2F." *El Universal*, 28 November.

Martz, John D. 1968. *Acción Democratica: Evolution of a Modern Political Party in Venezuela*. Princeton, N.J.: Princeton University Press.

———. 1995. "Political Parties and the Democratic Crisis." In *Lessons from the Venezuelan Experience*, edited by Louis Goodman, Johanna Mendelson Forman, Moisés Naím, Joseph S. Tulchin, and Gary Bland, 31–53. Baltimore: Johns Hopkins University Press.

Mayobre, José Antonio. 1992. "Desde el 1936 al año 1976." In *Política y economía en Venezuela: 1810–1991*, edited by Alfredo Boulton, 275–92. 2d ed. Caracas: Fundación John Boulton.

Mayorca, Javier Ignacio. 2000. "Coronel de la FAV denuncia a general que ascendió con un año de antiguedad." *El Nacional*, 14 September.

———. 2002. "Alianza de militares activos precipitó la caída de Hugo Chávez." *El Nacional*, 13 April.

———. 2003. "En manos del Ejército comité de informática de la industria." *El Nacional*, 7 March.

McCoy, Jennifer L. 1989. "Labor and the State in Party-Mediated Democracy: Institutional Change in Venezuela." *Latin American Research Review* 24 (Spring): 35–67.

———. 2004. "What Really Happened in Venezuela?" *Economist*, 2 September.

McCoy, Jennifer L., and Harold Trinkunas. 1999. "Venezuela's Peaceful Revolution." *Current History* 98 (March): 122–26.

McCoy, Jennifer L., and William C. Smith. 1995. "Democratic Disequilibrium in Venezuela." *Journal of Interamerican Studies and World Affairs* 37 (Summer): 113–79.

McCubbins, Matthew, and Thomas Schwartz. 1984. "Congressional Oversight Overlooked: Police Patrols versus Fire Alarms." *American Political Science Review* 28 (February): 165–79.

McSherry, J. Patrice. 1997. *Incomplete Transition: Military Power and Democracy in Argentina*. New York: St. Martin's Press.

Medina, Oscar. 2003. "Las mechas del 23." *El Universal*, 15 June.

Mendoza, Tomás. 1949. Letter to Eloy Pérez Alfonzo. Doc. 275, Vol. 7, Fundación Rómulo Betancourt, Caracas, Venezuela.

Millett, Richard L. 1994. "Beyond Sovereignty: International Efforts to Support Latin

American Democracy." *Journal of Interamerican Studies and World Affairs* 36 (Fall): 1–23.

Moe, Terry. 1984. "The New Economics of Organization." *American Political Science Review* 28 (November): 739–77.

Mohr, Cynthia Jane Bruce. 1976. "Revolution, Reform, and Counter-Revolution: The United States and Economic Nationalism in Venezuela, 1945–48." Ph.D. diss., Graduate School of International Studies, University of Denver.

Molina Vargas, General Victor. 1992. Former director of counterinsurgency campaign during the 1960s. Interview by the author, 28 July, Caracas, Venezuela.

Molina Vega, José. 2000. "Comportamiento electoral en Venezuela: Cambio y continuidad." Paper delivered at the annual meeting of the Latin American Studies Association, 16–18 March, Miami, Fla.

Mollejas, Carlos. 2003. "Solo 14 funcionarios investigan 25 homicidios en actos políticos." *El Universal*, 5 January.

Mommer, Bernard. 2003. "Subversive Oil." In *Venezuelan Politics in the Chávez Era*, edited by Steve Ellner and Daniel Hellinger, 131–46. Boulder, Colo.: Lynne Rienner.

Monaldi Marturet, Francisco. 2005. Professor, Universidad Católica Andrés Bello, Caracas, Venezuela. Personal communication with the author, March.

Montiel, General Maglio. 1994. Chief of the Joint Staff. Interview by the author, 21 October, Caracas, Venezuela.

Müller Rojas, Alberto. 1989. "Rómulo Betancourt y la política militar." In *Rómulo Betancourt: Historia y contemporaneidad*, 407–26. Caracas: Editorial Fundación Rómulo Betancourt.

———. 1992. *Relaciones peligrosas*. Caracas: Editorial Tropykos and APUCV/IPP.

———. 1995. Retired army general, professor of political science at Universidad Central de Venezuela, and Hugo Chávez's 1998 presidential campaign manager. Interview by the author, 20 January, Caracas, Venezuela.

Naim, Humberto, and Ramón Piñango. 1989. *El caso Venezuela: Una ilusión de armonia*. Caracas: Ediciones IESA.

Naím, Moisés. 1993. *Paper Tigers and Minotaurs: The Politics of Economic Reform in Venezuela*. Washington, D.C.: Carnegie Endowment for International Peace.

Néry Arrieta, General Francisco. 1992. Former commander of the Guardia Nacional. Interview by the author, July, Caracas, Venezuela.

Norden, Deborah. 1996a. *Military Rebellion in Argentina: Between Coups and Consolidation*. Lincoln: University of Nebraska Press.

———. 1996b. "The Rise of the Lieutenant Colonels: Rebellion in Argentina and Venezuela." *Latin American Perspectives* 23 (Summer): 74–86.

———. 2001. "The Organizational Dynamics of Militaries and Military Movements: Paths to Power in Venezuela." In *Civil-Military Relations in Latin America: New Analytical Perspectives*, edited by David Pion-Berlin, 109–34. Chapel Hill: University of North Carolina Press.

————. 2003. "Democracy in Uniform: Chávez and the Venezuelan Armed Forces." In *Venezuelan Politics in the Chávez Era*, edited by Steve Ellner and Daniel Hellinger, 93–112. Boulder, Colo.: Lynne Rienner.

Nordlinger, Eric A. 1977. *Soldiers in Politics: Military Coups and Governments*. Englewood Cliffs, N.J.: Prentice-Hall.

Nunn, Frederick M. 1983. *Yesterday's Soldiers: European Military Professionalism in South America, 1890–1940*. Lincoln: University of Nebraska Press.

————. 1995. "The South American Military and (Re)Democratization: Professional Thought and Self-Perception." *Journal of Interamerican Studies and World Affairs* 37 (Summer): 1–56.

O'Donnell, Guillermo. 1979. "Tensions in the Bureaucratic Authoritarian State and the Question of Democracy." In *The New Authoritarianism in Latin America*, edited by David Collier, 285–318. Princeton, N.J.: Princeton University Press.

————. 1996. "Illusions about Consolidation." *Journal of Democracy* 7 (April): 34–51.

O'Donnell, Guillermo, and Philippe Schmitter. 1986. *Transitions from Authoritarian Rule: Tentative Conclusions about Uncertain Democracies*. Baltimore: Johns Hopkins University Press.

Olivares, Francisco. 2002a. "La Fuerza Armada fracturada." *El Universal*, 21 April.

————. 2002b. "El pánico se desató al mediodía." *El Universal*, 29 April.

————. 2003. "FAN revolucionaria." *El Universal*, 8 June.

————. 2004. "Cinco años por opinar.". *El Universal*, 24 October.

"Oposición convocó a paro nacional el 2 de diciembre." 2002. *El Nacional*, 3 December.

Otaiza, Eliéce. 1994. Former MBR-200 participant and chief of political police DISIP during Chávez administration. Interview by the author, 4 October, Caracas, Venezuela.

Palacios, Marianela. 2003. "Diputados denuncian los círculos bolivarianos." *El Nacional*, 14 March.

Penfold Becerra, Michael. 2000. "El colapso del sistema de partidos en Venezuela: Explicación de una muerte anunciada." Paper delivered at the annual meeting of the Latin American Studies Association, 16–18 March, Miami, Fla.

Pérez Rodríguez, Solbella. 2002. "Refugiados en la Plaza Altamira." *Tal Cual*, 24 October.

Pérez, Carlos Andrés. 1995. Former president, 1974–79 and 1989–93. Interview by the author, 14 February, Caracas, Venezuela.

Perlmutter, Amos. 1997. *The Military and Politics in Modern Times*. New Haven, Conn.: Yale University Press.

Perrow, Charles. 1986. *Complex Organizations: A Critical Essay*. 3d ed. New York: McGraw-Hill.

Pew Center Global Attitudes Project. 2002. *What the World Thinks in 2002*. Washington, D.C.: Pew Research Center for the People and the Press.

Piñango, Ramón. 1992. Professor, Instituto de Estudios Superiores de Administracíon (IESA). Interview by the author, 4 August, Caracas, Venezuela.

Pion-Berlin, David. 1989. "Latin American National Security Doctrines: Hard- and Softline Themes." *Armed Forces and Society* 15 (Spring): 411–29.

———. 1992. "Military Autonomy and Emerging Democracies in South America." *Comparative Politics* 25 (October): 83–102.

———. 1997. *Through Corridors of Power: Institutions and Civil-Military Relations in Argentina*. University Park: Pennsylvania State University Press.

———. 2001. "Civil-Military Circumvention: How Argentine State Institutions Compensate for a Weakened Chain of Command." In *Civil-Military Relations in Latin America: New Analytical Perspectives*, edited by David Pion-Berlin, 135–60. Chapel Hill: University of North Carolina Press.

Pion-Berlin, David, and Craig Arceneaux. 2000. "Decision-Makers or Decision-Takers? Military Missions and Civilian Control in Democratic South America." *Armed Forces and Society* 26 (Spring): 413–36.

Plan Andrés Bello, 1990–2000. 1990. Academia Militar de Venezuela, Ministerio de la Defensa, República de Venezuela.

Poleo, Patricia. 2002. "Factores de poder." *Nuevo País*, 17 April.

"Proyecto de reglamentación para la Comisión Interpartidista." Not dated. Doc. 30, Vol. 36, Fundación Rómulo Betancourt, Caracas, Venezuela.

PROVEA. 2002. "Informe anual, 2002–2003." <http://www.derechos.org.ve/publica ciones/infanual/2002_03/>. Accessed June 2004.

Quiróz Corradi, Alberto. 1992. Former president, MARAVEN oil company. Interview by the author, 17 August, Caracas, Venezuela.

Rangel, Beatrice. 1992. Former chief of staff under President Carlos Andrés Pérez. Interview by the author, 20 August, Caracas, Venezuela.

Rangel, Domingo Alberto. 1949a. Letter to Rubén Castellanos, June 27. Doc. 6, Vol. 9, Annex B, Fundación Rómulo Betancourt, Caracas, Venezuela.

———. 1949b. Letter to Rubén Castellanos, August. Doc. 10, Vol. 9, Annex B, Fundación Rómulo Betancourt, Caracas, Venezuela.

———. 1957a. "Anteproyecto de tesis para Acción Democrática." Vol. 35, Annex A, pp. 24–27, Fundación Rómulo Betancourt, Caracas, Venezuela.

———. 1957b. Memorandum for Central Comité. Doc. 9, Vol. 35, Annex A, Fundación Rómulo Betancourt, Caracas, Venezuela.

———. 1988. *La revolución de las fantasías*. Caracas: Editorial Grijalbo.

Remmer, Karen. 1991. *Military Rule in Latin America*. Boulder, Colo.: Westview Press.

Rey, Juan Carlos. 1989. *El futuro de la democrácia en Venezuela*. Caracas: IDEA.

Rial, Juan. 1996. "Armies and Civil Society in Latin America." In *Civil-Military Relations and Democracy*, edited by Larry Diamond and Marc Plattner, 47–65. Baltimore: Johns Hopkins University Press.

Rios, Argelia. 2002a. "Un referendo consultivo sera respetado por el Ejército." *El Universal*, 24 October.

———. 2002b. "La Fuerza Armada espera el humo blanco electoral." *El Universal*, 4 November.

Roberts, Kenneth M. 1996. "Neoliberalism and the Transformation of Populism in Latin America: The Peruvian Case." *World Politics* 38 (no. 1): 82–116.

———. 2003. "Social Polarization and the Populist Resurgence in Venezuela." In *Venezuelan Politics in the Chávez Era,* edited by Steve Ellner and Daniel Hellinger, 55–72. Boulder, Colo.: Lynne Rienner.

Robledo, Marcos. 2004. Senior advisor to Chilean minister of defense. Personal communication with the author, October.

Rodriguez, Fernando R. 1989. "El camino hacia la democracia: Militares y política en la transición española." Ph.D. diss., Universidad Complutense.

Rodríguez, Francisco. 1992. "Tras el intento de golpe del 4-F: Política y militares en Venezuela." *Politeia* 15: 109–20.

Rodríguez, Gustavo. 2002. "Terrorismo estremeció ciudad." *El Universal,* 26 February.

"Rodríguez Araque: Venezuela no tiene carrera armamentista." 2005. *El Universal,* 21 February.

Rodríguez Iturbe, José. 1984. *Crónica de la década militar.* Caracas: Ediciones Nueva Política.

Rodríguez-Valdes, Angel. 1992. *Los rostros del golpe.* Caracas: Alfadil Ediciones.

Rojas, Alfredo. 2004. "Baduel invoca 'alerta' del Ejercito." *El Universal,* 25 June.

Romero, Aníbal. 1987. *La miseria del populismo.* Caracas: Ediciones Centauro.

———. 1990. *Aproximación a la política.* Caracas: Ediciones de la Comandancia General del Ejercito.

———. 1994. *Decadencia y crisis de la democracia.* 2d ed. Caracas: Editorial Panapo.

———. 1995. "Rearranging the Deck Chairs on the Titanic: The Agony of Democracy in Venezuela." Paper presented at the annual meeting of the Latin American Studies Association, September, Washington D.C.

———. 1996. "Venezuela: Democracy Hangs On." *Journal of Democracy* 7 (October): 30–42.

Romero, Dubraska. 2002a. "La historia secreta de un fracaso militar." *Tal Cual,* 16 April.

———. 2002b. "Cacería en la GN dejó 29 generales sin cargo." *Tal Cual,* 22 May.

———. 2002c. "La estrategia militar después de 11A." *Tal Cual,* 15 October.

———. 2002d. "Intriga en el alto mando," *Tal Cual,* 21 November.

Romero, Dubraska, and Veruska Romero. 2002a. "Alas rotas." *Tal Cual,* 20 June.

———. 2002b. "Fragatas obsoletas." *Tal Cual,* 21 June.

———. 2002c. "Adiós a las armas." *Tal Cual,* 25 June.

Romero, Gustavo. 1992. Political analyst. Interview by the author, 9 July, Caracas, Venezuela.

Roquié, Alain. 1989. *The Military and the State in Latin America.* Berkeley: University of California Press.

Ruiz Pantin, Efraín. 2002. "Asociación de Alcaldes rechaza intervención de la Metropolitana." *El Nacional,* 19 November.

Salieron, Victor. 2002. "La economia se desplomó 10%." *El Universal,* 27 December.

Sanín (Alfredo Tarre Murzi). 1984. *Rómulo.* 2d ed. Caracas: Vadell Hermanos Editores.

Sanoja Hernández, Jesús. 2000. "FAN: Arianos y bolivarianos." *El Nacional*, 30 March.

Sarmiento, Tomás. 2003. "Analistas preven la peor contracción económica de la historia Venezolana." *El Universal*, 12 June.

Schaposnik, Eduardo. 1985. *Democratización de las Fuerzas Armadas Venezolanas.* Caracas: Editores ILDIS–Fundación Gonzalo Barrios.

Schmitter, Philippe. 1971. "Military Intervention, Political Competitiveness, and Public Policy in Latin America: 1850–1967." In *On Military Intervention*, edited by Morris Janowitz and Jacobus van Doorn, 426–503. Rotterdam: Rotterdam University Press.

———. 1995. "The Consolidation of Political Democracies: Processes, Rhythms, Sequences, and Types." In *Transitions to Democracy*, edited by Geoffrey Pridham. Aldershot, U.K.: Dartmouth Publishing Company.

Schumpeter, Joseph A. 1976. *Capitalism, Socialism, and Democracy*. New York: Harper and Row.

Servicio de Inteligencia de las Fuerzas Armadas. 1958. Multiple memorandums to military high command regarding political activities and affiliations of Rómulo Betancourt. Docs. 51, 53–70, 77, and 79, Vol. 35, Annex B, Fundación Rómulo Betancourt, Caracas, Venezuela.

Sonntag, Heinz R., and Thaís Maingón. 1992. *Venezuela: 4-F 1992: Un análisis sociopolítico*. Caracas: Editorial Nueva Sociedad.

Sosa A., Arturo. 1989. "La política social de Rómulo Betancourt." In *Rómulo Betancourt: Historia y contemporaneidad*, 343–71. Caracas: Editorial Fundación Rómulo Betancourt.

Soto Tamayo, Carlos. 1986. *Rómulo: Democracia con garra*. Caracas: Editorial Texto.

Soto Urrútia, General José Radamés. 1994a. Professor at Venezuela Air Force General Staff School. Interview by author, 7 October, Caracas, Venezuela.

———. 1994b. Interview by the author, 29 October, Caracas, Venezuela.

———. 1995. Interview by author, 21 February, Caracas, Venezuela.

Stambouli, Andrés. 1980. *Crisis política, Venezuela, 1945–58*. Caracas: Editorial Ateneo de Caracas.

———. 1994. Interview by the author, November, Caracas, Venezuela.

Stepan, Alfred. 1974. *The Military in Politics: Changing Patterns in Brazil*. Princeton, N.J.: Princeton University Press.

———. 1986. "Paths toward Redemocratization: Theoretical and Comparative Considerations." In *Transitions from Authoritarian Rule: Comparative Perspectives*, edited by Guillermo O'Donnell, Philippe Schmitter, and Lawrence Whitehead, 64–84. Baltimore: Johns Hopkins University Press.

———. 1988. *Rethinking Military Politics*. Baltimore: Johns Hopkins University Press.

Stockton, Paul. 1995. "Beyond Micromanagement: Congressional Budgeting for a Post–Cold War Military." *Political Science Quarterly* 110 (Summer): 233–59.

Subero, Carlos. 2002. "Más de 60 generales sin cargo." *El Universal*, 13 May.

Tarre Briceño, Gustavo. 1994a. *El espejo roto: 4F 1992*. Caracas: Editorial Panapo.

————. 1994b. Former chair of the finance committee in the Chamber of Deputies. Interview by the author, 30 September, Caracas, Venezuela.

————. 1994c. Interview by author, 14 October, Caracas, Venezuela.

Tarre Murzi, Alfredo. 1983. *Los Adecos en el poder.* Caracas: Producciones SELEVEN.

Taylor, Charles Lewis, and David A. Jodice. 1983. *World Handbook of Political and Social Indicators.* 3d ed. New Haven, Conn.: Yale University Press.

Toro Hardy, José. 1992. *Venezuela: 55 años de política económica.* 3d ed. Caracas: Editorial Panapo.

Trinkunas, Harold A. 1999a. "Crafting Civilian Control of the Armed Forces in Emerging Democracies." Ph.D. diss., Stanford University.

————. 1999b. "The Observation of the 1998 Venezuelan Elections." The Carter Center, February.

————. 2000. "Crafting Civilian Control in Emerging Democracies." *Journal of Interamerican Studies and World Affairs* 42 (Fall): 77–109.

————. 2002a. "The Crisis in Venezuelan Civil-Military Relations: From Punto Fijo to the Fifth Republic." *Latin American Research Review* 37 (no. 1): 41–76.

————. 2002b. "The Reemergence of the Venezuelan Armed Forces as a Political Actor." *Journal of Iberian and Latin American Studies* 8 (July): 165–78.

Tugwell, Franklin. 1975. *The Politics of Oil in Venezuela.* Stanford, Calif.: Stanford University Press.

U.S. Arms Control and Disarmament Agency. 1984. *World Military Expenditures and Arms Transfers.* Washington, D.C.: U.S. Government Printing Office.

————. 1995. *World Military Expenditures and Arms Transfers.* Washington, D.C.: U.S. Government Printing Office.

Vaca, Senator Eduardo. 1995. President of Senate national defense committee. Interview by the author, 7 October, Buenos Aires, Argentina.

Valenzuela, Arturo. 1978. *The Breakdown of Democratic Regimes: Chile.* Baltimore: Johns Hopkins University Press.

Valenzuela, J. Samuel. 1992. "Democratic Consolidation in Post-Transitional Settings: Notion, Process, and Facilitating Conditions." In *Issues in Democratic Consolidation,* edited by Scott Mainwaring, Guillermo O'Donnell, and J. Samuel Valenzuela, 57–104. Notre Dame, Ind.: University of Notre Dame Press.

Valero, Jorge. 1994. *Como llegó Acción Democrática al poder?* Caracas: Ediciones Tropykos.

Valsalice, Luigi. 1979. *La guerilla castrista en Venezuela y sus protagonistas: 1962–1969.* Caracas: Ediciones Centauro.

Varas, Augusto. 1988. "Autonomización castrense y democracia en América Latina." In *La autonomia militar en América Latina,* edited by Augusto Varas, 13–29. Caracas: Editorial Nueva Sociedad.

Vargas, Lieutenant Colonel Mario. 1949. Letter to Captain Tomás Pérez Tenreiro. Doc. 275, Vol. 7, Annex A, Fundación Rómulo Betancourt, Caracas, Venezuela.

Velásquez, Ramón J. 1995. Historian and former president. Interview by the author, 3 April, Caracas, Venezuela.

Veneconomía. 1995. *Perspectivas económicas, políticas y sociales de Venezuela, 1995–2000.* Caracas: Veneconomía.

"Venezuela planea comprar un lote de armas rusas." 2004. *El Universal*, 26 November.

Verbitsky, Horacio. 1987. *Civiles y militares: Memoria secreta de la transición.* Buenos Aires: Editorial Contrapunto.

———. 1995. Senior investigative reporter for *Pagina/12*. Interview by the author, 27 June, Buenos Aires, Argentina.

Villegas Poljak, Ernesto. 1996. "Caldera ha callado el ruido de sables." *El Universal*, 5 August.

———. 1999. "Glorificación del 4F dividió a las FAN." *El Universal*, 7 February.

Vivas, Mercedes. 1994. Professor, Academia Militar de Venezuela. Interview by the author, 11 November, Caracas, Venezuela.

Weber, Max. 1958. *From Max Weber.* Oxford, U.K.: Oxford University Press.

Weffer Cifuentes, Laura. 2002. "El Alto Mando me traicionó, cobardes!" *El Nacional*, 17 April.

Welch, Claude E., Jr. 1975. *Civilian Control of the Military: Myth and Reality.* Buffalo: Council on International Studies, State University of New York at Buffalo.

———. 1992. "Military Disengagement from Politics: Paradigms, Processes, or Random Events." *Armed Forces and Society* 18 (Spring): 323–42.

Weyland, Kurt. 2000. "Neopopulism and Market Reform in Argentina, Brazil, Peru, and Venezuela." Paper delivered at the annual meeting of the Latin American Studies Association, 16–18 March, Miami, Fla.

Wickham-Crowley, Timothy. 1993. *Guerrillas and Revolution in Latin America.* Princeton, N.J.: Princeton University Press.

Wilson, Scot. 2000. "Chavez Taps into Military to Fill Top Civilian Posts." *Washington Post*, 27 October, A24.

Wolpin, Miles. 1986. *Militarization, Internal Repression, and Social Welfare*, New York: St. Martin's Press.

Yánez Mondragón, Alfredo. 2004. "Eduardo Roche Lander: Controles inexistentes." *El Universal*, 1 April.

Yépez Daza, Colonel Jacobo E. 1980. *Los fundamentos de la defensa en Venezuela.* Caracas: Trabajo de Investigación Individual, IAEDN.

———. 1995. Former director of planning for the Joint Staff. Interview by the author, 6 March, Caracas, Venezuela.

Zagorski, Paul. 1992. *Democracy vs. National Security: Civil-Military Relations in Latin America.* Boulder, Colo.: Lynne Rienner.

Zambrano Sequín, Luis. 1995. "Sobre lo que hemos hecho y lo que todavia podemos hacer." In *Venezuela, la democracia bajo presión*, edited by Andrés Serbín, Andrés Stambouli, Jennifer McCoy, and William Smith, 89–106. Caracas: INVESP/Editorial Nueva Sociedad.

Zapata, Juan Carlos. 2002a. "Así cayó Carmona." *Tal Cual*, 15 April.

———. 2002b. "El hombre de la chaqueta morada." *Tal Cual*, 2 May.

Zaverucha, Jorge. 1993. "The Degree of Military Autonomy during the Spanish, Argentine, and Brazilian Transitions." *Journal of Latin American Studies* 25 (no. 2): 283–99.

Ziems, Angel. 1979. *El Gomecismo y la formación del ejército nacional*. Caracas: Editorial Ateneo de Caracas.

Zimmermann, Ekkart. 1983. *Political Violence, Crises, and Revolutions*. Cambridge, Mass.: Schenkman Publishing Company.

INDEX

■

Academia Militar, 30–31, 32–33, 161–62, 180–81

AD (Acción Democrática): Communist affiliation, 53, 92, 265 (n. 7), 267 (n. 9); goals of, 72; hegemony, 52–53, 104–5, 142–43, 148–49, 208; 1958–73, 92, 267 (n. 9); 1952–58, 72–75, 188, 266 (nn. 1, 3); 1945–48, 29, 35–41, 46–48, 50–52, 59–60, 259; party militia, 58, 266 (n. 9); party split, 72, 75, 114, 266 (n. 5); youth wing, 73–75, 114, 116, 266 (nn. 3, 9). See also Betancourt, Rómulo

AD–Junta Patriótica alliance, 83

AD-UPM alliance, 36–39, 41, 238

AD-URD alliance, 76

AD-URD-COPEI alliance, 75–77

Agüero, Felipe, 17, 64

Alexander, Robert J., 63

Alfonsín, Raul, 241–43, 245–46

Amnesty for political crimes, 125, 199

Andrés Bello plan, 161–62

Andrés Pérez, Carlos, 141, 177

Appeasement strategies: AD, 29, 40–41, 46–48, 60; Argentina, 242, 243–44; Argentina and Venezuela compared, 258; Betancourt administration (1959–64), 109, 112, 125–26, 130–32, 140, 152–53; Caldera administration (1993–98), 199; collapse of, 157, 173–79; defined, 10–11; Gallegos administration, 29; Leoni administration, 145; military dominant, 68–69

Appeasement strategies, types of: amnesty for political crimes, 125, 199; compensation, 109, 112, 130–32, 145, 152–53, 164–65, 191, 201–2; defense allocations, 145–46, 164–65, 191; education, 67–68, 131–32, 140; modernization, 67, 131, 140

Arcaya, Ignacio Luís, 115

Arceneaux, Craig, 147

Arellano, Gámez, 55, 57

Argentina: transition to democracy, 3, 16–19, 65 66, 116 17, 236–37, 240–47, 257–60

Arias Cardenas, Francisco, 212–13, 216

Armaments purchases as appeasement strategy, 67, 131, 140

Armed forces (1908–45), 30–40

Armed forces (1973–89): appeasement strategies used for, 164–65; autonomy of, 160–61, 166–67, 169; corruption/malfeasance in, 165–66; divide and conquer strategies, 183–84, 186–87; economic development projects, 161, 163–64; external defense role, 160, 164–65; factionalization in, 161–67, 179–83; internal security role, 161, 168; jurisdictional boundaries, limiting, 163, 166, 167; jurisdictional boundaries deconsolidation, 167–69; MBR-200, 173, 179–87, 191–96

Armed National Liberation Front. See FALN

Autonomy: degrees of, 6; military, 40–
41, 46–50, 59–60, 133, 146–47, 160–61,
166–67, 210
Aylwin, Patricio, 248, 250
Azuaje, Major, 85

Baduel, Raúl, 227, 228
Barcelonazo, 120
Belief systems: traditional military
norms, 22–24
Betancourt, Rómulo: Communist
affiliation, 103, 112, 140, 267 (n. 9);
military power, 47, 56, 72–73, 74;
voluntary exile of, 57–58, 265 (n. 8).
See also AD
Betancourt, Rómulo (1945–48 administration): coup attempts against, 45;
divide and conquer strategies, 46–
47; military, civilian control of, 111;
military, relationship with, 43, 111;
military autonomy, 40–41, 46–50,
59–60; military power struggle, 42–
50, 59, 60; opportunity structure,
42; opposition to, 52. See also AD;
Venezuela, 1945–48 democratization
Betancourt, Rómulo (1959–64 administration): anti-Communist position,
112, 114; appeasement strategies,
109, 112, 125, 126, 130–32, 140, 152–
53; assassination attempt on, 119;
civilian control by oversight, 109;
civil-military relations, 110, 141–42,
152; coalition government, 113, 115;
coup attempts against, 118–23; divide
and conquer strategies, 109, 112, 125–
29, 132–34, 140–41, 152–53; external
defense, 134; foreign policy, 114–15;
internal security, 133–34, 139; jurisdictional boundaries, consolidating,
132–35; military, relationship with,
102–7, 109–13, 124–25, 141; military autonomy, 133; monitoring strategy, 109,
124–25; 1958 election of, 102–6; 1963
presidential election, 138–39; opportunity structure, 80, 103–4; opposition
to, 114–16, 120–21; popular support
for, 118–19, 137, 139–40, 142; regime capacity, 109, 134–35, 154–55, 259; regime
leverage, insurgency threat used for,
111, 113, 117, 135, 139–42, 151–52; sanctioning strategies, 25, 117–23, 141, 152.
See also AD; PCV/MIR insurgency
Biaggini, Angel, 39
Bigler, Gene, 64
Bolivarian Revolutionary Movement
200. See MBR-200
Bolivia, 74
Bravo, Douglas, 121, 144, 149, 180
Briceño Linares, Antonio, 104, 118, 120,
122, 126–28, 138–39

Cabello, Diosado, 220
Calcaño, Rincón, 45
Caldera, Rafael: 1994–98 administration,
1, 197–205; 1968–73 administration,
148–51, 187; Pact of New York, 77
Calvo Sotelo, Leopoldo, 255
Carmona Estanga, Pedro, 206, 220
Carnevali, Alberto, 266 (n. 1)
Casa Militar, 125
Casanova, Roberto, 83, 86, 87
Castro, Cipriano, 30, 118
Castro, Fidel, 115
Castro León, Jesús María, 92–96, 98, 103,
118–19
Catholic Church, 52, 78
Causa R, 189, 196–97, 209
César Vargas, Julio, 39, 45
Chávez Frias, Hugo: 4F coup attempt, 1,
3, 156–57, 170, 185, 187, 263–64; leader-
ship role in MBR-200, 180–83, 191–92,
193–94, 199, 261; military support
for, 191; 1998 elections, 209; popular
support for, 187

Chávez Frias, Hugo (1998– administration): civil-military relations, 210–17, 221–24, 261, 263; divide and conquer strategies, 214; economic and social policies, 228, 229–30, 231; 11 April coup attempt, 209, 217–24, 231, 263, 264; external defense, 227; foreign policy, 218; internal security, 211, 216–17, 224–27; military, politicization of, 212–14, 261, 263; military dominance over civilian control, 210–12, 214, 216, 232–33; military expansion under, 215–17, 263; 1998 political campaign and election of, 208–10; opposition, 206, 217–19, 222, 223, 224–31; Plan Bolívar 2000 social program, 215–16; sanctioning strategies, 207, 215, 221–22, 223; summary, 1–2, 25–26, 229–33; 2000 political campaign and election of, 212–13; 2004 recall referendum, 213; 2002 return to power, 220

Chile: transition to democracy, 18–19, 28–29, 65–66, 116–17, 235, 236–37, 247–53, 257–60

Círculos Bolivarianos, 224

Civilian control: consolidating, 4, 20–24; crafting, 4–5, 8–13, 260–61; deconsolidation of, 168–69; defined, 5; institutional collapse of, 157, 173–79, 232–33; institutionalizing, 23, 234–35, 263–64; institutions of, 13–16, 22–23, 239–40; jurisdictional boundaries for measuring, 7–8, 19–21; maximizing, 4–8; military acceptance of, 110, 150–51, 152, 153; military expansion threatens, 197–98; military jurisdiction reduced by, 106–7; minimizing, 5–6; PCV/MIR insurgency results in, 139–42, 151–52; purpose of, 14; regime capacity-regime leverage correlation, 17–20; success components, 153–54

Civilian control by containment, 18–19, 21, 64–66, 149–50, 199, 202–3, 263–64

Civilian control by oversight, 5–6, 18–19, 21, 109, 236–37, 247–56

Civilian control strategies: Argentina, 3, 245–47, 258–59; Betancourt administrations, 110–11, 126, 152; Caldera administrations, 150–51, 153, 204–5; Chile, 3, 235; Junta de Gobierno, 95–96, 106–7; 1958 democratization, 85–86, 258; 1945–48 democratization, 259, 260–61; Pérez administration, 157, 173–79, 197–98; Punto Fijo period (1958–73), 153–54; Spain, 3–4

Civilian control strategies, military dominant: appeasement, 68–69; Betancourt administration (1945–48), 40–41, 46–50, 59–60; Chávez Frias administration, 210–12, 214, 216, 232–33; Gallegos administration, 29, 54–55, 60; institutional collapse with, 232–33; internal security, 48–49; Leoni administration, 146–47; Pérez Jiménez administration, 68–69; political influence, 29, 68–69, 211–12, 214, 216

Civilian defense expertise, 101, 109, 204–5

Committee of Independent Political Electoral Organizing. See COPEI

Communism: AD and, 53, 92, 265 (n. 7), 267 (n. 9); Betancourt and, 103, 112, 114, 140, 267 (n. 9)

Compensation as appeasement strategy, 109, 112, 130–32, 145, 152–53, 164–65, 191, 201–2

Competition as control strategy, 97–98, 128–29, 166–67

Conde López, Horacio, 43

Confederación General de Trabajadores, 224

Contreras, Manuel, 251

Coordinadora Democrática, 222, 224–25, 228, 231

COPEI (Comité de Organización Política Electoral Independiente), 53, 75–77, 188–89, 208

Coppedge, Michael, 159, 170, 209

Cuba, 75, 115, 137–38, 140, 141

Davies, Thomas M., 40

Defense allocations as appeasement strategy, 145–46, 164–65, 191

Delgado Chalbaud, Carlos, 39, 48, 49, 53, 54, 55–60, 66

Democratic Action Party. See AD

Democratic consolidation process, 4, 20–24

Democratic Republican Union Party. See URD

Desch, Michael, 14

Development projects, 68–69, 77–78, 144, 161, 163–64

DIM (Directorate of Military Intelligence), 181–82, 186, 190

DISIP (Dirección de Servicios de Inteligencia y Prevención), 181–82, 186

Divide and conquer strategies: AD, 72–73, 75; Argentina and Venezuela compared, 258; armed forces (1973–89), 183–84, 186–87; Betancourt administrations, 46, 109, 112, 125–29, 132–34, 140–41, 152–53; Caldera administration (1993–98), 199, 201–2; decentralization, 97–99, 125–29, 132–34, 140–41; defined, 11; Junta de Gobierno, 96–101, 108; Pérez administration, 193, 195–96; *reincorporados*, 97, 126; service limits enacted, 100. *See also* Factionalization strategy

Education as appeasement strategy, 67–68, 131–32, 140

11 April coup attempt, 206–7, 209, 217–24, 231, 263, 264

Ellner, Steve, 159

El Proceso, 241

Escalante, Diogenes, 34, 37, 38

Escuela Básica, 67, 99

Estrada, Pedro, 79

External defense, 7, 134, 160, 164–65, 168, 178, 200, 202, 227

Factionalization strategy: armed forces (1973–89), 161–67, 179–83; Chávez Frias administration, 214, 264; Medina administration, 40; Pérez administration, 181–87, 190, 191–96; Pérez Jiménez administration, 80–86. *See also* Divide and conquer strategies

FALN (Fuerzas Armadas de Liberación Nacional), 122, 136–39, 144–45, 148–51

FARC (Fuerzas Armadas Revolucionarias de Colombia), 200

Feaver, Peter, 15

FEDECAMARAS (Federación de Cámaras y Asociaciones de Comercio y Producción), 93, 104, 224

Federation of Chambers and Associations of Commerce and Production. *See* FEDECAMARAS

Fernández, Eduardo, 188

Fernández, Rómulo, 70, 82–84

Fifth of July Movement conspiracy, 193–96

Fitch, J. Samuel, 22, 23, 260

FLN (Frente de Liberación Nacional), 122

4F coup attempt, 1, 3, 156–57, 170, 183–93, 197, 263–64

Frei, Eduardo, 249, 250

Frente Institucional Militar, 214

Gallegos, Rómulo (1948 administration), 50–59

García Carneiro, Jorge, 223, 228
García Ponte, Gabriel, 79
García Villasmil, Martín, 103, 105, 118, 212
Garrido, Alberto, 180
Gaviria, Cesar, 225, 229
Global Acquisitions Plan, 177
Gobierno de Ancha Base coalition, 143
Gómez, Florencio, 143
Gómez, Juan Vicente (1908-35 adminis-
   tration), 30-34
González, Felipe, 255, 256
Grüber Odremán, Hernán, 193-94, 195
Guardia Nacional, 33, 49, 133-34, 145,
   161, 168, 175, 193, 196, 226

Hellinger, Daniel, 159
Herrera Campíns, Luis, 76, 167
Holy Week rebellion of 1987, 242, 244
Human rights, 241-42, 250-51, 267 (n. 4)
Huntington, Samuel, 5-6, 14, 15, 19

IAEDN (Instituto de Altos Estudios de
   la Defensa Nacional), 163
Institutional Military Front, 214
Intelligence and Prevention Services
   Directorate. See DISIP
Internal security: Betancourt administrations, 48-49, 133-34, 139; Caldera
   administration (1993-98), 200, 202-
   3; Chávez Frias administration, 211,
   216-17, 224-27; defined, 7; Junta de
   Gobierno, 94; Leoni administration, 147; military dominant, 48-49;
   Pérez administration, 173-75, 198;
   Pérez Jiménez administration, 69, 70,
   75, 81-82, 84, 103-4; types of, 139,
   200, 202-3, 211, 224-27; Venezuela
   (1908-45), 33

Jiménez Sánchez, Iván, 189
JRG (Junta Revolucionaria de Gobierno), 40-49

Junta de Gobierno (1958): civilian control of armed forces, 95-96, 106-7;
   coup attempts against, 92-95, 103, 267
   (n. 9); divide and conquer strategies,
   96-101, 108; internal security, 94;
   military factionalism during, 88-91;
   monitoring during, 96-97; 1958 presidential elections, 100-106; popular
   support for, 93-94; regime capacity,
   101, 108-9; sanctioning during, 95;
   summary, 106-9
Junta Militar de Gobierno (1958), 86-88
Junta Patriótica, 79-80, 82, 83-84, 87,
   267 (n. 7)
Jurisdictional boundaries: consolidating,
   132-35; IAEDN-NSD in removing,
   163; importance in emerging democracies, 261-63; measuring, 7-8, 19-21;
   military secrecy laws reduce, 166;
   politicization reduces, 169; types of,
   21

Karl, Terry, 63, 170
Kirchner, Nestor, 247

Lagos, Ricardo, 252
Lamberti, Blas, 88, 92
Lanz, Vallenilla, 78, 79
Larrazábal, Carlos, 87, 89, 98
Larrazábal, Wolfgang, 86, 87, 88-89,
   91-94, 104-6
La Sagrada, 32, 33
Leoni, Raul (1963-68 administration),
   138-39, 143-48
Levine, Daniel, 28, 63
Llovera Páez, Luis, 59, 83, 84
López Contreras, Eleazar (1935-41), 33,
   34, 36, 38, 45
López Henrique, Josué, 105
LOSD (Ley Orgánica de Seguridad y
   Defensa), 163
Los Notables, 182-83

Loveman, Brian, 40
Lugo, Avendaño, 28
Lusinchi, Jaime (1983–88), 172, 177

Maldonado Michelena, Victor, 68
Manrique Padrón, Luis, 194
Martz, John D., 63
MAS (Movimiento al Socialismo), 149,
    189
MBR-200 (Movimiento Bolivariano
    Revolucionario 200), 173, 179–87,
    191–96, 199, 263
McGill, Samuel, 30, 31
Medina Angarita, Isaías, 33–40
Mendoza, Eugenio, 88, 92
Mendoza, Tomás, 56
Ménem, Carlos, 241, 244–47
MEP (Movimiento Electoral del
    Pueblo), 148
MIR (Movimiento de la Izquierda Revo-
    lucionaria), 114–16. See also PCV/MIR
    insurgency
Modernization of military as appease-
    ment strategy, 67, 131, 140
Molina, Antonio Tejero, 255
Molina Villegas, Jesús, 121–22
Moncada Vidal, Juan de Dios, 93, 136
Monitoring strategy: Betancourt admin-
    istrations, 47, 109, 124–25; defined,
    11; Junta de Gobierno, 96–97; Leoni
    administration, 145, 147–48; Pérez
    administration, 181–83, 185–86, 190–
    91, 198; Pérez Jiménez administration,
    69
Moreno León, José Ignacio, 188
Moros, Marco Aurelio, 105–6
Movement of the Revolutionary Left.
    See MIR
Movement toward Socialism Party. See
    MAS
Movimiento Quinto de Julio (Fifth of
    July Movement) conspiracy, 193–96

Müller Rojas, Alberto, 183
Muñoz León, Radamés, 196, 197–98, 199

National Liberation Front. See FLN
9 April general strike, 206, 218–19
Niño, Eleazar, 45
Nixon, Richard, 92
Norden, Deborah, 13, 242
Nuevo Ideal Nacional (New National
    Ideal), 67, 69
Nunn, Frederick, 22

Ochoa Antich, Fernando, 156, 182, 185,
    188, 189, 197
O'Donnell, Guillermo, 40
Ojeda, Fabricio, 79, 122, 145
Operación República II protection,
    138–39
Opportunity structure for transition:
    Argentina, 257–58; Betancourt ad-
    ministrations, 42, 80, 103–4; broad,
    defined, 8–9, 11; Caldera administra-
    tion (1993–98), 203–5; Chile, 257–58;
    narrow, defined, 8–9, 11; 1958 democ-
    ratization, 85–86, 238, 248, 257–58;
    1945–48 democratization, 238, 257–58;
    Spain, 257–58
Ortega, Carlos, 218
Osorio García, Jorge, 162

Pact of New York, 76–77, 102
Pact of Punto Fijo, 102–3, 104, 115
Parada, Martín, 81
Parra, Gastón, 218
Partido Democrático Venezolano, 36
Partyarchy, 170–75
Patriotic Military Union. See UPM
PCV (Partido Comunista de Venezuela),
    75, 76, 114–16
PCV/MIR insurgency: arrest of
    PCV/MIR legislators, 141–42;
    beginnings, 120–22, 136, 261; civilian

control as result of, 139–42, 151–52;
counterinsurgency campaign, 137,
139, 140–48; counterinsurgency ends,
148–51; Cuban support for, 137–38,
140, 141; FALN split, 144–45; goals,
135–36; leadership, 136; membership,
136–37, 142; popular opposition to,
137, 139, 140; prisoner interrogations,
267 (n. 4); Puerto Cabello insurrection, 122; rural front collapse, 144–45;
rural guerrilla groups, 137–38; urban
terrorism, 136–37
PDVSA (Petroleos de Venezuela, S.A.),
213, 218, 225, 226, 228
Peña, Alfredo, 224
Peñaloza, Carlos Julio, 181, 184–85
People's Electoral Movement. See MEP
Pérez, Carlos Andrés, 141
Pérez, Carlos Andrés (1988–93 administration): appeasement, collapse of
institutions of, 157, 173–79; appeasement strategics, 191; civilian control
threatened by military expansion,
197–98; coalition government, 188–
89; corruption/malfeasance of armed
forces, 177–78; divide and conquer
strategies, 193, 195–96; economic
policy, 157, 172–75; factionalization
strategies, 181–87, 190–96, 264; 4F
coup attempt, 1, 3, 156–57, 170, 183–
93, 197, 263–64; impeachment of, 1,
196; internal security under, 173–75,
198; monitoring by, 181–83, 185–86,
190–91, 198; Movimiento Quinto de
Julio conspiracy, 192–93; opposition
to policies of, 187, 189, 192; political
and economic turmoil under, 157–58;
privatization policies, 178; sanctioning strategies, 190, 198; summary,
196–202; 27 November rebellion, 157,
192–96
Pérez Jiménez, Juan, 45

Pérez Jiménez, Marcos (1945–48), 38, 39,
42, 45, 47, 48–49, 54, 55–60
Pérez Jiménez, Marcos (1952–58 administration): appeasement strategies,
67–68; armed cronyism, 67; collapse of, 71, 75–85; crony capitalism
under, 69–70; development projects
of, 68–69, 77–78; external security,
70; factionalization strategies, 80–86;
internal security, 69, 70, 75, 81–82, 84,
103–4; military, 67–71, 73, 74, 79–85;
monitoring by, 69; opposition groups,
78, 82–84; plebiscite, 77, 79, 81; public
policy of, 70; regime ideology, 67, 68–
69, 77–78; regime leverage, 67–69;
sanctioning strategies, 84. See also AD
Pietri, Arturo Uslar, 143
Pinochet, Augusto, 247, 251
Pion-Berlin, David, 6, 147
Plan Bolívar 2000 social program,
215–16, 231
Plan Global de Adquisiciones (Global
Acquisitions Plan), 177
Poleo, Patricia, 219
Ponte, Gabriel García, 79
Ponte Rodríguez, Manuel, 122, 136
Prieto Figueroa, Luís Beltrán, 148
Programa Mínimo de Gobierno, 102–3
Public policy, 7, 70, 133
Punto Fijo period (1958–73), 2–3, 151–55.
See also Betancourt, Rómula (1959–
64 administration); Caldera, Rafael:
1968–73 administration; Leoni, Raul
(1963–68 administration)

Quintana, Maucó, 194

Rangel, Domingo Alberto, 73–75, 105,
114, 261, 266 (nn. 3, 5, 9)
Rangel León, Lieutenant Colonel, 57
Rangel Rojas, Pedro, 181
Regime at risk, 17–18, 29, 59

Regime capacity, 4–5, 15–16, 17, 236–37, 247–53, 259–60
Regime leverage in Argentina, 242–44
Regime leverage maximization strategies, 9–13
Regime persistence, 18–19, 21–22
Reincorporados, 97, 126
Revolutionary Armed Forces of Columbia. See FARC
Revolutionary Governing Council. See JRG
Rincón Calcaño, Colonel, 45
Rincón Romero, Lucas, 206, 219
Roberts, Kenneth M., 209
Roche Lander, Eduardo, 216
Rodríguez, Valmore, 47
Rojas, Patricio, 250, 251
Rosendo, Manuel, 222

Saenz, Irene, 209
Sáez Mérida, Simón, 114
Salas Romer, Henrique, 209
Sanabria, Edgar, 104, 105, 106
Sanctioning strategies: Argentina, 242, 243–44; Argentina and Venezuela compared, 258; Betancourt administration (1959–64), 25, 117–23, 141, 152; Chávez Frias administration, 207, 215, 221–22, 223; Junta de Gobierno, 95; Pérez administration, 190, 198; Pérez Jiménez administration, 84; Spain, 12
Schmitter, Philippe, 8
Seguridad Nacional, 81–82, 84, 103–4
Seineldín, Mohamed, 244
Serra, Narciso, 255–56
SIFA (Servicio de Inteligencia de las Fuerzas Armadas), 92
Spain: transition to democracy, 3–4, 12, 18–19, 65–66, 236–37, 253–60
Stepan, Alfred, 6
Suarez, Adolfo, 255

Tarre Briceño, Gustavo, 162
10 December general strike, 217–18
Trejo, Hugo, 79, 81, 87–88, 89–91
Trienio. See Venezuela, 1945–48 democratization
Trujillo, Rafael, 119
27 November rebellion, 157, 192–96
2 February referendum, 225
2004 recall referendum, 227–31
2002–3 general strike, 224–27, 231

United States, 28, 92, 140, 188–89, 249
UPM (Unión Patriótica Militar), 35, 37–40, 42–44
URD (Unión Republicana Democrática), 53, 75–77, 102–4, 115, 139, 143
Uruguay, 116–17
UTC (Unidades Tácticas de Combate), 137

Vargas, Julio César, 45
Vargas, Mario, 41, 42, 44, 54–57, 265 (n. 6)
Vásquez Velasco, Efraín, 206, 219
Velásquez, Ramón J., 118, 125, 196–97
Venezuela: democracy's future in, 1–3; economy, 34–36, 62, 71, 77–79, 113–14, 199, 201–2, 215, 228, 230; history of, 1–3, 30, 76; 1908–45, 30–40; 1988–99 overview, 25; 1984–88 democratic reform, 208–10; 1958–98, 62–66, 237–40; 1948 and 1958 compared, 237–40; 1948–52 interregnum, 66; 1945 revolution, 34–40; 1990s instability, causes of, 157–60; 1973–89, 163, 165–66; power-maximizing strategies, 239–40; regime capacity, 16, 239. See also Armed forces (1973–89); and specific administrations
Venezuela, 1945–48 democratization (Trienio): Chile's transition compared

to, 258–59; civilian control, role of ideas in crafting, 260–61; civilian control strategies, 259; civil-military jurisdictional boundaries, 261–63; failure, causes of, 50–52, 73, 237–38; Gallegos administration, 50–59; history of civil-military relations, 3; jurisdictional boundaries' importance in, 261–63; 1948 coup d'état, 27, 29, 55–60; opportunity structure, 238, 257–58; regime capacity, 238; regime leverage, 238; Spain's transition compared to, 257; summary, 59–61. *See also* Betancourt, Rómulo (1945–48 administration)

Venezuela, 1958 democratization: Argentina's transition compared to, 236–37, 257–60; Chile's transition compared to, 236–37, 248, 250, 251, 257–60; civilian control by containment, 263–64; civilian control strategies, 258; jurisdictional boundaries' importance in, 261–63; 1945–48 compared to, 237–40; opportunity structure, 85–86, 238, 248, 257–58; regime capacity sources, 259–60; regime leverage, 238; Spain's transition compared to, 236–37, 257–60; success, components of, 238–39; transitional government, 86–88

Venezuelan Communist Party. *See* PCV

Venezuelan Congress, 128–29, 134, 140, 147, 166

Venezuelan constitution, 127, 209, 210–17, 264

Venezuelan Petroleum Corporation. *See* PDVSA

Villalba, Jóvito, 45, 74, 75–77, 102–4, 267 (n. 7)

Villate, Romero, 81, 83, 86, 87

Visconti, Francisco, 193–94, 195

Weyland, Kurt, 209

Zárraga, José Giacopini, 56–58, 265 (n. 8)